Post-Metropolitan Territories

D0706153

Processes of multi-scalar regional urbanization are occurring worldwide. Such processes are clearly distinguishable from those of the nineteenth and twentieth centuries due to the shifting concepts of both the city and the metropolis. International literature highlights how what we have historically associated with the idea of cities has long been subjected to consistent reconfiguration, which involves stressing some of the typical features of the idea of "cityness".

Post-Metropolitan Territories: Looking for a New Urbanity is the product of a research project funded by the Italian Ministry for Education, Universities and Research (MIUR). It constitutes a thorough overview of a country that is one of Europe's most diverse in terms of regional development and performance: Italy. This book brings together case studies of a number of Italian cities and their hinterlands and looks at new forms of urbanization, exploring themes of sustainability, industrialization, de-industrialization, governance, city planning and quality of life.

This volume will be of great interest to academics and students who study regional development, economic geography and urban studies, as well as civil servants and policymakers in the field of spatial planning, urban policy, territorial policies and governance.

Alessandro Balducci is Full Professor of Urban Planning and a member of the PhD Program in Urban Planning and Policy Design at Politecnico di Milano, Italy.

Valeria Fedeli is Associate Professor in Urban Planning at Politecnico di Milano, Italy.

Francesco Curci is Research Fellow at the Politecnico di Milano and lecturer at the Ca' Foscari University of Venice, Italy.

Routledge Advances in Regional Economics, Science and Policy

Post-Metropolitan Territories

Looking for a New Urbanity

**Edited by Alessandro Balducci,
Valeria Fedeli and Francesco Curci**

LONDON AND NEW YORK

First published 2017 by Routledge

2 Park Square, Milton Park, Abingdon, Oxfordshire OX14 4RN
52 Vanderbilt Avenue, New York, NY 10017

Routledge is an imprint of the Taylor & Francis Group, an informa business

First issued in paperback 2019

British Library Cataloguing in Publication Data
A catalogue record for this book is available from the British Library

Library of Congress Cataloging in Publication Data
Names: Balducci, A. (Alessandro), editor. | Fedeli, Valeria, editor. |
    Curci, Francesco, editor.
Title: Post-metropolitan territories and urban space / edited by
    Alessandro Balducci, Valeria Fedeli and Francesco Curci.
Description: Abingdon, Oxon ; New York, NY : Routledge, 2017.
Identifiers: LCCN 2016036735| ISBN 9781138650480 (hardback) |
    ISBN 9781315625300 (ebook)
Subjects: LCSH: Metropolitan areas—Italy. | Urbanization—Italy. |
    Regional planning—Italy. | Urban policy—Italy.
Classification: LCC HT334.I8 P67 2017 | DDC 307.76/40945—dc23
LC record available at https://lccn.loc.gov/2016036735

ISBN: 978-1-138-65048-0 (hbk)
ISBN: 978-0-367-24954-0 (pbk)

Typeset in Times New Roman
by Swales & Willis Ltd, Exeter, Devon, UK

This book is dedicated to Daniele Pennati, post-doctoral fellow in urban planning and active member of our research team who, thanks to his exceptional knowledge in web design, has been the designer of our atlas of post-metropolitan territories, the instrument around which we have developed our research project.

Daniele had the extraordinary capacity of making complex problems understandable, and for us his dramatic death, with the sudden interruption of his young life, has been a great loss, completely incomprehensible.

Contents

Illustrations

Figures

Tables

Moroni, 2009), *L'apprendimento come esperienza estetica. Una comunità di pratiche in azione* (2011) and *La strada che parla. Dispositivi per ripensare le aree interne in una nuova dimensione urbana* (with Leonardo Lutzoni, 2016).

Daniela De Leo is a tenured researcher and Assistant Professor in Urban Planning at the Sapienza University in Rome, Italy. She has conducted and coordinated national and international research activities in Nablus, in East Jerusalem, in Beirut, and as Visiting Scholar at IURD (Institute of Urban and Regional Development), UC Berkeley, 2013. She has also been associate researcher at the DUSP (Department of Urban Studies and Planning) at MIT, 2011–13. Her research focuses on challenges for planners and urban planning theories and practices in the face of the Mafia, in conflicts and contested space, and in areas with strong asymmetry of powers and inequalities.

Valeria Fedeli is Associate Professor in Urban Planning and Policy at Politecnico di Milano, Italy, where she teaches socio-spatial analysis and European Urban policies. She is also responsible for the Jean Monnet Course EU Regional and Urban Policy at master's level and she is currently a member of the PhD Board Urban Planning, Design and Policy. She is also a member of the Advisory Board of EURA (European Urban Research Association); a member of the scientific committee of Urban@it (Centro nazionale di studi per le politiche urbane); and a scientific member of the Scientific Coordination Committee of the Programme Urban Futures (LABEX. PRES, Universitè Paris-Est). Among her research interests are: strategic planning, metropolitan governance, inter-municipal cooperation, and processes of regional urbanization and urban change. She was responsible for the operative coordination of the PRIN 2010 project: 'Post-metropolitan territories as emergent forms of urban space: coping with sustainability, habitability, and governance'. Among her recent publications on these research topics, she was co-author of the book *Strategic Planning for Contemporary Urban Regions: City of Cities: A Project for Milan* (2011).

Laura Fregolent is Associate Professor of Urban and Regional Planning at the Department of Design and Planning in Complex Environment, University IUAV, Venice, Italy. Her research fields are focused on the analysis of the structural characteristics of urban and territorial transformations and how the uses of land, city and spaces influences the insurgence of social movements. She is co-director of the journal *Archivio di studi urbani e regionali*.

Luca Garavaglia, PhD in information society at the University of Milan-Bicocca, is a post-doctoral research fellow at the University of Eastern Piedmont, Italy. He is editor of the scientific journal *Studi Organizzativi*. His research interests focus on local development, urban studies and regional socio-economic networks.

Giovanni Laino is Associate Professor of Urban Planning at the 'Federico II' University of Naples – Department of Architecture, Italy. He is a member of the IUAV School of Doctorate Studies – doctorate course Architecture, City and Design (Venice). His research explores urban planning and public policies and deals mainly with the agency of fragile populations. He has published several articles and two monographs. He is a social planner engaged for many years in a wide range of urban regeneration programs aimed at improving deprived areas. With reference to Naples, he recently produced the video *Which Post Metropolis From The South?*, which received the honourable mention of local authorities in Sele award 2014.

Laura Lieto is Professor of Urban Planning at the 'Federico II' University, Italy. She writes extensively on planning theory, urban informality and transnational urbanism. She is the managing editor of the planning journal *CRIOS*. Her most recent publications are: *Planning for a Material World* (with R. Beauregard (eds), 2016), and 'Does Actor Network Theory Help Planners to Think about Change' (with R. Beauregard) in: Y. Rydin and L. Tate (eds) *Actor Networks of Planning* (2016).

Francesca Lotta is a planner and has a PhD in urban and regional planning in the co-tutorship thesis program with the Polytechnic University of Madrid, Spain. Her principal research interests revolve around environmental issues. Her PhD thesis is focused on the local ecological network, and over the years she has examined the issues of public space, peri-urban agricultural areas, transformation of the agricultural landscape and, recently, Italian metropolitan reform, which affects the environment at the planning level.

Francesco Lo Piccolo is Full Professor of Urban Planning and coordinator of the BSc and MSc Program of Urban, Regional and Environmental Planning, Department of Architecture, University of Palermo, Italy. He is the deputy of the rector for the PhD programs of the University of Palermo. Fulbright Fellow and Marie Curie TMR Fellow, his research is mostly directed to social exclusion, ethnicity and diversity, conflicts and power relationships in planning, with specific interests in ethics and justice. He is the editor – with Huw Thomas – of *Ethics and Planning Research* (2009). He has published on these issues in *International Planning Studies, Planning Practice and Research, European Spatial Research and Policy, Journal of Policy Research in Tourism, Leisure & Events, International Journal of E-Planning Research, Planning Theory and Practice, Town Planning Review* and *Planning Theory*. He is a member of the editorial board of *Town Planning Review*. He was the president of AESOP (Association of European Schools of Planning) from 2014–16.

Fabio Lucchesi graduated in architecture from the University of Florence, Italy, in 1994 and obtained his PhD in urban, territorial and environmental planning in 2001. He has been a faculty member in architecture and in spatial planning at the University of Florence since 2001, and Associate Professor in Urban Planning in the Architecture Department since 2014. He is currently teaching urban design and GIS technologies for spatial planning. His research activity, both theoretical and applied, mainly concerns the role of description and representation in planning activities and the use of geographical information technologies in the description of territorial identity. He has been involved in many research projects carried out at both local and national levels. Since 2014 he has been the head of LCart (Laboratory of Cartography and Spatial Analysis) at the Architecture Department, University of Florence.

Iacopo Zetti gained his master's degree in architecture in 1994 and PhD in urban, territorial and environmental planning in 2000. He is Associate Professor in the Department of Architecture at the University of Florence, Italy, where he teaches urban and territorial planning. He took part in several national research projects within groups active in the section of urban planning at Florence University and within international research groups. He has worked as a researcher at Florence University and at the Regional Institute for Economic Planning of Tuscany, dealing with topics such as the monitoring of planning activity in Tuscany, urban planning and environmental sustainability, and participation of citizens in public policies. He was a consultant for several urban plans, in Italy and abroad (Niger, Cuba, China). His research activity covers several fields, including: the participation of inhabitants to the urban project and to planning policies; GIS and cartography as knowledge instruments for urban planning; and the transformation of public space under the pressure of the global economy.

Acknowledgements

The editors and authors would like to thank the International Advisory Board: Professor Peter Ache (Radboud University Nijmegen, Netherlands), Professor Louis Albrechts (emeritus, Catholic University of Leuven, Belgium), Professor Simin Davoudi (Newcastle University, UK), Professor Christian Lefèvre (Université Paris-Est Marne-la-Vallée, France), Professor Klaus R. Kunzmann (emeritus, Technical University of Dortmund, Germany), Professor Willem Salet (University of Amsterdam, Netherlands), Professor Iván Tosics (Metropolitan Research Institute, Budapest, Hungary).

The authors would also like to thank all the partner institutions and single members of the extensive network of the PRIN. In particular, the editors would like to acknowledge the research teams of the Politecnico di Bari (coordinated by Professor Nicola Martinelli), University of Bologna (coordinated by Professor Valentina Orioli) and University of Genoa (coordinated by Professor Roberto Bobbio), who have embraced the overall methodology and research purposes, providing their contribution to extend the *Atlante dei territori post-metropolitani* to three more territories.

Finally, the editors would like to thank all of the colleagues at the Department of Architecture and Urban Studies (DAStU), Politecnico di Milano, with whom they had the opportunity to discuss the research objectives and results during the last four years.

A sincere and special thought goes to Edward W. Soja, who has inspired the research project and passed away during its accomplishment.

Credits

The research on which this book is based comes from the Research Project of National Interest (PRIN 2010–11) 'Post-metropolitan territories as emergent forms of urban space: coping with sustainability, habitability, and governance' (*Territori post-metropolitani come forme urbane emergenti: le sfide della sostenibilità, abitabilità e governabilità*), funded by the Italian Ministry for Education, Universities and Research (MIUR) and coordinated by Professor Alessandro Balducci (Politecnico di Milano).

PART I

Building an atlas of post-metropolitan Italy

1 Post-metropolitan territories as emergent forms of urban space

Alessandro Balducci, Valeria Fedeli and Francesco Curci

Post-metropolis: an inspiring conceptualization

Processes of multi-scalar regional urbanization are occurring worldwide, with characteristics that clearly distinguish them from those studied by nineteenth- and twentieth-century urban studies through the traditional concepts of both the city first and the metropolis later. International literature highlights how all that we have historically associated with the idea of cities has long been subjected to a consistent reconfiguration, which involves and stresses some of the typical features of the idea of "cityness" (Sennett, 2007) – in other words, what we consider the typical urban characteristics to be, what makes the city a specific phenomenon that can be distinguished from other forms of social life. Size, density and heterogeneity were accounted for by Wirth and the Chicago school as the distinctive characteristics of "the urban"[1] (Dematteis & Lanza, 2011); the processes that have occurred since the end of the twentieth century in Europe and in the United States have produced relevant challenges to these features. So far, literature has focused its attention on the description of the new forms and size of the city, elaborating a large amount of new terms to describe its new characteristics: conurbations, (global) city-regions, megalopolis, megacities, polycentric regions (Geddes, 1915; Gottmann, 1957; Borja et al., 1997; Sassen, 2001; Florida, 2006; Hall & Pain, 2006; Florida et al., 2008; Scott, 2011), and so on. At the same time, the international debate has also shown that, together with their size and form, the nature and identity of cities are being profoundly modified. In the European context, in particular, some historical characteristics seem to be at stake (Le Galès, 2002, 2006, 2011, 2015) – social heterogeneity, political autonomy and governmental asset, roles and functions, lifestyles and landscapes, political orientation – so much so that, on the one hand, urban multiplication and diffusion become categories no longer clear and significant (Amin & Thrift, 2005), while on the other, in the face of *planetary urbanization* (Brenner, 2014), the city appears to be just one of the forms of the contemporary urban condition. In this respect, the city has become, for scholars, politicians and policymakers, an ambiguous object (Martinotti, 1999), the description (and government) of which is particularly complex because it has become more and more difficult to isolate the contemporary urban fabric in terms of a stable and definitive socio-spatial fact that is clearly distinguishable from the non-urban realm.

For many years, these kinds of processes have been interpreted in terms of decentralization, dispersion or even disloyalty to the constituent characteristics of the historical city, reproducing an interpretative model typical of the nineteenth century, counterposing the center to the periphery, concentration to dispersion, homogeneity to heterogeneity, proximity to distance. In this sense, according to several scholars, including Edward Soja, much of the literature that initially came to terms with the so-called new urban dimension has not really renewed the vocabulary and the concept of the city (Soja, 2011). Even when trying to describe the new metropolitan condition, a great part of the literature has simply expanded the "city" framework for the interpretation and judgment of processes that could not be framed anymore with the same concepts (Soja, 2011). Not only images such as that of agglomeration and conurbation (the former being the result of the growth around the compact city, the latter the result of the welding of neighboring agglomerations), but also the same idea of metropolitan areas seems, in this respect, still based on the idea of a clearly identifiable relationship between the central city and its neighboring territories, or an area of influence of the central city.

Such traditional interpretations of urban change have been questioned by a number of authors who have proposed thinking, a decade from now, in new terms about the contemporary urban, looking at the unfolding processes of regional urbanization that are completely reshaping the urban, but also looking at size, density and heterogeneity (just to mention some of these new definitions: the "città infinita", introduced by Bonomi & Abruzzese, 2004; the "open city", proposed by Sennet, 2007; the "endless" city, discussed by Burdett & Sudjic, 2007). The American geographer Edward Soja – looking in particular at urban phenomena on the West Coast of the USA, but extending his exploration outside of the United States – proposed in 2011 focusing on new socio-spatial phenomena that seemed to have erased or fundamentally altered the relationship between urban and suburban as conceptualized, first, within an urban model, and then within a metropolitan one. In particular, he proposed exploring and dealing with "the emergence of a distinctive new urban form, the extensive polynucleated, densely networked, information-intensive and increasingly globalized city region [. . .], to a polycentric network of urban agglomerations, where relatively high densities are found throughout the urbanized region" (Soja, 2011, p. 684).

Three epiphenomena, according to Soja, could be detected and studied under the concept of "post-metropolis," as reformulated by the author in 2011: (1) the flattening and shrinking of the gradient of urban density; (2) the progressive erosion of the boundary between urban and suburban; and (3) the homogenization of the urban landscape as well as an increasing differentiation and specialization of the suburban. Among the effects, Soja (2011) listed: (1) the disappearance of significant differences in lifestyles between urban and suburban, with the emergence of different (sub) urban ways of life; (2) the mixing of urban and suburban forms; (3) the combination of paradoxical forms of decentralization and recentralization, tied on the one hand to the expulsion of some urban functions in peri-urban contexts, capable of generating new centers and, on the other, to the shaping of new geographies in the suburban and the reverse; and (4) the emergence of a new urban form, that of "polynucleated, densely networked, information-intensive, and increasingly globalized city region" (Soja, 2011, p. 684). In the post-metropolis conceptualized by Soja, the traditional density gradients from the center to the periphery get thinner; the boundaries between the city and the countryside fade away; peripheries become more and more differentiated and host strategic urban functions; decentralization and recentralization recombine and produce new sets of centralities and new systems of voids. These effects could express and configure not only a new urban form, but also a "new urban question" that reformulates, rather than simply amplifying some of the typical problems of the twentieth-century city, such as environmental degradation, social polarization, inequalities in the distribution of and access to resources. The new urban regional scale seems to behave like a constitutive element not only of spatial recomposition, but also social and economic processes. This element questions the idea of socio-spatial cohesion traditionally linked with the urban fact, and lets new destructuring and restructuring processes emerge, deserving new analysis, interpretation and policy approaches.

We came into this reconceptualization of post-metropolis in terms of regional urbanization on the occasion of a seminar organized in Paris by the City Councilor Pierre Mansat, the purpose of which was to discuss the challenges of metropolitan governance in the case of similar urban contexts (Paris Metropole, *Le defi de la gouvernance*, 2011). We found it to be an interesting and challenging hypothesis of research to use as a starting point, a few months later, when we initiated a research proposal to be submitted to the national call for research projects published by the Italian Ministry for Education, Universities and Research (MIUR). The discussion that took place in Paris with Edward Soja seemed promising and stimulating. Once back in Italy and looking for a challenging research framework to propose, we suggested to other colleagues in Italy to assume some of the questions that the discussion had generated in our minds.

Could Soja's reasoning be assumed also to explore the Italian context? Were Italian cities facing the emergence of new complex and diverse forms of the urban, characterized by the above-mentioned processes? Could this interpretative framework allow us to unveil a new urbanization phase and, together with this, help us identify new forms of social inequalities, a more heterogeneous and divided city, characterized by new social differentiation or plagued by significant environmental problems as proposed by Soja? Alternatively, was the Italian case impossible to describe according to the hypothesis developed with reference to the USA context? Was there the need for a specific and peculiar interpretative framework?

In our minds there was also the idea that the last 20 years of research on regional urbanization in Italy had produced quite consistent results in terms of conceptualization of urban change (Boeri et al., 1993; Lanzani, 2003; Clementi et al., 1996; Secchi, 2005; Balducci & Fedeli, 2007; Balducci et al., 2008; Balducci et al., 2011), but with limited international resonance. Indeed, the Italian case could contribute to enriching the international debate, proposing possible alternative interpretations to international mainstreaming (Roy, 2009). Since the 1990s, the Italian debate has generously focused on the interpretation of the consistent processes of socio-spatial change occurring in some of the largest urban areas in Italy. And since the 1960s, in fact, a series of important changes have affected some of the most lively urban contexts in Italy, attracting the attention of several urban scholars (among others, De Carlo, 1962; Samonà, 1959; Quaroni, 1967; Indovina et al., 1990; Boeri et al., 1993; Turri, 2000; Secchi, 2005; Perulli, 2012). In particular, some of the concepts introduced in the early 1960s – in a dialogue with the international debate, by authors such as Quaroni, Samonà and De Carlo, for example the *città-regione* (De Carlo, 1962) – to describe the first evident effects of urban regionalization in contexts such as the Milan urban region have been reused and adapted to discuss more recent processes that occurred during the late 1980s and early 1990s and which have been interpreted through the concept of *città diffusa* (Indovina et al., 1990). This umbrella term is used in different ways by different authors to describe the contradictions and potentialities, the threats and opportunities of a kind of urban development with new forms, size and meaning, both in more typical metropolitan conditions (the case of the Milan urban region) and in non-metropolitan ones (the Veneto region). In this respect the Italian debate has focused on the one hand on the contradictions and potentialities of a diffuse urbanization, altering the traditional reference to the city, and on the other on the proposal of new urban landscapes and lifestyles, which deserved not only appropriate descriptions but also design attention. In particular, a part of the debate has stigmatized the externalities of a "diffuse urbanization" and suggested the necessity to govern the "urban diffusion" (see in particular Indovina, 1990). This part of the literature has at the same time clarified that the diffuse city was different in nature from the concept of sprawl: the Italian diffuse city was a mixed-use city, not necessarily low density and not necessarily rich and suburban. The other part has tried to acknowledge the dignity of this new form of urbanity, looking at it as a positive planning challenge (see Lanzani, 2003; Secchi, 2005), and in particular trying to produce new analytical categories able to grasp the new settlement patterns but also with attention to the socio-economic dynamics that produce them. In the mid-2000s the exploration of large conurbations covering entire parts of the national territory – in particular along the Turin-Milan-Venice axis in terms of *città infinita* by Bonomi and Abruzzese (2004) – further contributed to developing the idea of a new urban dimension, which is not only infinite, because it is lacking in boundaries, but infinitely complex in all its components – meaning in this sense that the complexity of problems and opportunities offered by the traditional urban areas can be found even in apparently suburban or traditionally peripheral contexts. The historical polycentric nature of the Italian context and the conceptualization of the Third Italy in the economic sphere have further contributed to the debate, confirming the special attention to the richness of the urban structure on the one hand, and on the other focusing innovatively on the production of urban formations based on a peculiar interaction between a small and medium-sized manufacturing system and the historical urban grid in specific parts of the country (namely in the Lombardy, Veneto, Emilia Romagna, Toscana and Marche regions). In this respect, the idea of post-metropolis could appear only partially able to contribute to this articulated debate.

We also had a final urgency in our scholarly agenda: that of putting forward a research project that could, almost 20 years after one of the last systematic attempts in Italy to interpret socio-spatial change processes produced by an academic research project (Clementi et al., 1996), recognize and thematize the emergence of new and plural "urban forms"/"forms of urbanity" and contribute to supporting decision-makers and policymakers in shaping a more consistent urban agenda and new forms of urban governance. The frequentation of the international debate had in fact convinced us that a systematic exploration of the urban phenomenon had been lacking in Italy for a long time (at least since the 1980s). This void in the production of knowledge was even more dramatic in terms of policy agenda: not only had the urban become an increasingly unidentified object (CSS, 2011), but it was also feeding a void in the field of public policies and institutional design. No explicit urban policy has, in fact, been (and is even now) available in Italy for a long time (Urban@it, 2016). At the same time, some of the recent institutional reforms are based on an interpretation of urban regions still built on a metropolitan imaginary, thus further contributing to enlarge the debate between the *de facto* city and the *de iure* city (Calafati, 2014).

A research project of national concern: main challenges and expectations

Assuming this perspective in an exploratory way, discussed by several strands of international literature and which we started synthetically to indicate with the concept of the "post-metropolis" (Soja, 2011), we submitted a PRIN research project entitled "Post-metropolitan territories as emergent forms of urban space: coping with sustainability, habitability, and governance." The project, which was funded and run between 2013 and 2016, involved nine universities in Italy (Politecnico di Milano, Università del Piemonte Orientale, Politecnico di Torino, IUAV Venezia, Università degli Studi di Firenze, Università di Roma La Sapienza, Università di Napoli Federico II, Università di Palermo, Università di Sassari) and other research centers (in particular ISPRA, Istituto Superiore per la Protezione e la Ricerca Ambientale) with a large and interdisciplinary network of scholars and researchers.[2] We aimed to explore major urban areas in Italy, with particular attention on the production of urban regionalization, or "regional urbanization" processes (Soja, 2011), trying to produce both a theoretical and an empirical contribution to the construction of analytic and interpretative frameworks able to describe what we considered as the emergence of multi-scale processes of urbanization, based on a complex interaction between path-dependency and innovations and consistently challenging the fields of urban studies, planning and urban governance. In this perspective, the project aimed to provide significant indications also in the practices and policies field, being interested in developing interpretative scenarios able to suggest innovative policy approaches, in particular in terms of livability, sustainability and governability.

The research activities developed during the three years focused in particular on the emergence of new scales, dimensions, morphologies and typologies of "urban" that seemed to escape, also in the Italian context, the traditional center-periphery paradigm and the related policy treatment. An unaccomplished metropolitan season seems in fact to distinguish the Italian context from other ones – both from the settlement pattern and the institutional process point of view. On the one hand, the historical polycentric urban network has, in fact, interacted with specific effect on the growth of capital cities, producing something that cannot be classified in terms of metropolitan, nor in terms of sprawl of suburbanization; on the other, the historical polyarchy and central role of municipalities have so far not allowed the real implementation of supralocal or regional authorities able to intercept and deal with the new scale of processes, bypassing the traditional municipal and city boundaries. Facing this specificity, we were interested in testing if the post-metropolis paradigm could introduce us to a different interpretation of the current urbanization phase. In this perspective, the research project was developed along three main axes during the three years: the construction of interpretative images (*explorations*), the identification of problems linked with the nature of the current urbanization processes (*questions*) and the design of innovation scenarios (*scenarios*).

In the first direction, the research project developed an in-depth investigation of transformation processes occurring in major Italian urban areas, based on the production of a quantitative database responding to key research questions. In particular, a research protocol was developed which aimed at providing an answer to a set of research questions: which kind of processes are main Italian urban areas experiencing? Can they be described according to the traditional metropolitan concept or can the post-metropolis conceptualization provide an interesting framework to describe new forms of urbanity? In particular, can we recognize the emergence of new problematic urban challenges or, on the contrary, a new urbanity offer, as an outcome of the new dimension, size and nature of the urban phenomena explored?

In implementing the research project, a large part of our effort was concentrated on the development of a research framework useful for producing new analytical and interpretative portraits of large urban areas in Italy. The production of this was a central step in the consolidation of research questions and the construction of research devices able to develop them. The decision was taken to make use of a quantitative research approach in order to select indicators that could measure and describe processes of social, economic, environmental and political change. On the basis of this research protocol, supported by GIS (geographical information system) and web technologies, it produced the so-called "Atlas of post-metropolitan territories" (*Atlante dei territori post-metropolitani*; see Chapter 2 for details), an open web resource thought of as an observatory prototype to be used by researchers, scholars, practitioners and decision-makers, but also everyday citizens.[3]

The quantitative research protocol has been applied to nine case studies (Turin; Milan; Venice and Veneto; Florence and Tuscany; Rome; Naples; Palermo; south-eastern Sicily; Gallura – the latter two as counter-cases), selected because they are representative of major urban areas in Italy or unexpected processes of post-metropolitan nature in non-typical urban contexts. The delimitation of the cases, together with their selection, and the construction of the protocol, can be considered as some of the most significant elements of the research project, both in terms of methodology and content. The research protocol was in fact applied to two different strategic exploration devices: the so-called *squares* (in Italian, originally *tasselli*) and the *corridors* (TEN-T Core Network Corridors).

The *squares* are 100 × 100 km wide (a bit smaller in the insular cases) observation "windows" inside which the exploration was developed, trying to overcome administrative boundaries and observe the nature, dimension, forms and significance of the social, political, economic, institutional and environmental challenges affecting main urban areas in Italy. The *squares* are thought to explore, in a manner that cannot be taken for granted, the emergence of new socio-spatial patterns and test the gradient hypothesis proposed by Edward Soja. They are positioned over the map, as each chapter will argue, in relation to some original research hypotheses on the specific nature of the urban regions explored, in particular taking into account the complex interplay between path-dependency and innovation. The *squares* are, in this respect, used to enlarge the viewpoint, unbundle it from traditional administrative geographies, possibly exploring new boundaries and measuring the nature of observed processes that question the traditional center–periphery dimension. The *squares* are thought to check processes of socio-spatial differentiation inside each urban region while providing a common spatial reference aid for comparing the consistency and nature of phenomena observed inside the different urban areas explored. In particular, the explored *squares* cover the most important urban areas in Italy, where one could expect to better test the post-metropolis conceptualization. Two additional counter-cases were originally selected in order to test it in non-traditional urban contexts: eastern Sicily and northern Sardinia. They are two island territories, affected in the last decades by important urban change linked to different models of tourist development, which seemed to be experiencing some interesting processes of urban change with traces of post-metropolization (emergence of urban density profiles; complexification of the social structure; hybridization of landscapes; erosion of the urban/non-urban boundaries).

The *corridors* were introduced as a counterbalance: they represent the main infrastructural and logistic corridors as defined by the European Union: by crossing the *squares* they help test the necessity to overcome the center–periphery logic in a transcalar and relation scale, and they provide the opportunity to explore an unedited urban geography. The *corridors* were studied in particular by the local research unit of Piemonte Orientale, interested in developing an observation and understanding of regional urbanization processes able to intercept and describe the formation of large urban regions all over the Italian territory.

Each research unit contributed to the production of the research framework and to its application in a specific territorial context, basically corresponding to the reference territory of the local research units and teams, with the aim of producing in-depth interpretations of local cases, as well as contributing to a discussion at national level. On this basis, every research unit produced a report-monography dedicated to the different *squares*, which we decided to call *regional portraits*. The idea was to produce a series of interpretative portraits of the urban regions explored, based on a common research protocol that was not necessarily comparative, but which could express significant research hypotheses at both local and national levels. Indeed, each research unit developed the portrait not only adopting the protocol in the background, but assuming specific key perspectives considered relevant to the discussion of peculiar processes of change, as will be evident when reading the chapters of this book. It proposes a collection, a *gallery*, of regional portraits, where each portrait is conceived as a highly interpretative picture of the case as well as a contribution to the general research hypothesis in a non-linear and holistic representation of post-metropolitan Italy. All in all in this sense, as we argue throughout the book, it provides an image of urban Italy that is quite different from the uniform, continuous and homogeneous urban region described by Soja and Kanai (2007) – and even more from the "Rom-Mi-Tur" depicted by Florida (2008, p. 55) – as the outcome of a complex interplay between path-dependency and innovation.

This book: structure and contents

This book has three major aims: (1) to contribute to the international discussion and in particular to the debate on the necessity of a new urban theory (Brenner, 2014); (2) to introduce and discuss some of the most relevant methodological challenges related to the exploration and interpretation of the current forms of the contemporary urban world; and (3) to present and discuss an updated portrait of contemporary Italian urban phenomena. In this perspective, the book is characterized by a balance between theory and empirical findings, being at the same time a relevant resource for discovering the Italian context and aiming at producing a significant contribution to urban theory and research.

These objectives are achieved both in the introductory chapters, presented in Part I, and in Part II, which is dedicated to illustrating the regional portraits. In particular, Chapter 2 presents the main methodological challenges related to a key output of the PRIN research: the "Atlas of post-metropolitan territories" (*Atlante dei territori post-metropolitani*) designed and implemented with the ambition to build an observatory on urban regionalization processes in Italy (PRIN Postmetropoli, 2015). Part II collects the nine regional portraits developed by the different research units involved in the project: the chapters were constructed following a shared line of observation, according to which the case is presented highlighting its specificity in the Italian context and the reasons behind the positioning of the *square* framing a specific territory. Each regional portrait reflects on three different dimensions of change, trying to unveil the complex interplay between path-dependency and innovation: the social, the spatial and the institutional, adopting the hypothesis that social change often precedes spatial change and that institutions often follow social and spatial change at a certain distance. This approach was discussed during the research seminar held in Milan in February 2015, during which the international advisory board of the project was invited to discuss preliminary results.[4] The regional portraits also anticipate some specific key issues, in relation to its implication on the specific case. In this respect, the regional portraits proposal situated arguments on a number of key issues, which are more generally presented in Part III of the book. This is composed of six different contributions which provide critical elements on several key issues. The chapter by Perulli, Lieto, Garavaglia and Pennati illustrates the *corridor* dimension and copes with the transcalarity of processes of regional urbanization. The role of physicality and territory is discussed by Paba and Perrone. The challenges in the field of governance and citizenship are exposed by Fedeli, while De Leo and Palestino argue about the relevance of regulation and "s-regulation" matters. The chapter by Fregolent and Vettoretto (with Bottaro and Curci) presents the results of a socio-economic cluster analysis and synthetically proposes to identify different urban typologies of contemporary Italy. Finally, the chapter by Cellamare and Vettoretto puts forward some final hypotheses on the peculiarity of the Italian context. The final chapter presents conclusions by the editors about the results of the research project and argues about the relevance of the post-metropolis conceptualization in the Italian context, in particular with some implications on the policy dimension and on the sphere of spatial planning.

Notes

1 The substantive use of the adjective "urban," which will be quite frequent in this book, derives from the lexicon of Henri Lefèbvre (1970).
2 For a complete list of the colleagues that have participated in the PRIN research project, read the initial note in each regional portrait and in the chapter by Perulli, Lieto, Garavaglia and Pennati.
3 The *Atlante* is designed to be implemented over time, also with the contribution of researchers not formally members of the original network. During the second and third years, for example, the construction of the atlas has been extended to other urban areas – Genoa, Bologna and Bari – with the contribution of other research units with the aim of promoting further information on related cases (see PRIN Postmetropoli, 2015).
4 The international advisory board was composed of: Professor Peter Ache (Radboud University Nijmegen, Netherlands), Professor Louis Albrechts (emeritus, Catholic University of Leuven, Belgium), Professor Simin Davoudi (Newcastle University, UK), Professor Christian Lefèvre (Université Paris-Est Marne-la-Vallée, France), Professor Klaus R. Kunzmann (emeritus, Technical University of Dortmund, Germany), Professor Willeem Salet (University of Amsterdam, Netherlands), Professor Iván Tosics (Metropolitan Research Institute, Budapest, Hungary).

References

Amin, A., and Thrift, N. (2005). *Cities: Reimagining the Urban*. Cambridge: Polity Press.
Balducci, A., and Fedeli, V. (Eds.). (2007). *I territori della città in trasformazione: tattiche e percorsi di ricerca*. Milano: FrancoAngeli.
Balducci, A., Fedeli, V., and Pasqui, G. (Eds.). (2008). *In movimento: Confini, Popolazioni E Politiche nel territorio milanese*. Milano: FrancoAngeli.
Balducci, A., Fedeli, V., and Pasqui, G. (2011). *Strategic Planning for Contemporary Urban Region*. Aldershot: Ashgate.
Boeri, S., Lanzani, A., and Marini, E. (1993). *Il territorio che cambia, Ambienti, paesaggi, immagini della regione milanese*. Milano: Aim-Segesta.
Bonomi, A., and Abruzzese, A. (Eds.). (2004). *La città infinita*. Milano: Mondadori.
Borja, V., Belil, M., Castells, M., and Benner, C. (1997). *Local and Global: The Management of Cities in the Information Age*. United Nations Centre for Human Settlements. London: Earthscan Publications Ltd.

Brenner, N. (Ed.). (2014). *Implosions/Explosions: Towards a Study of Planetary Urbanization*. Berlin: Jovis Verlag GmbH.

Burdett R., and Sudjic, D. (Eds.). (2007). *The Endless City: The Urban Age Project by the London School of Economics and Deutsche Bank's Alfred Herrhausen Society*. London: Phaidon.

Calafati, A. (2014). *Città e aree metropolitane in Italia* (GSSI Urban Studies Working Paper No. 1). L'Aquila: Gran Sasso Science Institute. Retrieved from http://ssrn.com/abstract=2369323

Clementi, A., Dematteis, G., and Palermo, P.C. (1996). *Le forme del territorio italiano, vol. I, Temi e immagini del mutamento, vol. II, Ambienti insediativi e contesti locali*. Bari: Laterza.

CSS, Consiglio italiano per le Scienze Sociali. (2011). *Società e territori da ricomporre: Libro bianco sul governo delle città italiane*. Roma.

De Carlo, G. (1962). Relazione finale. In Istituto Lombardo di Scienze Economiche e Sociali. (Ed.), *Relazioni del seminario "La nuova dimensione della città, la città-regione". Stresa 19–21 gennaio 1962*. Milano: Ilses.

Dematteis, G., and Lanza, C. (2011). *Le città del Mondo*. Torino: UTET.

Florida, R. (2006, July 3–10). The New Megalopolis: Our Focus on Cities is Wrong, Growth and Innovation Came from New Urban Corridors. *Newsweek International Edition*. Retrieved from http://www.msnbc.msn.com/id/13528839/site/newsweek/

Florida, R. (2008). *Who's Your City? How the Creative Economy Is Making Where to Live the Most Important Decision of Your Life*. Toronto: Random House of Canada.

Florida, R., Gulden, T., and Mellander, C. (2008). The Rise of Megaregions. *Cambridge Journal of Regions, Economy and Society*, 1(3), 459–476. doi: 10.1093/cjres/rsn018.

Geddes, P. (1915). *Cities in Evolution*. London: Williams and Norgate.

Gottmann, J. (1957). Megalopolis or the Urbanization of the Northeastern Seaboard. *Economic Geography*, 33(3), 189–200.

Hall P., and Pain, K. (2006). *The Polycentric Metropolis: Learning from Mega-City Regions in Europe*. London: Earthscan.

Indovina, F. (1990). La città diffusa. In F. Indovina, F. Matassoni, M. Savino, M. Torres, and L. Vettoretto (Eds.), *La città diffusa* (pp. 19–45). Venezia: Iuav-Daest.

Indovina, F., Matassoni, F., Savino, M., Torres, M., and Vettoretto, L. (Eds.). (1990). *La città diffusa*. Venezia: Iuav-Daest.

Lanzani, A. (2003). *I paesaggi italiani*. Roma: Meltemi.

Lefebvre, H. (1970). *La révolution urbaine*. Paris: Gallimard.

Le Galès, P. (2002). *European Cities: Social Conflicts and Governance*. Oxford: Oxford University Press.

Le Galès, P. (2006). *Le città europee: società urbane, globalizzazione, governo locale*. Bologna: il Mulino.

Le Galès, P. (2011). *Le Retour des villes européennes: sociétés urbaines, mondialisation, gouvernement et gouvernance. 2ème édition augmentée d'une préface inédite*. Paris: Presses de Sciences Po.

Le Galès, P. (2015), *Esiste ancora un modello europeo di città?* [Lecture/Video]. Urban@it Seminar, Università di Bologna, October 2. Retrieved from https://www.youtube.com/watch?v=QVvjNTcb0iA.

Martinotti, G. (Ed.). (1999). *La dimensione metropolitana*. Bologna: il Mulino.

Perulli, P. (Ed.). (2012). *Nord: Una città-regione globale*. Bologna: il Mulino.

PRIN Postmetropoli. (2015). *Atlante web dei territori postmetropolitani* [web atlas]. Retrieved from http://www.postmetropoli.it/atlante.

Quaroni, L. (1967). *La torre di Babele*. Padova: Marsilio.

Roy, A. (2009). The 21st Century Metropolis: New Geographies of Theory. *Regional Studies*, 43(6), 819–830.

Samonà, G. (1959). *L'urbanistica e l'avvenire delle città*. Bari: Laterza.

Sassen, S. (2001). Global Cities and Global City-Regions: A Comparison. In A.J. Scott (Ed.), *Global City-Regions* (pp. 78–95). Oxford: Oxford University Press.

Scott, A.J. (Ed.). (2011). *Global City-Regions: Trends, Theory, Policy*. Oxford: Oxford University Press.

Secchi, B. (2005). *La città del XX secolo*. Bari: Laterza.

Sennet, R. (2007). The Open City. In R. Burdett and D. Sudjic (Eds.), *The Endless City: The Urban Age Project by the London School of Economics and Deutsche Bank's Alfred Herrhausen Society* (pp. 290–297). London: Phaidon.

Soja, E. (2011). Regional Urbanization and the End of the Metro-polis Era. In G. Bridge and S. Watson (Eds.), *New Companion to the City* (pp. 679–689). Chichester: Wiley-Blackwell.

Soja, E.W., and Kanai, M. (2007). The Urbanization of the World. In R. Burdett and D. Sudjic (Eds.), *The Endless City: The Urban Age Project by the London School of Economics and Deutsche Bank's Alfred Herrhausen Society* (pp. 54–69). London: Phaidon.

Turri, E. (2000). *La megalopoli padana*. Venezia: Marsilio.

Urban@it, Centro nazionale di studi per le politiche urbane. (Ed.). (2016). *Rapporto sulle città, Metropoli attraverso la crisi*. Bologna: il Mulino.

2 Towards an observatory of urban Italy

Methodological challenges of the 'Atlas of post-metropolitan territories'

Alessandro Balducci, Valeria Fedeli, Francesco Curci and Fabio Manfredini[1]

Cities are central places in the contemporary world, which is becoming more urban: not only because more than 50 percent of world population is concentrated in cities (OECD, 2012) – more than 80 percent in the Italian context (CSS, 2011) – but because it is more and more difficult to distinguish between urban and non-urban places (Brenner, 2014). In this perspective, it is even more urgent than in the past to reflect on a diffuse and plural condition of urbanity that questions the same nature of the urban and opens to dramatic challenges, both from the theory point of view, and the policies and practices point of view. At the same time, it seems necessary to understand if the urban question is still a central one in the contemporary social question: in other words, if observing the city is still a crucial act for understanding societal challenges and the urban has a central role in the social question of the twenty-first century (Donzelot, 2009).

A sort of chronic absence characterizes the Italian context from this perspective: not only have we been missing for a long time a national policy dedicated to cities (d'Albergo, 2010; Cremaschi, 2005, 2006, 2010), but we have also never had an observatory on urban change and on the problems of cities. In 2011 the *Libro bianco sul governo delle città* (CSS, 2011) – a white paper on cities promoted by academics – denounced this lack of attention from public policies towards cities and called for not only a new analytic exploration, but also a new policy and institutional treatment of cities which is able to guarantee their role as a resource for the country and as an essential foundation for the democratic future of the country. More recently, a number of Italian universities founded Urban@it, a national center for urban policy, in order to reinforce the debate on the urgency of a national urban policy, which is also connected with the European debate on an urban agenda (Urban@it, 2016).

Actually, a number of local or sectoral observatories are available, promoted at regional level, together with some supra-local ones promoted and supported by cities and their associations which produce and make available some relevant data.[2] At a national level, the National Statistics Institute (ISTAT) and the National Council for Economics and Labor (CNEL) have recently been working on the production of indicators focused on the urban condition, elaborating the so-called BES (an indicator of well-being associated with the urban scale and condition).[3] Finally, the diffusion of open data is producing a vast amount of data on the web, but in quite a fragmented and opaque modality. Despite these efforts, the Italian context does not have an organized and systematic observatory on the urban condition that is able to provide a state-of-the-art image that produces and diffuses organized and usable knowledge for stakeholders, decision-makers, scholars and citizens.

At university level, the last attempt to produce an observatory on territorial change dates to the late 1990s: the research project "Itaten" tried to map the process of spatial and social change characterizing Italy at the end of the twentieth century (Clementi et al., 1996). A previous relevant effort was the so-called "Progetto 80" (Ministero del Bilancio e della Programmazione Economica, 1969; Renzoni, 2012) launched by the Ministry of Finance and Economic Affairs, which aimed to provide relevant implications on public policies. Since then no additional effort has been promoted, confirming a void that becomes more and more problematic, particularly in the current climate of growing uncertainty. The uncertainty that contradistinguishes the contemporary world, exacerbated by the economic crisis of the late 2000s, has generated a growing demand for usable knowledge, knowledge that can be used in private and public decision-making processes. City mayors, deputy mayors, city councilors, as well as other public decision-makers look for knowledge that can contemporaneously produce effectiveness and legitimacy in decision-making processes. At the same time there is – particularly in this moment of institutional reform – a growing demand for knowledge in connection with the new transcalar nature of processes. Against the backdrop of the general challenging interplay between local and global dimensions, recent institutional reforms – introducing metropolitan government institutions and discussing the nature, role and boundaries of large-scale institutional levels such as provinces and regions[4] – push for a new geographical dimension of processes to be developed that can overcome official administrative boundaries, which are increasingly unable to intercept the networked and transcalar nature of social practices and urbanization (Brenner, 2000).

At an international level, a new interest in quantitative studies has recently emerged on the basis of the amount of data that can now be generated and made available by information technologies. "The new science of cities," as Michael Batty (2013) defined it in his recent book, paves the way for new focus on quantitative methodologies and, at the same time, opens up several challenges in terms of both methodology and content, particularly in relation to the need to consider the implications of network theory and complexity theory. As proposed by Brenner, important methodological changes should be introduced, while looking for a new urban theory, in order to introduce data that is not based on census geography and which can represent flows rather than stocks (Brenner, 2014).

The *Atlante dei territori post-metropolitani*

Some of these challenges have been central nodes in our research project, in particular when we decided to dedicate the first year to the production of a quantitative database capable of describing socio-economical, politico-institutional and environmental transformation processes affecting large urban areas in Italy. The result of this effort of producing a new observatory on urban change, focusing in particular on large urban areas in Italy, is the "Atlas of [the Italian] post-metropolitan territories" (*Atlante dei territori post-metropolitani*; see PRIN Postmetropoli, 2015). This is an interactive web atlas that integrates maps, data, graphs and rankings, and it can be used to produce geographic representations of the major phenomena mapped through the collection of data and indicators, both simple and complex, selected on the basis of their relevance to the research hypothesis and research questions put forward by the PRIN project. The first and major section of the final product – divided into six families of simple indicators, for a total of more than one hundred interactive maps – resembles other international observatories on urban change, since it also provides general data and information on the whole national territory and all the municipal bodies in Italy. In its second section, dedicated to complex indicators, it presents a more oriented observatory on urban change in large urban areas: the composite and synthetic indicators provided here are in fact the outcome of advanced elaborations aimed at testing the post-metropolis conceptualization in the Italian context. The final section of the web atlas collects, among others: composite indicators of human density; urban hardship; physiographic resistance to urbanization; economic, demographic and financial dynamism; synthetic indexes of road accessibility; mobility; self-containment; residential attractiveness; and so on.[5]

The construction of the *Atlante* was, from this perspective, a test field in four methodological directions, if compared with other similar experiences and the international debate (see Brenner, 2014, for the debate on the methodology of research to be developed to explore processes of planetary urbanization), in so far as:

- *It experiments with new geographies of analysis*: even if largely based on census data, traditionally linked to the municipal boundaries, the *Atlante* proposes looking at urban areas through the 100 × 100 km *square*[6] and the *corridors* geography. This means that maps and data-generating maps are both available with a municipal scale, but can be read and analyzed through statistical elaboration generated inside the *squares* (see next point). This makes it possible to explore and acknowledge new geographies and boundaries linked with regional urbanization processes. In this perspective, the *Atlante* highlights and tries to deal with the necessity to produce a knowledge framework able to deal with the new scales and geographies of processes. The idea is that an urban phenomenon does not end at the municipality boundary but, in some way, it continues according to its real spatial dimension and intensity.[7]
- *It experiments with a transdisciplinary and interpretative perspective, the only thing able to measure a complex concept such as urbanity*: it is organized in different sections, which collect indicators and data in relation to spatial, socio-demographic, economic, environmental and energetic, political and institutional processes, trying to provide elements for a transdisciplinary portrait of urban change. The section dedicated to synthetic indicators in particular provides more complex elaborations based on a transdisciplinary

logic, aimed at reading the urban fact as the outcome of plural and complex processes, heterogeneous and articulated, and as such destined to be governed through non-sectoral but integrated policies. By crossing traditional urban data with less used ones (such as income profiles, voting geography, systems of opportunities, accessibility, institutional fragmentation, mobility indexes), the Atlas aims to identify ways to measure and assess the emergence and consistence of new forms of "urbanity" and "cityness" (Sennet, 2007; Sassen, 2010). This is a major methodological challenge: correlation between multidisciplinary data is the central point in trying to describe and interpret new urban facts, together with the emergence of new urban or "post-metropolitan" urban questions. The Atlas aims to build a multifaceted portrait of contemporary urban processes, making them comparable.

- *It experiments with the use of new data*, non-traditional data or the strategic reuse of census data: on the one hand, the availability of non-census data is increasing the range of information that can be used to describe traditional phenomena; on the other, it also allows, at times, the interception of practices and processes that traditional census data cannot describe, in particular for their transcalar, networked nature. The *Atlante* aims to produce a first exploration of these potentialities. In particular, it collects many different sources of data: authoritative, such as those provided by official statistical institutions or by other institutions (for example, Italian Revenue Agency, European Environment Agency, ISPRA), and crowdsourced, such as OpenStreetMap, which is used for obtaining information on the distribution of main urban facilities at the national scale (stadium, multiplex, harbors, and so on) that is difficult to find through conventional data providers. During the research we experimented with the necessity of integrating conventional data that were more flexible and more capable to overcome the hard constraints of the census data in terms of spatial (municipality boundary) and temporal resolution. From this perspective, the *Atlante* can be integrated with other sources of data, such as user-generated data and in particular mobile phone data, that have a very fine spatial and temporal resolution, are very flexible and can well describe and explain urban dynamics (Pucci et al., 2015).

- Finally, the Atlas has been built as an *open resource*, open to consultation for the research community, as well as for the policy community and society at large. It aims to offer the opportunity to explore a structured, updated and open database through geographical representations. In this respect, it is not a traditional repository of data: it produces geographic and infographic representations that allow the acknowledgement of geographies of observed processes and together a simple representation of basic statistical elaborations. It also makes available original data for consultation. In addition, it is thought of as a resource to be used and implemented by those who are using it: people consulting data and maps for their research can do so without having to pay, but are required to acknowledge the credits and at the same time share the results of their analysis with the community of the *Atlante* users. In this respect, it proposes a way of delivering the logic of open-source data, not as much in terms of direct access to raw data, but more in the capacity of the Atlas to show the multifaceted complexity of contemporary cities. The website can be explored in many ways and at different scales. For each page, it is possible to produce an overall map in national scale, to zoom on the *squares*, to customize classes and colors, to display road and rail lines as well as administrative boundaries, to perform specific analyses and visualizations by selecting specific ranges, exporting maps and charts as vector graphics. Each operation on the map corresponds to a consequent update on the graphs and vice versa. The Atlas therefore represents an interesting and useful tool for exploring dozens of complex urban questions in an intuitive and communicative way.

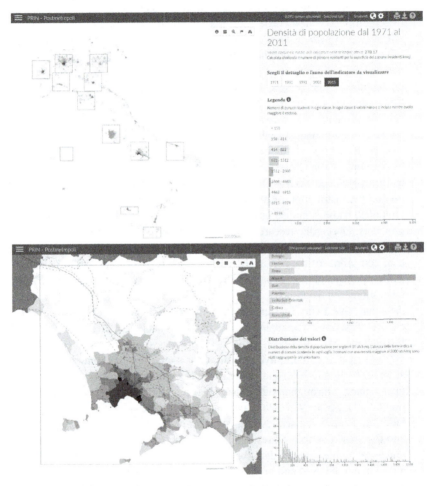

Figure 2.1 Atlante dei territori post-metropolitani [web atlas]: examples of cartograms and interactive charts

Source: PRIN Postmetropoli (2015)

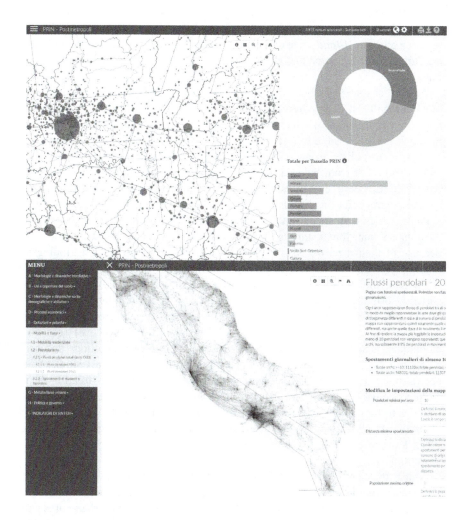

Figure 2.2 Atlante dei territori post-metropolitani [web atlas]: examples of interactive
maps of points (hubs and nodes) and arcs (flows)

The image also shows the indicators menu.

Source: PRIN Postmetropoli (2015)

About the role of the *square*

During the course of the PRIN research, as already mentioned, an important analytical role has been played by the so-called *square* (or *tessera*). Accordingly, it
seems important to devote part of this introductory chapter to summarize some

of the reasons that form the basis for this choice. This means trying to explain the function and the logic that in many ways the *square* assumes within our research and our *Atlante*, responding to various questions about where and how the "urban" (urbanization and urbanity) is changing inside and around the major Italian cities.

First, the *square* is both an observation device and a measurement tool. Metaphorically, it is together a lens, a caliber or a meter. Its use was originally motivated by the need to select and compare multiple portions of Italian territory in which it was possible to test empirically and quantitatively the discourses on the post-metropolis with particular reference to center–periphery gradients (Soja, 2000, 2011). Far from being a merely analytical tool, the *square* should not be conceived as a perimeter or as a geometric representation of urban phenomena. On the contrary, its function is to emphasize the extent and scale of some phenomena, which may appear totally but also partially inscribed in it. In fact, those phenomena that "break through" the *square* are especially relevant, not only because of their size, but also because of their morphology and positioning in relation to urban and regional systems and infrastructures.

Second, the geometrical, symmetrical and Cartesian choice (the *square* is perfectly oriented north–south/east–west, and it was never rotated) is dictated by the awareness of geo-morphological differences that characterize the Italian territory: the "obliquity" of the peninsula, the plentiful presence of seas and mountains, islands and sub-peninsulas. The uniformity of proportions and orientation in this sense can help detect and pinpoint the different case studies in a neutral manner, putting them, at least to start, on the same plane, treating them in the same way and avoiding pre-characterizations that anticipate interpretation. In order to maximize the relevance of the purviews, principally in the presence of particular physiographic characteristics, the only discretion granted to each PRIN local research unit was that relating to the positioning – by translation – of the *square.*

Third, the size of the *square* is dictated by the need to operate a leap of scale necessary to answer the research questions. Its bulk, in fact, calls for an enlargement of the gaze, "zooming out" from central cities and urban cores and emancipating both from metropolitan hierarchical monocentricity (Soja, 2011) and administrative boundaries.[8] Furthermore, the size of the *square* questions the very concepts of "urban" and "urbanization" returning to their epistemological roots (Brenner, 2014).[9]

Finally, the *square* is also motivated by more practical reasons related to its meaning and role within the *Atlante*. To allow the collection of data on a municipal basis, each local research unit has been commissioned to select a specific number of municipalities (even slightly external to the *square*) that constitute the defined set of statistical units. Although it is not comparative research, thanks to this operation it is now possible to compare the behavior of different urban regions, not only displaying their spatial patterns, but also comparing statistics (sums, averages, variances, and so on).

Figure 2.3 Squares and *corridors*

The map shows the *squares* explored by the PRIN local research units and reported in the "regional portraits" of Part II of this book (Turin, Milan, Venice and Veneto, Florence and Tuscany, Rome, Naples, Palermo, south-eastern Sicily, and Gallura). The dashed perimeter indicates the *squares* (Genoa, Bologna and Bari) that, already included in the web atlas, will be developed in the future thanks to the collaboration with other universities.

Source: PRIN Postmetropoli (2015)

Notes

1 Although this chapter should be considered a result of the common work and reflection of the three authors, A. Balducci took primary responsibility for the introduction, V. Fedeli and F. Manfredini took primary responsibility for the section 'The *Atlante dei territori post-metropolitani*', and F. Curci took primary responsibility for the section 'About the role of the *square*'.
2 See the websites and reports by Comuniverso (Ancitel) and Cittalia-Fondazione Anci Ricerche, promoted by the Association of Italian Municipalities (ANCI – Associazione Nazionale Comuni Italiani). See in particular the report edited by Testa (2013).

3 See the BES website: www.misuredelbenessere.it/.
4 See recent studies on macroregions by SGI (2014), Bruzzo (2016), and Ferri (2016).
5 See PRIN Postmetropoli (2015): "Idicatori di sintesi", § i.
6 As we will see, the *square* has a different dimension only in the Sardinian and Sicilian cases, principally because of geo-physical reasons. With specific reference to the two Sicilian cases, because of the rectangular shape, it was preferred to call it *tessera* instead of *square*. More precisely, the Gallura *square* is 75 x 75 km wide, the Palermo *tessera* is 100 x 40 km wide, and the southeastern Sicily *tessera* is 100 x 60 km wide (see PRIN Postmetropoli, 2015).
7 For this reason we also used census block data to develop a methodology aimed at producing maps and graphs based on a regular grid in order to obtain more homogeneous and continuous visualizations and statistics of spatial phenomena. An experimental representation of this approach has recently been published by Balducci et al. (2016).
8 An area of 10,000 km^2 (100 x 100 km) is about three times the average area of the Italian provinces and about two-thirds of the average area of Italian regions.
9 While not lying perfectly on the same level, Edward Soja's theory about post-metropolis and Neil Brenner's critical urban theory and radical cartography have both been useful in the construction of the PRIN research hypotheses and methodologies.

References

Balducci, A., Curci, F., Fedeli, V., and Pucci, P. (2016). Milano, post-metropoli? *Territorio*, 76, 35–45.

Batty, M. (2013). *The New Science of Cities*. Cambridge, MA: MIT Press.

Brenner, N. (2000). The Urban Question: Reflections on Henri Lefebvre, Urban Theory and the Politics of Scale. *International Journal of Urban and Regional Research*, 24, 361–378.

Brenner, N. (Ed.). (2014). *Implosions/Explosions: Towards a Study of Planetary Urbanization*. Berlin: Jovis Verlag GmbH.

Bruzzo, A. (2016). Riferimenti teorici per la delimitazione territoriale delle Regioni. *Argomenti. Rivista di economia, cultura e ricerca sociale*, 3, 31–56.

Clementi, A., Dematteis, G., and Palermo, P.C. (Eds.). (1996). *Le forme del territorio italiano* (Vol. 2). Bari: Laterza.

Cremaschi, M. (2005). *L'Europa delle città*. Firenze: Alinea.

Cremaschi, M. (2006). Politiche urbane: una assenza solo parziale. *Urbanistica*, 130, 12–19.

Cremaschi, M. (Ed.). (2010). *Politiche, città, innovazione*. Roma: Donzelli.

CSS, Consiglio italiano per le Scienze Sociali. (2011). *Società e territori da ricomporre. Libro bianco sul governo delle città italiane*. Roma.

d'Albergo, E. (2010). Urban Issues in Nation-State Agendas: A Comparison in Western Europe. *Urban Research & Practice*, 3(2), 138–158.

Donzelot, J. (2009). *Vers une citoyenneté urbaine*. Paris: Rue d'Ulm.

Ferri, V. (2016). La delimitazione territoriale dei governi sub-centrali: un'analisi comparata a livello europeo con particolare riferimento a Francia e Italia. *Argomenti. Rivista di economia, cultura e ricerca sociale*, 3, 57–92.

Ministero del Bilancio e della Programmazione Economica. (1969). *Progetto 80: rapporto preliminare al programma economico nazionale 1971–1975*. Roma: Istituto Poligrafico dello Stato.

OECD. (2012). *Redefining Urban Areas: A New Way to Measure Metropolitan Areas*. Retrieved from: http://www.oecd-ilibrary.org/urban-rural-and-regional-development/redefining-urban_9789264174108-en.

PRIN Postmetropoli. (2015). *Atlante web dei territori postmetropolitani* [web atlas]. Retrieved from http://www.postmetropoli.it/atlante.

Pucci, P., Manfredini, F., and Tagliolato, P. (2015). *Mapping Urban Practices through Mobile Phone Data*. Heidelberg, New York, Dordrecht, London: PolimiSpringerBrief. Springer.

Renzoni, C. (2012). *Il Progetto '80. Un'idea di Paese nell'Italia degli anni Sessanta*. Firenze: Alinea Editrice.

Sassen, S. (2010). Cityness: Roaming Thoughts about Making and Experiencing City. *Ex aequo*, 22, 13–18.

Sennet, R. (2007). The Open City. In R. Burdett and D. Sudjic (Eds.), *The Endless City: The Urban Age Project by the London School of Economics and Deutsche Bank's Alfred Herrhausen Society* (pp. 290–297). London: Phaidon.

SGI, Società Geografica Italiana (2014). *Per un riordino territoriale dell'Italia*. Roma.

Soja, E.W. (2000). *Postmetropolis: Critical Studies of Cities and Regions*. Oxford: Basil Blackwell.

Soja, E.W. (2011). Regional Urbanization and the End of the Metropolis Era. In G. Bridge & S. Watson (Eds.), *New Companion to the City* (pp. 679–689). Chichester: Wiley-Blackwell.

Testa, P. (Ed.). (2013). *Rapporto Cittalia 2013. Le Città Metropolitane*. Roma: Cittalia-Fondazione Anci Ricerche.

Urban@it, Centro nazionale di studi per le politiche urbane. (Eds.). (2016). *Rapporto sulle città. Metropoli attraverso la crisi*. Bologna: il Mulino.

PART II
Regional portraits
Looking inside the *squares*

3   Milan beyond the metropolis

*Alessandro Balducci, Valeria Fedeli and
Francesco Curci*[1]

The Milan urban region has been the focus of research explorations concerning regional urbanization processes since the 1960s. In fact, not only has it been one of the most evident cases of metropolitan development in Italy since the Second World War, but it can also be considered as one of the most patent cases of urban regionalization in the country.

In the 1990s several scholars conceptualized the case in terms of production of a spread-out city (*città diffusa*: Boeri et al., 1993), or an urban region (*regione urbana milanese*: Lanzani, 1991; Balducci, 2004), or a sort of endless city-region (*città infinita*: Bonomi & Abruzzese, 2004) that extends from Turin to Venice – one in which the extension, transcalarity, complexity, heterogeneity and acceleration of urbanization processes (Lévy, 2013) are the temporary outcome of the interaction among a historical polycentric structure inherited from the nineteenth century (De Finetti, 1969), forms of metropolitan organization that have renovated the city since the middle of the last century (Dalmasso, 1972; Mioni, 1975; Sernini, 1998; Moretti, 1999; Consonni & Tonon, 2001), regional-scale processes exceeding both traditional administrative boundaries and consolidated urban imaginaries, and conceptualizations that had already emerged in the late 1960s (De Carlo, 1962; Lanzani, 1991; Boeri et al., 1993; Clementi et al., 1996; Macchi Cassia, & Ischia, 1999; Secchi, 2005; Balducci & Fedeli, 2007; Balducci et al., 2008; Balducci et al., 2011).

In this perspective, the *square* of Milan was almost naturally centered in the city of Milan: this choice reflects on the one hand the central role that the city has historically played in the socio-spatial, economic and institutional organization of the regional space; on the other hand, it allows us to use the case to test some of the gradient hypotheses on which the conceptualization of post-metropolis is based (Soja, 2000, 2011), as this chapter will argue. The complex interplay between path-dependency and innovation that characterizes the case will be a second central aspect for interpreting the complex interaction among historical polycentrism and processes of metropolization and regional urbanization that have so far shaped a peculiar and at the same time exemplary urban region.

Post-metropolis, regional urbanization, urbanity: exploring the hypothesis of density gradients

The post-metropolis conceptualization proposed by Edward Soja in 2011 is based on several relevant assumptions (see Chapter 1). One of the most challenging arguments proposed by the author deals with the hypothesis based on the exploration of density gradients. According to this hypothesis, density – one of the most typical urban features – is no longer necessarily a prerogative of central cities. In particular, in Soja's hypothesis, the density gradient observed is related to population density, whose flattening curb provides an argument against the traditional center–periphery patterns and the need to acknowledge the emergence of a new urban condition. In this sense, the case of Milan, because of its historical radiocentric growth pattern, offers a great opportunity to test the hypothesis of the *bouleversement* of traditional center–periphery logics. At the same time, because of the legacy of the historical polycentric matrix developed before the twentieth century, it challenges methodologically the elaboration of a density gradient grounded on a metropolitan imaginary and offers the opportunity to test it in a typical European context.

In addition, this study formulates the hypothesis that the analytic potentialities of the density gradient could be extended beyond the sphere of demographic density to another density-related index, in the spatial, social, economic and institutional fields. In fact, this multiple and articulated interpretation and study of the density gradient is aimed at developing a quantitative possibility to measure and observe not only new urban density profiles, but also new patterns of "urbanity". The aim is to open an operative dialogue between Soja's hypothesis and other conceptualizations of urbanity proposed by authors such as Lévy (2013). In fact, Lévy proposes the idea of a *gradient d'urbanité*, where the density of relationships is taken into account in order to recognize places with strong or weak urbanity. In this respect, associating *density gradients* to *urbanity gradients* seems to give the possibility of distinguishing between urbanization and urbanity. In other words, the interest of this study is to try and test Soja's hypothesis beyond demographic density data in order to identify which kind of urban condition (urban life and offer, material and immaterial) is produced by processes of regional urbanization. Are we just facing more dense demographic patterns or urbanized patterns, or are we observing a thoroughly new socio-spatial organization, capable of providing a complex and vivid urban life to the inhabitants of a large urban region, exceeding the traditional idea of a center with its peripheries? An urban offer – a set of physical and social opportunities, but also a complex jigsaw of problems, conflicts and challenges – which would be available not only to the inhabitants of central cities, but in an open and differentiated way in different parts of the urban region. According to this hypothesis, we would observe the disappearance of (traditional) peripheries and the emergence of new polycentric urban conditions, not necessarily exempt from socio-spatial differentiation, but probably proposing non-traditional patterns and geographies – even in terms of center and peripheries.

The way to approach and measure *urbanity*, in this sense, becomes a key methodological and conceptual question, in order to contribute to a deeper interpretation of the post-metropolis concept. The aim is also to argue the relevance of the new urban scales in terms of production of a new urban question. In fact, the interest was not only to explore the spatial dimensions of regional urbanization processes, but also which kind (if) of urban conditions they are producing and which kind of urban problems they are generating. The Milan *square* provided interesting hints both from the methodological and content points of view.

The comparative study of the demographic density gradient of the Milan *square* within the national context reveals its peculiarity and uniqueness. In fact, the Milan *square* is characterized by a unique relevant phenomenon of density gradient flattening from the center of the city towards the rest of the urban region (Figure 3.1). This presents a completely different model compared with more metropolitan-like cases such as Turin, and non-metropolitan ones such as Venice (and Veneto) (Figure 3.2). In relative terms, the density of the population remains consistently higher than in any other Italian urban area at a distance of 30–40 kilometers from Milan's city center. While in the Turin case, the shift in the demographic density is already visible at a distance of 10–15 kilometers, reproducing a more traditional metropolitan behavior, in the Veneto *square*, the archipelago post-metropolis patterns do not even allow a measurement of density gradient from a defined central point.[2] From this perspective the Milan case, in particular when analyzed through cartograms, allows us to see different spatial behaviors: on the one hand, it is possible to see more typical density patterns in the first ring of municipalities, grown at higher rates in the economic boom after the Second World War, within a 10 km distance; on the other hand, highly dense patterns are evident again at a 30–60 km distance, where the other medium cities (provincial chief-towns) are located.[3] These two phenomena reflect the effects of more traditional metropolitan nature processes that took place between the 1950s and 1970s, producing a typical metropolitan ring around the city boundaries. They also show the historical polycentric structure of the urban region, producing historical networks of regional cities. What is new, or at least less ordinary than could be expected, is the consistency in terms of demographic density of the sector positioned between 10 and 40 kilometers, where demographic densities appear not at all different from the typical urban ones. These territories resonate with the idea of "in-between," as proposed by Sieverts (2003) and then reformulated by Keil (2011). Others, instead, see a non-traditional reading of the suburban space meant as a challenging urban condition which presents forms and characteristics that resemble, in terms of complexity of landscapes, more traditional city patterns. Far from being a space of sprawl (Lanzani, 2012), this in-between space is characterized not only by a high demographic density, but also by a dense profile of urbanization, where the diffusion of urban condominiums (rather than single-family housing patterns, as expected in most parts of the urban region) and land-take indicators show intense profiles of urbanization and models which are fairly different from sprawl.[4]

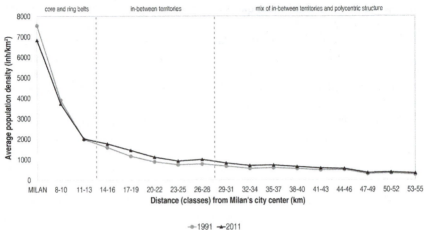

Figure 3.1 The flattening-out of population density gradient in the Milan *square* between 1991 and 2011

Source: Authors' calculation, based on data provided by ISTAT (Italian National Institute of Statistics) (Census data 1991, 2011)

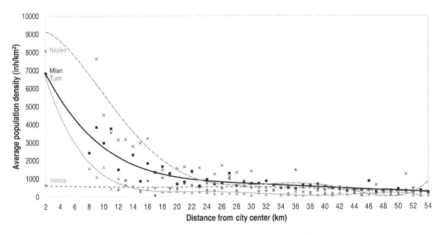

Figure 3.2 Population density gradients (2011): comparison between the *squares* of Milan, Naples, Turin and Venice

Source: Authors' calculation, based on data provided by ISTAT (Census data 2011)

Is this dense urbanization profile accompanied by an urban lifestyle? Once measured through density gradients of selected socioeconomic indicators, it is possible to notice – at a regional scale – the diffusion of conditions which traditionally belong to cities in the Italian context. From the demographic and socioeconomic point of view, in fact, citizens of the urban region show features that are quite comparable with those of the central city. For example, between 2001 and 2011, the linear curb of the rate of single-person households consistently flattened (down) in a space between 10 and 30 km; the ageing index, as well, dramatically flattened (up) outside Milan, with consistent peaks in the first ring, but also at a distance between 10 and 40 km. Both gradients appear increasingly flattened compared with the density gradient. What results from the analysis of the density gradients of the demographic data is that citizens of the urban region and citizens of the central city are less differentiated than in the past. Not only are ageing people concentrated in the central city or the regional ones, but the first ring of municipalities around Milan is experiencing a high concentration of ageing, and a general diffusion of ageing people can be registered all over the *square*. At the same time, singles, who traditionally chose the central city because of the opportunities it offers, are scattered in the urban region. Similar data can be observed in terms of concentration of immigrants and young families: the young families gradient is flatting down, while the immigrants gradient is flattening up. In both cases, the in-between space at a distance of 10–40 km has been the most affected by change in the last 20 years. The same is true for the central city, which is characterized by what could be defined as a sort of *implosion* – as we will argue in the next paragraph – with a return of typologies of inhabitants, young families in particular, that had abandoned the central city for decades. The same can be argued on the basis of social heterogeneity gradients. If traditionally we associate the idea of the city with a high degree of socio-demographic differentiation, the Milan *square* seems to be characterized by a growing *mixité* throughout the region. However, there is the exception of some residential enclaves of social homogeneity and isolation, mostly located beyond former industrial fringe municipalities.[5] Looking at the last two decades, for example, there has been a flattening-out of the ethnic mix gradient expressly up to a distance of 35 km from Milan.[6]

But are these citizens of the same kind? Do they have the same lifestyles and opportunities? As also shown by indicators such as income distribution, wealth distribution and hardship index, these in-between spaces present an urban profile increasingly comparable with that of cities, although in some cases still far from that of the city of Milan. The gradients of education, home property, housing types, unemployment rate and housing crowding highlight gentler curbs than in previous decades, while social polarization remains higher in the city of Milan than in its urban belt. Cartograms and gradients concerning per capita income and the Gini Index show the presence of rich and polarized territories located immediately after the belt municipalities of Milan. Nevertheless, even if "*clubbization*" phenomena have been observed through political and vote studies (Diamanti, 1996; Bonomi, 2008), the Milan *square* presents evidence of a flattening-out of diversities between the central city and the rest of the urban region. In other words, although it is still possible to identify different citizen profiles and orientations – as reflected in particular in political preferences – it is more and more complicated to distinguish between urban and suburban. In recent decades, the geography of votes has also witnessed a consistent change, with the central city of Milan becoming more oriented to the center-left and the metropolitan region observing the crisis of center-right coalitions (and Lega Nord traditionally representing the interests of a specific section of the electorate with a strong territorial base – conservative, small entrepreneurs, anti-immigrants).

Additional interesting evidence comes from the statistical processing of real estate data: although Milan stands out from its *square* – more than other big Italian cities, such as Florence and Bologna – the gradients of real estate market prices (average values of housing for sale and rent), as a form of measurement of the quality of life, reflect the existing wide offer of both basic and strategic urban functions. In fact, it is possible to see the wide range of cultural/educational, commercial and social functions all over the urban region that describe the presence of a typical urban life (kindergarten, for example, as a proxy of a family model in which women work).[7]

A further element that can reinforce this analysis concerns data on accessibility and mobility gradients. In this respect, the high degree of road (and railway) accessibility throughout the urban region does not go unnoticed, nor does the high level of mobility throughout it.[8] In particular, both the study of traditional mobility data and innovative data (based on telecommunication data) highlight an explosion of mobility all over the urban region. In particular, in the in-between area of 10–40 km, there is an interesting correlation with housing density profiles: on the one hand, there is a large section of the *square* with high urban density and high density of mobility; on the other hand, a more traditional low-density / high-mobility correlation can be detected in the southern part of the *square*, which seems to represent a more metropolitan model of mobility.[9]

From the socioeconomic point of view, data reflect a distribution gradient of innovative activities, confirming a changing economic profile – only partially due to the economic crisis that has affected one of the richest urban regions in Italy. Data also reflect a density gradient that confirms the strong economic relationship between the central city and the surrounding urban region, as we will argue in the following paragraphs. In fact, on the one hand, the employment crisis is producing new dependencies from the core cities; on the other hand, the in-between territories – most of which are suffering from the significant crisis in the manufacturing sector – appear particularly dynamic in terms of demographic and economic indicators, also because of recent technological and economic transitions. The change in the percentage of employees in innovative sectors (information, communication, finance, insurance, research, business services)[10] shows that, between 2001 and 2011, the modest growth of Milan, Bergamo and other centers, which slightly reduced their specialization, matched an increase of employees within the middle territories – namely in the south of Milan – which also increased its specialization.[11] These phenomena probably suggest the rise of new economic interactions and interdependencies – a sort of new supply chain – between core cities and neighboring territories (not excluding parts of the historical industrial districts). However, they also suggest the emergence of new local-scale demands for renewed competencies within rapidly changing territories. From this point of view, the proliferation as well as the numerous and dense infrastructural axes of new strategic commercial and leisure facilities (outlets, shopping centers, multiplex, amusement parks, and so on) contribute towards the growth of a diversified provision of services for territories less and less definable as suburban.

As a first general conclusion, the Milan *square* presents evident signs of post-metropolization characterized by new urbanity patterns producing some of the phenomena conceptualized by Soja (2000, 2011): (1) the flattening and shrinking of the gradient of urban density; (2) the progressive erosion of the boundary between urban and suburban; (3) the homogenization of the urban landscape as well as an increasing differentiation and specialization of the suburban.

In other terms, urbanity profiles and gradients also confirm a post-metropolitan profile with: (1) the disappearance of significant differences in lifestyles between urban and suburban, with the emergence of different (sub)urban ways of life; (2) the mixing between forms of urban and suburban; (3) the combination of paradoxical forms of decentralization and recentralization, linked to the expulsion of some urban functions in peri-urban contexts, capable of generating new centers and shaping new geographies in the suburban, as well as the reverse; (4) the emergence of a new urban form, that is "polynucleated, densely networked and information-intensive" (Soja, 2011, p. 684).

Milan post-metropolis between path-dependency and innovation: exploring the new boundaries of the urban

Is it possible to identify a new urban boundary – other than the municipal and metropolitan ones – capable of shaping a conversant institutional framework? If so, to what extent does it mirror processes similar to those observed by Soja (2000, 2011) in the USA's context? If so, to what extent is it the outcome of a complex interplay between the peculiarity of the milieu and the globalization of urban processes that seem to generate a "planetary urbanization" (Brenner, 2014)? In other words, what kind of path-dependency and what kind of innovations can be observed? And what do they say about the specificity of the Italian case against Soja's post-metropolis hypothesis?

Post-metropolis and polycentrism: evidence of spatial innovation and path-dependency

From the physical point of view, when compared with the others, the Milanese *square* can be described as one of the most urbanized and dense. It actually appears as a sort of "urban continuum" with the largest extension of artificial land covers in Italy.[12] On the one hand, this is the result of a lack of consistent obstacles to urbanization, being the region limited by mountains only in its very upper sector; on the other hand, it is due to its central geographical position within the northern Italian macro-region. This has generated a flow of urbanization dating back to the Middle Ages and exploding during the nineteenth century, producing one of the most urbanized regions in Europe. Inside this apparent "urban continuum," naturally open to host an "infinite" urban region (Bonomi & Abruzzese, 2004), three elements of path-dependency have been quite effective in shaping regional urbanization processes and generating a specific spatial pattern: (1) a natural (geophysical) north–south divide; (2) a historic polycentric regional structure; (3) a radiocentric shape model of expansion, communication and connection between Milan and other regional territories.

First, highly dense urban spaces are typical of the northern sector, while the southern one has for a long time been characterized by a consistent separation between compact urban settlements and rural areas. As a result, the boundary between the urban and the non-urban is almost evident along a line which goes east–west across Milan, the so-called "line of springs" (*linea delle risorgive*). This is the outcome of the geophysical structure that has historically characterized the region, where a clear boundary can be drawn between the southern humid plains and the northern dry territories, favoring, in the first case, agricultural uses and, in the second, residential and industrial developments.

Second, the *square* is based on a historical polycentric structure that is the outcome of the interaction between a process of intense spatial transformation of the historical urban "armor" and the more recent processes of metropolization that happened to the city of Milan. By exploring the growth of urban settlements all over the region in the last century, it is possible to see the interplay between the "explosion" of the city of Milan over the neighboring municipalities and provinces, and the parallel growth of the other historical regional poles over their adjacent territories. While the metropolization of Milan was taking place, the main regional chief-towns – located at an average distance of 40 km from the city of Milan – supported processes of urban and economic growth, especially in the second part of the twentieth century, securely based on small and medium enterprises which contributed to creating a quite peculiar (spatial and socioeconomic) urban model.

Third, a net of infrastructure, roads and railways has historically structured a radiocentric network centered in the city of Milan as the institutional, financial and cultural fulcrum of other less populated regional chief-towns (less than 100,000 inhabitants) and more similar, from social and economic viewpoints, to medium-sized cities in Italy and Europe. This radiocentric structure was actually the outcome of the late nineteenth – and early twentieth – century dynamics, when the urban growth model adopted by the first municipal spatial plans favored a concentric expansion around the city; this, interacting with the polycentric structure of the region, produced for a long time a sort of typical Christallerian spatial model, only recently cancelled by some innovations produced by regional urbanization patterns that have proposed non-radiocentric patterns and urban formations (Balducci et al., 2011).

The combination of these three path-dependency elements has shaped a regional space with approximately eight million residents: the current full *square* population (7,854,889) is about 1.5 times that of 1951 and equal to 13 percent of the national population. The first strong demographic growth occurred during the "Italian economic miracle" period (1950s–1970s) due to domestic migrations concentrated within Milan's municipal boundary and its first ring of municipalities. However, it was during the following decades (1970s–1990s) that processes of apparent suburbanization beyond the first ring of municipalities occurred. In this period, in fact, the population of the city of Milan started to decrease, while the surrounding provinces started to experience intensive waves of growth.[13] A consistent urban development took place all over the *square*, while the central city and the first ring of the surrounding municipalities started to lose population, together with the marginal mountain territories. This produced in the 1990s a dynamic and densely inhabited space even far beyond the central city, draining population directly from the most peripheral regions as well as from the municipality of Milan. This process was due to a number of individual choices, in particular linked to housing affordability, but also to a process of decentralization of the manufacturing spaces and deindustrialization of the city of Milan.

The multiple process – saturation of the city of Milan and first-ring municipalities, success of local economic districts reinforcing the historic polycentric network, decentralization of functions from the central city – produced thick demographic density and urbanization patterns all over the northern, western and eastern sectors, creating a dense and heterogeneous urban environment characterized by a strong functional mix in many regional sectors and some relevant innovations in relation to the past.

In fact in the last 30 years, the clear divide between the urban and non-urban has been challenged consistently all over the *square* – in particular, though, along the north–south line, where a quick and intense process of urbanization has eroded the natural divide between the northern and the southern sectors. Despite the preservation introduced in order to protect natural and environmental resources through the institution of an agricultural park (*Parco Agricolo Sud Milano*) within the boundaries of the Province of Milan, residential mobility and economic development have particularly affected the southern territories, as evident from both spatial and social data (PRIN Postmetropoli, 2015).

As regards the radiocentric structure (and spatially related processes), interestingly, in the last decade not only has the central city stopped losing population, but growth has been generally less consistent, even if still evident, and more concentrated in the southern sector and part of the north-eastern sector – along the corridor between Milan and Venice.[14] It is interesting to see that, while the first area – traditionally agricultural – is less dense and populated for historical reasons, the second is an already populated and more dense area, characterized since the 1970s by a strong economic role and a good balance between the environmental component and economic development. The recent economic crisis was more consistent in the highly urbanized north-western sector, which corresponds to the historical axis of growth of the urban region (the Simplon Axis). In this respect, the last decade has somehow confirmed the radiocentric development model. However, it has also produced some elements of "implosion" (Brenner, 2014), with the central city moving back on the scene and several consolidated territories losing their historical roles.

In terms of land-take, the *anthropic land use cover index*[15] highly exceeds the values of other Italian urban areas, especially because of the urbanization degree along the north-western and eastern sectors. On the other hand, a low degree of spatial fragmentation and dispersion characterizes the morphology of settlements if compared with others in Italy. Actually, since 1988, the Milan urban region shows the most consistent trend of urbanization in Italy: before, the record was held by Naples. Nevertheless, in terms of per capita land-take, Milan remains one of the most efficient urban regions in Italy, with 197 square meters per capita. In the last decade, the Milan urban region has been characterized by a less extended process of substitution of agricultural areas compared with other urban areas in Italy, as if a sort of acknowledgment of the limits to growth had been implicitly assumed. Impervious soils cover nine percent of the whole *square*. Indeed, together with the cases of Rome and Veneto, Milan was affected by the highest degree of land conversion into urban areas at national level during the same period: this is particularly true not only for the central areas, but also for those once considered peripheral places. In-depth analysis related to land-use transformations shows that the most relevant changes are related to conversion processes of the agronomic structure. A detailed analysis of the four macro-categories of land use demonstrates that the largest part of land-take in the Milanese *square* is generated by productive and commercial functions rather than by new residential uses.[16] This provides interesting elements for interpretation, since it describes an increasingly complex urban system, multifunctional and heterogeneous, rather than monofunctional and segregated. As a matter of fact, during the last 20 years, these processes were accompanied by the diffusion of relevant urban functions all over the regional space.[17] If analyses show the persistent role of the regional chief-towns in terms of concentration of public (urban) strategic functions, the large diffusion of some of them can be recognized in unexpected locations. As a matter of fact, museums, universities and research centers are no longer the prerogative of cities, but have adopted location strategies which have generated new profiles of centralities, or at least have moved from the central city to other regional poles. All in all, when observing the most recent data on land-take generated by new residential settlements, an urban discontinuous fabric can be identified, even if characterized by dense morphologies.[18]

Infrastructure constitutes five percent of the total amount of land-take in the last decade, following important infrastructure projects that have affected some new regional corridors and introduced both radiocentric and non-radiocentric elements within the polycentric network: the regional railway system reconnects the main regional chief-towns through an urban underground link crossing Milan; new highways, sometimes confirming and doubling the historical network, essentially enlarge the boundaries of the urban – for example, the new bypass road *Tangenziale Est Esterna*, which confirms the strategic importance of the eastern sector – or introduce a new non-Milanocentric axis, such as the new *Pedemontana*, a highway running horizontally north of Milan (at a distance of about 20–30 km) and connecting other regional cities without passing through Milan.

Comparing these data with the geophysical structure of the urban region, it is possible to see that the intense urbanization of recent decades has occurred all over the plain, also affecting traditionally excluded spaces that have become more attractive despite their refractory structure. In this sense, it is possible to conclude that the most recent processes of urbanization have partly challenged, cancelled or reinvented the geophysical structure explained above. However, even if urbanization patterns and land covers are crucial for this study on spatial innovations, the tendency to overcome the historical geophysical structures – exceeding both the urban and metropolitan boundaries and investing new regional spaces – relates also to demographic dynamics, as shown by the residential mobility analysis. Analyzing the residential movement patterns of the last decade, an uncommon attractiveness of the southern urban region has appealed to, in relation to its original population, a relevant number of newcomers – as shown by the index of residential attractiveness[19] – completely reversing the traditional north–south divide. These dynamic territories, where people arrive and leave, coexist with other shrinking territories, where there has been a consistent loss in terms of population. From a general perspective, it is possible to recognize: the stability in terms of attraction of the central city of Milan; the growing weakness of the first ring of municipalities in the central area; the stability of the intermediate northern territories, between the peripheral mountain areas and the typical metropolitan municipalities; the role of intermediate dynamic spaces of the southern region, where endowment of urban strategic functions is more limited but growing. These in-between regional "stripes," which have assumed a transversal structure, despite the original monocentric and centripetal origin, seem to struggle and confirm their strategic roles.

Post-metropolis and social practices: evidence of socioeconomic innovation and path-dependency

Physicality only partially (and slowly) reflects the complexity of socioeconomic and socio-spatial relationships: social practices anticipate large processes of unbundling and rebundling of the urban taking place in the Milan *square*. One of the most traditional and interesting sets of data that shows the nature of a highly connected urban society is the one related to people's mobility.

In the last decade of the twentieth century (1991–2001), mobility dynamics in the Region of Lombardy showed complex geographies of flows and a significant use of the territory. The obliged movements, for job and study reasons, were characterized by fixed schedules and defined paths – between an origin (home) and a destination (job/school). They typically describe a metropolitan organization of space and have an increasingly less significant weight than in the past, compared with the emergence of much more articulated movements in time and space, related to personal reasons, flexible types of jobs, leisure and purchases.[20] In other words, typical commuter patterns account only for a part of the mobility geography that occurred in the above described urban region. Forms of multidirectional mobilities related to less hierarchical and more complex relationships and practices intensified in the inter-census decade (2001–2011) and are reshaping spatial geographies inside the Milanese *square*, as evident by integrating the latest national census data by ISTAT[21] with specific data sources available in the Region of Lombardy (Regione Lombardia, 2002; Provincia di Milano, 2006).

An increasing mobility in commuting for job reasons is evident, in particular in terms of outflows from the municipalities of residence. Commuter flows between 2001 and 2011 were boosted (+9.2 percent), supported by a significant increase in outflows (+19.8 percent), compared with a decline of internal flows in each municipality. The density of movements (internal flows + outflows/ employed) increased more (+2.03 percent) than the average income per capita (+1.44 percent), which confirms, for the Milan urban region, a trend similar to other large metropolitan areas where mobility is growing faster than revenues.[22] More than 50 percent of employees work in a municipality in which they do not live. This phenomenon, which can be read in terms of loss of self-containment index, can be explained in relation to the recent residential expansion in the southern sector on the one hand, where there is a limited job offer and a strong integration with Milan's economic system, and on the other hand with the crisis of local economic districts in the northern sector, traditionally characterized by a strong integration between the workplace and home and short-range mobility. In this respect, it is possible to argue the emergence of a rather peculiar post-metropolitan condition: not only have the typical metropolitan patterns diminished during the past two decades with a sort of explosion of mobility all over the region, but they have also experienced processes of implosion in the last decade. In fact, the self-contained profile generated by the specific socioeconomic development model has suffered from a deep crisis that has unbundled a quite consolidated organizational model. Data show a process of recentralization of commuter flows towards the city of Milan. A stable equilibrium of inward-bound commuter flows (Milan) can be observed after a previous decade (1991–2001) characterized by a reduction in the catchment area of the capital in favor of dynamic external territories. The dependence of the municipalities in the Province of Milan on the capital city declined between 1991 and 2001 (–12.1 percent).[23] During the last decade, it remained stable, denouncing less dynamism in the surrounding areas where, in the past, mobility increased driven by the job offer, probably reflecting a recentralization dynamic in terms of strategic functions and residential attractiveness in the central city.

The observed dynamics are evidently related to socioeconomic and lifestyle transformations. After a first analysis, it is possible to argue that the previous decade contributed interestingly to describe a multi-central regional network, in which movements were dense and significant, whereas the current economic crisis has complicated mobility practices even further, reflecting a higher differentiation in terms of territorial attractiveness. In this respect, analyses clearly show the dynamism of an in-between regional space characterized by a dense network of municipalities in the sector between the first ring belt of municipalities and a larger one (30–40 km). The intensity of flows shows a fragmented pattern of multiple centralities that seem to exceed both radiocentric and polycentric hierarchies. In this respect, mobility data not only support the exploration of the interconnected nature of the *square*, but also highlight one significant feature of post-metropolitan processes, which could be defined in terms of sudden change of path. In the relationship between path-dependency and innovation, change seems to take place at high rhythms, completely reversing long-term trends at an unexpected pace.

Finally, quite interestingly the correlation study between urban density (calculated as a percentage of residential buildings with one and two floors) and mobility index (calculated as a ratio between inflows + outflows and employees) shows the new possible boundaries of this dense and highly interconnected urban region: a wide area with a profile based on high mobility and high urban density and some areas characterized by low urban density and low mobility, the majority of which are localized in the north-west of the Milan urban region and in the rural areas in the south-west. Municipalities with low urban density and low mobility are few in the north of Milan. A third typology of municipalities with high urban density and low-mobility index includes very different situations: attracting polarities such as Milan and Monza, characterized by a high internal mobility but a low value in outflows. This would confirm on the one hand the traditional dense urban center characteristics, and on the other hand the consistency of low-density / high-mobility situations.

This is even more interesting when one considers that both census and municipal registry data are not able to intercept complex and elusive migratory and residential phenomena (Pucci, 2014, 2015; Pucci et al., 2015). Nevertheless, it seems possible to say that the city of Milan – but also other regional cities – is the place with the highest presence of inhabitants not officially resident (non-resident but domiciled). It was possible to estimate this phenomenon, which affects especially the immigrant population, thanks to a census data on dwellings occupied only by non-residents.[24] Beyond the peculiarity of this phenomenon, analyzing migratory balance between 2002 and 2011, in relative terms (i.e. compared with the 2001 resident population), Milan has demonstrated a better performance compared with its belt municipalities.[25] Once again, these data suggest that after a period of sharp population decline in the main cities, some implosions are now occurring especially in Milan, which, despite the lack of reliable data, seems to be going through a phase of attractiveness and renewed labor – and urbanity – supply.

A new urban question?

If mobility practices describe the intense relationality involving a large urban region, the PRIN research also aims to explore to what extent the interplay between the spatial and the social dynamics producing regional urbanization can be associated with the disappearance of social cleavages funded on an urban–metropolitan imaginary and organization. In other words, can we identify a differentiated social geography? Are there new profiles of segregation or, rather, is there a diffuse social mix? Is it possible to distinguish profiles of social polarization on a different and unprecedented regional scale? A central question of the research project was associated with what was suggested by Soja (2000, 2011), correlating the new regional scale to the emergence of a new urban question – one not traditionally linked with a consolidated idea of centrality and peripherality, but connected with the formation of new profiles of social unbalances, where the regional and transcalar dimension have introduced non-ordinary phenomena. In the post-metropolis idea, is it possible to produce new considerations on spatial injustice, generated by the new spatial patterns? If so, how can an approach be found to explore social injustice that is less based on asset and stock, and capable of dealing with a trans-calar and fluid definition of citizenship (Davoudi & Bell, 2016)?

With reference to the Milanese case, analyzing the density gradients, as outlined above, four basic profiles of social differentiation were detected:

1   a *central city*, together with other mid-sized regional cities affected by consistent processes of social polarization, both at the regional and municipal scales;

2   a *first ring of municipalities*, originally the place of concentration of new families in the 1950s and 1960s, which are now experiencing typical urban, rather than suburban processes: ageing population, economic crisis, social frailty;

3   a *second ring of municipalities* which shows peaks of urbanity similar to Milan, at a distance of 14–15 km from the city of Milan. Interestingly, this second ring collects in all directions mid-sized cities that have attracted middle classes for different reasons, looking for interesting locations (from the infrastructural or environmental point of view). These places, once considered less competitive than the first ring, are now new sort of "edge cities" (Soja, 2000; Garreau, 1991) and attracting living spaces presenting characteristics which are not typical of suburbanization;

4   an *urban continuum*, where contrasting phenomena are taking place: an in-between space which better represents the idea of suburbanity with specific features, such as higher rates of home property and large residential spaces, but also more typical urban phenomena, such as unemployment and social unbalances. This is in contrast with the situation of the last 20 years, in which they were among the richest spaces in the region, expressing a political orientation towards secessionism and independence from the central city. It is no coincidence that these places were the home of new political movements, as well as institutional innovation (such as the Province of Monza and Brianza, detaching from the larger Province of Milan[26]).

In this respect, through all four cases, an interesting interplay can be identified between path-dependency and innovation.

As regards the household composition, typologies typical of the central city, such as single-person households, have spread all over the urban region in the last inter-census decade; on the other hand, large families are more clearly concentrated in the "suburban continuum," first in the eastern sector, but more recently in the southern one.[27] Home property is particularly consistent along the infrastructural axis in the northern and eastern sectors, while in a more scattered, but also consistent, way, it's taking place in the southern one.[28] The dimension of living spaces is particularly consistent in the southern sector, but also in the north-western one.[29] Single-family houses characterize the western sector (namely between the A4 and A8 highways), while condominiums characterize the eastern "flank" of Milan. In conclusion, a fragmented pattern of apparently suburban profiles can still be recognized mostly at a distance of between 30 and 50 km from Milan's city center, but with fuzzy boundaries and very differentiated physiognomies.

As regards the social composition, ageing population is no more simply a phenomenon typical of the central city, but strongly affects the northern regional space, also far beyond the first ring of the Milan area municipalities; while the southern territories, instead, are younger and dynamic.[30]

The immigrant population, in the 1990s, almost dispersed in the north-eastern sector along the infrastructural axis linking Milan to Bergamo, becoming increasingly concentrated in the whole eastern sector. The latter has features similar to, if not higher than, those of the city of Milan and the other regional cities.[31] In this perspective, the whole eastern sector of the *square* is, for different reasons, the regional space most affected by high percentages of immigrants (workforce in the north linked to the manufacturing system, in the south to agricultural activities).

Read in sequence, this information provides a quite differentiated mosaic of the Milan urban region, where specific sectors seem to be characterized by a more evident presence of specific characteristics of the population, on the one hand; and, on the other hand, as shown by other indicators, conditions typical of the central urban areas are quite diffuse in large sectors of the urban region, in particular not only in the first ring of municipalities around the city of Milan, but in a wider regional space. Not only has the distinction between center and periphery faded consistently during the last decade, but so has the profile of urban complexity: problems and challenges related to urbanity emerge in a scattered way all over the *square*, affecting small and medium-sized cities which have limited knowledge and economic resources to face the mix of social problems and demands that these processes produce.

Exploring traditional indicators – such as the percentage of residents holding a high school diploma, the unemployment index, the housing crowding index and the age dependency ratio – in order to investigate social differentiation, a composite index was produced based on a multiple set of indicators.[32] The map produced by this index describes a central city still characterized by a favorable positive situation if compared with the rest of the urban region, particularly if compared with its northern and southern contiguous municipalities. At the same time, positive values can be seen all over the urban region, with the exception of some clusters of municipalities mostly located in the eastern sector of the *square* between Milan, Lodi and Bergamo. On the other hand, when looking at the variations between 2001 and 2011, together with absolute data, evident problematic conditions are quite concentrated around the central city and the rest of the *square* characterized by a low index – whereas the current situation shows the emergence of new unexpected urban hardships in eastern sectors.[33] This seems to reduce consistently a specificity of an urban region traditionally characterized in the last decade by a pattern of opportunities almost equal in every part of the regional space.

As mentioned, looking at the Gini Index and the map of income distribution, it is possible to easily recognize the polarization occurring in the central city, where there is a concentration of highly differentiated conditions between rich and poor. Under a certain perspective, the urban region appears to provide much more balanced social conditions than the central city (Figure 3.3), but new inequality areas are visible, especially in the in-between territory of Brianza and around the lakes. When exploring, for

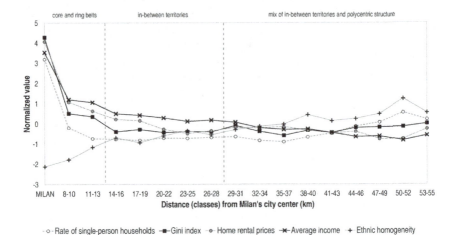

Figure 3.3 Socioeconomic gradients within the Milan *square*: comparison of
corresponding normalized values for different indicators (2011/12)

Source: Authors' calculation, based on different datasets provided by ISTAT (Census data 2011),
MEF (Italian Ministry of Economy and Finance) (2012) and OMI (Real Estate Market Observatory
belonging to the Italian Revenue Agency) (2012)

example, the situation of housing deprivation – which had progressively disappeared
all over the country between 1951 and 2001 (–90 percent of non-traditional kinds
of housing) – it is possible to see that during the last decade (2001–2011) the trend
seems to have reversed at national level. The same can be observed in the Milan urban
region, with similar data for the city of Milan, the first ring of municipalities around
it and – unexpectedly – in the traditionally rich north-western sector, but also in some
southern municipalities. These data can be compared with those related to the number
of people living in the same dwelling, confirming the emergence of highly problematic living conditions all over the urban region, unpredictable a few years ago.

These data are just the visible part of a problematic condition which could
become even more complicated in the future. In fact, when taking into consideration the stress that families are experiencing, even worse figures could be expected.
Considering the issue of housing affordability, a composite index of "housing
risk" was built based on monthly family incomes, average monthly rental rates
and shares of rented accommodation.[34] In this case, the central city together with
the northern, historically rich, sector of Brianza and the more recently developed south-western sector shows more problematic situations, while the eastern
sector shows less consistent processes, despite the fact it seems to be the space
for concentration of the immigrant population. Around and within all regional
chief-towns one can observe similar problematic conditions. Analyzing the Urban
Vulnerability Index as a composite index based on the above-mentioned vulnerability indexes, one can indeed see the emergence of the eastern and western
sectors of the urban region as particularly stressed conditions.

As a general and preliminary conclusion, the analysis at a regional scale, of social structure and processes, highlights the emergence of a growing strong differentiation, whose spatialization should be considered as a relevant issue. Concentration of specific social problems or conditions, on the one hand, polarization, on the other, could in fact define a new urban question and geography of social problems which is thoroughly different from that affecting the city and the metropolitan area. That is still largely invisible to policymakers and institutions. In this respect, a careful consideration of post-metropolitan condition should bring with it the emergence of a new urban agenda, where the new transcalar nature of social problems, its different spatialization of resources, should deal with the new challenges generated by a new (and still almost invisible to policymakers and institutions) condition of denied regional citizenship (Donzelot, 2009). In this respect, the role of mobility as generator of new social unbalances and exclusions appears much more consistent in relation to the scale of social phenomenon taking place in the context of regional urbanization processes (Cass et al., 2005).

Post-metropolis and the distance among social practices, spatial organization and institutional frameworks

On the one hand, density of inhabitants, functions and resources, multi-polarity and interconnections, and on the other hand heterogeneity of opportunity and roles, and complexity of urban problems across the wide urban region identified within the *square*, clearly indicate an *implosion/explosion* of the urban (Brenner, 2014) in which the relationship between the central city and the surrounding regional space can no longer be described in terms of an "inside" and "outside" of a center and a periphery, at least in a traditional way. As a consequence, when considering a series of recently available descriptions of the Milan urban region, it is possible to see that they all transcend traditional administrative boundaries. Moreover, they provide a different and non-converging identification of the urban region. According to the European Metropolitan Network Institute:

> the Milan Metropolitan Area, also known as "Grande Milano" or "Greater Milan," is the urban agglomeration around the city of Milan, [. . .] is home to 7 million inhabitants [. . .][and is] characterized by high institutional fragmentation. The area includes in total 249 municipalities; all municipalities in the Province of Milan and in the Province of Monza and Brianza; 49 in the Province of Varese, 43 in the Province of Como and 45 in the Province of Lecco (Meijers et al., 2012, p. 79).

This definition seems to be a hybrid of what the OECD territorial review identified in 2006 as the "Milan metropolitan region" (OECD, 2006) and what the OECD MetroMonitor has identified more recently adopting a new methodology.[35] On the basis of these parameters, as the OECD concluded, "Commuting flows suggest that socioeconomic linkages have expanded even farther than the boundaries of the Province of Milan, which then results in a definition of the Milan metropolitan region with more than 7 million people" (OECD, 2006, p. 26). More recently, the

OECD (2012) provided an interpretation based on new criteria, distinguishing between an urban core and urban hinterland.[36] The new functional urban region would thus be made of 147 municipalities, crosscutting the provincial boundaries: 122 municipalities from the Province of Milan, 47 municipalities from the northern Province of Monza and Brianza, 5 from Varese, 4 from Como, 5 from Bergamo, 12 from the Lecco, 25 municipalities from Pavia, 10 from Cremona, 20 from Lodi. The region identified covers more than 4 million people (2010 statistics), with a total land area of more than 2,600,000 km² and more than 3 million people concentrated in the 115 municipalities of the core area. Recently, a study coordinated by Calafati (2014) proposed a definition of the urban region based on functional urban area studies. Once again the study clearly shows the discontinuities and differences between existing institutional boundaries and social and spatial practices, measured on the basis of different available methodologies. This blurred condition has been the focus of a lot of scholarly and institutional debate. In 2014, a new law was issued which finally introduced the so-called "Città Metropolitana," that is, a new metropolitan government whose boundaries, for a number of reasons, were identified in a quite simplistic way, including the boundaries of the existing second-tier institution, the province, which was cancelled. Clearly, this does not introduce a relevant innovation in relation to governance problems in such a context, failing to reduce the gap between the *de facto* city and the *de jure* city (Calafati, 2014).

The *square* is apparently characterized by a high level of institutional fragmentation, including: 985 municipalities, 12 provinces, 3 regions. Milan urban region is the first, followed by Turin, with half the number of municipalities in Italy. This is not a recent development: the current situation is similar to that of 1921, almost a century ago. This high level of fragmentation, one further element of path-dependency, when compared with the demographic situation, provides a different interpretation. In fact, by measuring territorial fragmentation (number of municipalities/100,000 inhabitants /total population), it is possible to see one municipality for every 83,000 inhabitants, quite a different situation compared with Rome, where there is one municipality for every 10,000 inhabitants. In other words, municipalities are less proximate to cities than in other cases. When comparing this situation with the average dimension of municipalities, in spatial and demographic terms, the case of Milan is characterized indeed by the largest percentage of small municipalities (more than 50 percent is below 10,000 km²) mostly concentrated in the north central sector, where it is also possible to identify the most populated ones (almost all municipalities between 10,000 and 50,000 inhabitants are in this section). A final method of judging institutional fragmentation is by measuring geopolitical fragmentation, as proposed by Hoffmann-Martinot (2004). When taking into account the number of people living in the central area, the case of Milan is characterized by quite a limited geopolitical fragmentation very different from the Veneto case. As a general conclusion, despite the high number of small municipalities, fragmentation is not as high as one could conclude with a first generic analysis; in fact, the density of people, especially in the core area, made it apparently necessary to multiply the number of local governments.

Nevertheless, this high number of local municipalities that reflects the historical strong importance of the lowest level of local government in the Italian case makes governance processes in an urban region characterized by transcalar problems and challenges quite complicated. Lacking a form of metropolitan governance for decades (just instituted on 1 January 2015) and in a situation of high resistance to cooperation by the municipality of Milan towards the surrounding ones – dating back to almost the 1950s (with an exception in the 1960s) – and more recently by the region, the forms of cooperation among municipalities have multiplied, although remaining quite sectoral or limited in time and space. While the boundaries of the existing provinces have absorbed quite insufficiently some instances of coordination (spatial planning, transportation, infrastructure, environment, but all in a light and limited way), the latter has been mainly developed in specific fields and territories on a voluntary basis. In fact, a large number of sub-coordination policy areas can be identified, often related to a specific management objective and designed on the boundaries of the province – the second-tier institutional level instituted in the 1990s and now set to be redefined by recent reform. For example, a number of specific resource management issues and geographies (water management – ATO; districts for social and health care facilities – ASL) have been shaped on the boundaries of the provinces. In addition, the urban region can count on a limited number of forms of stable inter-municipal cooperation: 30 unions of municipalities were mapped (*unioni di comuni*) and 6 mountain inter-municipalities (*comunità montane*). In both cases, these are localized on the margins of the *square*: the former in the southern provinces, supporting forms of institutional cooperation among municipalities made available according to several laws, but not strongly supported in terms of resources or a competence framework by the regional law; the latter in the northern part, due to the nature of the form of cooperation, destined by law to small municipalities in the mountain areas.

Finally, a number of voluntary forms of territorial cooperation areas are visible, mainly bottom–up and voluntary, based on the cooperation among municipalities; sometimes supported at provincial level with special funds or resources, they are often cooperating on projects. A relevant source for cooperation has been the so-called PLIS, supra-local parks. At the moment, 33 are promoted by municipalities to preserve natural spaces with an inter-municipal extension. Other forms of local cooperation are related to facility provisions, in particular energy, water and waste disposal. While the issue of local development has been a central reason for cooperation in the last decade, the number of forms of local development agencies has consistently decreased. What is consistent, though, is the cooperation at local scale for public transportation, set to grow thanks to a new law, but still a weak point for the whole urban region. Even if both the region – with an integrated regional transport system – and the city of Milan – with its special agency for public transportation – ensure a good quality of interconnections, the whole area cannot count on a special authority capable of addressing the problems of movement of people all over a highly functional, interrelated urban region system.

New governance arrangements are researched and practiced in particular in specific fields, clearly showing the need for coordination. These appear more diffused in contexts characterized by relevant policy issues to be addressed, or some forms of political homogeneity. However, in general the picture has identified the multiplication of scattered and fragmented governance arrangements, with dense assemblages in specific areas, highlighting the relevance of the governance issue as part of the more general issue of regional citizenship and the emergence of a demand of institutional innovation, which so far has not found an appropriate answer. This provides interesting elements for reflecting on an exceeding post-metropolitan redefinition of governance patterns and a common institutional treatment.

Conclusions

Milan represents a unique case of regional urbanization in the Italian context. Among the areas investigated in the PRIN research, it is definitely the most suited to directly test the main post-metropolitan assumptions made by Edward Soja (2000, 2011). Actually, some constitutive elements of Soja's discourses are reflected in the recent phenomena arising in the Milan urban region. However, thanks to the assistance of the *Atlante dei territori post-metropolitani* (PRIN Postmetropoli, 2015), it is possible to observe behaviors and dynamics that still reproduce a metropolitan model. Nonetheless, in some cases, with different profiles and intensities depending on the specific sectors of the

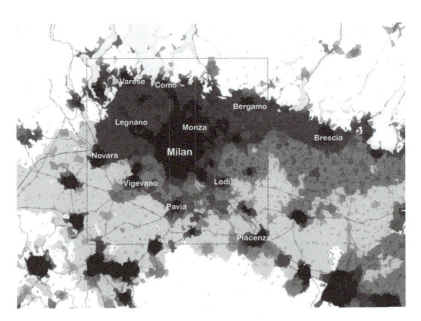

Figure 3.4 Urban gradients within and beyond the Milan *square*

Source: Authors' graphic based on PRIN Postmetropoli (2015)

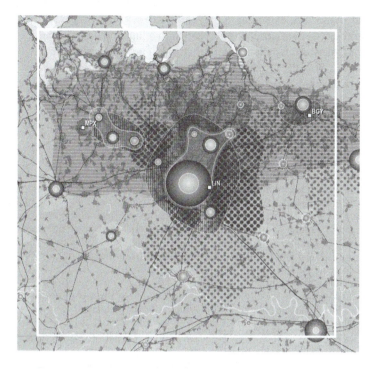

Figure 3.5 Synthetic map of the Milan *square*
Source: Authors' graphic based on PRIN Postmetropoli (2015)

square, the traditional and always recognizable geo-structural features of this over-investigated urban region are challenged by unprecedented phenomena going in two directions: on the one hand, towards new forms of *explosion* of the central city (Milan, but also of other chief-towns), not circumscribed to the population spread and different from traditional suburbanization processes; and on the other hand, new forms of *implosion* driven by a new attractiveness (mainly because of jobs and cultural offers) for Milan, but also for other emerging territories (especially located in the eastern and southern sectors) which are increasingly dense, infrastructured, dynamic, mixed, mobile, capable of economic innovation and residential attractiveness – but also as a consequence of the presence of increasingly variegated commercial and leisure facilities, landscapes, ecologies. It seems like urbanity redistributes itself among the old and new poles and "edge cities" of a polycentric and polynuclear urban region (Soja, 2011), diversifying and redefining itself. However, it also reconceptualizes polycentrism, rebalancing traditional density patterns and reorienting daily movements, migrations and spatial development.

These intense social, economic and spatial dynamics are consistently stressing the institutional framework extending to the entire urban region what was typical of the central city – immigration, polarization, ageing, and so on – but also changing central poles into functional platforms which are oppressing the city of residents producing pressures, tensions and potential socio-political conflictual arenas that could develop into a new urban question if not addressed in a smart and critical way.

Notes

1 Although this chapter should be considered a result of the common work and reflection of the three authors, A. Balducci took primary responsibility for the introduction and conclusions, F. Curci took primary responsibility for the "Post-metropolis, regional urbanization, urbanity" and "A new urban question?" sections, and V. Fedeli took primary responsibility for the "Milan post-metropolis between path-dependency and innovation" and "Post-metropolis and the distance among social practices, spatial organization and institutional frameworks" sections. During the development of the research project, P. Pucci and S. Salata made fundamental contributions, respectively, to mobility issues and land-use issues.
2 Therefore, the standard measurement from the Venice case would not provide any relevant result. Whereas the measurement from the centroid of the square positioned between Padua and Vicenza highlights a thoroughly different spatial pattern.
3 See PRIN Postmetropoli (2015): "Densità di popolazione dal 1971 al 2011", § a.1.3.
4 See PRIN Postmetropoli (2015): "Indice di condominialità – 2001, 2011", § i.2.6; "Consumo di suolo 2012", § 5.1.
5 Our processing of tax returns open data provided by the Ministry of Economy and Finance (MEF) reveals a particular concentration of socioeconomic wealth and polarization at a distance of 13 km from Milan.
6 We used 1991, 2001 and 2011 census data to calculate and compare the concentration index (assumed as an inversely proportional proxy for the ethnic mix) of the foreign resident population by continent of origin.
7 See PRIN Postmetropoli (2015): "Dotazioni e polarità", § E; "Scuole dell'infanzia e primarie per comune – 2012", § c.8.2.
8 See PRIN Postmetropoli (2015): "Indice di mobilità – 2011", § i.1.5.2; "Indice di accessibilità a strutture e poli urbani (stradale)", § i.3.2.
9 In particular, research on the topic of mobility has been developed by Professor Paola Pucci in the Milan research unit.
10 See PRIN Postmetropoli (2015): "Variazione percentuale degli addetti per settore 2001–2011", § d.4.4.
11 See PRIN Postmetropoli (2015): "Indice di specializzazione nei settori innovativi – 2001, 2011", § i.3.9.6;
12 See PRIN Postmetropoli (2015): "Consumo di suolo 2012", § 5.1.
13 In the most recent decade (2001–2011) this process seems to have stopped, although the 2011 population of the city of Milan was still less than it was in 1951.
14 In the first there is a more recent densification, especially within the municipalities located between Milan, Vigevano, Pavia and Lodi; in the second, a "welding" process occurred between the extended urbanized core and the infrastructural axis linking Milan to Bergamo.
15 See PRIN Postmetropoli (2015): "Percentuale di aree antropizzate (da fonte CLC) – 2006", § b.1.2.
16 During the period 1999–2012, the total amount of registered land-take (land-use transition from agricultural or natural land into urban land) was equal to 29,850 ha. In terms

of land-take processes, we can still see consistent flows from arable land to construction sites (2,100 ha); from arable land to urban parks and urban green areas (1,246 ha); from arable land to productive sites (1,999 ha); from arable land to discontinuous urban fabric (1,118 ha).

17 See PRIN Postmetropoli (2015): "Dotazioni e polarità", § E.
18 Interestingly, processing and comparing DUSAF databanks 1.1 (1999) and 4.0 (2012) (Ersaf/Regione Lombardia), "construction sites" constitute 10 percent of the total amount of land-take, while "urban green parks and urban green areas" constitute 8 percent.
19 See PRIN Postmetropoli (2015): "Indice di attrattività residenziale – 2001–2011", § i.3.4.
20 In the Region of Lombardy commuter flows in 2002 were only 29 percent of the daily mobility flows. The daily average trips were 2.65 trips/day (2.67 for women's trips; 2.55 trips/day in the Province of Milan). 91.2 percent of the sample performed sequentially two displacements (Regione Lombardia, 2002).
21 The 2011 Istat census provided a survey on daily mobility for work and study, with information only on the modal split and the average time of displacement which, however, does not contemplate the possibility to recognize movements over 60 minutes.
22 The Province of Milan concentrates 27.7 percent of commuter flows of the Region of Lombardy. These are 12.8 percent in the Province of Bergamo, 11.9 percent in the Province of Brescia and 10.7 percent in the Province of Monza and Brianza.
23 As regards the modality of movements, the use of the train is particularly important and has increased in the last decade, unlike the use of the car, the lowest percentage at national level. This trend may be related to the improvement that occurred in the last decade to the regional rail service, and, in particular, to the "suburban lines" (*Linee S*) with a significant supply of rail connections to Milan (two trains per hour per direction).
24 See PRIN Postmetropoli (2015): "Percentuale di abitazioni occupate solo da persone non residenti – 2001", § b.4.2.
25 See PRIN Postmetropoli (2015): "Indice di attrattività residenziale – 2001–2011", § i.3.4.
26 Looking at the political profile, based on the national elections data, two relevant peculiarities can be identified. On the one hand, participation in vote is high and consistent all over the square, if compared with national data (1994, 2013). Nevertheless, a more consistent participation in vote can be identified in the eastern sector, rather than in the eastern and north-eastern one. In terms of political identification, it is possible to see clearly a number of situations of political instability, particularly concentrated in the first ring of municipalities of Milan and in the Bergamo region, which are also rich and dynamic territories. See PRIN Postmetropoli (2015): "Media della percentuale di affluenza alle elezioni politiche del 1994, 2001, 2006, 2008, 2013", § h.2.1; Numero di vittorie delle coalizioni di Centrodestra o Centrosinistra nelle elezioni politiche del 1994, 1996, 2001, 2006, 2008, 2013, § h.2.2.
27 See PRIN Postmetropoli (2015): "Numero medio di componenti per famiglia – 2012", § c.2.1.
28 See PRIN Postmetropoli (2015): "Percentuale di abitazioni occupate da persone residenti per titolo di godimento – 2001", § c.4.1.
29 See PRIN Postmetropoli (2015): "Superficie media abitazioni occupate da residenti – 2011", § c.5.8.
30 See PRIN Postmetropoli (2015): "Indice di vecchiaia – 1991, 2001, 2011", § c.1.3.1; "Variazione dell'indice di vecchiaia – 1991–2011 e 2001–2011", § c.1.3.2.
31 See PRIN Postmetropoli (2015): "Indice di vecchiaia – 1991, 2001, 2011", § c.1.3.1.
32 See PRIN Postmetropoli (2015): "Indice composito di sofferenza urbana – 2001, 2011", § i.2.12.
33 Namely between Lodi and Piacenza, Lodi and Treviglio, Treviglio and Bergamo, Bergamo and Lecco.

34 See PRIN Postmetropoli (2015): "Indice rischio abitativo – 2011/2012", § i.2.9.
35 The OECD based its interpretations on four main criteria: "minimum population size of 1.5 million people; minimum population density of 150 people per km²; contained labour markets with a maximum net commuting rate of 10 percent of the resident population; and one city that is under the threshold of 1.5 million people but which accounts for more than 20 percent of their national population" (OECD, 2006, p. 83).
36 "An urban core consists of a high-density cluster of contiguous grid cells of 1 km² with a density of at least 1,500 inhabitants/km² and the filled gaps (. . .). An important innovation of this methodology identifies which urban areas have such a polycentric structure. This is done by simply looking at the relationships among the urban cores, using the information contained in the commuting data. Two urban cores are considered integrated, and thus part of the same polycentric metropolitan area, if more than 15 percent of the residence population of any of the cores commutes to work in the other core (. . .) Urban hinterlands are defined as all municipalities with at least 15 percent of their employed residents working in a certain urban core. Municipalities surrounded by a single functional urban area are included and non-contiguous municipalities are dropped" (OECD, 2012, p. 3).

References

Balducci, A. (2004). Milano dopo la metropoli. Ipotesi per la costruzione di un'agenda pubblica. *Territorio*, 29/30, 9–16.
Balducci, A., and Fedeli, V. (Eds.). (2007). *I territori della città in trasformazione: tattiche e percorsi di ricerca*. Milano: FrancoAngeli.
Balducci, A., Fedeli, V., and Pasqui, G. (Eds.). (2008). *In movimento. Confini, Popolazioni E Politiche nel territorio milanese*. Milano: FrancoAngeli.
Balducci, A., Fedeli, V., and Pasqui, G. (Eds.) (2011). *Strategic Planning for Contemporary Urban Regions City of Cities: A Project for Milan*. Farnham: Ashgate.
Boeri, S., Lanzani, A., and Marini, E. (1993). *Il territorio che cambia. Ambienti, paesaggi, immagini della regione milanese*, Milano: Aim-Segesta.
Bonomi, A. (2008). *Il rancore. Alle radici del malessere del Nord*. Milano: Feltrinelli.
Bonomi, A., and Abruzzese, A. (Eds.) (2004). *La città infinita*. Milano: Mondadori.
Brenner, N. (Ed.) (2014). *Implosions/Explosions: Towards a Study of Planetary Urbanization*. Berlin: Jovis Verlag GmbH.
Calafati, A. (2014). *Città e aree metropolitane in Italia* (GSSI Urban Studies Working Paper No. 1). L'Aquila: Gran Sasso Science Institute. Retrieved from http://ssrn.com/abstract=2369323
Cass, N., Shove, E., and Urry, J. (2005). Social Exclusion, Mobility and Access. *Sociological Review*, 53(3), 539–555.
Clementi, A., Dematteis, G., and Palermo, P.C. (1996). *Le forme del territorio italiano* (Vols. 1–2). Bari: Laterza.
Consonni, G., and Tonon, G. (2001). *La terra degli ossimori*, in Aa.Vv., *Lombardia. Storia D'Italia*. Torino: Einaudi.
Dalmasso, E. (1972). *Milano capitale economica d'Italia*. Milano: Angeli.
Davoudi, S., and Bell, D. (Eds.). (2016). *Justice and Fairness in the City: A Multi-disciplinary Approach to 'Ordinary' Cities*. Bristol, UK: Policy Press.
De Carlo, G. (1962). Relazione finale. In Istituto Lombardo di Scienze Economiche e Sociali. (Ed.), *Relazioni del seminario "La nuova dimensione della città, la città-regione"*. Stresa 19–21 gennaio 1962. Milano: Ilses.
De Finetti G. (1969). *Milano costruzione di una città*. Milano: Hoepli.

Diamanti, I. (1996). *Il male del Nord. Lega, localismo, secessione*. Roma: Donzelli.

Donzelot, J. (2009). *Vers une citoyenneté urbaine*. Paris: Rue d'Ulm.

Garreau, J. (1991). *Edge City: Life on the New Frontier*. New York: Doubleday.

Hoffmann-Martinot, V. (2004). *Towards an Americanization of French Metropolitan Areas?* Paper presented at the Department of Political Science and International Relations, Universidad Autónoma de Madrid, February 2004, and at the International Metropolitan Observatory Meeting, 9–10 January 2004, Bordeaux, Pôle Universitaire de Bordeaux.

Keil, R. (2011). Global Suburbanization: The Challenge of Researching Cities in the 21st Century. *Public*, 43, 54–61.

Lanzani, A. (1991). *Il territorio al plurale*. Milano: FrancoAngeli.

Lanzani, A. (2003). *Il paesaggi italiani*. Roma: Meltemi.

Lanzani, A. (2012). L'urbanizzazione diffusa dopo la stagione della crescita. In C. Papa (Ed.), *Letture di paesaggi*. Milano: Guerrini associati.

Lévy, J. (2013). Liens faibles, choix forts: les urbains et l'urbanité, *La Vie des idées*. Retrieved from http://www.laviedesidees.fr/Liens-faibles-choix-forts-les.html.

Macchi Cassia, C., and Ischia, U. (Eds.). (1999). *Un territorio urbano*. Milano: Franco-Angeli.

Meijers, E., Hollander, K., and Hoogerbrugge, M. (2012). *A Strategic Knowledge and Research Agenda on Polycentric Metropolitan Areas*. Retrieved from: http://www.platform31.nl/uploads/media_item/media_item/23/1/KRA_Polycentric_metropolitan_areas-1398346137.pdf.

Mioni, A. (1975). Le trasformazioni dell'assetto storico del territorio lombardo nell'età industrial. In A. Mioni and R. Rozzi (Eds.), *I centri storici in Lombardia*. Milano: Silvana.

Moretti, A. (Ed.). (1999). *Il paradigma del policentrismo. Conoscenza e trasformazione del territorio lombardo*. Milano: FrancoAngeli.

OECD. (2006). *OECD Territorial Reviews: Milan, Italy*. Paris: OECD Publishing. doi: http://dx.doi.org/10.1787/9789264028920-en.

OECD. (2012). *Redefining "Urban": A New Way to Measure Metropolitan Areas*. Paris: OECD Publishing. doi: http://dx.doi.org/10.1787/9789264174108-en.

PRIN Postmetropoli. (2015). *Atlante web dei territori postmetropolitani* [web atlas]. Retrieved from http://www.postmetropoli.it/atlante.

Provincia di Milano, Assessorato alla viabilità, opere pubbliche stradali, mobilità e trasporti. (2006). *Futuro in movimento. Scenari e prospettive della mobilità e dei trasporti nell'area metropolitana milanese*. Milano: Provincia di Milano.

Pucci, P. (2014). Identifying Communities of Practice through Mobile Phone Data. *Brazilian Journal of Urban Management*, 6(1), 75–97.

Pucci, P. (2015). Mobility Practices as a Knowledge and Design Tool for Urban Policy. In P. Pucci and M. Colleoni (Eds.), *Understanding Mobilities for Designing Contemporary Cities*. Heidelberg-New York-Dordrecht-London: Springer.

Pucci, P., Manfredini, F., and Tagliolato, P. (2015). *Mapping Urban Practices through Mobile Phone Data*. Heidelberg-New York-Dordrecht-London: Springer / PoliMI SpringerBriefs Series.

Regione Lombardia, Direzione Generale Infrastrutture e mobilità. (2002). *Indagine origine/destinazione regionale 2002*. Milano: Regione Lombardia.

Secchi, B. (2005). *La città del ventesimo secolo*. Bari: Laterza.

Sernini, M. (1998). *Una forma di città*. Catanzaro: Il Rubettino.

Sieverts, T. (2003). *Cities without Cities: An Interpretation of the Zwischenstadt.* London: Routledge.

Soja, E.W. (2000). *Postmetropolis: Critical Studies of Cities and Regions.* Oxford: Blackwell.

Soja, E.W. (2011). Regional Urbanization and the End of the Metropolis Era. In G. Bridge and S. Watson (Eds.), *New Companion to the City* (pp. 679–689). Chichester: Wiley-Blackwell.

4 Turin metropolitan region

From path-dependency dynamics to current challenges

Nadia Caruso and Silvia Saccomani[1]

Turin *square*: towards a regionalisation process?

The city of Turin is a well-known case owing to the peculiar characteristics of its social, economic and urban development in the twentieth century (Gabert, 1964) and, in particular, after the Second World War. It is an emblematic case of a Fordist city (the city of the FIAT car industry), and its development and territorial dynamics have influenced the surrounding area. From the 1960s this effect rose with increasing strength and, even if since the 1980s the patterns have been changing, the path-dependent character is still evident.

The so-called Turin *square* (*tassello*) is located in the Piedmont Region and has been analysed according to a dimension of 100 x 100 km; the centre of the *square* is nearly the city of Turin: this position is based on the history that linked the development of this territory to the development of the city of Turin. When the sight moves from the city to the *square*, another feature reveals its relevance in the territorial development dynamics: a great part of this area is mountainous to the west and north along the border with France and with the Valle d'Aosta Region, while in the south and east the territory is flat or hilly. Many valleys open up to the Turin plain: the most important among them is the Susa Valley, which connects the Turin plain with France by rail and highway. Many municipalities, especially in the mountain areas, are very small. Furthermore, the position of the Turin *square* in the Italian territory shows another specificity: it is the only *square*, among those analysed, located on an international border and it constitutes an important part of an international axis that connects various territories, the European Mediterranean Corridor (Lisbon–Kiev).

In addition, the city of Turin and its surrounding area have been affected by processes that are generally considered features of the transition towards new post-metropolitan models, broadly explored in international literature (Soja, 2011; Brenner, 2013; Diener et al., 2005) – such as economic restructuring, the transition from a Fordist to a post-Fordist industrial metropolis, the feeble boundaries between cities, suburbs and rural areas, the changes in everyday life brought in by the technological revolution, and so on. Despite this fact, just the above-mentioned characteristics of the city and the *square* imply a sort of difficulty to assume models and concepts of urban phenomena as able to explain the current dynamics, whereas those were defined based on different territorial contexts. The main research question of the national project – can the current changes taking place in the different Italian territories be explained as forms of transition towards post-metropolis? – has found only partial positive responses in the "portrait" of Turin. Therefore, other concepts, traditionally present in the Italian debate, have been used to better understand the current dynamics of urban areas. Metropolisation, for instance, is a concept that was defined a few years ago (Indovina, 2003; Indovina et al., 2009) in relation to studying Italian dynamics. According to Indovina and colleagues (2009), the metropolisation process is the result of the spreading on the territory of population, housing, activities, commercial centres, services, and so on. This trend is based on the widespread supply of public and private specialised activities in an increasingly broader area. It means a sort of auto-organisation process, which determines integration among these activities, but without a clear strategy, nor a coherent territorial structure. The result is the transition from a hierarchical territorial structure to a more polycentric territory, shaped according to local economic, cultural and social features. This metropolisation process is based on the economic and technological changes in the industrial sector and in the consumption models which have affected the territory with the development of the service economy, the changes in the chains of production and the innovation in transport and telecommunications technologies. Daily life is also changing: family structure, mobility and organisation of work, education needs, and so on. The private demands/needs have opened up a growing interest towards services, which become specificities of places, poles in the urbanised area. In this kind of metropolisation, the effects of auto-organising processes on the territory are also social inequalities, separation and selection, linked with real estate values. According to a trend of polarisation in both directions, the upper and the lower social classes remain in the core, while economic activities and middle-class families move to the outskirts where a better environmental quality and infrastructure and services are available. Private enterprises use the diversity in real estate values and the presence of infrastructures to spread in the metropolitan area.

Considering these general characteristics, in Turin *square* the metropolisation process has been strongly conditioned by world economic and technological changes; in particular, from the 1980s the process of economic restructuring marked the transition from a "Fordist city" to a "post-Fordist territory" (Bagnasco, 1990). Nevertheless, the process started earlier with urban spread: in the 1960s factories moved to the outskirts, and they were followed by the population looking for lower-cost housing. Then the different urban areas were incorporated and functionally integrated in a metropolitan area. However, this area has maintained a strong centre, the city of Turin, as a reference point for the rest of the territory. Over time, relations among the core and other parts have been changing: the hierarchical relationships have become less strict, giving rise to forms of polycentrism.

The dual morphology of this territory also had a role in these dynamics: the plain area has historically been marked by the processes of economic development, while the mountainous area has been characterised by scarce development and abandonment. The metropolisation process has invested especially growing parts of the plain area, enlarging what has been called the Turin metropolitan area (TMA),[2] while the mountain parts have remained mostly untouched.

Another characteristic of this *square* is the high level of fragmentation of public authorities. Most of the *square* belongs to the Province of Turin, which has a total population of more than 2 million and includes 315 municipalities out of the 500 encompassed by the *square*. Despite the slow polycentrism tendency, this fragmentation gives rise to the issue of how to govern this territory and with which institutional organisation. This is a crucial issue today in the new institutional framework put in place by the state in Italy with the establishment in 2015 of the metropolitan cities: one of them is Turin Metropolitan City (TMC), whose territory coincides with the territory of the old province. The effects of this top–down institutional design have to be addressed together with bottom–up processes that were stimulating the slow growth of a polycentric structure.

The question this regional portrait tries to explore is whether some of the dynamics taking place in Turin *square* are really changing the urban characteristics of its territory and fostering a regionalisation process. This general question will be addressed from three different perspectives: the socio-economic perspective, the spatial and functional perspective, and the institutional perspective, with a special attention to the governance processes taking place, trying to verify the role of path-dependency in the changing dynamics and the current challenges which have to be faced. Finally, some conclusions will be drawn.

Socio-economic perspective

Rise and fall of a one-company town

Owing to the morphology of the *square* territory, for a long time its socio-economic dynamics have been the result of what happened in the plain and especially in its socio-economic centre, the city of Turin. The broad area of the mountain municipalities has often been neglected in the literature since the main area of interest has been the highly developed and industrialised plain.

For centuries the city of Turin grew following principles of rigid and unitary organisation. From the 1950s a broad agglomeration grew around it, involving several rings of municipalities and establishing a large metropolitan area. This has never been governed and planned according to coherent principles. In the last 40–45 years the process of metropolisation of this area followed different dynamics according to territorial processes and without institutional borders.

After the Second World War the city of Turin developed according to the Fordist model and its development was mainly based on the automotive sector. FIAT was the company that triggered this development. This industrial model had its heyday in the 1950s and 1960s and the city grew accordingly. The population in those years could be divided into two main categories: the bourgeois class and the working class. The urban space could also be divided according to the population living there, identifying a social spatial division (Bagnasco, 1986). The workers lived mainly on an axis from north-east to south-west, while the upper classes lived on the eastern side of the city, on the hills.

From the 1970s a general deterioration of this economic model took place. Several triggers can be identified: the energy crisis of 1973 and the deficiencies of the Fordist model, based on large factories and a rigid organisation of work. The weaknesses of an economic development anchored only to the automotive sector also became clear. A general financial reorganisation process by FIAT took place, restructuring the technologies and the organisational model. Outsourcing to the rest of Italy and abroad was put in place, labour-saving technologies were adopted and, following a trend of specialisation, a number of components were produced by other small and medium-sized companies. This economic transition brought the Fordist model to a more flexible production in the 1980s, the "just in time" approach (Whitford & Enrietti, 2005). During the 1980s the employment rate in large companies decreased, while it grew in the small and medium-sized ones. This was a result of their empowerment, as they started to specialise and be independent from the leading company, strengthening their technological expertise (Antonelli, 1986). FIAT kept its leading role, but Turin started to lose its character of a "one-company town": the employment rate decreased in the industrial sector while it rose in the tertiary one, especially as services for industrial companies.

The economic transition of the 1970s and 1980s also affected the city and its spatial organisation: the population of Turin declined while there was a demographic movement towards the municipalities of the surrounding metropolitan area. In particular, the municipalities of the "third ring", those further from Turin, gained population from these suburbanisation movements. The municipalities located on the east side (hills) and on the west (hills and mountains) were the favourite places of middle- and upper-class families and professionals, and in these areas the average size of houses increased (Chicco et al., 1995). The working class moved especially to the suburbs in the municipalities close to Turin in the north-east and south-west directions (Conforti & Mela, 1995). In the 1980s the economic restructuring and the spatial movements of factories also had physical results in the urban areas, with a strong increase of vacant industrial areas and brownfields.

In the 1990s the demographic decline of the central city and the movements towards the rest of the metropolitan area continued (Mela & Conforti, 2008). These dynamics meant a strong growth of municipalities around Turin, following some directions (north, east and Susa Valley on the west). The mountain arc from north to south and the central city showed instead a decreasing trend.

In short, the changes which developed in the Turin area between the 1970s and the new millennium can be summarised as follows: the central city lost more than a quarter of its population, while the other municipalities around it increased by almost one third; the housing sector rose in the municipalities located further away from Turin, especially towards the west and the Susa Valley; the low density of these new settlements caused a high soil consumption and the massive use of private cars. The Fordist model vanished (Bagnasco, 1990), but the urban structure was still shaped on the spatial distribution of the different social classes. In the last thirty to forty years the dominance of Turin has decreased in the metropolitan area and the spread of services has allowed the growth of relations among new different poles and nodes (Buran et al., 2006).

The last 10–15 years: permanence and change

According to Mela and Conforti (2008), after the decline of the 1980s and 1990s, the population in the city of Turin started to grow again from 2000 to 2007. The data (+5.04%) is higher than the regional average and very close to that of Turin Province (+5.19%). This growth is entirely caused by immigrants coming from other countries. From 1991 to 2011 (ISTAT, census data, www.postmetropoli.it/atlante/), the immigrant population grew by more than 100% in the majority of municipalities of the *square*; the only area that did not register this increase is a part of the mountain arc in the north-east (Lanzo Valley) and this is clearly related to its traditional low-profile economic structure. The territorial concentration of immigrants is higher in the central city and fragmented in the rest of the *square*. Focusing on the percentage of the foreign population compared with the Italian one, in the decade 2001–11 its weight changed from 15% to 22%. The central city and the municipalities of the Susa Valley (those where the Winter Olympic Games took place in 2006) show the highest percentage. Outside Turin Province, municipalities belonging to Asti and Cuneo Provinces (still part of the *square*) also have a high percentage of foreign population.

The current demographic situation confirms the trends of the previous decades: according to the data, between 2001 and 2011, the population grew at higher rates in the municipalities of the external rings of the TMA, while Turin keeps a steady low increasing trend. The rate of ageing population also increased from 2001 to 2011: the mountain arc on the west side, from the north to south of the *square*, shows the highest rate of ageing index, while the plain area and the upper Susa Valley have the lowest index. In Turin the proportion of the population over 65 years old is higher than in the urbanised plain around it, showing the relation among population trends and the urbanisation paths.

Concerning education, in 2001 the population with higher levels of education was located mainly in the plain area, with high peaks in Turin and the municipalities of the hills on the east side and those of the "third ring" around the central city on the west side. Citizens with secondary and higher education were living also in the municipalities in the upper Susa Valley, showing again the strong link and the similarity of this area with the core of the *square*.

In addition, the economic characteristics of the population moving within the *square* seem to confirm some of the previous patterns. Population with higher incomes is concentrated in the highly urbanised central area: the municipalities with the peaks are located on the hills on the east of Turin or on the west in the "third ring". Also, Gini index confirms this income distribution: a stronger income homogeneity (lowest index) is present, especially in the plain area, while the municipalities in the upper Susa Valley, those located in the Alpine arc and the others on the hills (east side of Turin) show a high income disparity. Further from the core, the same trends can be noted in the municipalities at the foothills towards the north and especially in the plain towards the south and the Province of Cuneo.

In 2001 (2001 census data, the only data available), most residential buildings were located in the core area, in the main urbanised directions in the plain (towards north and south, south-east) and in the municipalities at the upper Susa Valley.

The above-mentioned central enlarged core of the *square* seems to have similar features to Turin as far as the concepts of heterogeneity and density are concerned. The central city is strongly linked to its rings, especially to the third one, chosen by the local population as a better environment to live. The situation is strongly different in the arc of municipalities located in the mountains from north to south. This area shows opposite trends: decreasing numbers of inhabitants, ageing population, low population density, low income, low education level. The upper Susa Valley is an exception, with few municipalities that have a situation comparable with the central urbanised area: high income due to the tourism economy (skiing sector), increasing population and density, high numbers of immigrants, low rates of ageing population and high rate of education.

These demographic trends reflect fairly similar economic dynamics. In the twenty-first century the manufacturing sector has been clearly reshaped by the changes in the automotive industry, while tertiary sector activities are growing. The economic transition has mainly affected the central city, where the industrial working class has lost its role in favour of employees in the service sector. Innovative industrial activities (electronics, robotics, telecommunications, and so on) started to locate in the Turin area, and a movement towards the "knowledge economy" was recognized (Conti & Vanolo, 2003). Many initiatives were undertaken in order to attract these sectors and their promotion was seen as a central goal in the second Turin Strategic Plan (Torino Internazionale, 2006).[3] As a whole, the *square* lost almost 100,000 jobs in the manufacturing sector and 100,000 in the agricultural sector, while in the commercial sector jobs grew by about 1 million between 2001 and 2011. In the tourism sector there was a growth of more than 1 million jobs as well, while the building sector saw a small rise.

In the decade 2001–11 the general picture of the spatial distribution of employment and plants shows a fragmented situation, with decreasing numbers of jobs in the northern part of the territory and around the central city, a low rise in the south and along the Susa Valley, while the low increase of plants is due to the process of economic specialisation. As a whole, this decade shows the increasing concentration of most of the economic activities in the central urbanised area and in the municipalities of the Susa Valley.

These data are not yet showing the strong impacts of the financial crisis of 2007–08, which affected Italy a few years later than the USA; the data from 2011 to today could be more meaningful to identify the crisis trends, the effects of austerity policies and the big challenges that this situation implies. The only recent available data are those related to employment and unemployment in the Piedmont region and in Turin Province. The Piedmont region has been strongly hit by the financial crisis compared with the other northern Italian regions:[4] recent data show a region strongly hit by labour reduction and restructuring.

According to Piedmont region and ISTAT data,[5] regional unemployment has been increasing since 2008, following the global financial crisis; in fact, the working population decreased (−4.5%) between 2008 and 2013, while the population looking for a job increased (113.1%). The employment rate (population 20 to 64 years old) decreased (−2.7%) in the same period, while the unemployment rate grew from 5.1% in 2008 to 11.3% in 2014. Focusing on the data of the provinces, Turin Province shows a worse trend than other provinces. Working population decreased between 2008 and 2014 (−6.4%) and the population looking for a job increased 57.13%, while southern Piedmont provinces such as Asti and Cuneo have a more positive trend: a lower decrease of working population (Cuneo −1.11%, Asti −4.2%), a lower growth of citizens looking for a job in Cuneo Province (+34.65%), not in Asti (+60.58%). In Piedmont, agriculture is the economic sector that lost more jobs (−21.74%) between 2008 and 2014, while in the same period the Province of Turin registered a stronger decrease (−78.3%).

In Piedmont the unemployment rate almost doubled between 2008 and 2014. The population from 15 to 24 years old was the most affected by this rise (from 15% to 42.2%). The highest increase of unemployment affected the population with higher education (university degrees) and mainly women (from 2.3% to 6.2% between 2008 and 2014). In the same period, in fact, the unemployment rate in Turin Province increased from 5.6% to 12.9%, while the best-performing province in Piedmont was Cuneo, showing a low growth in unemployment from 3.5% to 5.3%.

The census data show a permanence of the traditional socio-economic development without big changes in the economic engines or in their locations. Looking at these data, the traditional industrial structure does not look able to overcome the crisis by itself. The crisis gave a negative acceleration to those socio-economic processes that were already in place, but slowly developing, leaving this territory without a clear strategy to deal with it. Focusing on the strengths and abilities that the past has grounded in this territory could be a way to recover and address the crisis.

Spatial and functional perspective

In the Turin *square* the morphology of the territory has had an important role in shaping the development and urbanisation process in recent decades. Forty per cent of the *square* municipalities and 47% of those belonging to the Province of Turin (which includes about 65% of the *square* municipalities) are classified as totally or partially mountainous. Historically the plain has been the place of urbanisation and development, even if the different valleys have also played a role in the development of the *square*.

As explained in the previous section, the central plain area has many common features, but the mountain municipalities at the upper Susa Valley, which specialise in tourism, have some socio-economic features in common with it. The situation is different in the other mountain municipalities, where the population declined until the 1960s, in contrast with the increasing tendency in the whole *square* after the Second World War.

This demographic trend in the plain also had spatial and physical consequences: increase in population density and in soil consumption. In fact, data show a trend towards a growing population density in the central plain area in the period 1971–91, stronger in some of the municipalities closer to Turin, especially on the western part of the traditional TMA. Then, in the period 1991–2011, this growing density extended radially to become a larger territory; it also extends along the foothills towards the north, towards the south in the Province of Cuneo and in the most tourist municipalities of the upper Susa Valley. However, recently some of the municipalities closer to Turin on the west and the south of the TMA show a stable density, while the central city shows a decreasing density trend, which is linked with its demographic decline.

In the same period (1991–2011) the increase of the anthropic surfaces, which means an increase of soil consumption,[6] invested especially the municipalities of the outer rings of the TMA and grew along the infrastructure to Milan, the Susa Valley and also towards the south. This trend is confirmed by the distribution of the sealed soil per capita in 2009, which shows the amount of soil consumption in the tourist municipalities of the Susa Valley as well.

In the *square*, agricultural soil is present especially along a diagonal axis from north-east to south and in some municipalities of the Susa and Lanzo Valleys, but this presence is accompanied by a decrease of the used agricultural surfaces, especially in all the mountain areas and also in the eastern hill municipalities, while a small increase is shown only towards the Province of Cuneo in the south. Along the foothills or in tourist mountain municipalities this trend is accompanied by increasing anthropic surfaces, but in other areas there is no parallel increase of the anthropic surfaces, showing possible processes of abandonment of the agricultural activities in these areas. This tendency to abandon agricultural activities invests an extended area in the mountain part of the *square*.

The distribution of commercial activities confirms the role of some municipalities of the plain area, such as Chivasso and Ivrea in the north, Pinerolo in the south-west and others bordering the central city. They are the same cities identified recently by a study of the Department for Development and Economic Cohesion (DPS) as *Poli* (poles), while most of the mountain areas are classified as *aree interne* (inner areas).[7] The role of these municipalities and their relations with the central city have changed over time, leading also to changing definitions of what can be considered the TMA from a physical and functional point of view: recent international research has defined functional urban areas (FUAs) and morphological urban areas (MUAs),[8] which give a similar perspective of this territory (IGEAT, 2007).

The distribution of commercial activities in the *square* also highlights the influence of the motorway infrastructure in favouring the location of the biggest commercial centres: many of them are located around Turin and form a sort of ring along its western motorway ring road from north to south. The distribution of the university poles also confirms the same functional organisation of the territory and is the result of the decentralisation process of some courses by the two universities of the *square*, both located in Turin.

In contrast, there is a widespread presence of small cultural services, such as libraries and museums, in small municipalities or in the valleys. This suggests growing attention to cultural events and can also be seen as a sign of a trend by small communities to affirm their identities against possible processes of abandonment.

The network of transport infrastructure has also been strongly influenced by the morphology of the *square*: a dense network in the plain which extends towards the main valleys. Recently the railway network has been improved in the number of connections and frequency, establishing a so-called metropolitan railway network. From the point of view of mobility, the average mobility index (ratio between internal flows plus outflows and employees) increased between 2001 and 2011. This increase did not change significantly the geography of mobility, but mobility was extended especially to the municipalities of the southern part of the *square* and the Susa Valley. The decrease of the self-containment index (ratio between internal flows and employees) is significant, involving especially the foothill municipalities along a sort of north–south axis and the south border of the province. This means a prevalence of people who work outside the municipality where they live: consequently there is also an increase of the dependence index in the same municipalities (ratio between outflows and employees of the municipality).

From the spatial and functional perspective, the most significant features of Turin *square* are the role of the morphology in shaping the territory and, connected with it, the continuity and persistence of the urbanisation process which took place in the plain. The dynamics that developed over time, especially in recent decades, have not significantly changed these processes until now. This territory remains a dual territory (the plain and the mountains) (Saccomani, 2014) in which the functional and physical dynamics are connected, but still different.

Institutional perspective

The real challenge for a territory like the Turin *square* is how to govern its dynamics, and with which tools and which institutional and governance structures. This raises some questions: what are the difficulties that the territorial government encounters in such a fragmented situation? Have the described regionalisation processes, even if weaker than in other territories, influenced the institutional perspective and territorial governance? Has the less hierarchical and more polycentric spatial organisation fostered the emergence of new forms of governance? What are the administrative difficulties related to this perspective?

These questions became more serious with the recent national local authorities reform, Act 56/2014, which established ten metropolitan cities (MC) in Italy: one of them is the Turin Metropolitan City (TMC) and it introduced new challenges for such a territory. The territory of the TMC coincides with the former Province of Turin.

Before answering these questions, it is necessary to provide a more detailed description of the institutional structure of the *square*, because the current challenges are strongly dependent on it.

Table 4.1 Administrative units and fragmentation index: comparison between the Province of Turin and the average values of other Italian provinces

	population % variation (2001–11)	central city population over province population (2001)	central city population over province population (2011)	number of municipalities per 100,000 inhabitants (2011)	fragmentation index (2011)	total number of administrative units per 100,000 inhabitants (2011)
Turin Province	3.8%	40.3%	38.8%	14.0	36.1	17.5
Other provinces (average)	3.7%	45.8%	43.8%	5.1	13.3	6.9

Source: Authors' calculation on ISTAT census data

Administrative fragmentation and stable cooperation units

The provincial territory[9] is very fragmented from an administrative point of view, meaning a proliferation of government authorities in the same area (see Table 4.1). The fragmentation index is more than twice the average.[10] Taking into account the number of other institutional administrative units – institutional forms of cooperation[11] – and the number of municipalities, the fragmentation index[12] does not change much.

On the one hand, administrative fragmentation complicates the process of inter-institutional cooperation and can make new forms of territorial governance difficult to achieve. On the other hand, administrative fragmentation could mean a more widespread government power and can sometimes lead to new, more stable forms of governance over time.

Among the above-mentioned institutional forms of cooperation there are differences: their legal or voluntary origin, the kind of territory involved, the themes they address, the subjects involved. These differences influence their ability to stimulate a cooperative attitude and the ability to set up cooperative behaviour with broad objectives. For instance, the prevalence of local forces in the composition of the actors involved in the cooperation, such as in the case of municipalities unions,[13] rather than the prevalence of those deriving only from an institutional top–down design, could have a better chance of overcoming institutional fragmentation.

Governance networks and density

The governance networks taken into account in this analysis are mostly the result of voluntary cooperation (project cooperation, *cooperazioni mobili a progetto*). They are planning tools based on local, inter-municipality and sometimes multi-scalar initiatives. They are generally integrated programmes, based on coalitions and partnerships between public and private actors – often an expression of a local partnership – and their contents constitute an integration of policies and policy areas. They aim, more or less explicitly, at the exploitation of local resources (tangible and intangible) for the development of local areas. Most of them were the product of EU Structural Funds Programmes.

The choice to analyse this kind of cooperation excludes other, more bottom–up types not related to institutional initiatives. These are generally linked to initiatives of local actors (often NGOs), and are more difficult to identify and map. On an imaginary line from "government" (defined skills, objectives and spatial dimension) to forms of governance totally bottom–up (spatial dimension, objectives and competencies not previously defined), the chosen forms of cooperation are located in an intermediate position in which the spatial dimension tends not to be predefined. This is true except for the possible criteria which can limit its definition, as in the case of some national, regional or EU programmes. This characteristic leaves room for local aggregation initiatives. In many cases, all of the objectives and characteristics of the participants are also not defined.

These forms of cooperation can be looked at from two different points of view: the features of the networks and the density of their presence in each municipality. From the first point of view it is worth noting that nearly all the municipalities of the province were involved in at least one cooperation network in the period of observation (1990–2013): on average, each municipality entered into 4.7 networks, but the situation is different in different areas.

The municipalities strongly involved in the cooperation networks are those located around the central city. If we take into account the other municipalities whose participation is at least 10% above average, the resulting image is quite similar to the FUAs described by Espon, including the municipalities of the Susa and Lanzo Valleys. The municipalities whose involvement in cooperation networks is around average are located along the foothills in the north and south-west. The municipalities which are below average are instead located around two cities defined as *Poli* (poles) by the Department for Development and Economic Cohesion (DPS) (see above): Ivrea and the surrounding Eporediese area in the north, and Pinerolo in the south. Focusing on the stronger or weaker links between the different municipalities involved in cooperation networks, the role played by the central city and its surrounding area is confirmed. The stronger links involve three of the five DPS *Poli* (Turin, Moncalieri, Chivasso) and the DPS *Poli Intermedi* (intermediate poles), all located just around Turin. Nearly the same happens for the medium-strength links, except for some networks in the Olympic Valleys.

As a whole, taking into account governance networks and links, a confirmation of the historic monocentric structure of the *square* emerges, that is, the role of the TMA according to the way it grew in the last 40 years, especially along a west–east axis. So, the growth of the number of governance experiences seems to be influenced by traditional factors, especially the economic role of the municipality and the historic centre–periphery relationships.

At first glance the regionalisation processes, although weaker than in other *squares*, do not seem to have strongly influenced the capacity of the municipalities located outside the traditional (even enlarged) MA, to become active actors in the governance processes. The administrative fragmentation, the population dimension and the morphology of the *square* can explain this weakness.

To test this result it can be useful to take into account what was previously called density of cooperation, that is, to weight the number of cooperation in which each municipality is involved on the amount of its population. The hypothesis is that the density of cooperative processes can be a significant indicator of the process of regionalisation. It can be considered as evidence of a new local bottom–up capacity to address, in a cooperative way, the government of the changes taking place. This hypothesis emphasises as a positive element the emergence of new "soft spaces" of governance (Allmendinger & Haughton, 2009), more suitable than the institutionally designed entities to intervene in areas that tend to be polycentric.

The result of this kind of analysis significantly changes the above-described monocentric image. First, it shows the weaker involvement of the central city and also of the other towns classified as *Poli*, except Moncalieri.

Second, it reveals another geography of cooperation, articulated along two axes: one extends along the foothills area, from the west side of the MA north-eastwards; the other is a west–east axis from the lower Susa Valley to the hills of Chieri, extending towards Asti. Other experiences have emerged in the southern area of Pinerolo, where recent metropolisation processes have taken place.

Third, the municipalities showing a stronger attitude to cooperation are generally those in which the population has grown in recent years. A similar relationship can be seen with income distribution. The municipalities at the upper Susa Valley are an exception since they are characterised by high incomes but a weak attitude to cooperation, even during the Olympic period (2006).

Fourth, it is interesting to note that the municipalities with a stronger tendency to cooperate are generally those that showed a greater stability of political coalitions in the local elections (which took place between 1994 and 2013). This is generally true except for some of the municipalities of the lower Susa Valley, which has been a place of social conflict in recent years concerning the local opposition to the Turin–Lyon High Speed Train currently under construction. Political stability can be seen as a component of local institutional capacity (Healey, 1998) that has fostered the cooperation attitude.

No relation has been observed between the political "colour" of the local coalition (centre-left or centre-right) and the attitude to cooperation. This seems to be in contrast with the opinion of some authors (Allmendinger & Haughton, 2009; Haughton et al., 2013; Waterhout et al., 2013), who describe the proliferation of soft spaces of governance in some European countries. According to these authors, the "soft spaces" are identified as the product of the growing push towards neoliberal policies, as local voluntarism commits to a role that the public administrations are no longer able/do not intend to play; according to this interpretation, "soft spaces" of governance are an answer to a policy of disengagement by the public institutions from a direct intervention in a lot of social and economic situations, generally a characteristic of the attitude of centre-right coalitions.[14] On the other hand, the emergence of forms of cooperation on the part of small local communities on specific policies could be a contribution to the same growth of new, more institutional forms of management and associated functions (especially in an area with the characteristics of the Province of Turin). There is often a tendency in the studies to a "simplistic use of the neoliberalization process to explain any change in policy" (Le Galès & Vitale, 2015, p. 12, our translation).

Actors, times and themes

As far as the actors involved in this cooperation are concerned, nearly all of them are multi-scalar, including upper-level institutions (the regional or the provincial government). Given the prevalent origin of the cooperation mentioned above, this is fairly evident. There are many cases in which the role of upper-level institutions in starting and implementing initiatives is significant. However, more than 60% are public–private cooperation, either involving private actors or associations (trade unions, non-profit associations, civil society associations).

The prevalent theme in each cooperation has been classified as follows:[15] (1) rural development, (2) economic development and innovation, (3) local public transport, (4) urban regeneration, (5) environment and renewable energy, and (6) tourism, culture, environment and landscape, big events.

Most of the collected experiences started in the period 2000–06, while after 2007 their number decreased significantly. As a whole, there is a small prevalence of cooperation around tourism, culture, and economic development and innovation. The second theme is more present in the first period (1990–99), while both are also significant in the second period (2000–06). From 2000 to 2006, three other themes become more prevalent: rural development, urban regeneration, and environment and renewable energy. It is worth noting that in the third period (2007–13) the new initiatives show a stronger bottom–up origin, alongside a decrease in the total number of cooperation networks and the emergence of the theme of local public transport.

As far as the territories involved are concerned, cooperation density in the field of rural development has a clear territorial distribution pattern: a sort of arc from north to south on the east of Turin and along two valleys (Chiusella Valley on the north and Susa Valley on the west). Cooperation in this field involves small municipalities, generally in demographic and employment decline, especially in the valleys. Until 2011 they do not seem to have significantly changed the tendency to a decrease of used agricultural surface in these territories, except in the Pinerolese on the south. Over time the density of cooperation in this field moved from western and northern municipalities (Susa Valley and Canavese) to eastern and southern ones (Chieri, Pinerolo).

The initiatives of economic development and innovation have a sufficiently clear territorial distribution as well (two axes: along the foothill area and along Susa Valley). Cooperation concerning local public transport also has the same distribution. In some of these areas employment decreased in the last decade – for instance, in Canavese in the north foothills area. However, in these territories there is still a degree of specialisation in the manufacturing sector, despite the structural changes taking place.

All the forms of cooperation with a focus on the environment and renewable energy have started more recently (after 2007) and are located in the northern valleys and in the northern part of the MA. In the last area long-standing cooperation experiences have led to a stable municipalities union.

The distribution of cooperation focusing on urban regeneration shows a clear north–south axis, which surrounds and cuts off Turin, but involves other municipalities of the MA. All these initiatives started after 2000 and the more recent ones show a growth of new themes less related to the traditional urban regeneration approach, such as PIC Urban, and are more locally created.

Finally, cooperation focusing on tourism, culture and so on is concentrated in the mountains to the west, the hills to the east and in the MA, while these initiatives are poor or nearly non-existent in the south and in the north of the province, in spite of the presence of potentially attractive elements such as national and regional parks.

Looking through the square *from the government/governance perspective*

To understand the challenges the Turin *square* has to face from the point of view of government issues and governance practices, it is necessary to go over the steps and features which have especially marked government issues in the last 40 years.

The TMA never had a unitary form of government, even if in 1990 national Act 142/1990 had introduced a new institutional level – the metropolitan city (MC) – which, in the case of Turin, should have included the city and its metropolitan area. This law was not implemented in any Italian case in the following decades.

At the beginning of the new millennium the city of Turin started a strategic planning process involving part of the surrounding municipalities of the MA. It was the first Italian experience of strategic planning and of a governance process involving different stakeholders. It led to a First Strategic Plan in 2000 (Torino Internazionale, 2000), a Second Strategic Plan in 2006 (Torino Internazionale, 2006) and a Third Strategic Plan in 2015 (Torino Strategica, 2015). All three plans, albeit with different intensity, underlined the necessity to move towards some form of metropolitan government, including a number of municipalities (38 in the first plan, 22 in the second, and again 38 in the third) who voluntarily wanted to join the experiment, which in fact had a very weak result as far as the construction of a metropolitan government is concerned.

Finally national Act 56/2014 introduced the new metropolitan cities (MCs) that were established at the beginning of 2015 in ten Italian metropolitan areas. The MCs territory must coincide with the existing province territory. This solution stems essentially from the cuts to public expenditure proposed by the central government and not from a process of rethinking the role of local authorities and the institutional structure of the Italian territory.

So, Turin Metropolitan City (TMC) includes the 315 municipalities of the former province, without any real relation with the past studies about the dynamics that invested this territory, nor its morphological peculiarities or the governance processes which recently emerged. The only attention paid to such a particular territory was the decision by the new authority to set up the so-called "homogeneous zones": administrative divisions of the territory, foreseen by the national Act as a possible choice by each MC. The TMC territory is divided into 11 homogeneous zones.[16]

From the perspective of government issues, the case of the TMC poses several questions regarding both the planning tools available to this new institution, and the governance and government processes that this new institution can/should put in place.

From the point of view of planning, such an area needs plans that are traditionally defined as "regional plans", but also strategic planning processes able to define scenarios for its future development. Both perspectives are foreseen by the national law, but should be redefined in order to fit the specificities of this territory and its development (Barbieri & Giaimo, 2014). What has been done until now from this point of view is certainly not sufficient to answer the new situation. The strategic planning processes that took place in this area in the last 15 years, involving a very small number of its municipalities, are not an adequate answer to the new requirements of the law, nor to the evolution of the TMC territory and the governance processes previously described.

For instance, according to the new *Statuto* (statute, a sort of constitution) of the TMC, the homogeneous zones could participate in the definition of the strategic plan for their areas and this could foster a sort of bottom–up process that would end in the production of a strategic plan for the whole TMC. This could be an interesting perspective that might even find a basis in the past governance experiences. Nevertheless, the Third Strategic Plan, launched in 2015, involves instead only 38 municipalities which are part of six different homogeneous zones, and the production of the Metropolitan Strategic Plan that the TMC started in November 2015 seems to follow a rather centralized procedure for the time being.

From the point of view of the policies to be implemented, there is a clear need for a strong articulation according to the characteristics of this huge and diversified territory.

From whatever point of view we look at the issue, the particularities of the TMC strongly indicate a need for different levels, methods and tools for its government. In particular, it seems useful to take a step back from the institutional design and its problems and think more freely about aspects such as policy articulation and innovation vs. territorial dimension, and voluntary vs. institutionalised approaches. In a territory with these spatial, economic and social features, the cooperation of small local communities in specific policies could be a testing ground of the possible bottom–up contribution to the more institutional forms of associated management of municipal functions, that is, in such a territory governance "soft spaces" could pave the road towards more efficient institutional reform.

Conclusions

First of all, the natural and geographical features of the *square* territory (mountains and plain) have played and still play an important role in the socio-economic processes. This duality of a territory, shaped in the underdeveloped mountain area and the developed plain, is not new, and its social polarisation and inequalities can have been deepened by weaker interconnections. This partly explains the differences between the north and south areas of the mountain arc as well. This territorial structure influenced the socio-economic development in the past, but it still plays an important role, especially if we look at the data around population, income, housing, infrastructure and services.

Second, this territory still shows the permanence of a monocentric structure in which the central metropolitan area keeps its historic importance and the central city keeps its role of strong reference for an area, which has become more and more enlarged, while also showing signs of an increasingly softer hierarchy. Most of the demographic data confirm this territorial structure in which, starting in the 1980s, the lowest social classes remain in the core, while middle-class families move to the municipalities of the outer rings of the TMA – those further away from the central city, especially on the western and eastern hills, where a better environmental quality, infrastructure and services are available. In fact, the mobility data also show changes in the mobility directions: from a prevalent centre-to-the-closer-outskirts direction, to the tendency to link more efficiently larger parts of the territory in different directions.

In the last decade a regionalisation process has been taking place, fostering the emergence of some initial forms of polycentrism, especially along the foothills and in the southern part of the *square*. The possible extension of the metropolisation process towards the southern province (Cuneo) is unprecedented, while the increasing similarity to and relation with the metropolitan area of some municipalities of the Susa Valley is part of a traditional trend, which has been reinforced by recent events (Olympics), but possibly also by new ICT supply, which has affected economic restructuring.

The impact of the financial crisis on Turin *square* is another important issue bound to affect the future development of this territory, which has been severely hit. The traditional path-dependent and space-dependent characters of its development do not seem ready to effectively react, at least until now. Social inequalities and polarisation are growing, while private enterprises – which effectively used the diversity in real estate values between the centre and the periphery and the presence of infrastructure to spread in the metropolitan area – are currently those hardest hit by the crisis effects.

Third, focusing on the governance dimension, new dynamics can be seen in the governance processes based on "soft space" cooperation. These forms of cooperation throw a little light on the possibility of dealing with the effects of such a fragmented territory. The auto-organised character of these practices was based on the goal and ability of valorising the various territorial specificities, competences and tangible and intangible local resources, even if funds came generally from other institutional levels (EU, region or state). As said previously, the cooperation density pattern can be interpreted as a component of a new local institutional capacity, possibly consistent with a trend towards a regionalisation process.

From the point of view of this kind of practice, the current challenge is not only the new period of EU priorities, but also the coherence between the local communities' abilities to attract EU funding and the new institutional framework.

In fact, the new institutional framework – metropolitan city plus homogeneous zone plus municipalities unions – is the biggest challenge for this territory, alongside working out how to counter the effects of the economic crisis and restart a process of change and development. This requires both a consolidation of the new institutions capable of enhancing the legacies of governance practices, and an innovation, to be defined, in the instruments for governing, planning and managing this particular territory.

Therefore, answering the initial research question, the analysis of the Turin area opens up various issues and challenges. First of all, the socio-economic processes show an urban form in the phase of transforming itself with features such as: rising polycentrism, less hierarchical relations, enlargement of the urbanisation

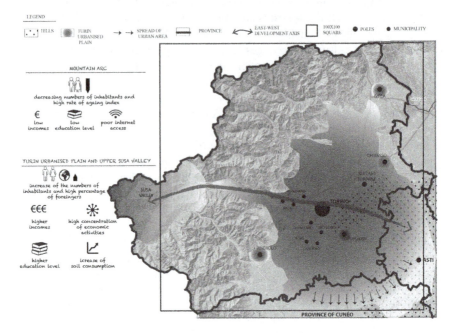

Figure 4.1 Turin regional portrait

Source: image by Elena Pede

without clear distinctions between urban and suburban, and changes in the demographic and economic structures. These characteristics can determine a slow transition towards a "post-metropolis". On the other hand, the role played by this territory's morphology, the strong *path-dependent* development, and the "weight" of its history on the current transition, highlight how this regionalisation process requires no schematic models, but methodologies which could be adapted to place-specificities.

Notes

1 Both authors contributed equally to this work and share responsibility for the presented data.
2 The first proposal for a delimitation of the TMA was launched in 1972 by the Piedmont regional government for analytical purposes without any institutional value: it included 53 municipalities, Turin and 23 municipalities of a "first ring" around it (directly bordering Turin) and 29 of a "second ring". This area was defined according to the industrial processes developed during the 1950s and 1960s and to the residential model linked to the location of the factories. In 1971, 48% of jobs in Piedmont were in this area and 41% of the regional population was living there. This is the area which is generally called the historic metropolitan area. Since the mid-1970s the economic transition of manufacturing activities and the changes in the socio-demographic conditions started to modify the borders of this TMA, leading to a densification of a "third ring" of municipalities further away from the central city and to an enlargement of the

conurbation, which fostered, after 1990, different new proposals for a larger delimitation of a TMA (Conforti & Mela, 1995; Spaziante, 1996), an area including more than 100 municipalities around Turin.

3 From 2000 the city of Turin and part of the municipalities around it took part in different phases of strategic planning. The first plan developed in 2000 was considered a good practice from the other Italian cities and it can be considered as a trigger of a strategic planning season in Italy. After the first plan, the city and its metropolitan area engaged in two more strategic plans: the second one in 2006 and the third in 2015.

4 For instance, in Piedmont the average of unemployment insurance (*cassa integrazione*) hours paid by public funds to support private enterprises in crisis added up to 304 hours (annual average for each worker) in 2013, 211 in Lombardy, 182 in Veneto and 175 in Emilia-Romagna (the national average is 222), and has been growing since 2009: it increased from 40 million paid hours per year before 2009 to 140 million each year after then. The use of unemployment insurance grew especially in the commercial and building sectors between 2006 and 2013, while in the manufacturing industry it has been decreasing since 2010/11. In 2013 the increase mainly affected small enterprises (professionals, associations, foundations, other entities) and it reflects the crisis in the tertiary sector, less affected at the beginning of the financial crisis.

5 Reference at: http://www.regione.piemonte.it/lavoro/osservatorio/quadro.htm and Regione Piemonte (2014).

6 In the 234 municipalities of the plain and the hills, soil consumption grew by 9% between 2000 and 2006, while the increase was only 2.2% in the following four years (Ballocca & Foietta, 2012), a sign either of a greater attention to the problem or of the effect of the economic crisis on the building sector.

7 DPS (Department for the Development and the Economic Cohesion) of the Italian Ministry of Economic Development, nowadays called Territorial Cohesion Agency, produced in 2012 a classification of the Italian municipalities based on the idea that the Italian territory is a polycentric territory, in which a dense network of municipalities offers basic facilities to the others. Municipalities are thus classified according to the level of facilities they can offer and their accessibility, reaching a classification which goes from poles (*poli*) to the more peripheral and deprived areas (called *aree interne*, inner areas), which are totally dependent on other municipalities as far as basic facilities are concerned (DPS, 2012). According to this classification, nearly all the municipalities of the mountainous part of the Turin Province belong to *aree interne*.

8 In recent years (2007 and 2011) ESPON (European Spatial Planning Observation Network) focused its research projects on the aim of identifying European metropolitan areas, or similar metropolitan territories, which led to the definition of two analysis units: functional urban areas (FUAs) and morphological urban areas (MUAs). FUAs are made of municipalities in which a significant population percentage moves for working reasons to a densely inhabited area called an MUA.

9 This analysis takes into account only the municipalities of the province, not those of the entire *square*, as it is necessary to refer to some institutional delimitation.

10 The average refers to the data concerning the seven provinces taken into account in the national research (Milan, Venice, Florence, Rome, Naples, Palermo, Turin), which became metropolitan cities.

11 Such as mountain or hill communities, ATOs (optimal territorial areas) for waste and water supplies, health districts, municipalities unions, regional and national protected areas.

12 "Since the magnitude of political fragmentation [of a metropolitan area] is directly proportional to the number of local governments per 100,000 inhabitants and inversely proportional to the percentage of the metropolitan population residing in the central city of [a metropolitan area], an Index of Geopolitical Fragmentation can be computed by dividing the first quantity by the second" (Zeigler & Brunn, 1980, p. 82) (cited in Kübler, 2005, p. 17).

13 The municipalities unions are special local authorities consisting of two or more municipalities who exercise their functions and manage public facilities in an associated way. They existed from the beginning of the 1990s, but were not implemented until recently, when Act 56/2014 tried to encourage their formation in order to decrease costs related to the number of local governments.

14 The recognised contrast between this theory and practices does not mean that the neoliberal turn in policy does not exist in Italy: this process is taking place, linked also with the crisis and austerity policies in all European countries. But often at the local level, practices, participation experiences and civil society actions can have an influence that goes over the ideological/political barriers. Neoliberal turn and its economic consequences is making the life of local authorities of all political colours hard; therefore bottom–up cooperation can make a difference.

15 This classification is the result of an analysis of the urban and territorial policies developed in Italy and the EU in the last 20 years and was chosen by comparing the investment priorities of the ERDF 2000–06 and 2007–13. The time thresholds at which each cooperation has been attributed are chosen according to the three European programming periods (pre-1999, 2000–06, post-2006) as well. They indicate the time frame in which the project started, which is presumably the time of the decision, while the implementation times were longer.

16 The central city as a whole (39% of the population of the TMC) is one of 11 homogeneous zones, surrounded by a ring formed by 5 zones that actually reproduce the territory of the TMA itself, while on the west most of the zones are drawn on the valleys system.

References

Allmendinger, P., and Haughton, G. (2009). Soft Spaces, Fuzzy Boundaries, and Metagovernance: The New Spatial Planning in the Thames Gateway. *Environment and Planning A*, 41(3), 617–633.

Antonelli, C. (1986). *L'attività innovativa di un distretto tecnologico*. Torino: Fondazione Giovanni Agnelli.

Bagnasco, A. (1986). *Torino. Un profilo sociologico*. Torino: Einaudi.

Bagnasco, A. (Ed.). (1990). *La città dopo Ford. Il caso di Torino*. Torino: Bollati Boringhieri.

Ballocca, A., and Foietta, P. (2012). *Territorio: maneggiare con cura. Torino*. Retrieved from http://www.provincia.torino.gov.it/speciali/2012/consumo_territorio/dwd/relazione.pdf.

Barbieri, C.A., and Giaimo, C. (2014). A New Model of Institutional Governance for New Planning Policies in Italy. *Urbanistica*, 153, 92–93.

Brenner, N. (2013). Theses on urbanization. *Public Culture*, 25(169), 85–114.

Buran, P., Mela, A., and Piperno, P. (Eds.). (2006). *La questione metropolitana nel Piemonte del Duemila. Una prima ricognizione analitica*. Torino: Ires Piemonte.

Chicco, P., Garelli, M., and Saccomani, S. (1995). Torino Metropolitan Area in the '80s: Urban Structure and Housing Policies. In L. Padovani (Ed.), *Urban Change and Housing Change: Evidences from four European countries* (pp. 176–208). Venezia: DAEST, Collana Ricerche, 19.

Conforti, L., and Mela, A. (1995). L'area metropolitana: un centro o una specificità. In IRES (Ed.), *Relazione sulla situazione economica sociale territoriale del Piemonte 1995* (pp. 129–165). Torino: Rosemberg and Sellier.

Conti, S., and Vanolo, A. (2003). Torino, Europa: scenari possibili. *Urbanistica Dossier*, 60, 5–9.

Diener, R., Herzog, J., Meili, M., de Meuron, P., and Schmid, C. (2006). ETH Studio Basel, Contemporary City Institute, *Switzerland: An Urban Portrait*. Basel-Boston-Berlin: Birkhäuser – Publishers for Architecture.

DPS, Dipartimento per lo sviluppo e la coesione economica. (2012). *Le aree interne: di quali territori parliamo? Nota esplicativa sul metodo di classificazione delle aree*. Retrieved from http://www.dps.tesoro.it/aree_interne/doc/Nota%20Territorializzazione%20AI_03%20 marzo_2013.pdf.

ESPON. (2011). *Espon 2013 Database: Quality rather than quantity . . . Final Report – March 2011*. Retrieved from: https://www.espon.eu/main/Menu_Projects/Menu_ ScientificPlatform/espondatabase2013.html.

Gabert, P. (1964). *Turin, ville industrielle; étude de géographie économique et humanine*. Paris: Presses universitaires de France.

Haughton, G., Allmendinger, P., and Oosterlynck, S. (2013). Spaces of Neoliberal Experimentation: Soft spaces, postpolitics, and neoliberal governmentality. *Environment and Planning A*, 45, 217–234.

Healey, P. (1998). Building Institutional Capacity through Collaborative Approaches to Urban Planning. *Environment and Planning*, 30(9): 1531–1546.

IGEAT, Institut de Gestion de l'Environnement et d'Aménagement du Territoire. (Ed.). (2007). *ESPON 1.4.3: Study on Urban Functions, Final report*, Brussels/Luxembourg: ULB/ESPON Monitoring Committee. Retrieved from: http://www.espon.eu/mmp/ online/website/content/projects/261/420/index_EN.html.

Indovina, F. (2003). La metropolizzazione del territorio. Nuove gerarchie territoriali. *Economia e società regionale*, Oltre il ponte.

Indovina, F., Doria, L., Fregolent, L., and Savino, M. (2009). *Dalla città diffusa all'arcipelago metropolitano*. Milano: FrancoAngeli.

Kübler, D. (2005). *Problems and Prospects of Metropolitan Governance in Sydney: Towards old or new regionalism?* Sydney: City Futures Research Centre, UNSW.

Le Galès, P., and Vitale, T. (2015). Diseguaglianze e discontinuità nel governo delle grandi metropoli. Un'agenda di ricerca. *Territorio*, 7–17.

Mela, A., and Conforti, L. (2008). *La configurazione sociale nei diversi ambiti spaziali della citta' di torino e i processi di mobilita' residenziale*. Torino: IRES – Istituto di Ricerche Economico Sociali del Piemonte, 1–68.

Regione Piemonte. (2014). *Il mercato del lavoro in Piemonte nel 2013*. http://www. regione.piemonte.it/lavoro/osservatorio/rapporti.htm

Saccomani, S. (2014). Torino: A Metropolitan City of 315 Municipalities. *Urbanistica*, 153, 102–105.

Soja, E.W. (2011). Regional Urbanization and the End of the Metropolis Era. In G. Bridge and S. Watson (Eds.), *New Companion to the City* (pp. 679–689). Chichester: Wiley-Blackwell.

Spaziante, A. (1996). Piemonte. In A. Clementi, G. Dematteis and P.C. Palermo (Eds.), *Le forme del territorio italiano II*. Bari: Laterza, 27–56.

Torino Internazionale. (2000). *Il Piano strategico per la promozione della città 2000*, Torino, http://www.torinostrategica.it/pubblicazioni/primo-piano-strategico/

Torino Internazionale. (2006). *Il secondo Piano strategico dell'area metropolitana di Torino 2006*, Torino, http://www.torinostrategica.it/pubblicazioni/il-secondo-piano-strategico-dellarea-metropolitana-di-torino/

Torino Strategica. (2015). *Torino Metropoli 2025*, Torino, http://www.torinostrategica.it/ pubblicazioni/torino-metropoli-2025/

Waterhout, B., Othengrafen, F., and Sykes, O. (2013). Neo-liberalization Processes and Spatial Planning in France, Germany, and the Netherlands: An exploration. *Planning Practice & Research*, 28(1), 141–159.

Whitford, J., and Enrietti, A. (2005). Surviving the Fall of a King: The regional institutional implications of crisis at Fiat Auto. *International Journal of Urban and Regional Research*, 29 (4), 771–795.

Zeigler, D.J., and Brunn, S.D. (1980). Geopolitical Fragmentation and the Pattern of Growth and Need. In S.D. Brunn and J.O. Wheeler (Eds.), *The American Metropolitan System: Present and future* (pp. 77–92). New York: John Wiley.

5 Genesis of a fluid metropolitan space

Urban metamorphoses in Venice and Veneto

Laura Fregolent and Luciano Vettoretto[1]

Illa gens non arat, non seminat, non vindemiat. (These folks don't plough, sow, harvest grapes)

Guglielmo di Puglia, with respect to the Venetians, *Honorantie* (around 1050).

Astonishing cities

We can understand the surprise of an educated inhabitant of a Greek-Byzantine town of southern Italy in the middle of the ninth century, seeing a city without a productive base and without its own rural territory, which produced a large amount of revenue almost entirely by trade developed on a global scale but without any significant spatial proximity. Probably, the description of Guglielmo di Puglia may have been intended as a metaphor: a city without fertile and productive ground means a city without roots, a city of nomads.

It would probably have been a similar surprise that visitors felt in some "shock cities", such as Chicago in the 1890s, Manchester in the 1840s or Los Angeles in the 1930s (Briggs, 1990, p. 56).

In the case of Venice (and Veneto, the administrative and geographic region that includes Venice as its capital), some astonishing situations have occurred over time, as a chain of metamorphoses produced different economies, societies and metropolitan patterns, in a game between path-dependency and more or less radical changes, endogenous dynamics, and external influences and impacts.

In this chapter, we will try to present such a chain of metropolitan metamorphoses, with particular reference to the second post-war period, discussing the emergence of a city-region connected to a larger and internationalized polycentric mega-city (at least for some kinds of flows), which is, however, still rooted in some basic cultural and social characters. In such a city-region, there is no coherence or clear order; tradition and innovation, cosmopolitanism and localism, modernity and postmodernity, industrial and post-industrial are all present in a fairly small physical space (if compared with metropolitan areas such as Paris or London). For a strange case of circularity in history, Venice became one of the most important metropolises of the world in the late Middle Ages as a reticular space of flows (Castells, 1989), and its destiny now is still linked to global flows.

The area

The Veneto region lies in the north-east of Italy and has a population of about 5 million. It is well known to scholars, as emblematic of a distinct industrial structure that has been very successful in terms of economic growth (Bagnasco, 1977, 1988).

The *square* (10,000 sq km) includes a significant part of the region, the *central plain* (18,391 sq km), equal to 54.4%. Such territory is the plain north of the Po River, which has a high level of transportation infrastructure, and includes four major cities and many smaller centres. The four cities are of a similar demographic size (Venice: 261,362, but the daily users – commuters, tourists, students – are more than 100,000; Padua: 206,192; Vicenza: 111,500; Treviso: 81,014, plus Verona with 252,520), with small distances between these cities (for example: Venice–Treviso: 27 km; Venice–Padua: 36 km; Padua–Vicenza: 30 km). Apparently, the area is morphologically polycentric.

European and Italian cities

According to Häusserman (2005), the European city has control over land use and spatial pattern, land ownership, public utilities including transportation, and is pioneer in urban regeneration. A city, then, that was different from American or Asian ones because of the strong presence of a kind of "municipal socialism", which contributed towards giving identity to its inhabitants. Such a definition is appropriate not only for contemporary European cities, but it is their *longue durée* character. The *longue durée* has to do with the "structure", not intended as a stable organization or consistent and lasting relationship among its elements, but rather as a fluid and dynamic assemblage of relations that can be of long duration, in a game of multiple temporalities (Braudel, 1958). According to Braudel, the interpretation of cities cannot rely on often misleading short-term events. Every city and every society, with its crises, should be seen in historical socio-economic and spatial relations with its territory and with the archipelago of cities to which it belongs (Braudel, 1958, p. 738). On the other hand, Lefebvre devotes much space to this question. In his opinion, "the city is a space-time and not just a projection of a social structure, of a global society in space" (Lefebvre, 1970, p. 148, editors' translation from French). "A space is nothing but the inscription in the world of a time, spaces are actualizations, inscriptions in the simultaneity of the outside world of a series of times, the rhythms of the city, the rhythms of the urban population" (Lefebvre, 1970, p. 224, editors' translation from French). There is no doubt that the contemporary European city is different from the American or Asian ones for the slowness of its transformation, the intertwining of different temporalities, which produces more complex urban spaces and social practices, and for the influence of its historical legacies.

Even if such a character seems to weaken over time, Italian, and in part, German cities, show an urban structure, in the *longue durée*, made up of a closely woven and rich texture of many cities. While France, Great Britain, Spain, and so on, became national states, in Italy a multitude of small states and city-states (such as Venice) survived, in different arrangements, until 1861. So, while France and Great Britain produced big city capitals and an urban implosion towards these cities (metropolis), in Italy the plurality of cities persisted. Some such cities were capitals, for example Venice, Rome, Milan, Florence, Naples, Turin, ... They were, at the same time and with different combinations, producer-, mercantile- (according to Max Weber, Venice was a case in point) or consumer cities (Weber, 1958). Such a combination made some of these cities into powerful economic nodes, but, because of the presence of important consumers (courts, merchants, bankers, and so on), they also developed a powerful and innovative "cultural and creative" industry.

Also for these reasons, the metropolitan character of the Italian cities cannot be only quantitative. The Italian metropolises are closer to the original meaning of the notion. Particularly in the Latin tradition, the metropolis is not associated with city size, but with the religious and administrative power, and influence on a territory (such a definition keeps some elements of the original Greek etymology; see Topalov et al., 2010). The idea of a metropolis as a very big city is fairly recent, with the idea of hierarchical arrangements and the associated instruments of economic geography. To our mind, metropolis is a difference in relational dynamics, structures and practices, which produces a thickening (by overlapping, complementarity, and so on) of networks among a plurality of actors, and, consequently, impacts/influences a wide physical and social urban structure.

Metropolis in the *longue durée*: metro-networks and metro-central places

Between 1842 (when von Thünen published his treatise on the *Isolated State*) and 1933 (Christaller's central place theory) an influential (descriptive and normative) model of order for the explanation and control of urban phenomena was produced. The location, size and relationships have been thought of as consequences of economic rationality, with particular reference to the relations between the cost of transport, market area and commodity prices, in a situation of general economic equilibrium with some basic assumptions: an isotropic space, no differences in habit or consumer preferences, the urban location of any kind of markets, homogeneity in transportation modes, a spatial pattern formed by a city and its hinterland. Such a sophisticated analysis produced an influential set of concepts: equilibrium, hierarchy, centrality, and its symbolism: the circle in von Thünen, the hexagon (which is an approximation of the circle) in Christaller.

It is obvious that some urban phenomena, in their physical concreteness, have similarities with the spatial image of Christaller. However, this is just one way of organizing regional spaces, depending on local and historical characters (Taylor, 2010; Batten, 1995).

Analysing European urban structure in the Middle Ages, Hohenberg and Lees (1985) recognized two ideal types of city: the reticular (Venice as a prime example) and the central place (Leicester as a prime example). The central-place city has its rural hinterland; it is a commercial city with a market of goods and services, some manufacturing activities mainly for its region, a hierarchical government and an orthogenetic-linear development, of which the drivers are artisans and peasants. The reticular city is basically mercantile, based on non-proximity trade networks, not necessarily with a hinterland, a city that exerts influence and hegemony both formally and informally, a heterogenetic (discontinuous, rhizomatic) development, of which the drivers are merchants and bankers, the main actors who make the city a gateway in long networks. A relationship between city and countryside is not necessary.

Among the many differences between European and American cities, we can find similarities only in the network model. Around 1700, expanding urban America was a "strange urban network", non-Christallerian, where cities (Boston, Philadelphia, New York, Newport, Charleston) were mercantile gateways not so much related to one another, but rather directly to transatlantic cities. Like Venice, they were located on spatial, temporal and social frontiers, between East and West, pre-modernity and modernity, mercantile and industrial capitalism (Monkkonen, 1988, pp. 49–51).

The first metropolis: a global gateway for multiple economic-urban corridors

Approximately halfway through the ninth century, the beginning of a period of economic growth, Italian cities (and Venice in particular) had significant competitive advantages: a long and particular urban tradition, based on the Latin idea of *civitas*. The *civitas*, in contrast to the *polis*, does not have any ontological status, rather it is the place of the *cives*, a multitude of individuals who agree to following the same laws and moral habits, regardless of any ethnic, religious, social memberships or territorial boundaries (Cacciari, 2004): a strategic position between East and West, North and South. Around 1100, Venice appeared as the most active commercial gateway in Europe, with networks of merchants across all of Europe and the East. It was a real global city, made up of flows of merchants, money, goods, artists and scientists, and supported by economic and technical innovations (insurance, loans, exchange, accounting techniques) and by a policy-making that assembled different policy instruments: war, threat, but, overall, *pacta* (contracts) with other cities regarding many issues, from trade to navigation rights. This history is well reconstructed in many essays (see, for example: Braudel, 1985; Jones, 1974; Lane, 1975; Romano, 1974). From 1050 to 1300, the economic growth was impressive, and produced at least two innovations: a system of autonomous city-states often with a democratic character, and hegemony based on trade. Such innovations were associated with a sharp demographic growth (not only urban, but also rural) and with the rise of urbanization, not only of the two largest European cities (Milan and Venice), but also in the medium and small-sized towns. Around 1300, the estimated population was: Venice 110,000–120,000, Milan about 150,000, plus a large number of cities with populations of between 20,000 and 40,000 (such as Bologna and Verona) or between 30,000 and 40,000 (such as Padua, Naples and Rome). In European comparative studies, a city with more than 25,000 inhabitants is considered very large, and cities with populations of between 10,000 and 25,000 large cities (Pounds, 1973, p. 358). In the same period, London had 40,000 inhabitants.

The first metropolitan form was a reticular one, where Venice was the gateway in a global system that connected flows of goods, money, people and ideas across Europe. Venice was mainly made up of flows, and often the networks were formally established by contracts. Information from notarial and accounting records show a particular link between Venice and Milan (Ugolini, 1985), and between Venice, Milan and the towns located at the access to the Alpine valleys and along the main rivers, particularly the Po River. Between 1050 and 1300, Venice and Milan appeared as the terminal gateways of a very rich urban corridor in northern Italy that was joined, in the case of Venice (and with long and intense conflict with the rival city-state of Genoa) to the Adriatic corridor and with north European networks. Because of its reticular (economic, political and physical) pattern, the towns near Venice (whose spatial pattern was more similar to the central places) enjoyed a certain level of autonomy. So during the *long durée*, a polycentric pattern was established, with relative autonomy between insular Venice and the urban mainland that constituted a character still present (Lanaro, 1984).

The first metropolitan metamorphosis: a regional capital, and the question of modernity

The crisis of this model began in the late thirteenth century, when the (maritime) flows came to a standstill. Loss of innovation in shipping technology, moving the focus to the Atlantic and fall of the price of spices forced Venice to adopt a different territorial strategy. To cope with the progressive loss of hegemony in maritime trade, Venice built a territorial state that included the whole north-east of Italy, part of Slovenia and Croatia, and a couple of Lombardy provinces. From the sea (but the role in maritime trade was still important) to the land, the metropolis changed, developing more than before an innovative industrial base (glass, soap, dyes, ships, wool, silk, a sophisticated printing industry, and so on). Rich merchants and aristocrats invested in innovative agriculture techniques and land reclaim, thus transforming the territory (Palladian villas, infrastructures, rural villages). Still retaining its role as a gateway between East and West, and becoming richer and richer, at least throughout the sixteenth century, the metropolitan metamorphosis was completed. The new, still opulent metropolis was much less reticular, and much more a capital city of a territorial state. In this new role, the relations with other cities, particularly Padua, became closer. Padua seemed to arise as a complementary pole, with its industry and, above all, its ancient university (partially subsidized and protected by Venice); according to Lane, Padua became a kind of gateway by which famous painters and humanists worked in Padua and Venice at the same time. Since the late fourteenth century, this new metropolis appeared as an enlarged city-region. Capital flowed from the city to the countryside and vice versa, and progressive specialization in luxury goods maintained Venice in international trade networks. At the same time, during the fourteenth century, despite the heavy defeat at the hands of the League of Cambrai (1509), and the many problems of a huge public debt, Venice undertook a vast operation of *Renovatio Urbis* (the public buildings in Piazza San Marco and the Rialto area are the best known), with a local interpretation of the Renaissance language that was so successful in Florence and Rome. Not a break with the past – renewal came with prudence, and "the *novitas* were confronted with the origins", a renewal "constantly pursued, but in the absence of 'catastrophic' decisions" (Tafuri, 1995, p. 13). The metropolis had found a new representation of itself, in the city and in the countryside.

The crisis arose at the end of the fourteenth century, and Venice appeared no longer able to react. The causes of the crisis were multiple (loss of income from sugar and cotton because of the flows from the Americas, the strength of the Ottoman Empire, the hegemony of Flanders, Britain and France in international trade, the difficulty to develop industrial capitalism and entrepreneurship (capitalism remained basically mercantile), outdated regulations, an obsolete political system, and devastating plagues (Lane, 1975). Until the end of the Republic (1797), there were successive positive and negative economic cycles. The old global metropolis had become a regional capital, maintaining an attitude of superiority towards other cities, which reinforced a kind of separateness between Venice and the Veneto. The capital was still rich, but the urban problems rose clearly (housing and sanitary conditions, poverty). The metropolis attracted international people, with its great number of theatres, celebrations and fairly free moral habits, and so on. According to Stendhal, the city of Venice was "the gayest in Italy and perhaps in the world, and certainly the least pedantic" (Stendhal, 1854, p. 100, editors' translation from French).

Around 1600 Milan was the largest Italian centre of the metallurgical industry that spread across the centres of the Milan–Venice corridor, where the textile proto-industry was also important. The central and northern cities developed complementary functions: Florence and Milan in industry, Venice and Genoa were nodes of commerce and transport on a large scale. Venice's decline was by then apparent, for the loss of competitiveness of its industry and trade and the fading of competitive advantages.

With the decline, the myth of decadent Venice began, as well as its renewed international attractiveness, not as "the greatest general store in the world" but for its architecture and "strange" daily life. At the same time the question of modernity emerged, and possible ways for the construction of a modern metropolis. Venice, as a dominant mercantile city, turned into a dominant city of beauty and anomaly, which needed an accurate conservation.

The powerful romantic myth of decadence, however, failed to see that the economically declining Venice, the great old global metropolis, was perhaps already beyond modernity. Simmel wrote about Venice and the metropolis of modernity. In the modern metropolis, Simmel discovered anthropological changes subsequent to the overload of stimuli and to the abstraction and objectification of monetary exchange. In Venice, Simmel found ambiguity and ambivalence, a separation between appearing and being, where the ostensible uniformity of architecture, places and habits was just a mask that hid the multiplicity of social situations and practices. The modern metropolis, but also Rome and Florence, did not lie: the correspondence between urban places and daily life was always clear, as was clearly visible the division of labour. "But in Venice, where all that is cheerful and bright, free and light, [the mask] has only served as a face for a life that is dark, violent and unrelentingly functional. The city's decline has left behind a merely lifeless stage-set, the mendacious beauty of the mask" (Simmel, 2007, p. 44). It appeared as a city of many floating islands, where the bridges did not separate or join a city with no roots, a surface without ground, at the same time sea and land, east and west, ancient and modern. This artificial city "has the ambivalent beauty of an adventure that is immersed in a life without roots, like a blossom floating in the sea" (Simmel, 2007, p. 46). A city of flows and merchants (nomads) does not produce roots but rhizomes. If the metropolitan individual reacts by putting a distance between himself and the world, Venice is the adventure (*adventura*, what will happen as an event, out of the continuity of ordinary life), possible only in a non-deterministic world, a world with soft ties and low levels of predictability.

"A hundred profound solitudes together compose the city of Venice – that is magic. An image for the men of the future" (Nietzsche, quoted in Malpass, 2015, p. 208). Solitude of Venice as detachment from tradition, emancipation from the slavery of social and cultural traps – there is no romantic nostalgia in such visions.

That was Venice at the end of its history as a global network metropolis and of the experience of capital-metropolis of a territorial state. Obviously, about six centuries of international and cosmopolitan relevance and a certain amount of innovation in practices of mercantile, industrial and agriculture capitalism have left deep traces.

Modernity and late modernity, and its metropolitan models

From 1730 onwards, the decline was progressive. At least until halfway through the nineteenth century, the old (no more?) metropolis became increasingly weak, even at a local level. From 1797, with the French occupation, Venice was no longer a regional capital. International treaties assigned Venice to Austria, which ruled Venice until 1866 (with a short period of French dominion), when it was incorporated in the young Italy.

During this period of decline (Austrians invested in Trieste's port, at the expense of Venice), the problem of modernity fully rose. Both the French and the Austrians carried out some modernization operations, partly on the urban structure. Napoleonic government tried to give a European character to some parts of Venice (public gardens in the Castello area, wider streets, an important building in St Mark's square, and so on). Austrians intervened on the modern infrastructures, building the Milan–Venice railway and the railway bridge that connects Venice to the mainland, radically changing the accessibility and direction of urban development.

Hohenberg and Lees (1985, p. 277) showed the ranking of the first 40 largest European cities in the past. In 1750, London and Paris were the largest cities, followed by Naples (another capital city). Venice was in eighth place in the ranking, with a relative decline in the long run (the population had not increased signif-icantly since the fourteenth century). However, the declining Venice was still more populated than Milan, Berlin, Hamburg and Barcelona. Between 1750 and 1850, the decline was very sharp, and Venice fell from eighth to thirty-first. In the same period, almost all the Mediterranean cities declined (Milan less rapidly), while the industrial cities (Liverpool, Manchester, Glasgow, Birmingham) had a very intense growth. In 1950, the decline was complete. Venice went out of the ranking, while the Italian cities of the "industrial triangle", based on Fordist modes of production, grew significantly. Milan, in particular, rose from twenty-first to fifteenth position, almost the same as the ranking it had had in 1750. The higher position of Rome was the outcome of its role as capital city and by the enlargement of its administrative borders required by the Fascist government in order to create the "great imperial Rome" which could compete in size with other European capitals.

So, the decline of Venice became a public issue, and the question of moder-nity arose, influenced by international groups. "This Venice is a problem for the 'moderns'. Fascinated by a crystallized continuity, which has been mistaken for banal organic unity – perhaps to be regained – they cannot tolerate the challenge that Venice hurls out at them" (Tafuri, 1985, p. xi).

Just after the union of Venice and the Veneto with the Italian state, some important modernization policies were implemented. In the first phase, such poli-cies were introverted and "insular" in character, trying to insert industrial plants and infrastructures into some peripheral areas of insular Venice, sometimes with foreign capital and entrepreneurship, opening of technical schools, improvement of health care, a new urban transit by boat – "vaporetti" – a new land-use plan, the aqueduct in 1884, and so on (Roverato, 1984; Franzina, 1986). Venice began to experiment with modernity, but modernity implies boundary-crossing, some kind of break with the past. The modern metropolis forged by industrial capitalism is not a linear evolution of the city, but something new which rearranges social rela-tions, economic practices, a new way of life.

In coping with modernity, Venice and the Veneto have experienced two radically different models, which produced not only radically different spatial patterns, but also profound differences in social and economic models. In this his-tory we can recognize three phases: the rise of industrial Fordist Venice, linked to an urban implosion, and, in the Veneto region, the progressive growth of a different industrial model which did not erase the links with rural life, producing a much less impressive urban growth (from around the 1930s until the 1960s); the crisis of the Fordist industry and the rise of the Third Italy, a very powerful economy based on (Marshallian) industrial districts, a society coherent with the economic structure, and a model of scattered industrial location and urbanization, the *città diffusa*, diffuse city (late 1960s–1990); the crisis of the model of the Third Italy, processes of industrial restructuring, the progressive disappearance of the Marshallian districts, a kind of "back to the city" and new spatial relations on any scale (1990 onwards).

Two models: urban and economic implosion and concentration vs. soft modernization (1930–60)

For many years, the Veneto region hosted two very different models of modernization.

Venice, the old metropolis, plunged into modernity pushed by some local and national élites, starting from the late 1920s. One of the leading figures was Giuseppe Volpi (entrepreneur, Ministry of Finance in the Fascist regime). In these years, a very powerful and influential idea of Venice as a modern metropolis was established. According to this idea, Venice should have expanded its modern element on the mainland, and preserved the beauty of its insular old centre, which was considered an international pole of arts, culture and entertainment. This project began to become reality around 1917, when Porto Marghera (in a huge territory on the mainland, right in front of insular Venice) was constituted by a concentration of national industrial and financial groups. The idea was to build an enormous, very modern industrial zone, based on advanced basic industry (electrometallurgical, chemical, mechanical, shipbuilding, energy, and similar), a great commercial port, a waterway connection to insular Venice, logistics and intermodal infrastructure, a "garden city". The effective take-off of this industrial zone was around 1930, with 5,100 employees, which rose to 15,700 in 1945 and eventually 32,968 employees in 1965 . Fordist Venice was thus accomplished, and one of the major national industrial poles was built. In the meantime, according to the local élites' ideas, Venice significantly reinforced its role as international capital of culture and high society. After the establishment of the *Biennale d'arte* in 1893, the first in the world, the International Festival of Contemporary Music (1930) and the International Film Festival were created in 1934 (again the first in the world). Luxury hotels, restaurants and modern infrastructure were built, for example the car bridge parallel to the train bridge, the car and bus terminal (1935) and two new bridges on the Grand Canal. A competition for the new railway station of Santa Lucia was launched, the highway Padua–Venice was constructed in 1933 and the more recent highway connection with Milan in 1962, Padua–Bologna in 1970 and the international airport in 1961 (Roverato, 1984; Franzina, 1986; Zucconi, 2002). The administrative territory of the municipality of Venice was enlarged by a national law under the Fascist regime, including in the greater Venice area some local municipalities which were historically autonomous (Mestre is the best known).

The old metropolis was to become a new metropolis, but it was also dependent on national industrial and financial capital. The plan was to construct a modern metropolis with a clear spatial division, where Venice was to be the place of international (conspicuous) consumption and production of art, culture, history, architecture, as well as being picturesque, while the ancient district of Mestre (with Marghera), the contemporary space of Fordist production and place of transportation and logistics infrastructure, was to be transformed into a blue-collar periphery. According to this plan, a new spatially separated urban society should have been produced: the upper-class inhabitants and users in insular Venice (with a certain number of native people, as "actors on stage" and, perhaps, a new servile class for the affluent users of Venice), physically separated from the "*classes dangereuses*" of mainland Venice.

But this *pole de croissance*, invented 30 years before the Perroux theory (1964) – which, beginning from an exogenous industrial location should have triggered the formation of externalities, demographic and urban growth, increase in demand of good and services – worked only in part.

The Porto Marghera operation brought about a sophisticated idea of modernity, and brought Venice back towards metropolitan status, which was, of course, much weaker than in the past. But this plan of modernization clashed with the historical conditions. The huge urban implosion of mainland (Mestre) was only in part dependent on a traditional movement from the countryside, which was a large pool of redundant labour force, towards the industrial city. A significant number of employees did not move to the city, but still lived in their rural houses, combining agricultural activities with their work in industry (Piva & Tattara, 1983). For a long time, the identity of the blue-collar worker will still be linked to the traditional rural background and to its practices. From the point of view of the entrepreneurs, this meant an extraordinary instrument of social control and avoidance of class conflicts. Meanwhile the Fordist firms demanded low-skilled, low-paid, mobile workers, whereas the blue-collar inhabitants in insular Venice were specialized and their wages were medium to high (*idem*). A segmentation of the labour market occurred, with an increase of unemployment in insular Venice, which emphasized social clefts within the lower class.

For a long time this was a kind of modernization with little social change. Certainly, it was a period of urban implosion, but the (morphological) polycentricism was not eroded. The sharp demographic growth on mainland Venice (Mestre) was to a large extent the result of an "exodus" from the insular Venice of the under- and lower classes, which had been forced to move out because of very critical housing conditions (families living in ground floor apartments liable to flooding at high tide, overcrowding, no light or air, poor sanitary conditions) and the number of evictions.

Demographic statistics (see PRIN Postmetropoli, 2015) show the permanence of the polycentric character of the Veneto region, and the limited attractiveness as residential choice of Venice (insular plus mainland) with regard to the other cities. At that time particularly, Verona was increasingly approaching Venice, which suggests the hypothesis of a region with two urban terminals fairly separated. These dynamics are apparently different from the case of Milan's growth. At least until 1960, Lombardy, differently from Veneto, developed a classical process of centred metropolitan development. At the same time, the urban implosion did not seem to empty the hinterland of insular and mainland Venice, which continued to grow. Until the 1970s, the demographic growth of the hinterland was ascribable to the positive natural balance (due to the persistence of rural habits and culture and the younger age of the population), while residential mobility towards the first and second rings appeared high starting from the 1970s and 1980s (urban diffusion/

explosion). Migration from abroad was very considerable for both urban and extra-urban locations from 2000 onwards. At the same time, employment in the increasingly de-industrialized Marghera dropped to 11,391.

The old metropolis gained control and influence over a (limited) territory, because of some élite and authoritarian state actions. Notwithstanding the presence of a huge and advanced basic/Fordist industry, the spatial patterns showed limited phenomena of urban implosion. The new industrial metropolis did not alter the morphological polycentrism, nor did it significantly absorb its hinterland. This is because the spatial pattern of Veneto had not become diffused or scattered, the diffusion of many medium or small centres, villages, and so on, constituted, together with a dense road infrastructure, an original character of the territory that still supports contemporary urbanization.

But this metropolis had a limited urban implosion as well because of competition from another very powerful model, that of diffuse industrialization. In the same years (from the end of 1800 to the first years of the twentieth century), a different model was experimented with, mainly in the Vicenza and Treviso territories (Franzina, 1990; Lanaro, 1984; Roverato, 1984). In this case, too, historians tell us there were élites and leading figures at work (mainly the entrepreneur Alessandro Rossi), and a kind of benevolent paternalism had been shifted from rural life to industry. The key elements were the camouflage of the industrial plants in the rural landscape, the de-concentration of firms across the territory (but in the presence of financial concentration), small (but with advanced organization of labour) dimensions of each plant in order to avoid urban concentrations, diffused model of industrial location, a tailor-made welfare system, mainly provided by the entrepreneurs (including housing, education, health care), the avoidance of severing families from their rural background. This model is that of a self-organizing society, with a minimal presence of the state, a very flexible labour market, no significant social conflicts, and a model of a very soft transition to modernization. The governance network was made up of local rural notables, church, local politicians and economic actors, who acted, simultaneously, at both national and local level (sometimes with important roles in national government, and a substantial influence on some policies about migratory flows, rural and industrial credit policy, social policy). In 1911, the Veneto region was fourth among the most industrialized regions (after Lombardy, Piedmont and Tuscany), with a fair number of advanced sectors. Vicenza, in those years, appeared as one of the most industrialized Italian provinces. The economic and urban landscape was characterized by a significant industrial presence, immersed in a mainly rural world, made up of small and medium productive units along the high Veneto plain. Such a model, which is quite the opposite of the "great Venice" model, would overcome the challenges of modernization, producing the well-known "Third Italy". It can be viewed as a particular model of development, strictly connected to local history and cognitive frames, re-used as a powerful resource in the apparently anti-Fordist modernization process. As in the first phase of its life, Venice was *de facto* disjointed by its regional territory.

A new urbanization cycle: diffused city, diffused industrialization, industrial districts (1970–90)

The situation described above evolved from the well-known Italian model of development based on the SME systems, which often constituted Marshallian industrial districts, with some relevant changes compared with the past: the paternalistic attitude transformed into remarkable, non-conflictual industrial relations; welfare was guaranteed by a mix of family and public welfare; the roots with the rural world weakened; the scattered character of industrial and housing location exploded.

This phase has been studied by many scholars (see, for example, in English: Amin & Thrift, 1992; Asheim, 2000; Becattini, 1989, 2003; Brusco, 1986; Garofoli, 1991), and the model has been used as a policy example in many countries, so we can be very brief on this point. Some typical characters of such economic arrangements are: a limited territory with a population of industrial and service firms sharing the same economic interest; some degree of sectorial specialization, and a high degree of internal connections, local economic systems fairly restricted and self-sufficient, with a certain variety of sizes of firms, external economies, a favourable public regulation and infrastructure policy, a fairly cohesive and low conflictual society that facilitates trust relations and economic exchanges, reducing transaction costs, high level of mobility among firms and upward social mobility, particularly from the position of skilled workers to entrepreneurs. High performance was also attributable to a high level of adaptive capability, partially linked to a flexible labour market, and support by public institutions.

The link of the Marshallian districts with their territory produced revenue that was invested in the same territory, in part for industrial investments, in part for an upgrading of consumption, particularly addressed to housing, with similar dwelling models across the territory: low density, ownership, single-family housing, a model that should have represented the new social status of the formerly poor peasants. Between 1971 and 1991, the sprawl was impressive (see the maps in the quoted *Atlante*), as the result of two trends: the first one was a movement from the city towards the first and second rings, particularly by young couples, both for affordability and for the search of a new non-urban (but neither rural) style of life, linked to some neo-traditional values, perception of security and safety (from pollution and congestion too) and high social value of home ownership. The second trend was the endogenous growth due to the will to upgrade the housing conditions, show off a new and more adequate self-image, reusing family assets (land, the old rural family house, family savings), but still maintaining the links with the enlarged family of origin (as a very important welfare provider). The combination of the two movements produced the *città diffusa* (Indovina et al., 2005; Fregolent, 2005), a dense and diffuse network/patchwork of homes, workplaces and places of consumption (retailing, malls, discos, and so on), with a high level of mobility mainly supported by private/individual transportation. As the *Atlante*'s maps show, the territory of the highest growth forms a continuous corridor between Milan and Venice, by the side of the highway, with a particular concentration in the Milan urban region and in the Veneto large *città diffusa*, where the two patterns of physical growth described above are well evident. The location of various kinds of shopping centres (see the *Atlante*'s map) confirms the existence of an urban corridor and the role of the main road infrastructure in the production of spatialities. As already mentioned, the diffuse city was not a novelty, but a distinct character and a historical legacy, so the growth overlapped existing centres (particularly if they were located at road junctions), ran along all roads, forming a continuous and ostensibly chaotic sequence of fields, scattered housing, linear housing, small centres, medium towns, industrial and commercial zones, compact cities, and so on. In contrast to metropolitan Venice of the previous phase, in such a territory there is no spatial distinction between production and consumption. In this case the differences are more temporal (the timing of spatial practices) than spatial. At the same time, the impressive sprawl produced severe negative externalities (congestion, pollution, and so on) which jeopardized the economic model, triggered environmental conflicts and called for different, more sustainable, development practices.

Cities, in such a situation, are the places which serve their wider or narrower territory, depending on the functions located in the urban space. Above all, in such socio-economic configuration, cities are the place of higher education, better equipped healthcare facilities, location of public bureaucracy and of supra-local political bodies, urban entertainment and places of culture and the main location for some less common tertiary activities. In the *città diffusa*, cities are just thicker nodes.

This model reached a crisis in the 1990s, when globalization began to have a significant impact on the economic model; the economic and financial crisis of 2009 produced a strong acceleration to profound economic, social and spatial changes.

After the Third Italy: a fluid metropolitan space (1990–2015)

From the 1990s, mainly because of the globalization process, the Veneto has changed radically. The changes, which combine historical legacy, local innovations and exogenous influences, are the progressive depletion of the Marshallian industrial districts, the thinning of the Third Italy social formation and the new influent roles of cities.

Veneto as the "industrial district" of the northern urban corridor, and the rising economic mixité

Between 2001 and 2011, industrial employment fell by almost 16%, compared with the national average decline of 11%, while service industries accounted for 54% of the total and employment in the non-profit sector increased by 38% (national average 28%). The regional economy underwent a major restructuring process, with significant selective changes in the manufacturing sector and a wide expansion of service industries. Both of them significantly impacted on social and urban change. At the same time, the expansion of non-profit activities showed a relevant local activism on social issues (health care, care for the elderly and children, help for migrants, sports, culture), which supported and complemented the local public welfare, strengthening social cohesion.

Despite the decrease of employment, the central and Piedmont area appeared to be a kind of "industrial zone" of northern Italy (and, particularly between 1965 and 1995, one of the main engines of national economic growth), as the *Atlante*'s maps show. Such a selective shrinking of the manufacturing base did not produce dramatic problems. The employment to population ratio was 65%, against a national average of 57%, and the unemployment rate was 6.8% (national average 10.7%). The excess labour force was absorbed into the tertiary sector. The economic restructuration dissolved the Marshallian districts, which were the foundation of the regional economy and society. Scholars agree in recognizing some trends: financial, value-added, turnover concentration in fewer companies, opening up of relational networks to the outside districts, business strategies internationally played along the entire global value chain, the weakening of traditional friendly industrial relations, different cultures and values brought by migrants, and so on. In short, firms have become ever more footloose and international, the proximity they need is no longer spatial (as in the Marshallian districts), but cognitive and located on international nodes of the value chain (see Grandinetti et al., 2010; Grandinetti, 2013). The territorial-communitarian model is gradually disappearing, with impacts on the cement of society. Investments have shifted to technology and knowledge-intensive industries (which have grown significantly), while traditional industry has swiftly declined. Positive data on the export and trade balance (Veneto is the second region in Italy in export, particularly in the Piedmont provinces of Vicenza and Treviso) demonstrate a high degree of internationalization, particularly in some productions named "beautiful and well done" (clothing and fashion, agrifood, furniture, footwear, eyewear, gold and jewellery).

The divorce of industry from its territory radically changes the models of society, governance and urbanization. It is probable that, at least partially, the growth of the service industry, particularly the so-called knowledge-intensive business services (KIBS) or advanced producer services (APS), is linked to the new global conditions. As we noted above, in the Veneto, growth has been fairly impressive. The value added in the service-producing industry rose by 1.2% in the period 1995–2011, more than the value added in the goods-producing industry (0.7%). While plant location, even in the era of Marshallian industrial districts, was fairly independent of the territory, service industry, particularly in the KIBS/APS sectors, looked for urban location, maximum accessibility, centrality and prestige. So, one of the results of the economic restructuring is the return of the cities as the nodes that support international industrial competitiveness. Choice of location by the advanced service industries, particularly in the case of medium or large firms, is a choice that involves many enlarged spatial strategies. *Atlante*'s maps show the distribution of KIBS in the Italian urban areas, and relationships to the GDP per capita. Apparently, Milan is the major Italian node for advanced services (followed by Rome). The cities of the Veneto (the first is Padua) have a ranking close to the average (which rises when the whole polycentric area is taken into consideration), and their distance from Milan's ranking has recently been reduced. The presence of KIBS has a very good correlation with the GDP per capita (the Pearson correlation index is 0.77), to demonstrate the multiplier impact of advanced services; moreover, Milan was the only urban area with a positive rate of growth of GDP per capita between 2001 and 2011. This result was confirmed by the network analysis carried out by Taylor (Taylor, 2012; Taylor et al., 2013), which shows the importance of Milan in the global networks. Similar results are obtained by analysing the location choice of the main logistics companies, which are a key component of the global dynamics (Antoine et al., 2014).

In brief, the last 15 years have significantly transformed the metropolitan landscape, specializing the space according to globalization dynamics. Milan appears to be the main Italian gateway, and the reference node of a large northern polycentric texture of cities and territories. The north-east appears, at least partially, as one of the main industrial districts of such assemblage, which develops network relations at many levels (25% of private investments in R&D is located outside the Veneto region, mostly in the Milan metropolitan area). This area appears to be a set of fluid urban and territorial assemblages, composed of local and global networks. Because of the complementarity of cities, a functional polycentrism has been confirmed: Padua in higher education, R&D and APS; Venice in international culture and tourism, logistics and transportation; Vicenza and Treviso in manufacture, a kind of thick network in the whole northern urban corridor and global flows.

The networks have become more and more complex with the increasing differences in the economic structure. There is not only a globalized industrial structure: tourism, for example, is highly internationalized (in 2012, 40 million out of 62 million overnight stays were foreigners) and increasingly managed by global players and smart technologies. Some increasingly important niches (such as agritourism, congress tourism, and so on), and the important sector of agrifood (Veneto is a leader in export of certain products) require local systems with a very high quality of life and landscape, and the capability to invest in strategic points of the global value chain. The same can be said for the rising interest in agriculture, which is going through a phase of rationalization, attracting young entrepreneurs and more appropriate organizational practices (the rural landscape, as well as the urban one, is distributed along all the urbanized and industrialized Po Valley: see Figures 16.1 and 16.3 in Chapter 16). Meanwhile, the cultural and creative industry (not only in tourism) is rising very swiftly, reaching, according to some estimates, approximately 130,000 employees (54% of total employment) and 5.8% of the total added value, similar to some advanced manufacturing sectors or finance and insurance. Such industries (which include a wide range of activities: visual and performing arts, printing industry, music, TV, radio and similar industries, design, cultural tourism, communication, live performances, international exhibitions, cultural and artistic heritage) have strong relationships with both manufacture and services (fashion, furniture, and so on), and they are, as the KIBS/APS, typically urban and they are strengthening the role of the cities. These changes are associated with a further population growth along urban corridors, which is very attractive in the location choice of households and firms (see *Atlante*'s map).

A more segmented society

The economic and demographic transformation change has had a heavy impact on the social composition. The main elements are the following (empirical data are taken from: Regione Veneto, 2013, and *Atlante*'s maps).

- **The ageing population** – the percentage of young people aged 18–34 dropped from 26% to 18% (a decrease of 23%) between 1998 and 2009. The geographic distribution of the old-age dependency ratio confirms the dynamics of the urban corridors, but with spots of an ageing population not only, as usually in Italy, in cities, but also in the belts. The cycle of suburbanization and outer-cities as the residential choice of young families has gradually decreased, and some cities are again starting to attract people (along the Milan–Venice corridor, Padua, Treviso, Vicenza, Brescia and Bergamo increased their population between 2001 and 2011, Milan and Verona remained stable or the decline slowed down; only Venice continues to lose population).
- **The sharp increase of migrants** – location choices of migrants are quite different. In the Milan region, the location is mainly urban. In the case of Veneto, location is urban too (but less intensive) but, above all, migrants live in the former industrial districts and/or wealthier rural areas. However, because of the loss of employment in manufacture, the provinces with the highest rate of growth are Padua and Venice. The more tertiary city has become the new magnet for many different populations.
- **A blocked social mobility and a shrinking of middle classes** – an ad hoc survey (Regione Veneto, 2013, p. 245) depicts a situation where the Veneto has a very low presence of middle classes because of its high percentage of employment in manufacture, and, for the same reason, a high presence of lower class. Between 1998 and 2009, the middle class declined further still, while the upper class increased to 58% and the lower class remained stable. This means that upward mobility has been from the middle to the upper class, and that the jump from the lower class to the middle class (or the upper class) is substantially blocked. In the time of Marshallian districts, class divisions were scarcely perceived, because of the high mobility from skilled dependent employment to self-employment. Social distinctions are now multiple (social class, race, age) and much more visible.
- **The increasing demand for low-skilled and low-paid occupations**, mainly service-oriented (2005–11: +21% in commercial services, +16% in other low-skilled-oriented service jobs), particularly in health care, tourism, restaurants, low-level personal services and transportation, caregivers and domestic workers) – at the same time, scientific and technical professions increased by 23% (life science, health care, engineering, creative professions, economic management) and the traditional artisans and blue-collar workers decreased by 2.7%. As Scott (2012, pp. 41–42) noted, a new servile class (as in the old cities) is growing, in order to allow the social reproduction of globalized upper class

in the technology and knowledge-intensive industries, business and financial services and cultural/creative economy. Part of the public welfare is now provided by this population, which is partially composed of migrants.

−   **Families are changing** not only in size and form, but also in habits – young people remain long in their family of origin – no longer by choice, but because of economic problems, particularly housing affordability. Residential proximity with the family of origin is now less strong than it once was, signalling a less important role of the family in social reproduction and as welfare provider.

−   **The informal proximity networks of solidarity continue to constitute an extraordinary support for individuals and families** – in 2012, 35% of the adult population helped non-family or non-friends (national average 30%), 82% said they had relatives or friends to rely on (average 76%), 15% volunteer.

−   Society has partially lost its territorial distinctiveness, as has the economy.

Fluid economies, hard societies: the undefined space of city-regions in global flows – post-metropolis?

The Veneto region appears a fluid city-region. It is fluid because its boundaries are fuzzy, and constructed from time to time by social and economic practices: the narrow and local boundaries of the declining traditional manufacture, the larger of the old and progressively dissolving Marshallian districts, the local space of informal solidarity networks or of rising local (often environmental) conflicts, the regional space of welfare facilities, the daily sphere of housework and house-shopping trips, the northern space or national space of the flows of goods, services, individuals, ideas, the global nodes of the chain of value. It is fluid because of the progressive divide between economy and territory, even when the territory is an important element in the added value of some products (for example, agrifood) and the territory is "invented" in some point of the chain value; and because the model of society does not seem to be a characteristic of a territory any longer.

Economies live on flows and are very fluid and adaptive; society seems to mirror such fluidity and adaptivity more and more, producing an unequal structure, with an upper class with a plurality of cultures and skills, and a cognitive proximity with the nodes of global networks, and a lower class that serves the needs of the upper class. In such a situation, the old blue-collar workers appear to be midway between the two, particularly if they are sufficiently skilled to upgrade the traditional productive knowledge (in furniture, clothing and so on) in the new technology-intensive processes. The more fluid the economy, the more society seems to stifle itself in social cages, partially mitigated by informal solidarity networks.

The Veneto city-region is without doubt morphologically and functionally polycentric, its boundaries are variable, crossed by many flows and networks. According to the Brookings Institution, which has analysed the 300 wealthiest metro-areas in the world, Venice-Padua (considered as one single metropolitan area) has a GDP per capita similar to Turin and Florence, in a group that includes, among others, Osaka-Kobe, Barcelona, Marseille, Berlin, Bordeaux,

Manchester, Seoul and Strasbourg. Milan has the highest ranking, close to some Japanese, Taiwan and American cities, followed by Bologna and Rome. The urban centres then have a high status, and seem well equipped to play in international networks.

The Perulli hypothesis of a global city-region in northern Italy seems convincing (Perulli, 2010, 2012). In such a mega-city-region, the Veneto acts as a local system for some functions, as an autonomous part of international networks for others (tourism, agrifood, peculiarity of cultural and artistic heritage, and so on), and as a part of the global northern city-regions for others.

Some empirical data seem to confirm such interpretation. The flows of transported goods show the close relationship in the Northern corridors: in 2013, 32% of goods transported outside Veneto had their final destination in Lombardy (18% in Emilia-Romagna); 22% of goods transported outside Lombardy reached their final destination in Veneto (22% Emilia-Romagna and 21% Piedmont). Commuting increasingly involves more trips between Veneto and Milan, along the highly infrastructured Milan–Venice corridor (highway, railways, two major airports located at the cosmopolitan terminal), and thanks to the increase of railway accessibility (Alampi & Messina, 2011).

Flows, megacities and city-regions – ostensibly full of opportunities, but not for everybody. Perhaps the very issue and limitation in exploiting opportunities is the rising social inequality that seems inherent in this phase. Is this a post-metropolis? Venice has been a post-metropolis many times in its history ... According to Soja (2000), the post-metropolis is associated with six discourses: post-Fordism and flexibility; cosmopolitanism; exopolis, a new urban form in which the main figures are the edge cities, outer-cities, exurbia, and so on; metropolarities, new social centralities and marginalities; carceral archipelagos, fortress cities, gated communities; simcities and the restructuring of urban imagery, such as theme parks. The Veneto city-region has been, simultaneously, Fordist and post-Fordist; cosmopolitan for centuries and localist; and Venice is certainly (also) a theme park. However, in the Veneto city-region, we do not find urban American elements, such as in the edge cities, because the territory has been historically produced by many centralities, and the same category of suburb does not fit the Veneto case, where the sprawl has been not only of housing, but is also linked to a model of a historical diffuse urbanization with a vibrant local life.

Ultimately, we think that the post-metropolis has no ontological status. It can rather be thought of as a historical trend, similar to the break between the modern metropolis and the city of the *ancien régime*. In this regard, we can certainly find profound differences from the modern industrial metropolis, and we can consider ourselves as being immersed in a new post-metropolitan phase.

Note

1 Research Unit of the IUAV University of Venice coordinated by Professor Luciano Vettoretto, Department of Design and Planning in Complex Environments (DPPAC).

References

Alampi, D., and Messina, G. (2011). Time-Is-Money: i tempi di trasporto come strumento per misurare la dotazione di infrastrutture in Italia. In Banca d'Italia. (Ed.), *Le infrastrutture in Italia: dotazione, programmazione, realizzazione* (pp. 137–174), Collana seminari e convegni, 7. Roma: Banca d'Italia.

Amin, A., and Thrift, N. (1992). Neo-Marshallian Nodes in Global Networks. *International Journal of Urban and Regional Research*, 16(4), 571–587.

Antoine, S., Sillig, C., Ghiara, H., and Ginet, P. (2014). How Logistics Link Italian Cities. *GaWC Research Bulletin*, 438(A).

Asheim, B.T. (2000). Industrial Districts: The Contribution of Marshall and Beyond. In G.L. Clark, M.P. Feldman, M.S. Gertler (Eds.), *The Oxford Handbook of Economic Geography* (pp. 413–431). Oxford: Oxford University Press.

Bagnasco, A. (1977). *Tre Italie. La problematica territoriale dello sviluppo italiano*. Bologna: il Mulino.

Bagnasco, A. (1988). *La costruzione sociale del mercato*. Bologna: il Mulino.

Batten, D.F. (1995). Network Cities: Creative Urban Agglomerations for the 21st Century. *Urban Studies*, 32(2), 313–327.

Becattini, G. (1989). Sectors and/or Districts: Some Remarks on the Conceptual Foundations of Industrial Economics. In E. Goodman and J. Bamford (Eds.), *Small Firms and Industrial Districts in Italy* (pp. 123–135). London: Routledge.

Becattini, G. (2003). *Industrial Districts: A New Approach to Industrial Change*. Cheltenham: Edward Elgar.

Braudel, F. (1958). Histoire et Sciences sociales: La longue durée. *Annales. Économies, Sociétés, Civilisations*, 13(4), 725–753.

Braudel, F. (1985). *La Méditerranée*. Paris: Flammarion.

Briggs, A. (1990). *Victorian Cities*. London: Penguin (first edition 1963).

Brusco, S. (1986). Small Firms and Industrial Districts: The Experience of Italy. In D. Keeble and E. Wever (Eds.), *New Firms and Regional Development in Europe* (pp. 184–202). London: Croom Helm.

Cacciari, M. (2004). *La città*. Rimini: Pazzini.

Castells, M. (1989). *The Informational City: Information Technology, Economic Restructuring, and the Urban Regional Process*. Oxford and Cambridge: Blackwell.

Franzina, E. (1986). *Venezia*. Bari-Rome: Laterza.

Franzina, E. (1990). *La transizione dolce*. Verona: Cierre.

Fregolent, L. (2005). *Governare la dispersione*. Milano: FrancoAngeli.

Garofoli, G. (1991). The Italian Model of Spatial Development in the 1970s and in the 1980s. In G. Benko and M. Dunford (Eds.), *Industrial Change and Regional Development* (pp. 85–101). London: Belhaven Press.

Grandinetti, G. (2013). *Dove stanno andando i distretti industriali?* (Paper No. 73). Venice: Ires Veneto.

Grandinetti, R., Furlan, A., and Campagnolo, D. (2010). Crescita aziendale, territori e imprese-rete. In P. Perulli (Ed.), *Veneto* (pp. 1–70). Milano: Bruno Mondadori.

Häusserman, H. (2005). The End of the European City? *European Review*, 13(2), 237–249.

Hohenberg, P.M., and Lees, L.H. (1985). *The Making of Urban Europe 1000–1950*. Cambridge, MA: Harvard University Press.

Indovina, F., Fregolent, L., and Savino, M. (2005). L'area centrale veneta: diffusione in evoluzione. In F. Indovina, L. Fregolent and M. Savino (Eds.), *L'esplosione della città* (pp. 200–223). Bologna: Editrice Compositori.

Jones, P. (1974). Dalla caduta dell'impero romano al secolo XVIII. L'economia delle tre Italie. In R. Romano and C. Vivanti (Eds.), *Storia d'Italia* (Vol. IV, pp. 1496–1810). Turin: Einaudi.

Lanaro, S. (1984). Genealogia di un modello. In S. Lanaro (Ed.), *Storia d'Italia. Le regioni dall'unità ad oggi. Il Veneto* (pp. 5–96). Turin: Einaudi.

Lane, F.C. (1975). *Venice: A Maritime Republic*. Baltimore: The John Hopkins University Press.

Lefebvre, H. (1970). *Du rural à l'urbain*. Paris: Anthropos.

Malpass, J. (2015). "We Hyperboreals". Toward a Nietzschean Topography. In J. Young (Ed.), *Individual and Community in Nietzsche's Philosophy* (pp. 195–213). Cambridge: Cambridge University Press.

Monkkonen, E.H. (1988). *America Becomes Urban: The Development of U.S. Cities & Towns 1780–1980*. Berkeley: University of California Press.

Perroux, F. (1964). *L'économie du XXème siècle*. Paris: PUF.

Perulli, P. (Ed.). (2010). *Nord regione globale. Il Veneto*. Milano: Bruno Mondadori.

Perulli, P. (Ed.). (2012). *Nord. Una città-regione globale*. Bologna: il Mulino.

Piva, F., and Tattara, G. (Eds.). (1983). *I primi operai di Marghera*. Venezia: Marsilio.

Pounds, N.J.G. (1973). *A Historical Geography of Europe*. Cambridge: Cambridge University Press.

PRIN Postmetropoli. (2015). *Atlante web dei territori postmetropolitani* [web atlas]. Retrieved from http://www.postmetropoli.it/atlante.

Regione Veneto. (2013). *Rapporto statistico*. Venice: Regione Veneto.

Romano, R. (1974). La storia economica dal secolo XIV al Settecento. In R. Romano and C. Vivanti (Eds.), *Storia d'Italia* (Vol. IV, pp. 1813–1931). Turin: Einaudi.

Roverato, G. (1984). La terza regione industriale. In S. Lanaro (Ed.), *Storia d'Italia. Le regioni dall'unità ad oggi. Il Veneto* (pp. 165–230). Turin: Einaudi.

Scott, A.J. (2012). *A World in Emergence*. Cheltenham: Edward Elgar.

Simmel, G. (2007). Venice. *Theory, Culture and Society*, 24(7–8), 42–46 (German original edition 1907).

Soja, E.W. (2000). *Postmetropolis: Critical Studies of Cities and Regions*. Oxford: Blackwell.

Stendhal (1854). *Vie de Rossini* (Vol. I). Paris: Le Divan. Retrieved from http://www.gutenberg.org [Accessed 20 August 2015].

Tafuri, M. (1995). *Venice and the Renaissance*. Cambridge, MA: The MIT Press (Italian original edition 1985).

Taylor, P.J. (2010). Urban Economics in Thrall to Christaller: A Misguided Search for City Hierarchies in External Urban Relations. *Environment and Planning A*, 41(11), 2550–2555.

Taylor, P.J. (2012). Milano nella rete delle città mondiali. In P. Perulli (Ed.), *Nord. Una città-regione globale* (pp. 177–191). Bologna: il Mulino.

Taylor, P.J., Hoyler, M., and Sànchez-Moral, S. (2013). European Cities in Globalization: A Comparative Analysis based on the Location Strategies of Advanced Producer Services. In J.R. Quadraro-Roura (Ed.), *Service Industries and Regions: Growth, Location and Regional Effects* (pp. 285–304). Berlin: Springer.

Topalov, C., Coudroy de Lille, L., Depaule, J.-C., and Marin, B. (Eds.). (2010). *L'aventure des mots de la ville*. Paris: Laffont.

Ugolini, P. (1985). La formazione del sistema territoriale e urbano della Valle Padana. In C. De Seta (Ed.), *Storia d'Italia. Insediamenti e territorio* (Annali 8, pp. 161–240). Turin: Einaudi.

Weber, M. (1958). *The City*. New York: The Free Press (German original edition 1921).

Zucconi, G. (Ed.). (2002). *La grande Venezia. Una metropoli incompiuta tra Otto e Novecento*. Venezia: Marsilio.

6   Territory matters

A regional portrait of Florence and Tuscany

Giancarlo Paba, Camilla Perrone,
Fabio Lucchesi and Iacopo Zetti[1]

Introduction

The picture outlined in this chapter is a portrait of Tuscany. Tuscany is a well-known region of Italy, rich in history, commonly considered a country of art and culture. Tuscany is an ancient urban region, a country of autonomous cities, proud of its identity. The network of cities that has been consolidated since the Middle Ages is still the backbone of the urban system. However, over recent decades a fundamental change has been happening in the very nature of the urbanization processes. The scenario which is constitutive of the urban in Tuscany nowadays can be defined as a shift from a "mode" supported by dynamics of centralization to one featured by a decentralization process of functions, new forms of economic activities, the emergence of a new urban–rural interplay and the emergence of different lifestyles. The most recent transformations and the economic crisis have profoundly changed the region: the processes of urbanization have consumed land and natural resources; the crisis has affected the economy and the traditional industrial districts; in larger cities there have been increasing manifestations of old and new poverty; social and environmental conflicts have severely worsened the political climate. At the same time in cities and urbanized areas, a new energy for change is emerging, movements that fight for the quality of life and the right to the city, innovative proposals in the field of social solidarity, shared dwelling and the ecological conversion of the economy.

These changes could be labelled as post-metropolitan, borrowing Soja's suggestion (Soja, 2011). The post-metropolitan transition in Tuscany is analyzed with reference to the role of geo-historical matrices in determining a polynuclear pattern of settlements and a reticular organization of inter-institutional cooperation. These phenomena are interpreted through the categories of physicality and path-dependence. The study highlights the regionalization of urbanization, according to the hypothesis of Soja, though in a different historical and geographical context.

The *square* includes northern Tuscany from inland areas (Florence and Prato) to the coast (Massa, Lucca, Pisa and Livorno). The city of Florence is not located in the center of the *square*. The reason for this choice is the following: Tuscany could be defined as a polynuclear region; Florence is certainly the largest and most important city, but it is a part of the large multipolar and urbanized ellipse formed by a ring of medium-sized cities and the valleys behind. In some cases (especially when the relationship between space and governance has been analyzed), the whole region of Tuscany has been taken into consideration.

The choice not to have Florence in the center of the *square* has proved appropriate to show some post-metropolitan trends: the reduction of hierarchy between the capital of the region and the other cities; the polynuclear layout of the Tuscan urban landscape; the weakening of center/periphery and city/country opposition. Changes and innovations of the post-metropolitan landscape are not tied to the traditional factors of concentrated urban agglomeration, but they are distributed in the regional space, making the territory tormented and rough, and the density gradient broken and unpredictable.

The portrait takes into account the following themes, considered to be particularly important for Tuscany.

The first point introduces the question of physicality as the interpretative perspective through which the portrait is depicted. The second point describes the role played by geo-historical features in the disposition of settlements, and the "rule of the persistence of territorial matrices" in the regional urbanization processes, showing the resistance of the polynucleated urban landscape.

The third point explores some relevant changes of the socio-economic landscape in Tuscany, and the way in which they modify the traditional economic geography and strengthen translocal networks. The fourth point describes the regionalization of the governance processes and their spatial consequences, which are referred to here as "physicality of governance." The reasoning concerns the geography of inter-institutional cooperation and area-based coalitions.

Finally, a first synthetic representation of the regional portrait is built. To do so, some fundamental components of the post-metropolitan transition in Tuscany are highlighted in order to measure the gradient of multi-layered density convergence.

Looking through the *square* from the perspective of physicality

Traces

The *squares* of the *Atlante* show the dissemination of *urban traces*, meant as the effects on the land of human interactions, whether the traces are dots or surfaces, extended or concentrated, tidy or haphazard. In the *squares* showing diachronic information, the changes appear rapid and at times impetuous. They give the sensation of defined territories and consolidated landscapes being overwhelmed. They seem to break boundaries, hide stories and traditions, and connect everything with everything else.

Changes in cities have a multidimensional and complex nature; they concern the following three aspects: the actual material(ity) of the territory; flows, movements, communications; and activities, happenings, events. The matter of the human settlements extends and becomes thicker and denser (this is land consumption: the extension and thickening of the human footprint). The grooves in the territory also become more intense and widespread. Both the tangible traces of the material transfers, and the intangible signs of the digital transfers, branch out, supporting each other[2]. Lastly, in urban concentrations events and uses become denser, the mesh of relations and performances becomes more complex – Ingold would define this figure of the urban landscape as a *task-scape* (Ingold, 1993). The transformation therefore concerns stocks, flows and interactions, generally making them more intense (but we can say that it is the interactions, the essence of the urban, that determine the consistency of the stocks and flows). The depiction of corridors and movements shows the tendency of socio-economic connections to extend horizontally in space, creating constellations in which cities disappear, becoming dots of light in milky ways, galaxies, filaments, corridors.

As shown later on, in particular in the case of Tuscany, it is precisely the entwining of place and world, assets and connections, local and global, fixity and motion (Schmid, 2015), which characterizes the recent evolution of contemporary urban landscapes. The depiction of the historical-geographical patterns tells the subtle *game* between the pervasiveness of the urbanization processes and the physical (but also institutional and social) roughness of the territory.

Physicality

The concept of *physicality* has been the interpretative device used by the research in two different fields: urbanization dynamics and governance processes. In particular: (a) the analysis of the urbanization processes in Tuscany shows the persistence of the physiographic and geo-historical patterns; (b) the interpretation of the governance processes shows how the cooperation between municipalities designs geographies that cross the institutional borders while adapting to the physiographic features of land.[3]

The analysis starts from the awareness that what happens affects the physical shape of the territory. This consideration is developed in two directions: the first deepens some recent analyses on the linkage between physical spaces, territory and planetary urbanization (Brenner & Schmid, 2014; Schmid, 2015); the second takes a new slant on some historical-genealogical roots of regional planning, from Geddes to Benton MacKaye (Batty & Marshall, 2009; Paba, 2011; MacKaye, 1928).

Brenner and Schmid made a critical analysis of the "urban age thesis," discussing its scientific bases and disputing its capacity to interpret the urbanization processes taking place in the regions of the world (Brenner & Schmid, 2014). In the most common version, based on aggregate and generic figures, the urban age thesis imagines a flat, liquid, indistinct urban universe, covered by an undifferentiated wave of building sediments, homogeneous, the same everywhere. Brenner and Schmid propose a different vision: "This emergent planetary formation of urbanization is deeply uneven and variegated, and emergent patterns and pathways of socio-spatial differentiation within and across this worldwide urban fabric surely require *sustained investigation* at various geographic scales" (Brenner & Schmid, 2014, pp. 747–8).

To take up an old book by Benton MacKaye, a "new exploration" is needed, extending in time and space, to grasp the effective characteristics of the transformation of the cities and the spread of the urban. In rebuilding the interplay between geosphere and sociosphere, and the unshakeable specificity of every regional environment, this new exploration, this sustained investigation starts precisely from the mere physical, the thing, the original, primeval characteristics of the territory where we live (MacKaye, 1928, p. 57).

Schmid seems to literally draw from that historical regionalist line of argument: "Urban space thus has an initial basis: the physical space formed by nature. And it is on this basis that a society produces its social space with its own features; it inscribes itself into the land, into the terrain" (Schmid, 2015, p. 292). In studying the processes of urban spread "we have to understand how general tendencies and abstract processes materialize, how they become a physical reality, consolidate, and inscribe themselves onto a territory" (Schmid, 2015, p. 290).

(Geo-bio) history matters

Settlement systems, above all in territories shaped by man since ancient times, have formed in a long process of reciprocal adaptation between the geographical, environmental, urban and cultural. During this process a recognizable and relatively stable settlement configuration comes into being through: the arrangement of built-up areas in the space defined by geophysical aspects; the relationship of towns and cities with the old road network; the distinction between city and country; the particular physiognomy of the landscape; the spatial layout of urban areas, which could be centered, polycentric, linear, hierarchical, and so on.

It is possible to give the visible and recognizable upshot of this process many titles: arrangement, pattern, configuration, morphology, cluster, organization, structure – Saverio Muratori used the definition of *impianto territoriale* (Muratori, 1967). Perhaps we can say that at a certain point the settlement patterns can achieve a kind of *efficacy in the spatial arrangement*, which tends to remain, resist, reproduce in time (also through a – open and not linear – game of variations, modifications, adaptations).

Urban and territorial settlements could be considered a sort of *mineralization of humanity*: "human-made structures are very much like mountains and rocks: the accumulation of materials hardened and shaped by historical processes" (De Landa, 2000, p. 55). Formed and hardened in/by historical processes, settlement clusters indeed tend to remain, keeping some aspects constant, changing others, and inventing others still. Nothing is deterministic in all this: territory is an invention – the outcome of an open and unpredictable game between geosphere, biosphere and anthroposphere – but, once invented (Muratori, 1967; Ferraro, 2002; Paba, 2008; Ravagnati, 2012), the territory tends to reproduce itself in time, directing the transformations, even when they are profound and "destructive." In conclusion, while at the urban scale it is possible to speak of "the law of the persistence of the plan" (according to Poète, Lavedan, and so on), on a regional scale it is possible to speak of "the law of the persistence of territorial matrices."

The regional urbanization process in Tuscany
(history, territory, polynuclearity)

Since medieval times and throughout history, Tuscany has been one of the most important urban regions in Europe. Between the thirteenth and fourteenth centuries, it was possible to count seven cities (Florence, Arezzo, Siena, Pistoia, Lucca, Pisa and Volterra). Around these larger cities a network of smaller settlements had already formed, which nevertheless had a recognizable urban character (Prato, San Gimignano, Colle Val d'Elsa, Massa Marittima, Borgo San Sepolcro, Montepulciano, Cortona). In the following centuries, some cities would decline, others emerge, but the nature of the Tuscan multipolar urban landscape would remain. Florence would soon prevail as a center of a higher rank, in dialectic with the other cities that would vary over time. However, the demographic and economic domination of Florence has never completely obscured the different urban networks of which Tuscany is composed (Cherubini, 2013).

The traditional descriptions of Tuscany are often characterized by a stereotype, with a basis of truth, which emphasizes the extreme variety of places within a fundamental unity of territory and culture: Tuscany as a "very harmonious and discordant symphony" of cities, landscapes and environments (Palazzeschi, 1934). This variety is still a fundamental feature of the Tuscan territory and it can be seen (this is the question that guides our research) to be the result of interplay between geomorphological "mountain-ness" and "hilliness" on one hand and the economic, cultural and social features on the other.

It is not our goal here to give a detailed reconstruction of the evolution of the Tuscan urban landscape. However, we can say very briefly that in recent decades the Tuscan territory has been affected by several processes of "incomplete metropolization" that have in some cases altered the original polycentric character of the region. It is important in particular to stress the following processes: the formation of two metropolitan agglomerations in northern Tuscany, in which demographic, economic and social resources have been concentrated (the metropolitan areas of Florence and Pisa-Livorno); the spread of settlements, often in the form of urban sprawl, which has affected the plains and margins of the metropolitan areas (the Florence-Prato-Pistoia basin, the Lucca plain, Versilia, the Arezzo plain, and so on); the consolidation of a linear city along the Tyrrhenian coast, driven by mass tourism and the leisure economy; the strengthening of the connections between urban systems caused by logistic and infrastructure policies.

Our research aims, however, to verify the role that geographical, bio-physical, historical and cultural matrices perform within the processes of settlement dissemination, and to analyze the persistence of a polynucleated urban landscape (Lucchesi et al., 2015).

"Streams and levees" in the regional urbanization process

The physiography of Tuscany is very complex. A series of hill ranges parallel to the coast, some volcanic areas and the curve of the north portion of the Apennines produce a very distinct relief form and a nervous system of valleys, frequently closed or interconnected through small clefts.

In ancient history we can identify several different phases of settlement growth and a succession of preferences for hills or valleys as the location for new villages. But if we relate to a more recent path of the development of a network of cities, it is evident how the complex structure of the valley system forced the location and distribution of the settlements along some main axes.

By working with topographic data, on a map it is relatively easy to separate the land we define as "levees" (soils with high gradient, wetland and swamps, natural parks and protected areas) from what remains, on the contrary: the floodplains, the intermountain basins and the coastal plains. This second space (what we have defined as "streams") is the domain where, from a certain point on in history, the settlement system of northern Tuscany found its location.[4]

A simple cartographic superposition of layers could immediately show the relationship between the dimension, form and distribution of the built areas and the "streams." Here the geosphere has coerced the settlements into a polynuclear structure, starting from the growth of population and settlements in the Middle Ages and thereafter, when a great expansion of the built environment was forced inside this very complex form of reliefs. A deeper analysis of the geological and geomorphological condition of the area would reveal several interesting reasons behind the location of the main settlements of the region and the chain of relationships linking towns and countryside.

Making a big jump in history we can consider how, starting from the first half of the twentieth century, the Italian population and the population of Tuscany began to grow quickly, the rate becoming particularly impressive after the 1950s. In this period not only was the natural growth rate high, but also a combined phenomenon was the migration of the rural population toward the main towns in the area.

Moving forward in our description of Tuscany, we can consider this phase as divided into two different periods, which can be depicted with the general census data from 1921 to 1971 and, with more details, from 1971 to 2011. In the first period, the cities that were already the biggest tended to grow more quickly and intensely with respect to the others. The first five municipalities for density growth were, in order: Florence, Prato, Viareggio, Forte dei Marmi and Montecatini Terme. While, on the contrary, the areas of decreasing population were located in the "levees" and just outside the floodplains. We can define this phase of urban history as the descent from the "levees" to the "streams."

The following phase (1971–2011) is characterized by the population's redistribution inside the "streams," more than by its growth. The more significant changes are only located in the valley municipalities, while the areas on the levees did not experience any significant variations. Density tended to grow primarily on the borders of the provincial capitals. The five municipalities where most growth took place were Poggio a Caiano, Campi Bisenzio, Prato, Calcinaia and Uzzano. The historic cities faced a phase of population decrease, or stagnation, with the exception of Prato, where population density has shown a steady increase since 1921 because of reasons that should be thoroughly investigated.

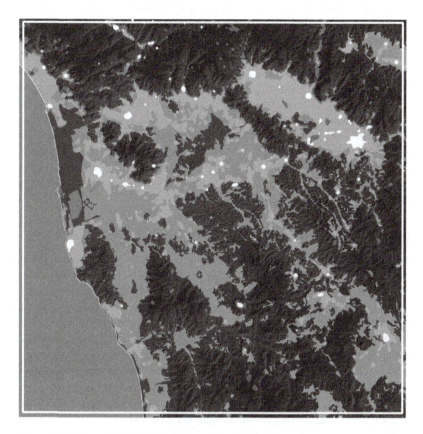

Figure 6.1 Polynucleated urban landscape in the Tuscany *square*

Darker colors represent the resistance to the urbanization processes played by the geophysical features ("levees"). Light gray and white represent the extension and density of settlements in the most
favorable areas ("streams").

Source: Elaboration by the authors

The five municipalities where density decreased more significantly are, in order:
Florence, Forte dei Marmi, Livorno, Siena and Pisa.

The result of the above-mentioned processes was the widening of the impervious soils in the streams, along the axes of the valleys. The complex structure
of internal rifts was gradually covered by the main roads and railways, and
along this network the real estate market found a good opportunity to develop
its activity. A comparison of any map of the built areas at the beginning of the
twenty-first century, compared with one from the end of the 1950s, gives a clear
idea of the process.

The resulting urban environment covers the majority of the "streams" in a
way that gives visibility to the influence played by physiographic features. What

seems lost, or difficult to find, is the polynucleated structure of the settlement system that was the starting point of our portrait (Batty, 2001, 2008).

Nevertheless, some considerations about the density gradient of the urbanization can help in inquiring if and to what extent we can still recognize a polynucleated urban structure. As a matter of fact, if we calculate and combine (for the minimum units of surface in use in the census) the density of population, workers and impervious soils, we can produce a sort of composed density. In the built-up area along the streams, this density has a certain average, but if we draw attention to the sites where this average is overtaken, a polynuclear landscape again emerges from the undifferentiated urban texture. The original imprinting given to the settlements is therefore still active and, under the surface, goes on guiding the process of urbanization at the regional scale (Batty, 2001; Dieleman & Faludi, 1998; Burgalassi, 2010).

The persistence of the polynucleated urban landscape

As said before, the nature of the Tuscan multipolar urban landscape has been a specific feature of the region since at least the fourteenth century and any map from the 1950s can easily show the persistence of this polynucleated network. Historically, Florence has been the main urban center since the Middle Ages, and before that in the Roman period, but this has not forced the entire urbanization phenomenon into a mononuclear pattern (Cherubini, 2013).

In analyzing the historical evolution of the settlement at regional level we can take advantage of the availability of a set of regional data regarding the presence of built objects in a series of historical maps, starting from the first half of the nineteenth century (Lucchesi et al., 2015). Based on this information, it is possible to elaborate a series of density maps (using a kernel density algorithm weighted on the dimension of the area covered by buildings) representing the distribution of the built objects at different moments in time.[5]

In the 1950s it is relatively easy to recognize the hierarchy, historically established, between the main towns, medium-sized settlements and a plurality of small villages that are not comparable with the main urban cores in terms of population, but that could be considered urban in terms of functions and services for the surrounding population.

The cities are characterized by an identifiable form, still connected to their history and not strongly transformed by a massive growth in urban population. We can identify a partial exception along the coast where a linear welding of the built environment is already visible in the north, connected with the development of the leisure area of Versilia.

The post-Second World War history recounts the evident and well-known impressive expansion of the settlements, mainly directed in the area we have defined as "streams," but the question we address here is related to the possibility of recognizing a persistence in the polynucleated organization of the settlement system as a whole.

While starting from a point in history where the relationship between local communities, cities and villages, and between built and natural environment, was clearly understandable (in our case from the cartography of the first half of the nineteenth century), and observing the present urban tissue, which seemingly is more similar to a sprawled uniform townscape, we can ask ourselves how far the historical figure of the Tuscan settlement has and is orienting the dynamics and patterns of growth.

If we measure the density gradient along some lines corresponding to the central axis of the internal valley and to the coast, we discover that the peaks of density increase from the nineteenth century to today, but at the same time that, in a graph, the position of the peaks tends to coincide.

Exceptions are present, but the general geographical persistence of the main point of density accumulation seems to define a sort of rule, and this helps to demonstrate the durability of the historical framework even in areas where the massive growth of buildings, seemingly, drives the urban environment toward an undifferentiated, uniformly dense continuum.

In this context, the polynucleated nature of the built environment is a historical fact. In the past centuries, the relationship between valley systems and settlements, and the very complex physiography that has shaped the development patterns of the villages, were central elements to be interpreted by local inhabitants in order to produce a suitable territory for their lives. If we look at some maps of Tuscany before the beginning of the nineteenth century, we can recognize something similar to a density map from the middle of the 1800s, but the imprinting given to the territory by the first trace of local communities is still strong enough to be mapped and recognized today, as we have tried to demonstrate (Batty, 2001; Burgalassi, 2010; see also Figure 6.1).

Territory, urban suffering and economic transition

Growth of urban suffering and housing policies

The *Atlante* provides data and useful maps giving a picture of the spread of urban suffering and spatial injustice in Italy, and in Tuscany.[6] The crisis that hit the world economy in 2008 has simultaneously exacerbated poverty and accentuated the inequalities between people, families and communities. The recession has affected various aspects of people's economic condition through job losses, increased employment insecurity, lower personal and family incomes, higher taxes and tariffs, and cuts to services and the welfare system.

The attention is, however, focused primarily on the spatial consequences of the crisis, on what can be defined as "urban suffering." The spatial manifestations of the crisis in Tuscany can be summarized as follows: impoverishment of the cities, and deterioration of neighborhoods; expansion of informal and illegal settlements; ineffectiveness of social housing policies; increase in homelessness; decline of traditional manufacturing districts; decay of traditional commercial districts; degraded urban enclaves in historic centers; erosion and privatization of public space; cuts in the provision of urban services and infrastructures; weakening of the artistic and cultural city life; reduction of public

transport; lower quality of life and environment; drastic decrease in public support to local communities; spatial and social isolation of the elderly, lonely
people, the poor and the homeless.

The living conditions in cities and regions affect individual and social poverty, emphasizing the consequences of the economic crisis. In collaboration with
the Michelucci Foundation in Fiesole, partner of our research group, aspects of
the Tuscan population's living conditions and how urban suffering has increased
were analyzed (Fondazione Michelucci, 2014).

A new form of poverty has spread in Italy, and therefore in Tuscany, due to
the conditions of urban life, and especially to housing conditions. The housing
situation can, even in itself, cause a condition of poverty; for an increasingly wide
stratum of the population, it can determine the passage from a condition of economic tranquility to a condition of poverty from which it is difficult to get out.

The condition of poverty, if we exclude housing costs, affects 17 percent of all
Italian families; this percentage rises to 21.7 percent if one includes the direct and
indirect costs arising from housing. In Tuscany, the percentages are, respectively,
14 percent and 18.5 percent. Poverty caused by the cost of housing in Italy is
8.3 percent, 3.5 percent induced both by housing and income, and 5.3 percent
induced by the cost of the dwelling alone (Palvarini, 2014). In Tuscany, the
percentage of family poverty has doubled (from 4 percent to 8 per cent) owing to
the sole effect of housing policies.

The housing policies followed by national and local governments in Italy
in recent decades (the encouragement to buy houses, pushing of bank loans,
block on public housing, ineffectiveness of social housing policies, increase
in tariffs and indirect costs of housing, increase in property taxes) are thus the
origin of a significant increase in urban poverty: a case in which the poverty
of places accentuated by neoliberal urban policies has resulted in an increased
poverty of the people.

Industrial landscape, districts and local development

The economic landscape of Tuscany is characterized by the concentration of
industry in the urbanized central ellipse, more specifically in the two metropolitan
areas of Florence and Pisa-Livorno.[7] This concentration, due to the high density
of agglomeration factors – population, markets, services, logistics, universities,
research, infrastructure – is integrated by the traditional landscape of widespread
small factories, making up a mosaic of local economic systems emerging within
well-identified and defined geographical areas. Among these local systems, the
districts formed by networks of small enterprises, generally linked to the Made in
Italy label, hold particular importance, belonging to a production cycle or to a set
of interrelated production cycles (Becattini, 2009).

These are the typical "Marshallian districts" which have played a key role in
the economic development of many regions, namely in central Italy. In Tuscany
they support the regional economy from the Valdinievole to Santa Croce
(leather), from Prato to Empoli (textiles), from Poggibonsi to Sinalunga (wood

and furniture), from Arezzo (gold industry) to Capannori (paper), from Carrara (marble) to Poggibonsi (wood and furniture), and so on.

The characteristics of the traditional manufacturing districts are the following: the key role of the territory which welcomes and protects the enterprise system; the importance of external economies that reduce production costs for the individual enterprises; the tendency to vertical integration of the production cycle; the process of incremental innovation; the ability to adapt to changes in technology and the market; the significant role of tacit knowledge and implicit cooperation between operators; the function of "accompaniment" and support played by public policies and local governments.

From local economic districts to translocal networks

The deep transformations in the global economic system and the long ongoing crisis, however, have had an impact on the metabolism of the Tuscan economy in general and on the industrial districts in particular, enabling processes of widespread modification (like in the case of the Prato's district, in which strong Chinese immigration has resulted in the growth of the garment industry alongside traditional textile activities).

What are the macro-global trends that will change the relationship between economy and territory in Tuscany in the coming years? What form of the territory and new economic geography can be imagined? It is possible to identify the following directions of change: a process of "planetary decomposition of production cycles" in which industrial districts need to find a different location; the centrality assumed by "intellectual technology production" which "changes the interactive structures in which individuals, organizations and countries are immersed;" the creation of a "global intelligence space," characterized by "ubiquitous access to information" increasing information flows, spatially distributed intelligence that surpasses physical barriers; the consolidation of "global value chains" and "global production networks" that go beyond places and countries (Lombardi & Bellanca, 2010).

Besides the traditional geographical proximity, which was at the origin of the birth and fortune of the traditional industrial districts, other forms of proximity, which can be defined as topological and relational, are taking over: cognitive, organizational, institutional and social proximity (Lombardi & Bellanca, 2010; Storper, 2009; Boschma, 2005). The strengthening of these forms of proximity causes the formation of translocal spaces, tied both to local context and global networks. "The space has global product thickness, density and irregularities, and therefore is not indifferent to living and working in one place or another" (Lombardi & Bellanca, 2010, pp. 22–23): therefore the world is not flat, nor, more than other regions of the world, is Tuscany flat, rather it is hilly and rough, physically, economically and socially. This happens because the Tuscan local "contexts," both intertwined and distinguished from "places," are able to insert the intelligence and capacity for innovation contained in the territories into the translocal networks of global economic development.

(New) traditions and (old) innovations

In the new geography created by the economic and social transition, two seemingly opposed phenomena occur. On the one hand, old and new districts appear to be even more deeply tied to the local territories and resources; on the other hand, new high-tech companies are emerging, both in the major urban centers, and in some old industrial districts.

In the first case we can speak of neo-traditional districts: that is, economic areas that strongly enhance the character of the territory, in particular high-quality agriculture, locally produced energy, heritage, culture, art, fashion, tourism – all sectors making great transformations in the dynamic development of the global economy. The geography of these neo-traditional economic niches therefore follows the geographical coordinates of the historical concentrations of territorial resources and "contextual" knowledge (Magnaghi, 2013; Boschma, 2005).

In the second case, still at an early stage, it is possible to observe the growth of young high-tech companies, linked more directly to the global networks of production, especially as far as the tech and innovative research-intensive sectors are concerned. In this case the contextual and relational proximity is enhanced: innovative enterprises develop the resources of intelligence, large metropolitan areas, and some of the most dynamic manufacturing districts, where there are significant factors such as research and development, universities, services, an advanced tertiary sector and a good quality of urban life.

Physicality of governance

Regionalization of the governance strategy (implosion/explosion, cooperation, coalitions)

This point focuses on the regionalization of the governance processes and their spatial consequences,[8] which are referred to here as "physicality." The reasoning concerns the geography of inter-institutional cooperation and area-based coalitions, while outlining their implications in governance and planning. To do so, changes in spatial boundaries and institutional borders are described along with the processes of transition and the challenges raised by the new post-metropolitan urban landscape.

The result of this research task is a first draft of the *portrait of governance in Tuscany*. It is an attempt to identify processes and strategies, which have been occurring for more than half a century. The analytical focus is therefore addressed toward capturing three main tendencies of governance and its "physicality:" (1) processes of implosion/explosion under which the geographies of governance widen or shrink; (2) multi-scalar cooperation among institutional bodies; (3) single-issue coalitions and deliberative democracy experiences (Granatiero et al., 2015).

This work takes its first steps from the empirical observation of coexisting dynamics, which have produced variability and instability in governance over the past decades. New economic and socio-spatial trends are addressing transcalar processes, which are blind to borders – whether urban, metropolitan, provincial

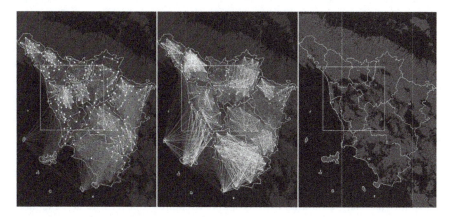

Figure 6.2 Tuscany: physicality of governance

On the left: network of bounded (area-based) institutional cooperations. At center: network of institutional fluid (issue-based) cooperations. On the right: interaction between cooperations and geophysical features.

Source: Elaboration by the authors

or municipal. Simultaneously, policy-making, planning tools and deliberative decision-making processes – which together form the apparatuses of governance – are not able to fully grasp the complexity stemming from this economic and socio-spatial change.

The regional urbanization processes have expanded or dissolved the perimeters of the settlements, while undermining the institutional domains of government and planning. In a first phase (from the 1950s to the 1980s), planning tools have tried to manage the changes by adjusting the scale of intervention to the largest dimension of the processes of urbanization.

From the 1990s onwards both a narrowing and an implosion of the domains of policy, governance and spatial planning have occurred. The research has studied the relationship between the spatial dimension of regional urbanization processes (which has been summarized in the concept of the Florence Urban Region) and institutional spheres of government and planning.

The *Florence Urban Region* has indeed experienced both implosion and explosion. It has been alternatively referred as the very core of the city, and a large metropolitan area including the so-called "Florence-Prato-Pistoia Plain" (understood as geographical domain, rather than institutional). Nowadays, in contrast to a trend of extension of the urbanization processes to a regional domain, we are witnessing a sort of shrinkage of the institutional domain of the metropolitan area, which includes just the province of Florence. This tendency is occurring simultaneously with the opposite trend: the spread of many forms of cooperation among municipalities that exceed the boundaries of the metropolitan area.

The coexistence of these different tendencies shows the shift from a fundamental centralized governance model to an interscalar, exploded and networked "governance strategy." More generally, this scenario can be defined as a shift from a "mode" supported by dynamics of centralization to one featuring the following processes: decentralization of functions; regionalization of the governance strategies; spreading of deliberative experiences in the management of conflicts; networking of new cognitive economies (Brenner, 2014; Storper, 2014; Heley, 2013; Haughton & Allmendinger, 2008; De Roo & Porter, 2007).

A portrait of post-metropolitan governance: geographies and questions

Tuscany, with specific regard to the northern area (the region's urban core), shows a mix of overlapping urbanization patterns, ranging from the traditional compact city to what can be defined as metropolitan features – at least under a number of aspects – from polycentrism to conurbation, from sprawl to suburbanization (Burgalassi, 2010; Hall & Pain, 2006; Keil, 2013; Ekers et al., 2012; Neuman & Hull, 2009). Several contributions have attempted to describe the tricky nature of the urbanization processes that have occurred in the urban core of Tuscany. As briefly mentioned above, over many decades, governance and planning have conceptually focused on the Florence Urban Region, each time denoting a different spatial domain. Then, the understanding of the progressive "adjustment" of the governance geography needs to take a fundamental question into account: the geographical entity we refer to as *Florence Urban Region* (FUR) has been redefined in its borders and extent each time that a new regulatory or strategic planning tool has been devised to treat challenges emerging from the dynamicity of the economy and its spatial effects. Accordingly, the *first question* of a post-metropolitan governance in Tuscany deals with the dilemma of whether to maintain the FUR borders or reshape new regional borders under the discourse of the "regionalization of the urban." The Florence Urban Region (which has become a fluid and fuzzy entity) no longer exists, at least with the same features that have addressed governance and planning until now. The metropolitan area has changed profoundly, insofar as its extension cannot be captured within the borders of the old institutional bodies.

The *second question* deals with the planning units in both the domain of statutory and strategic planning (Albrechts, 2013; Balducci, 2011). The story of planning in Tuscany as a tool of government/governance produces evidence, in accordance with the international trends (Katz & Bradley, 2013; Keil & Young, 2011), about the fact that the problems, challenges and opportunities that cities are facing – whether city-regions, networks of cities or regions – cannot be adequately tackled with traditional spatial planning. In an urban region such as Florence, traditional planning tools are unsuited to governing the processes of urban transformation and the governance implications of the post-metropolitan transition.

The *third question* deals with public decision-making, deliberative/participatory democracy and, of course, citizens' actorship. The Tuscan region has embedded deliberative/participative democracy issues in its laws and governance practices (Fayman et al., 2011). A regional law issued in 2007 (RL 69/07) and revised in 2013 (RL 46/13) has helped aim for better and more inclusive governance. The law provides both for ordinary participatory processes related to specific area-based problems, and mega-infrastructural regional projects to be managed through the "public debate" (a deliberative democracy technique inspired by its French cousin *débat public*). On the one side, Tuscany has become a remarkable "laboratory" for testing the validity of deliberative participation in the real world (Perrone & Morisi, 2013; Paba et al., 2009). On the other side, the sizeable number of post-metropolitan territorial conflicts still open shows the weakness of this approach or at least of its management when detached from the change occurring in the urbanization processes defined as regionalization of the urban.

A reference to the timeline supports the acknowledgment of the changing geography of the governance in Tuscany while clarifying new problems, challenges and opportunities. In northern Tuscany, at least three seasons of planning for the Florence Urban Region – a large territorial entity that includes the urban areas of Florence, Prato and Pistoia – can be recognized. They refer to different planning systems, reflect similar government/ance "templates" and are inspired by distinctive models of urban and economic development.

The first season (1950s and 1960s) was characterized by a hierarchical planning system (national law 1150/42), understood as a *government tool* providing for more than one municipality to make spatial plans through cooperation agreements, alongside the regular statutory planning at municipal, provincial and regional level. The metropolitan system that included Prato and Pistoia became the planning and governance entity. Some attempts to redesign the development of the metropolitan area were made in this period, without any kind of practical effects.

The second season (1980s) produced an interesting planning tool called the "structural scheme." It was aimed at embedding the interscalarity of the urban development and treating its complexity in terms of multifaceted spatial, environmental and political issues. Unfortunately, it was focused on the strictly urbanized areas of the Florence-Prato-Pistoia Plain (the surrounding territory was excluded). Again, nothing happened after this work.

The third season (1990s to present day) represents a shift from a hierarchical planning system to an institutionally cooperative and subsidiary one, following a new regional law system that has transformed planning into a tool of a multi-agent governance. Unfortunately, the two main regional provinces are the only units of reference for the attempts of either planning or governance to deal with metropolitan dynamics. In fact, planning and governance seem to identify two main metropolitan cores: the Pisa and Florence metropolitan poles. As a result of such a vision, the regional dimension of urbanization dynamics is flattened out and zipped up in the "old-fashioned" metropolitan mode that made northern Tuscany into a strange "two-headed metropolis" incapable of capturing and setting value by the complex urbanization process occurring in the meantime. Even the last strategic plan (2002) chose the provincial level as the reference unit, despite attempting to capture the changing nature of regional urbanization. Under the latest Italian national law (Law 56/2014), which represents the final step toward an implementation of a new institutional level of metropolitan government in Italy, the scale and the borders of metropolitan government and planning yet coincide with the territory of provinces, which is an institutional area too restricted if compared with the scales of regional urbanization processes.

The first step toward an effective governance approach to the post-metropolitan question is set out in the "Regional Strategic Framework 2014–2020" paper for a reform of the cohesion policy, issued by the Tuscan region in 2014. The framework is based on three main goals: (a) redesigning the central urban core of Tuscany with a specific focus on the flourishing of territorial capital, the improvement of a smart and soft mobility network, climate change adaptation, the development of projects such as the agricultural park of regional interest of the Florence-Prato-Pistoia Plain; (b) supporting the economy of the coastal territories led by medium-sized towns such as Livorno and Pisa; (c) improving the unsteady development trajectories of the inland areas (Apennine mountain areas and areas of southern Tuscany) through local participatory development.

Transitions and challenges: method of analysis

The methodological attempt to grasp the changing nature of the governance – its post-metropolitan essence and consistency – is based on the three following assumptions:

1   The analysis focuses on institutional governance processes with specific regard to the kind of cooperation among institutional entities (both issue- and area-based) and the typology of governance instruments; it includes cooperative networks that act within (stable cooperations) and outside the strict "cage" of institutional governance (voluntary and fluid cooperations).

2   The research highlights the inter-institutional fluid cooperations (issue-based cooperations) that explode outside the municipal and provincial boundaries. They are grouped in five subcategories: (a) territorial agreements (i.e. watershed agreements); (b) programs and projects; (c) strategic plans; (d) inter-municipal structural plans; (e) deliberative/participative projects.

3   The empirical work makes use of a threefold methodological framework inspired by Wirth's categories of "urban" – size, density, heterogeneity (Wirth, 1938). They have been redefined as features of post-metropolitan governance while taking into account the nature of contemporary processes and their regional dimension. The urban, understood as a combination of size, heterogeneity and density, is therefore no longer concentrated in major urban areas; it is instead organized at a regional dimension. Accordingly, as well as the regionalization of the urban has produced a polynucleated and networked settlement structure, the same way the cooperation, both institutional and voluntary, seems to reproduce geographies of regionalization of governance.

Density is defined as the *intensity* of "governance gestures" within an area with blurred borders. This research lens helps to design a *new polynuclear geography of post-metropolitan governance* and eventually to test the theory of density convergence as the effect of governance choices.

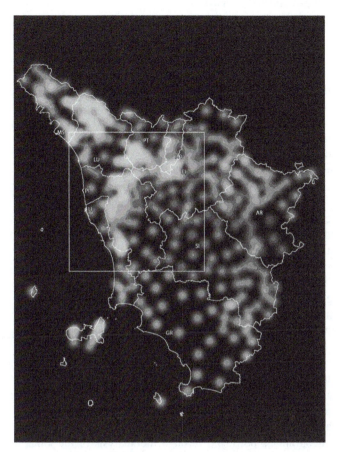

Figure 6.3 Tuscany: density of institutional cooperations

Light and dark gray stand for gradients of density ranging from higher to lower values.

Source: Elaboration by the authors

Heterogeneity is understood as diversity in terms of nature, objectives and issues of governance instruments (renewable energy, innovation and economic development, local public transport, urban regeneration, rural development, tourism and culture, environment and landscape, mega-events).

Size is stressed to include the *interscalarity* of government and governance actions, connections and cooperations between institutional bodies, and *interdependency* among territories and institutional bodies, which generates or is generated by acts of governance.

The intersection of these three categories highlights the extension/explosion and differentiation of governance throughout the region, beyond the major urban agglomerations, strengthening the post-metropolitan dynamics observed in the preceding paragraphs.

A synthetic representation of Tuscany: toward the new regional city

The portrait outlines the Tuscan landscape changes during the multi-scalar regional urbanization process characterizing the post-metropolitan transition (Soja, 2011). The result is a multifaceted portrait represented through the maps of the *Atlante*, layer after layer. In particular the portrait of Tuscany emphasized the following significant aspects: the role that the physiographic and spatial patterns play in the regional urbanization processes; the closely associated implications for governance and regional planning.

The choice of these two aspects is determined by the effort to verify the post-metropolitan transition features, taking into account the historical and geographical specificities of the Tuscan region. This specificity is linked to historical territorial matrices, in particular to the role played by the dense network of small and medium-sized cities.

Tuscany is indeed a polynuclear territory, expression of a path-dependence linked to geo-historical matrices that generated a plural network of urban centers, as well as to innovations that have marked the recent transition phase, characterized by a small enterprise structure, leaning against a dense network of small and medium towns.

The study then examined the coexistence of two trends: the one, toward density convergence theorized by Soja; the other one, the traditional settlement polynuclear organization linked to the geophysical structure that also embodies the maintenance of local identity and vitality of urban networks.

Accordingly, the portrait emphasized how these dynamics play an important role in addressing the regional governance also affected by the aforementioned polynucleated urban landscape. It also embodies the "physical" array of formal and informal cooperations, inter-institutional relations, stressing their interaction with the geophysical and geo-historical matrices.

The governance geographies portrayed through the analysis of the kinds of cooperation and the degree of coordination between institutional bodies show a balance of roles between urban areas and inland regions, emphasizing the trend toward a density convergence in the processes of regional urbanization. The post-metropolitan governance processes work as a tool of organizing the cooperations, anticipating the transition from an institutional area-based mode to an interscalar and polynuclear mode.

Although most of the governance instruments have been designed with reference to institutional and geographical entities that no longer include phenomena and processes unfolding through the region, the scenario emerging from the analysis shows some dynamics of transition toward the regionalization of governance – whether they are framed as stable cooperation for the management of services or fluid issue-based cooperation.

In a range that includes small and medium-sized cities, polycentric systems, metropolitan and post-metropolitan agglomerations (polynuclear structures organized in a regional domain), networks of rural settlements, rural/urban regions with a functional emphasis (such as the winemaking regions), and a complex

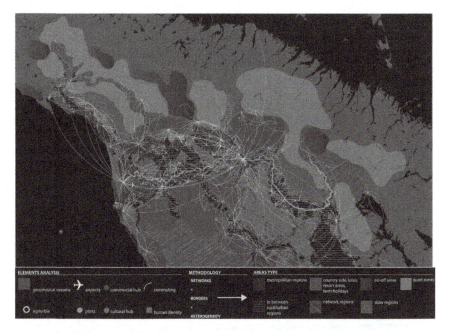

Figure 6.4 Tuscany: regional portrait

The map shows the resistance of the polynuclear urban landscape and the emergence of post-metropolitan spatial features (in-between regions, network regions, slow areas, quiet zones, streams and levees, rural/urban interstices, agriurbia, etc.).

Source: Elaboration by the authors

intertwinement between rural and urban spreading, Tuscany seems to become a laboratory for testing a new generation of governance model.

The final steps of the research have led to a first attempt of a synthetic representation of the regional portrait. This picture is an attempt of meta-geographical visualization of post-metropolitan transition in Tuscany. The synthetic image shows the trend toward the regionalization of the urban and suggests a possible configuration of the Tuscan region so as to redesign planning and governance policies.

Particularly, in this synthesis, the following aspects emerge:

–   the role of the geographical features in the regional urbanization dynamics and in the governance processes ("streams and levees");
–   the resistance of the traditional configuration of the Tuscan urban structure (polynucleated urban landscape);
–   the emergence of new spatial hierarchies and new characterizations of the Tuscan territories: in-between regions, network regions, slow regions, quiet zones, on-off areas, cultural hubs, rural/urban interstices, agriurbia, etc.;

-    the reshaping of the two pre-existing metropolitan urban areas around Florence (inner region) and Pisa-Livorno (coastal region) into an urban structure less hierarchical and more decentralized;
-    the effects of the regionalization of governance cooperations in the strengthening of role of peripheral regions (northern and southern Tuscany).

The resulting image portrays the multi-scalar process of urban regionalization in Tuscany, which the research defines as the emerging "new regional city" that lays over a new identification and interdependency rules of the various territorial components, which acquire significance within a regional dimension (with reference to the debate under way on the spatial turn and new regionalism) (Storper, 1997; Soja, 2011, 2015; Paasi, 2013).

Notes

1   This chapter provides a synthesis of the collective work done by the research unit. However, G. Paba and C. Perrone took primary responsibility for the introduction and the section "Looking through the *square* from the perspective of physicality," F. Lucchesi and I. Zetti took primary responsibility for the section "The regional urbanization process in Tuscany," G. Paba took primary responsibility for the section "Territory, urban suffering and economic transition," and C. Perrone took primary responsibility for the sections "Physicality of governance" and "A synthetic representation of Tuscany"; Antonella Granatiero and Maddalena Rossi contributed to the drawing of figures and maps.
2   See PRIN Postmetropoli (2015): "Densità e forma" § i.1.
3   The discussion on the validity of a physicalist paradigm is very complex. The interpretation of this paradigm adopted here does not correspond to either the idea of a radical physicalism or materialism, and it is closer to the critical spatial thinking, described by Soja as spatial turn (Soja 2010, 2011). In our interpretation, the physical dimension of the urbanization processes is not understood as deterministic in its manner. Rather we feel closer to an idea of physicalism *as an attitude* (Ney, 2008): "it claims that everything is physically constituted, not that everything should be studied by the methods used in physical science" (Papineau 2001, p. 25).
4   See PRIN Postmetropoli (2015), "Indice di resistenza delle matrici fisiografiche", § i.2.17.
5   See PRIN Postmetropoli (2015): "Indice di polinuclearità", § i.3.10.
6   See PRIN Postmetropoli (2015): "Indice composito di sofferenza urbana – 2001–2011", § i.2.12.
7   See PRIN Postmetropoli (2015), "Indice di dinamismo socio-eonomico", § i.2.1.
8   See PRIN Postmetropoli (2015), "Indice di propensione alla cooperazione", § i.3.12.

References

Albrechts, L. (2013). Reframing Strategic Spatial Planning by Using a Coproduction Perspective, *Planning Theory*, 12(1), 46–63.
Balducci, S. (2011). Strategic Planning as Exploration, *Town Planning Review*, 82(5), 529–546.
Batty, M. (2001). Polynucleated Urban Landscapes, *Urban Studies*, 38(4), 635–655.
Batty, M. (2008). The Size, Scale, and Shape of Cities, *Science*, 319, 769–771.
Batty, M., and Marshall, S. (2009). The Evolution of Cities: Geddes, Abercrombie and the New Physicalism, *Town Planning Review*, 80(6), 551–574.
Becattini, G. (2009). *Ritorno al territorio*, Bologna: il Mulino.

Boschma, R.A. (2005). Proximity and Innovation: A Critical Assessment, *Regional Studies*, 39(1), 61–74.

Brenner, N. (Ed.) (2014). *Implosions/Explosions: Towards a Study of Planetary Urbanization*. Berlin: Jovis Verlag GmbH.

Brenner, N., and Schmid, C. (2014). The Urban Age. In *Question, International Journal of Urban and Regional Research*, 38(3), 731–755.

Burgalassi, D. (2010). *Defining and Measuring Polycentric Regions: The Case of Tuscany*, MPRA Paper, Munich: University Library of Munich.

Cherubini, G. (2013). *Firenze e la Toscana: Scritti vari*, Pisa: Pacini.

De Landa, M. (2000). *A Thousand Years of Nonlinear History*, New York: Swerve Edition.

De Roo, G., and Porter, G. (Eds.) (2007). *Fuzzy Planning: The Role of Actors in a Fuzzy Governance Environment*, Farnham: Ashgate.

Dieleman, F.M., and Faludi, A. (1998). Polynucleated Metropolitan Regions in Northwest Europe, *European Planning Studies*, 6(4), 365–377.

Ekers, M., Hamel, P., and Keil, R. (2012). Governing Suburbia: Modalities and Mechanisms of Suburban Governance, *Regional Studies*, 46(3), 405–422.

Fayman S., et al., (Eds.). (2011). *Good Policies and Practices to Tackle Urban Challenges (The Case of Florence)*, Study commissioned by European Commission, Paris.

Ferraro, G. (2002). *Il libro dei luoghi*, Milan: Jaca Book.

Fondazione Michelucci. (2014). *Case e non case. Povertà abitative in Toscana*, Firenze: Seid.

Granatiero, A., Perrone, C., and Rossi, M. (2015). Geografia della governance in Toscana. In Agnoletti, C., Iommi, S., and Lattarulo, P. (Eds.), *Rapporto sul territorio: Configurazione urbane e territori negli spazi europei*, Firenze: IRPET.

Hall, P., and Pain, K., (2006). *The Polycentric Metropolis: Learning from Mega-city Regions in Europe*, London: Earthscan.

Haughton, G., and Allmendinger, P. (2008). Soft Spaces in Local Economic Development, *Local Economy*, 23(2) 138–148.

Heley, J. (2013). Soft Spaces, Fuzzy Boundaries and Spatial Governance in Post-devolution Wales, *International Journal of Urban and Regional Research*, 37(4), 1325–1348.

Ingold, T. (1993). The Temporality of Landscape, *World Archeology*, 25(2), 152–174.

Katz, B., and Bradley, J. (2013). *The Metropolitan Revolution: How Cities and Metros Are Fixing Our Broken Politics and Fragile Economy*, Washington, DC: Brookings Institution Press.

Keil, R. (Ed.) (2013). *Suburban Constellations: Governance, Land and Infrastructure in the 21st Century*, Berlin: Jovis Verlag.

Keil, R., and Young, D. (2011). Post-Suburbia and City Region Politics. In Phelps, N., and Fulong, W. (Eds.), *International Perspectives on Suburbanization: A Post-Suburban World?* London: Palgrave-MacMillan.

Lombardi, M., and Bellanca, N. (2010). *Le traiettorie reticolari dell'innovazione territoriale*, Working Paper, Firenze: Dipartimento di Science Economiche, University of Florence.

Lucchesi, F., Paba, G., and Zetti, I. (2015). La persistenza delle matrici geo-fisiche e storiche nei processi di urbanizzazione regionale. In Agnoletti, C., Iommi, S., and Lattarulo, P. (Eds.), *Rapporto sul territorio: Configurazione urbane e territori negli spazi europei*, Firenze: IRPET.

MacKaye, B. (1928). *The New Exploration: A Philosophy of Regional Planning*, New York: Harcourt, Brace and Company.

Magnaghi, A. (2013). The Role of Historical Rural Landscapes in Territorial Planning. In Agnoletti, M. (Ed.), *Italian Historical Rural Landscape*, Firenze: Springer.

Muratori, S. (1967). *Civiltà e territorio*, Rome: Centro Studi di Storia Urbanistica.

Neuman, M., and Hull, A. (2009). The Futures of the City Region, *Regional Studies*, 43(6), 777–787.

Ney, A. (2008). Physicalism as an Attitude, *Philosophical Studies*, 138, 1–15.

Paasi, A. (2013). Regional Planning and the Mobilization of 'Regional Identity': From Bounded Spaces to Relational Complexity, *Regional Studies*, 47(8), 1206–1219.

Paba, G. (2008). Invenzione del patrimonio e trasformazione del territorio. In Bertoncin, M., and Piase, A. (Eds.), *Pre-visioni di territorio: Rappresentazioni di scenari territoriali*, Milano: FrancoAngeli.

Paba, G. (2011). Le cose (che) contano: nuovi orizzonti di agency nella pianificazione del territorio, *CRIOS*, 1, 67–78.

Paba, G., Pecoriello, A.L., Perrone, C., and Rispoli, F. (2009). *Partecipazione in Toscana: Interpretazioni e racconti*, Firenze: Florence University Press.

Palazzeschi, A. (1934). *Sorelle Materassi*, Firenze: Vallecchi.

Palvarini, P. (2014). Come cambia la povertà in Italia dopo le spese abitative. In Fondazione Michelucci, *Case e non case: Povertà abitative in Toscana*, Firenze: Seid.

Papineau, D. (2001). The Rise of Physicalism. In Gillett, C., and Loewer B.M., (Eds.) *Physicalism and its Discontents*, Cambridge: Cambridge University Press.

Perrone, C., and Morisi, M. (Eds.), (2013). *Giochi di potere: Partecipazione, piani e politiche territoriali*, Novara: Utet.

PRIN Postmetropoli. (2015). *Atlante web dei territori postmetropolitani* [web atlas]. Retrieved from http://www.postmetropoli.it/atlante.

Ravagnati, C. (2012). *L'invenzione del territorio. L'atlante inedito di Saverio Muratori*, Milan: FrancoAngeli.

Schmid, C. (2015). Specificity and Urbanization: A Theoretical Outlook. In R. Diener et al. (Eds.), *The Inevitable Specificity of Cities*, Zürich: Lars Muller Publishers.

Soja, E. (2010). Cities and State in Geohistory, *Theor. Soc.* 36, 361–376.

Soja, E. (2011). Regional Urbanization and the End of the Metropolis Era. In Bridge, G., and Watson, S. (Eds.), *New Companion to the City*, Chichester: Wiley-Blackwell.

Soja, E. (2015). Accentuate the Regional, *International Journal of Urban and Regional Research*, 39(2), 372–381.

Storper, M. (1997). *The Regional World Territorial Development in a Global Economy*, New York: The Guilford Press.

Storper, M. (2009). The Economy of Context, Location and Trade: Another Trade Transformation, *The Handbook of Industrial Districts*, Birmingham: Elgar.

Storper, M. (2013). *Keys to the City: How Economics, Institutions, Social Interaction, and Politics Shape Development*, Princeton, NJ: Princeton University Press.

Storper, M. (2014). Governing the Large Metropolis, *Territory, Politics, Governance*, 2(2), 115–134. doi: 10.1080/21622671.2014.919874.

Wirth, L. (1938). Urbanism as a Way of Life, *American Journal of Sociology*, 44(1), 1–24.

7 Transformations of the "urban" in Rome's post-metropolitan cityscape

Carlo Cellamare

Introduction

Rome is located in central Italy, not far from the sea, in the centre of a vast territory, mainly characterized by agricultural and urban uses, with several groups of hills and mountains all around. The river Tevere (Tiber) crosses the city and its territory.

As is well known, Rome has a long history and has seen great stratification over the centuries. Its territory, as well, has been involved in the evolution of the capital, so it represents a long series of transformations over time. Rome is fundamentally characterized by a great archaeological, cultural and artistic heritage, one of the most important in the world – and this is a main identity factor of the city and of its territory and the related landscape.

Rome, as the capital of Italy and of Christianity, presents many main central functions and is part of a global network, with international flows of tourists and migrants. In the context of Italy, it maintains a fundamental role of attraction for most central (and southern) regions. In this way, along with Milan, the city is the main national and international node of the transportation system, with its airports, the railway and motorway network.

The area addressed in this research is larger than the square used in the national common work, the PRIN research, because of the vast influence that Rome has on a broader territory. The area is positioned with Rome near to the centre because of its centrality within a vast territory and because the development of the settlements and of the socio-economic relations follows all directions around the city. The square is positioned to consider the presence of the sea on the west side and to show the large range of relations (socio-economic fluxes, commuting, soil consumption, spatial distribution of settlements and so on) between Rome and a vast region of central Italy. Because of this, the sample square reaches all the provincial capitals of the Lazio region as well as the neighbouring regions of Umbria in the north and Abruzzo in the east.

Processes of urbanization and inhabitability

This regional portrait provides a first interpretive reading of the transformations of the "urban" in the context of Rome's territory. By using the term "urban", the intention is to interpret not only the physical-spatial or socio-economic transformations according to the best known studies, but the evolution of the complexity of the relationships between such different aspects. It aims to look at the complexity of socio-spatial relations, such as the organization of daily life, the ways of living in different territories, transportation modes, the relationship with the place where people live, the organization of time, the use of resources, and so on. Included in this are immaterial relations that refer to different lifestyles, to the cultural and social models, and to residents' relationship with daily life.

Rather than search the Roman context for a predefined or ideological template as to what is "urban", or the transition from an ideological "urban" in an equally ideological "metropolitan" (or "post-metropolitan"), this chapter attempts to reconstruct and investigate the processes of urbanization (Brenner, 2014; Diener et al., 2006). It addresses those elements that represent the "constitutive essences" of urban Rome today, the local ramifications of the process of "extended urbanization" that is a global phenomenon.

The attention to process requires new analytical tools and forms of interpretation. It requires stepping back from the territory itself to the readings and eventually to the interpretative models, refusing to search the "urban" only there where ideal models place it.

Lefebvre (1970; Schmid, 2012) portrayed the city as a mediator between local processes and their effects on the daily lives of the inhabitants and on the organization of space. Today this mediating role is played by the extensive territory and cannot be taken for granted; indeed, it must be investigated and interpreted. From this account, and with reference to the specific context, research has tended to read and recount the ''urban'' from an interpretation of the processes of urbanization, not given *a priori*. In this interpretation, given by the research, the territory – and the city – is the mediator between global processes of urbanization and the local conditions of daily life and the organization of space. Therefore, we can understand the transformations of the "urban" by studying the new organization of the territory and the conditions and ways of living that shape the urban landscape. Following this approach, the work on transformations of the "urban" in the context of Rome has tried to investigate the research questions of the national group with an emphasis on inhabitability.

In this way, the topic of living has been investigated through several relevant thematic areas:

– **Dwelling** – including an analysis and interpretation of the relationship between the displacement of populations, the search of housing, the trends and the geography of the real estate market, the advantages of site (presence of infrastructure, benefits or services related to mobility, quality of the environment, and so on), the education of new inhabitants and the reasons that led them to move on to different territories.
– **Morphologies of settlements and the service components which contribute to the quality of life** – this aspect addresses the analysis of settlement morphologies, corresponding to diverse socio-spatial patterns of dwelling,

and of all that support them directly, and in particular the issue of services and their accessibility.

– **The relationship between the organization of a settlement and organization of everyday life** – the interpretation and evaluation of forms of territorial reorganization are developed on two levels. First, this takes place at the level of the new territorial structure (the main lines of development, localized conveniences, the relationship between dwelling and infrastructure, territorial frameworks, dispersed or sprawling settlements, the reorganization of productive functions, regional mobility, the capacity of the new commercial centres to reorganize settlements, and so on). Second, there is the level of morphologies of social settlements, that is, the prevalent types and spatial forms adopted by new developments (closed and/or introverted residential enclaves, *villettopoli* or clusters of single-family homes, squatter settlements, large residential developments indifferent to the environment, developments inserted within surrounding rural areas, the recovery of historic centres, and so on). The goal is also the interpretation and evaluation of the effects of this territorial reorganization on the conditions and forms of organization of everyday life, both in its spatial qualities and in its temporality.

– **The experience and culture of lifestyles** – this dimension is predominantly immaterial (though closely related to the physical and material). It addresses the social and cultural aspects, which requires specific methods of investigation, with particular reference to urban practices in specific contexts of investigation, considered emblematic of the new processes of urbanization. This also allows one to investigate the multi-scale and multi-dimensional relationships that develop between the inhabitants and their urban context, relationships that extend well beyond the limits of their immediate residential territory.

This point of view allows one to integrate both the material and the intangible dimensions that characterize the processes of urbanization and which have been emphasized by several authors in different ways (Soja's "third space" and his concept of "post-metropolis", 1996, 1999; Brenner, 2014; Schmid, 2014; Harvey, 2006) recovering the original and foundational interpretation of Lefebvre (1974). Following Schmid (2014) we have to consider three dimensions of urbanization: "According to Henri Lefebvre's theory of the production of space, the urbanization process can be analyzed in three dimensions – first, the production of material elements and structures; second, the processes of regulation and representation; and third, socialization and learning processes" (p. 211).

In order to develop these considerations, the research has been carried out through an interdisciplinary approach: through the elaboration and analysis of quantitative data, as well as through the consideration of existing studies, but even through a qualitative study in the field (with more anthropological and sociological approaches) which covered the areas undergoing major urban and territorial transformations.

The research methodology was aimed at promoting a careful approach to the dimension of daily life, as a fundamental factor in interpreting the processes of urbanization with particular attention to the quality of life of people and to urban policies (Cellamare, 2011). In considering the territory as a "mediator" it has turned attention, on the one hand, to the relationship between global processes and economies and their local effects on the organization of the territory and, on the other, to the theme of conflict and social roles, both as a warning about the contradictory effects of spatial development and its local impact, and also as an important action of transformation and appropriation by the inhabitants and populations (both residents and immigrants).

This is not so much a redefinition of the urban in general, as much as an assessment of the changes in Rome and its territory. Thus, it presents an interpretation of this city's urban transformations and a reflection on what "extended urbanization" means given the specific conditions of Italy's capital and its territory. The working method has grown out of a dual process. On the one hand, an interpretation of the present conditions of urbanization and, as we have explained above, the related forms of living; and on the other, a reconstruction of the historical development that has produced the current process of urbanization. In line with Brenner's methodology, the research proposes (2014): "first, an account of (contemporary) patterns of urbanization; and second, an investigation of the (historical) pathways of urbanization that produced those patterns" (p. 211).

Rome has always been seen through broad stereotypes and corresponding generalized "images". The first is its role as capital of Christianity and the second is related to having been the capital of a great historical power, the Roman Empire. To the presence of a large and important archaeological heritage is added the huge historical and cultural heritage, both of global significance, which has accumulated over the course of the city's long history. In many ways, Rome lives *in* and *of* its history, or through more "transcendental" images such as religion. Its present constitution is linked to its being the capital of Italy, which leads to other stereotypes, the image of corruption, the negative role of politics and, in fact, the recent legal proceedings of "Mafia Capitale" confirm that this is not just a cliché. All these stereotypes, in fact, are not merely "images" (even if they lead to preconceptions), but contain a large degree of reality. They do not, however, comprise the entire and complex reality of this great Italian city and its surrounding metropolitan area, with its problems, its organization and its daily life. Regarding this point, there is still a dearth of content in contemporary scientific studies.

Rome presents, in fact, its own specificity and therefore its own specific interests. It's particular role is as a large bridge city between the Global North – as the capital of a Western country of advanced capitalism – and the South, which is also globalized, the Mediterranean, with a totally different culture both of lifestyles and of government and public policy.

Rome: global city?

It would be very difficult to consider Rome a "global city" in the generally accepted sense, as laid out in the much-discussed studies of Saskia Sassen. Incidentally, in the recent past, most of the transnational corporations (or simply national ones with a network of international activity), especially those in banking, finance, insurance, and so on, that still had offices in Rome have left definitely, preferring, with regards to Italy, their Milan office. Still, however, some major international companies or national ones, public and private, with a capacity for international activities, continue to operate out of Rome.

Nevertheless, there is no denying that Rome is, in its way, a global city with an international character, integral to a network of economic and financial flows of goods, energy and services, of human migration, and so on. A recent study (Thomassen & Clough Marinaro, 2014) highlighted the specific characteristics of Rome's different way of being a global city, acting as a bridge between the highly developed Western countries of northern Europe and North America and the Mediterranean countries, gateway to a network of relations with the Global South.

Rome, as is known, is a number of capitals in one, a situation that shapes its different ways of being a "global city". In the first place, of course, it is the political capital of Italy, with all the pros and cons of this role, and it is still the largest Italian city, with a dominant role throughout the south-central peninsula. But it is also the capital of another state, the Vatican, and more generally, it is the capital of Christianity, as well as a place of reference for many faiths, the target of massive pilgrimages and religious events, often strongly influenced by the media. Then it is a cultural capital, to the extent that it holds a unique archaeological and historical-artistic position, able to attract considerable tourist flows (added to those of religious tourism). The numbers (12.635 million tourists per year, 2013) are massive with respect to the resident population. Against this international character, a clear weakness or even absence of both international policies and policies towards "internationalization" must be recognized (d'Albergo & Lefèvre, 2007), revealing a strong "structural" weakness in this area.

As is well known, Rome has never been an industrial city. It saw a weak modernization in the nineteenth century when it was still the capital of the State of the Church and a conscious decision was taken, upon its becoming capital of Italy and even more so during the fascist era, not to allow industrial development. Intended to prevent the formation of "dangerous" social classes, this has always left Rome on the edge of productive development related to industry and big business, but powerfully oriented towards the development of public administration and towards the service sector. By the way, as a contradiction, it has become in recent years the second industrial town of Italy (behind Milan). But they are most of all small or medium enterprises, a weak and widespread fabric, more dependent on the local market than export.[1]

The construction industry has always played a special role and it has often taken on a speculative character, advancing hand-in-hand with the financial projects of real estate development. In fact, economists point out that the building cycle and its related processes (including the system of credit, mortgages, securities and all related financial transactions) make up about 40% of the GDP for this large urban area. This is especially true for Rome, where it was precisely this building activity and the development of residential areas that propelled the Roman economy, along with the areas of trade and tourism, in its boom phases culminating in the bubble of 2008, before the explosion of the economic crisis. Urbanization is one of the engines of the Roman economy, just as it is globally in the context of an evolution of advanced capitalism that puts value on the processes of urbanization in the world (Brenner, 2014; Brenner & Theodore, 2002). Rental income, but also more widely associated processes of commodification and financialization of the city's settlement process, is recognized as the real protagonist of urban transformation, not only for the city of Rome but for the whole urban region (Pizzo & Di Salvo, 2014). It was precisely that type of economy, based on a prevailing "bullish" character and on the constant (and thus, unsustainable) consumption of resources, which defined the well-known "modello Roma" in the early 2000s. This model was as striking for its positive effects on the city's GDP, as it was criticized (AA.VV., 2007) for its negative effects on the overall development of the capital, on the quality of the environment and the conditions of daily life of its inhabitants, and finally, for its eventual counterproductive role in the economic crisis of 2008.

The presence of the central state, as well as some local authorities that are very important as the Municipality of Rome and the Lazio Region, plays a vital role in the Roman economy. In a first meaning, this regards their role in developing employment and asking for services and induced activities. But, in a second meaning, this regards the influence on the organization of the private sector and the way in which its headquarters are present. The proximity to the political and institutional, in fact, means proximity to procurement and other systems of allocation of public resources. It is no coincidence that in Rome, offices of the companies involved in public works, infrastructure and procurement are present with the greatest concentration in Italy, while headquarters of the great banking, financial and insurance institutions fell short in time. The regime of the *Urbs* (d'Albergo & Moini, 2014) is based on a logic of collusion, not strictly in the legal sense (although some processes as recent as "Mafia Capital" are emblematic of that), as more fully in the agreement, even informal, between parties that allows you to delete or suspend the competition and encourage some people rather than others, in a logic of exchange and mutual advantage. That creates a complementarity between political and economic processes.

We witness in Rome to a claiming for a modernization process, without there being a real process of modernization of the economy, within restructuring and innovating production and infrastructure sectors.

The processes of transformation of the "urban" in Rome, then, also emerges against the background of a profound change in the economy in a neoliberal sense.

A supra-regional polarity and its expansion

A supra-regional polarity and its effects on daily life

In addition to being a point of reference nationally and internationally, Rome continues to act as a major attractor locally and regionally, drawing around it a wide area of influence. In particular, Rome represents an extremely strong pole of attraction in relation to the context of central (and, in part, southern) Italy, with regard to employment, the system of opportunities, services, and so on. This is especially true for: health services (high skill and ability; also in connection to a regional policy of centralization and specialization in the organization of health); commercial attractions (business parks, large shopping centres, outlets, and so on); centres of leisure and of free time; universities (with a hugely important branch network in Lazio attracting a percentage of students from other regions that is virtually unmatched in Italy, except – to a much lesser extent – in Milan).

Rome's strong attraction is reinforced by the weakness of its adjoining territory. Rome is surrounded by a territorial "void" that strongly characterizes the centre of Italy, a "void" that covers all of Lazio, Abruzzo, Umbria and, in part, (southern) Tuscany, Marche, Molise and (northern) Campania. The closest urban and metropolitan realities, structured in a comparable way, are as distant as Florence to the north and Naples to the south. Moreover, unlike other regions, there are no medium-sized cities in Lazio and the surrounding regional areas which might constitute a significant reticular system with Rome, with respect to which they would still be subordinate (despite the distance). The growing influence of Rome, in the end, has increased its own polarization and has weakened the attraction of smaller centres, even that of the traditional and historical local poles.

The strong level of centralization is projected at the local level, thus characterizing the daily life of dwelling. It is evidenced by the inflows, the very obvious large area of influence and range of influence that covers and exceeds the square, requiring an enlargement of the area of study. Rates of over 35% of inflows derive from neighbouring provinces, and high percentages even come from other regions, producing daily commute numbers and a very high radius of mobility, which is cause for serious concern.[2]

Finally, we can recognize the existence of a close working relationship, at a supra-local level, even with Naples[3] (Lazio Region, CREL, University of Rome, 2011), as some studies have suggested (Brenner & Katsikis, 2013). A Rome–Naples "corridor", although not fully developed in terms of residential and commercial development (that is, there is no territorial continuity along this route, despite being a reference for the development of settlements), definitely exists in functional terms.

In the following paragraphs, we will deepen the socio-economic perspective, taking into account its relationship with the spatial perspective.

The territory assailed by development and its "peripheralization"

For several years, the territory of the city of Rome has been undergoing a profound change.

The territory over-run by human settlement, in particular, is increasing at a rapid pace. The vast "metropolitan" area of Rome is primarily an extension of the capital. It is Rome's way of projecting itself outward, as a city that spills beyond its traditionally consolidated borders. This is essentially due to two factors. First, there is the extension of the City of Rome, as noted, the largest municipality in Italy,[4] with a surface (1,287.36 sq km) comparable with that of the Province of

Milan.[5] The great phenomenon of urban growth has historically developed within these boundaries. Second, there is the extension of settlements and the attractiveness of the city, which have no match in the surrounding areas, and this leads to an overwhelming dominance by the capital. To study the metropolitan area of Rome means first and foremost to study the Municipality of Rome.

In many ways, in the territory of Rome, the regionalization of the "urban" assumes the character of a multiplication (and diversification) of the outskirts of the city, a sort of regionalization of the suburbs. Those suburbs have a predominantly residential function. As a result, the real estate market has a prevailing role in the processes of urban development currently under way – not the manufacturing economies nor the government of the territory.

Conversely, this urbanization process often involves a "peripheralization" of the incorporated areas, whether small towns or intermediate zones.

These new "suburbs" are, however, less violent and confrontational, more "detached" and characterized by less internal congestion. Although the interpretive centre–periphery dichotomy, traditional to Rome, has today lost its effectiveness and should be totally rethought, it does maintain some significance in terms of the inequality of development and levels of urbanity.

This vast territory, first considered an extensive "*plaga agricola*" (vast agricultural area), is today an "inhabited" territory, not only in terms of settlement, but also in terms of its use and fruition (a clear expression of what has been termed "extended urbanization"). This vast process has developed without much consideration, but has meanwhile changed the physiognomy of the city and its surroundings. The effects have been a large human settlement, a large displacement of the population with a tendency to live further and further away (as far out as Orte), an increase in commuting, an extension of the basin and the area of influence that takes on a supra-regional character. In particular, today, the focus is above all on the territory beyond (or close to) the city's ring road, the GRA, where the development of settlements in the last 15 years has occurred, and where there are major population dynamics. Between 2001 and 2011, the population within the GRA (about 70 km in circumference and with a radius of about 11 km) has not grown, but rather decreased slightly. At the same time, a strong increase (23.4%) has been seen in the population that lives between the GRA and the municipal boundary, while there has been a 16.2% increase in residents in the rest of the sample area.[6] This is, in fact, a process that had already begun before 2001, but one that has taken off in the last 10–15 years. Furthermore today, following varying lines of growth, the continuity of settlements between areas inside and outside the ring road and the neighbouring territories has become a reality: the axis to the east (towards Guidonia and Tivoli), the major south-east axis along the Via Casilina, and the axis south to the *Castelli*.

Second, there is a *relevant settlement development outside the City of Rome.* As shown by the *Atlante* (the *Atlante web dei territori postmetropolitani*), a shift of population to the municipalities outside the City of Rome has been recorded, with percentages in some cases extremely high (around 10% per year). This shift mostly affects some directions: the north (not just the Tiber valley, but also the areas of Cassia and Flaminia, the two main national roads towards the north, and that of the Bracciano lake), the south-east (limited to Colleferro), the two coastal areas (north coast and south coast), and again in part to the east and the Castelli, the hill area south of Rome (with gradients decreasing as you move outwards). This population shift evidently corresponds to a strong settlement development that also involves a high consumption of soil and a dangerous growth in impermeability of land.

The reasons to move to municipalities outside Rome are linked both to the performance of the housing market, which in Rome is increasingly unaffordable for the lower income levels, and to a search for a better quality of life, involving in this case wealthier classes as well.

Such development dynamics are strongly related to the presence of major infrastructural systems, both motorways (A1 Rome–Florence north, A1 Rome–Naples to the south, A24 Roma–Aquila eastward, the Fiano-Valmontone belt to the east, the A11 Rome–Civitavecchia and Rome–Fiumicino Airport to the north-west and on the main coast road) and of railways, with particular reference to the metropolitan and regional railways. A specific study of the local research group, deepening the *Atlante*, has revealed that almost all of the increase of settlement along the main north and south-east axis is contained within a radius of 5 km of highway exits or railway stations.

Then there is a *close correlation between income and the performance of the housing market*. The cost of housing in Rome is very high, even in comparison with the national situation. The population that moves outward is often looking for a more affordable home. It should be noted, however, that the housing market does not collapse immediately, but decreases slowly moving outwards. This corresponds to a decreasing population stratification by income away from Rome (without regard to the direction). This means that it is not (or not only) the most disadvantaged who move to the fringes, but also the middle and lower-middle classes.

Field studies developed by the local research unit show how many residents leave the City of Rome because they cannot sustain the price of the property market in Rome, but also for other reasons, such as finding an improved quality of life (also social life), a better quality environment and landscape or a better relationship with the rural context. They seek accommodation outside Rome, if anything in those territories, which are more accessible, served by rail lines or highways.

The "peripheralization" of the territories, generated by the processes of urbanization under way, is "democratic" in nature, that is, it makes no social distinctions: all varying social categories, even if with different motivations, choose to move beyond the Municipality of Rome. Instead, they generate internal borders that mark uneven situations.

This process produces situations of amalgamation, such as those that characterize the area east of Rome and the surrounding municipalities, Guidonia, Fonte Nuova, Tivoli. In these contexts, a phenomenon of social mixité (frequently advocated by many) seems to emerge, but in reality it is a juxtaposition of realities that do not communicate among themselves: exclusive residential complexes within golf courses, illegal residential areas, technological campuses, industrial zones, isolated agricultural areas, ordinary residential districts, service facilities well beyond the local level, "betting cities" (metropolitan-level gambling centres) and Roma camps.

In this evolution and in this flow to the outside, there is a redefinition of what is considered "urban" and the city itself changes its nature.

Conflicts and inequalities

At the same time, significant conflicts, especially environmental ones, are generated (d'Albergo & Moini, 2011).

The territorial reorganization does not result in a particularly pronounced and obvious stratification, nor in a particular social hierarchy, in particular that of the centre–periphery kind. Even the immigrant population shows a geography of territorial distribution without involving additional levels of inequality. Indeed, in some ways, the immigrant population looks for territories beyond the "urban periphery" of Rome where they are often targets of hostility,[7] finding in these outer territories, first, fewer conflicts and less discrimination and, second, more possibilities for reception and integration. Conversely, nowadays migrants to these territories are the greatest protagonists and the strongest engine for the recovery of the historical centres, which, because of their degradation and reduced accessibility, are by and large abandoned by the original inhabitants.

More than a geography of social inequalities one can speak of an inequality of territories, in terms of allocation of urbanity, infrastructure and services, environmental pressures, political engagement, and so on.

The areas outside the City of Rome are often those where the population in exodus settles, but with no corresponding increase in services (or at least not at sufficient levels). At the same time there are the areas to which the capital "exports" unwanted features, from junkyards to logistics hubs. For this, they are perceived as territories of a "lower level".

However, this does not mean that these territories, particularly those outside of the City of Rome (and, in particular, for instance, the whole northern area), are lacking in a specific quality, for which they are often sought out. Either because they are not yet overwhelmed by urban development or because hitherto characterized by good political management, they are often characterized by several qualities, such as a certain kind of landscape or environment, a certain quality of life, or a significant dimension of sociability.

Rather, then, these territorial inequalities determine, first, strong and unprecedented conflicts, both between the centre and the periphery (that is, between the City of Rome and some neighbouring territories), and within local areas: (1) environmental conflicts (for example, the location of new landfills or incinerators, and so on); (2) conflicts related to the inadequacy of services (for example, the great problem of commuters, or conflicts related to the closure of hospitals and health services delocalized over the territories, under a policy focused on budget cuts and on centralization and specialization of the health facilities); (3) conflicts, within the territories undergoing population growth and urbanization, between historic residents and new populations, that is, around issues of identity.

Conversely, in these areas, new forms of self-organization or collaboration are emerging between institutions and citizens (in some cases, thanks to the collaboration with the local municipalities, for example, in the management of green spaces or social problems). They express the reaction of populations "over-run" by the development against the pressure and the disease, which new situations have created.

The phenomenon of group purchasing and "zero kilometre economies" expresses the effort to rebuild a closer relationship between producers and consumers, and between urban and neighbouring territories, promoting the recovery or reactivation (or even the activation) of productive activities so characteristic of the Roman context in the past.

Urbanization: a stratification of settlements and problematic polycentric structure

Persistence and innovation in the processes of urbanization

Deepening the spatial perspective, we can recognize that some settlement processes constitute a continuity over time, while others have an innovative character. Among the first is definitely the issue of residential expansion, mentioned previously, with its associated consumption of land – which is one of the gravest phenomena in contemporary Italy – resulting in a devastating increase in impermeable land. The breadth and scope of the development of illegal settlements in Rome and surrounding territories also remains absolutely relevant and constitutes one of the most characteristic phenomena of human settlement in the Rome area, a self-made city that brings with it a model of living, based on the private interest, on do-it-yourself construction and on sociability, but also on the lack of attention to the city's public dimension, on the appropriation and control of the territory.

Within the City of Rome alone, one third of the urban residential fabric is illegal and around 800,000 inhabitants live in areas originally developed without proper planning permission (Cellamare, 2013). These values are particularly egregious for a capital of a Western nation, considered among the most developed countries. In the outlying territories, particularly in the south-east and along the coastal territories, the values of illegal building are no less significant. In some cases, the phenomenon takes on different and peculiar characteristics (Fiano Romano in the north, Velletri in the Castelli area), while some municipalities are instead able to develop containment policies and a good control of the territory (Monterotondo in the north).

These are processes that no longer concern the problem of housing and emergency housing. Rather, they are illegal settlements for convenience, if not of a speculative nature, which seek to achieve a residential quality outside the formal market, creating a *de facto* parallel one. The illegal settlement of today has a character of broad shareholder of rental income.

Other phenomena instead have rather innovative, although problematic, characteristics:

First, the great development of some centres of a metropolitan or regional functional level. They are related also to the policy of "centrality" promoted by the 2008 Master Plan of Rome, but the real process of development has reduced their significance and revealed a great ambiguity. Thought to be poles of central functions, to promote polycentrism and regeneration of the peripheries, these are mainly commercial or entertainment and leisure centres. They are localized, with regards to Rome's municipality, close to the GRA and the large road infrastructures, with a catchment area which is supra-regional and with high numbers of users. For instance, the "centrality" and the related shopping centre *Porta di Roma*, in the Bufalotta area, north of Rome, located at the intersection of the A1 with the GRA, recorded more than 16.5 million visitors a year (more than the number of tourists visiting the Colosseum; 2008 figures). It has a catchment area that includes the Umbria and Abruzzo regions, in addition, of course, to the provinces of Rieti and Viterbo. To this list we might also add some single-functional centres, such as Rome's new convention centre, the University of Tor Vergata, or some great service centres, particularly those providing health care. The development of shopping centres has taken place throughout the metropolitan territory, where there are now more than 40 of these settlements. Among these, special attention is due to Valmontone, near the exit of the A1 Rome–Naples highway, which boasts an outlet (among the largest in Italy and with the greatest economic flows) and the Rainbow Magicland amusement park. Besides, the mall is emblematic of the connection to the global networks, both in terms of intangible flows and systems and in terms of economic processes. It constitutes the territorial "dock", the local node in a global network of trade. Following Brenner (2014), "Urbanization necessarily implies the materialization of global tendencies in local contexts," and large, mostly commercial "centralities" are the expression of this pattern. This is one of the most significant development phenomena in Rome's recent development, and one that has resulted in a major territorial reorganization, emblematic of a change in lifestyle (Figure 7.1).

Second, the development of some "new cities", often without any connection to the consolidated city. In reality, these are agglomerates or nuclei spread over what was once the Roman countryside. Occasionally private or speculative initiatives, they are very often either illegal or, alternatively, "planned", as a result of plans activated in the past but left incomplete, but which are nevertheless inhabited today, despite their precarious conditions.

Third, the development of agglomerations of settlements outside the city centres (also in the neighbouring territories) and frequently close to major motorways and rail lines (more precisely to the motorway exits or railway stations), differentiated according to the territorial situations. For example, the south-east axis is composed mainly of informal settlements scattered throughout the territory, while along the northern axis new residential complexes prevail, replicating (albeit in a more socially accessible manner) the model of gated communities.

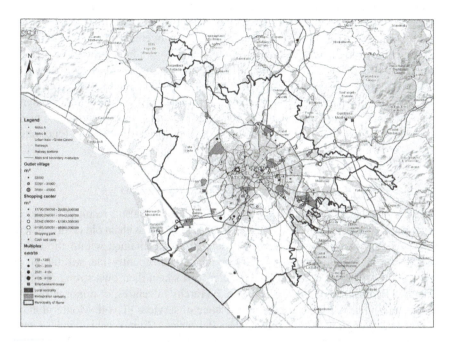

Figure 7.1 The "centralities" of the new Master Plan of Rome and the main commercial
poles

Source: Dario Colozza

Fourth, even more emblematic is the development of so-called "city of the
GRA", the evolution of the city's ring road from the boundary between the compact
city and the countryside to become a grand urban boulevard, a structural axis, and
an attractor of residential development (AA.VV., 2005; Pietrolucci, 2012; Bassetti
& Matteucci, 2013). Parallel to the large population shift to outside the GRA, this
infrastructure has become the reference axis for the localization of the main "centralities" provided by the new Master Plan of Rome (Cellamare, 2013, 2014). The
GRA was then transformed into a sort of large six-lane urban boulevard around
which the whole structure of a settlement system revolves (the "city of the GRA"
in fact). It is able to attract and absorb an extremely high percentage of vehicle trips
without requiring them to further penetrate the city. This has brought about an inver-
sion of the flows within the city; once predominantly towards the historic centre,
they now point outwards, a decidedly new phenomenon for Rome.[8]

Fifth, a reorganization of urban hierarchies, with particular regard to services,
in neighbouring territories with different situations: some functions remain in historically consolidated urban centres (that is, the Castelli area, Tivoli in the east
side, and so on), some intermediate centres which were relevant in the past (for

example Poggio Mirteto in the north) lose their role in favour of a direct dependence from Rome or other service centres. Meanwhile, some traditional service centres face an explosion in demand due to the movement of people and their intermediate role (that is, Monterotondo for schooling). Finally, intermediate service centres (such as Passo Corese, for education) are born with reverse flows.

Sixth, a renewed focus on peri-urban agricultural land and natural areas and, in particular, the parks that are gradually surrounded by residential development. These are increasingly taking on the character of "urban parks", and then a place for recreation, leisure and outdoor sports activities (primarily "urban" functions), but on a regional scale.

Spatial-temporal stratifications of the urbanization process

The current characters of the process of urbanization are also a result of historical evolution. As late as the 1970s, Rome was just a big city with an old centre, where most of the main activities were concentrated, all contained within the GRA, which was an outer limit, a limit between the city and countryside, still far out of reach. The territories bordering the smaller towns kept their own strong identity, historically rooted, and there was a local hierarchy of centres, of minor attraction because of their importance and the presence of services (Tivoli, Monterotondo, Bracciano, Poggio Mirteto, the castles, Palestrina, Civitavecchia, and so on). Rome had its strong pre-eminence over this territory, but its area of influence was definitely smaller. Even in the 1980s and 1990s, discussions about metropolitan Rome limited themselves almost exclusively to the Province of Rome, possibly excluding the municipalities of mountainous inland areas and those of the outer ring. But since the 1980s and 1990s we have witnessed a process of urban expansion, an explosion of the suburbs, mainly residential, which concerns not only Rome, but also some important centres or clusters: mainly Tivoli and Guidonia to the east, the Castelli Romani to the south, the centre of Pomezia on the Pontina main road, and the Roman coast. It is a process that overlaps the previous condition and that, in general, does not call into question the established role of some towns. It does, however, widen significantly the area of influence of Rome and results in a bleeding at the outer edges.

Finally, the current phase which is not only greatly expansive, but also multiplicative (in terms of the multiplication of centres and self-referential polarities), able to break down the historically consolidated geographies and produce a new hierarchy of centres. For instance, newly formed centres take on a greater importance than those centres recognized historically (see the relationship between the new settlement of Passo Corese and the historical centre and traditional pole of Poggio Mirteto, in the north). In other cases, we have the multiplication of dual cores with growth of those close to the major transport infrastructure (see, for example, the relationship between the old centre on the hill Monterotondo and the new Monterotondo Scalo near the railway station). These geographies of urbanization and the corresponding geographies of living overlap with one another, recombining without necessarily aligning.

The metropolitan area of Rome is therefore characterized by spatial and temporal stratifications of diverse processes and urban organizations, which often give rise to different, and quite specific, combinations: still surviving structures from pre-metropolitan (in some cases even rural) times; extending of urban and traditional metropolitan phenomena ("regionalization of the urban"); the overlap of new types of "urban" as illustrated so far.

The territory is a palimpsest of the processes of urbanization that have taken place over time, resulting in specific combinations in the various local contexts. In this perspective, the dichotomy between cities and urban, or between urban and non-urban, has little relevance. Developing what was in embryo in Lefebvre and on which Brenner elaborates, contemporary urbanization is (the outcome of) a layering of different forms of "urban", forms which often coexist and that are practised simultaneously by the inhabitants, even at varying scales (in a multi-scale dimension).

A subordinate polycentrism and non-governed development

Thanks to the development of poles, of the "city of the GRA" and processes of urbanization, which have been mentioned, a polycentrism is emerging that is calling into question, at least in part, the attractiveness of the centre of Rome. In parallel, in a complementary form, central Rome is losing its attraction and becoming primarily a district for tourism and trade and a citadel of politics. At the same time, residential functions are shrinking within the centre and the process of gentrification, prevalent in the historical centre, is now affecting the historic Roman suburbs, just outside the Aurelian walls.

While an emerging polycentrism can be recognized, it is mainly happening within the municipal boundaries (and, in fact, close to the GRA and other large infrastructures) and is being carried out all around residential and commercial "centralities", or in a few cases logistics and service centres. This polycentrism is thus without doubt a problematic one. Even outside of the City of Rome, some centres have emerged that can redirect some flows, but their strength is much lower compared with the great attractiveness of Rome, and though they are harbingers of change, they are still too weak. It is a subordinate polycentrism, still reflected on transportation flows.[9]

These processes of urbanization and urban transformation are the result of an unregulated development, played out in an environment of ambiguity and in a latent conflict between Rome and its neighbouring municipalities. On the one hand, these seek their own autonomy (even conflicting) from the dominant role of the capital. On the other, they pursue an alleged "metropolitan city" model, seeking apparent opportunities for development, but which in reality is stifling. With respect to these opportunities, the minor centres are unable to propose an independent alternative (at least in terms of production), except for those historically consolidated territories, which are structurally a bit stronger (the Castelli area, the area of Tivoli, Pomezia and the southern production zones). This situation causes conflicts and those contradictory effects, which we have mentioned. Some further

important adverse effects include the emerging difficulty of some municipalities in managing basic services (in particular schools), minor centres assailed by
population growth but inadequately equipped and lacking political support, as in
the case of Monterotondo.

Non-institutional implicit policies prevail, with on the one hand the legitimate property and real estate market and on the other illegal and private interests
(mostly in the illegal areas) playing an important role – in short, an absence of
formal policies which breeds a "formalization" of informal policies.

An anthropological mutation, a different way of dwelling

Along with the physical set-up of territory, the social-spatial relationships are also
undergoing change. Deepening the socio-economic perspective in relation with
the spatial perspective, we can see such a change, for instance, referring to some
key aspects:

- **Changes in social behaviours or in the organization of life of the inhabitants** –
  for instance, we can look at the role that free time and leisure has taken on in
  the organization of life of the inhabitants; or to the increasing commuting time
  that is considered acceptable; or the strong role that mall-going has taken on, far
  beyond the simple functional utility tied to the purchase of goods and services.
- **The relationships that evolve towards the city of Rome** – for instance,
  many reasons for moving (and also for daily moving) have, as reference, sites
  and activities throughout the greater Rome area, not just within the consolidated city. In addition, inside Rome's municipality, many poles of attraction
  are now located outside even the traditional and established city – and not just
  of the old town – leading to changes in the orientation of main flows, from
  the inside out. Therefore, changing the role and use of some sites, there are
  changes in the recognition of the values and significance of places. Flows are
  reversed – even if in limited degrees – even from Rome's municipality to the
  outside, not only for special functions and activities (such as, for instance,
  tourism and leisure time activities related to the coastal areas), but also for
  ordinary daily activities.
- **The relations that the inhabitants have with the territories in which main
  changes are developing** – for example, the residence (as a complex social activity) is increasingly divorced from the territory in which it happens, in terms of
  space and localization. Many activities (including children's schooling) are held
  elsewhere; it means in territories that do not belong to the area of daily action,
  much less in places within walking distance (or reachable by public transportation) or in a reasonable commute time. You live in several places at once. You
  live delocalized; you deconstruct memberships and the relationship with the
  places, not only in the consciousness of the people, but also in physical function.

The emergence of new socio-spatial relationships and new ways of using space
are primarily related to the reorganization of dwellings, the reorganization

of certain services (especially higher level) and the development of the commercial and recreational centres. This, however, also profoundly changes the experience of the city, our social patterns and, by consequence, the forms of the "urban". Thus, a different spatiality experienced by the inhabitants corresponds to different territorial phenomena.

Temporal aspects are also undergoing changes with a strong spatial-temporal fragmentation emerging in the lives of residents. The transformations of the urban, indeed, can be read not only in the reorganization of land and ways of using spaces, but also in a different temporality. They are reflected in the reorganization of the pace of life in the city (and its surroundings) and the pace, daily and otherwise, of its inhabitants. Here are just three examples: (1) the people who have settled in the residential enclaves in the towns north of Rome commute to the city during the day for work and also for their children's school, while they stay in the privacy of home in the afternoon and evening, with a clear separation of the two times of life; (2) shopping centres break the pattern of daily and weekly temporal rhythms, maintaining a continuity of activities throughout the day (until the end of the last film), and during the whole of the week (and especially the weekend, the period of maximum attendance, when whole days are spent in malls); (3) the "city of gambling" that has popped up on the city's eastern side, the Tiburtina "Las Vegas", lights up and comes alive only (or almost exclusively) at certain hours, the evening and night.

Many of the changes taking place are immaterial rather than spatial, in the physical sense of the term. This has been shown through the social behaviour and patterns of living, the evolution of temporality, the identifying characteristics and the relations with the places. We can also highlight the specific role played by the imaginary and by symbolic dimensions.[10] The imaginary, and in some cases the simulacra of urban environments defined elsewhere, are able to draw, define and "produce" territories.

The local as a resource

Against the backdrop of this game of distances, expulsions and the search for autonomy on the part of local territories, on the one hand, and of proximity and entrapment, often suffocating, on the other, by the central urban area, new dynamics are emerging. They are not only conflicts, but also processes of a new taking-root by recent inhabitants. These processes are not so vast but they are significant, and they often take place alongside a deep-rooted experience and feeling in which the local long-time residents continue to defend their local identity. These processes can be of a "subordinate" nature, or less extensive than the fundamental daily dependence on Rome. They are often "second generation" phenomena, affecting the newly arrived population. In some cases, the new inhabitants may revive traditional but outdated local identities, which remain in the collective imaginary, adopting the conduct of the native population (the festivals, a fictitious folk tradition, festivals, customs, and so on). In other cases, on the opposite end of the spectrum, the new grounding and taking-root of the population that moves into the external territories may be the result of a deliberate quality of life choice or merely based on the effect of daily life. A clear example is the experience of new families who build their networks around their young children's schooling. In all cases, it resumes a process of rebuilding relations within the local context, although within the varied (and often extraterritorial) relationships, which constitute the lives of the local inhabitants. Considering the social potential and the large range of environmental and territorial qualities, the "local" of the territories surrounding Rome could be considered as a "resource".

In addition and consequently, we can see in the territories surrounding Rome local forms of re-appropriation and self-management, which are relevant in many cases. Frequently, a vast social initiative and capacity of action are a response to the lack of government and institutional action, which is a general problem in these territories faced with the prevailing influence of the capital.

The lack of policy

The debate on Rome's "metropolitan area" in the 1980s and 1990s proved inconclusive, imbued with rhetoric and with no connection to the real processes taking place in the city and the surrounding areas. Regarding the institutional perspective, the resumption in recent years of discussions about the "metropolitan city" and "Rome capital", which is leading to a major reorganization, has the same characteristic of inconclusive rhetoric. In addition, such an institutional reorganization seems to be defined more around administrative questions than looking at general policies and strategic design of government. Neither the substance nor the approach to the issues seems to have changed, nor are the serious questions being asked about meaningful methods of governing these territories.

In this institutional perspective, the actual land-use and socio-economic dynamics, moreover, seem to be mainly the outcome of unregulated processes and a clear lack of comprehensive policy, with a mix of several institutional players who failed to cooperate, or cooperated only marginally. The Municipality of Rome has always focused on the problems of the city itself, perhaps considering the neighbouring territories as places to relegate certain issues (such as waste or logistics) which could not always be solved within the municipal area. The province, recently suppressed in the Italian institutional organization, was always too weak and limited its action, focusing on protecting and supporting, as far as possible, the towns in the hinterland against the influence of Rome. The region, in a difficult competition with a subject such as the City of Rome which dialogues and has close ties with the national government, preferred to deal with the management of its powers reversing the construction of any overall policies. The neighbouring territories, therefore, whenever possible, have organized themselves independently and often in opposition to the capital, trying to develop some projects on specific topics (typical and high-quality agriculture, cultural and historical heritage, the environment) that they would create a minimum of autonomy and would allow the acquisition of funding (especially in Europe through regional grants). This organizational capacity has grown especially in areas with a history of collaboration, which often has its roots in territorial federations of the old PCI (Italian Communist Party): the area of the Castelli towards the south, the Sabina and Tuscia regions towards the north. Today, the partnership focuses especially on environmental issues, whether as a response to environmental conflicts (waste), or by looking for alternative development projects, ones that exploit local resources and are not entirely dependent on Rome, as in the case of the emerging river contract initiative.[11] These are the timid responses to the lack of planning in the territories, fielded by networks of local actors, both institutional and otherwise. The lack of planning, policy and strategic vision is really the key point for the development of Rome's "post-metropolitan" territory. The newly formed metropolitan city as of yet does not seem ready to address this objective of strategic vision and governance, but surely this must be the focus of the future work of all those involved in various ways in the development of the metropolitan area of Rome.

Notes

1 The Roman economy is structurally weak, although it is now the second industrial city of Italy for number of employed in this sector. It experiences high unemployment rates and a prevalence of tertiary sectors (in particular, trade and public administration), tourism and construction. An interesting role is played by some sectors (with a high number of total employees): scientific research and development (with the presence of universities and the network of research institutes related to CNR); motion pictures, video and television, sound and music recording, programming and broadcasting activities (think of the presence, among others, of Cinecittà, RAI, Sky, and so on); production of software, consultancies and related activities (think of all the activities in support of the vast range of services and sectors of public administration).

2 There have been, however, some interesting differentiations in the distribution of internal flows: (1) the area of influence includes some municipalities of the inner belt (extending in all directions) from Fiumicino to Monterotondo, from Guidonia to Ardea, a sign of increasing transverse mobility between these municipalities (and their attractive roles); (2) the City of Rome shows a clear, strong phenomenon of self-containment (the highest in Italy in 2001 and at a similar level in 2011; see also the index of mobility); as mentioned previously, given its size it manages to keep most of the dynamics affecting its population within its city limits – to take particular account of the displacement of the municipal population outside the GRA (but we note an obvious ambiguity with respect to the attractiveness); (3) taking into account the displacement of the population outside of the City of Rome, the dependence on Rome and commuting becomes even more significant; and (4) an ambiguity, as regards the first belt of municipalities around Rome and other bordering municipalities, which show at the same time a discrete index of attraction (especially true for Ardea, Fiumicino, Guidonia and the lower zone of the Castelli Romani) and a strong (dominant) ratio of dependency; this can be understood to mark a strong connection among these municipalities – and between them and Rome – and a largely residential role (as confirmed by the displacement of the population and the already mentioned area of influence, as well as the dynamics of housing).

3 As evidenced by the number and frequency of train connections daily between the two cities (Lazio Region, CREL, Roma Tre University, 2011) and the daily flows of people between the two urban centres. The travel times of rail transport for people was reduced to 1h 10min between the two urban centres, absolutely comparable and compatible with the normal travel time within the urban (and underground) area of Rome.

4 It is also the nation's largest agricultural municipality.
5 It could also contain within its territory the top eight provincial capitals in terms of population (Milano, Torino, Napoli, Bologna, Venezia, Palermo, Firenze, and so on).
6 To be precise, Rome's population in 2011 was 2,628,026 inhabitants, while for the sample "square" the population is 4,745,458. The population of the Municipality of Rome in 2011 was 55.4% of the entire sample area. This proportion has dropped since 2001 when the city population was 2,526,342 (58.1% of the sample "square"), while that for the entire sample area was 4,348,391. In the territories outside the GRA, in the last ten years, there has been an increase of 23.4% (the population went from 568,296 to 701,429 inhabitants, while inside the GRA the increase is slightly lower) with a demographic weight within the City of Rome passing from 22.5% to 26.7%.
7 Often becoming scapegoats for the difficulties and tensions that the resident population experiences.
8 Analogously the flows from without no longer necessarily penetrate the city but rather are distributed around the ring belt.
9 Some basic effects of reorganization and restructuring of human mobility, considering even the fact that people are willing to accept slower commutes and greater distances. First, a strong increase in commuting, both by rail, still largely limited to Rome, and by road, with effects of incredible congestion, traffic and discomfort. The territory affected by this phenomenon is increasingly vast: not only the whole sample area (with the exception of the inland areas and mountain) but also areas external to it. Second, a change in the geography of the movement that are adapting to the new centrality, connected to the GRA. These phenomena mainly affect the territories outside of the City of Rome and include some areas and some centres of the first belt of municipalities outside of Rome.
10 Some examples: The new residential complexes, built along the axis of the new expansion to the north of Rome, offer not only new homes and possibly quality of life, but also promise true "models of living" or "lifestyles", as in the Bufalotta complex, in the Park of the Sabine, near the *Porta di Roma* shopping centre. This is true in the new residential enclaves in Castelnuovo di Porto, Riano, and so on, north of Rome, that replicate models of the medieval village. It applies in *Terre dei Consoli* (*Consuli Lands*), in Monterosi (north of Rome), a residential complex inserted in a golf course (actually called "golf club"), where it is explicitly sold as a "lifestyle" founded on totally private dimensions, on the quality of the environment and of the home, on a sense of security.
11 A river contract is an agreement between different actors, institutional, socio-economic and of the civil society, to support and act a common project of sustainable local development in territories strictly related to a river. The project will start from the enhancement of the river qualities, environment and landscape, local products and activities, local resources.

References

AA.VV. (2005). Grande Raccordo Anulare. *Gomorra – Territori e culture della metropoli contemporanea*, 9. Roma: Meltemi.
AA.VV. (2007). *Modello Roma. L'ambigua modernità*. Roma: Odradek.
Bassetti, N., and Matteucci, S. (2013). *Sacro romano Gra: Persone, luoghi, personaggi lungo il Grande Raccordo Anulare*. Macerata-Milano: Quodlibet Humboldt.
Brenner, N. (Ed.) (2014). *Implosions/Explosions: Towards a Study of Planetary Urbanization*. Berlin: Jovis Verlag GmbH.
Brenner, N., and Katsikis, N. (2013). Is the Mediterranean urban? *New Geographies*, 5, 215–234.
Brenner, N., and Theodore, N. (Eds.) (2002). *Spaces of Neoliberalism: Urban Restructuring in North America and Western Europe*. Oxford: Blackwell.

Cellamare, C. (2011). *Progettualità dell'agire urbano: Processi e pratiche urbane.* Roma: Carocci.

Cellamare, C. (Ed.) (2013). Roma, "Città fai-da-te" / Rome, "Self-Made Urbanism". *UrbanisticaTre – Quaderni,* 2. Roma: Università Roma Tre.

Cellamare, C. (2014). Ways of living in the market city: Bufalotta and the Porta di Roma Shopping Centre. In I. Clough Marinaro and B. Thomassen (Eds.), *Global Rome: Changing Faces of the Eternal City.* Bloomington, IN: Indiana University Press.

Clough Marinaro, I., and Thomassen, B. (Eds.) (2014). *Global Rome: Changing Faces of the Eternal City.* Bloomington, IN: Indiana University Press.

d'Albergo, E., and Lefèvre, C. (Eds.) (2007). *Le strategie internazionali delle città.* Bologna: il Mulino.

d'Albergo, E., and Moini, G. (Eds.) (2011). *Questioni di scala. Società civile, politiche e istituzioni nell'area metropolitana di Roma.* Roma: Ediesse.

d'Albergo, E., and Moini, G. (2014). *Il regime dell'Urbe. Politica, economia e potere a Roma.* Roma: Carocci.

Diener, R., Herzog J., Meili M., de Meuron P., Schmid C., and ETH Studio Basel, Contemporary City Institute (2006). *Switzerland: An Urban Portrait.* Basel-Boston-Berlin: Birkhäuser.

Harvey, D. (2006). *Spaces of Global Capitalism: Towards a Theory of Uneven Geographical Development.* London-New York: Verso.

Lefebvre, H. (1970). *La révolution urbaine.* Paris: Gallimard.

Lefebvre, H. (1974). *La production de l'espace.* Paris: Éditions Anthropos.

Pietrolucci, M. (2012). *La città del Grande Raccordo Anulare.* Roma: Gangemi Editore.

Pizzo, B., and Di Salvo, G. (2014). Il nodo della rendita immobiliare. In E. d'Albergo and G. Moini (Eds.), *Il regime dell'Urbe: Politica, economia e potere a Roma* (pp. 82–97). Roma: Carocci.

PRIN Postmetropoli. (2015). *Atlante web dei territori postmetropolitani* [Web Atlas]. Retrieved from www.postmetropoli.it/atlante

Regione Lazio, CREL (Consiglio Regionale dell'Economia e del Lavoro), Università di Roma Tre. (2011). *Roma nel Centro Italia: Mappe e sentieri del rapporto tra Roma e il territorio.* Roma: Mimeo.

Schmid, C. (2012). Henri Lefebvre, the right to the city, and the new metropolitan mainstream. In N. Brenner, P. Marcuse and M. Mayer (Eds.), *Cities for People, not for Profit: Critical Urban Theory and the Right to the City.* New York: Routledge.

Schmid, C. (2014). Patterns and Pathways of Global Urbanization: Towards Comparative Analysis. In Brenner, N. (Ed.), *Implosions/Explosions. Towards a Study of Planetary Urbanization* (pp. 203–217). Berlin: Jovis Verlag GmbH.

Soja, E.W. (1996). *Thirdspace: Journeys to Los Angeles and Other Real-and-Imagined Places.* Oxford: Basil Blackwell.

Soja, E.W. (1999). *Postmetropolis: Critical Studies of Cities and Regions.* Oxford: Blackwell.

Thomassen, B., and Clough Marinaro, I. (Eds.) (2014). *Global Rome: Changing Faces of the Eternal City.* Bloomington: Indiana University Press.

8 The Neapolitan urban kaleidoscope

Giovanni Laino

A post-metropolis?

The square chosen for this research encompasses all the towns in the Provinces of Naples and Caserta, many of those in the Province of Benevento, and the most urbanized zones of Salerno. The urban area of Naples fits within an 80 km wide and 60 km high rectangle, and thus is smaller than the square. It shares the characteristics of Naples itself: high population and building density, and a scarcity of facilities and services. The area shows a compresence of globalization dynamics and survivals of modes of production, lifestyles and spatial morphologies that have ancient roots. Over the last 20 years, the dependence of the interior on the coast has diminished. Urban sprawl has progressively become denser, eventually morphing into a continuous overcrowded area extending over about 2,500 square kilometers.

While until the 1990s it was still possible to distinguish individual towns connected to the largest city in the south, today we are confronted with a built-up continuum with evanescent boundaries. In a context which had always been marked by polycentrism, several towns and some corridors have become increasingly dense and structured. We can distinguish a de facto city constituted by Naples and the towns in its province, which form an urban continuum with other towns in the southern Province of Caserta and with those along the Salerno–Avellino axis. The boundary of this de facto city, of course, is not a line but rather a strip, but it nevertheless marks a sharp transition to non-urban territory. This speaks against Soja's understanding of this area as a post-metropolis.

In this extended city, informal and illegal activities are still rife, and the institutions appear to have been going through a long and serious crisis of governance. While the number of young people seeking employment outside of this area has increased,[1] the area has drawn in many immigrants, who have made an important contribution to the reproduction of wealth and living conditions. The prevalence of employment of these immigrants in ancillary jobs reflects the character of local society, whose economy is urban rather than manufacturing, being based on services to families, commerce and tourism. This socioeconomic structure demands and draws many subaltern low-cost workers.

Comparing the square under study with the urban areas of other large cities, there are many similarities with Milan – notably in certain metropolitan characteristics of the Neapolitan area – and, to a certain degree, with Turin, especially in the dualism between the hills and the coast or plain, respectively.

The size of the square was extended to include the islands of the Bay of Naples and the city of Salerno. The lower Latium area was also investigated to determine whether there was a densification of the corridors between Naples and Rome, but no evidence was found for this. Conversely, there is an evident and significant transformation along the Salerno, Fisciano, Solofra and Avellino axis. Within the investigated square, the Neapolitan area is certainly the most significant, because of its position looking out onto the sea, its connection with the three islands just off the coast, and its two ports with significant flows of commodities and passengers.

The ground hypothesis of the research unit was to assess the intensity of dynamics of differentiation, s-regulation and resilience in this area. Here a multi-focal, trans-scale and multidimensional perspective is adopted to single out forms and types of habitation, some of the social morphologies impacted by the ongoing transformation, and some specific settlement environments. In the following pages, contexts will be described where variations in density – along with the passage and anchoring of flows – variations in building forms, compresence of functions and populations, and of places built and managed in a more or less orderly way can be interpreted by hypothesizing spatial transformation dynamics. All this is linked to the hypotheses put forward by the national research.

Looking through the *square*

Dadapolis: a very stratified corpus of interpretations

In the corpus of studies on the Neapolitan area, we find frequent recourse to extreme images (Laino, 1989; Hughes & Buongiovanni, 2015). In many narratives, Naples is a city adrift, a land of active volcanoes, devastated by structural, environmental and sociopolitical crises. The paradigm of the crisis of peripheries in the globalized world finds a particular expression in the cognitive and legal crisis that has characterized the recent history of Italy (Donolo, 2011). All this takes place in a regional context that still shows a significant gap with north-central Italy. No matter what indicator or criterion is used to judge competitiveness and attractiveness, southern cities still lag far behind the cities of the north and center of the country. It is worth remarking that, given the limited area occupied by Naples, the regional capital, and the existence of a de facto city encompassing the whole territory of the Province of Naples and part of the territories of the Provinces of Caserta and Salerno, narrations dealing with Naples actually refer to its urban region as a whole.

Objective analyses, carefully taking into account internal articulations, without downplaying the serious problems plaguing the region, have also highlighted some positive factors and some growth dynamics. Alongside a growing deficit of development and organizational capabilities, some social groups, companies, networks and spaces are not only resisting, but even manage to be competitive and produce innovation. Today in the south, in middle-sized towns and some areas in the big cities, life conditions are quite good, especially for the upper classes. Campania,[2] which is no longer defined as the area of influence of Naples, is in the process of setting up one of the best integrated public transportation networks in Italy, in spite of serious problems of maintenance of the railway lines and the trains. Everywhere, even in the most marginal areas, one observes an extremely variegated geography of local dynamisms, although the legality of some is doubtful. Although the main poles are still the strong vertices of the regional urban structures hosting them, the historical gap between the coast and the interior has become attenuated. There is a clear trend to a decongestion of the large urban coastal areas in favor of a more polycentric distribution (Calafati, 2014, 2015). A chaotic evolution has led to the rise of an "urban region" encompassing an area extending between Mondragone, Caserta, Avellino and Salerno, which is the largest conurbation in, and the gate to, the Italian South. There are arguments in favor of the hypothesis that this is one of what Sassen (2014) calls "systemic edge", a place where the contradictions of contemporary development dynamics emerge more dramatically than elsewhere.

This area has one of the largest Italian universities – the Federico II, with over 80,000 students – and houses eight more.[3] The ports of Naples and Salerno are important, at least in terms of passenger traffic. A high-speed railway line provides easy access to Rome and the big cities of the north. Connections between southern cities, instead, are not nearly as good. It takes only one half hour more to travel from Naples to Milan than from Naples to Bari (about three hours by car or bus). Table 8.1 clearly shows that, although Turin and Milan, which are regional capitals of northern Italian towns, are about 800 kilometers from Naples, while Bari, the regional capital of Puglia, is only 250 kilometers from Naples, due to inadequacies of the railroad network train travel is much easier from south to north, between Naples and Milan, than from west to east, for example between Naples and Bari.

In the urban region, the hegemony of the capital is still strong. Naples is a city of 1 million inhabitants in the middle of a de facto city of over 3 million. To describe its conurbation with a slogan, we can say that it constitutes a compact and dense city, overcrowded with people and buildings. The vast central area is an ancient city, mostly composed of old and timeworn buildings, overall scarcely modernized, and with a very extensive historic center. It is a city that is

Table 8.1 Distances and travel times between Naples and other big Italian cities

	Distance (km)	*Travel time by high-speed train (minutes)*
Naples–Rome	225.6	70
Naples–Bari	262.0	230
Naples–Reggio Calabria	464.0	248
Naples–Milan	781.4	260
Naples–Turin	869.1	340

Source: data processing by Giovanni Laino

massively inhabited by families that are rooted in its neighborhoods or in the towns of the conurbation. It houses a mixed population and mixed activities and vital spaces. Open public spaces are scarce and small, there are few truly seg- regated areas and, compared with other European cities, there is little Cartesian specialization of space. The urban area boasts a higher young population com- pared with the worrying trend observable in other large Italian cities, but in some areas and social classes structural unemployment soars above 30–40 percent. The city does not just have unemployed individuals; it has whole unemployed families, with hundreds of thousands of people living in poverty. For many ser- vices in this area, unofficial channels are often activated alongside official ones to obtain what one seeks earlier and better. This is a scarcely disciplined, very porous and adaptive city, with widespread informal, illegal and criminal activi- ties. It is an urban area with many neighborhoods where life on the streets is intense. It is a kaleidoscopic city, with hypermodern features right next to tes- timonies from Greco-Roman history. It is the object, the scene and the site of a merging of pre-capitalist residues and signs of late modernity. The area is also an immense marketplace, with large hypermarkets as well as significant income "*à la valise*" nourished by thousands of immigrants, including many entrepreneurs, who experience the dimension of the frontier city between Tangiers, Naples and Istanbul (Peraldi, 2011). This area also houses one of the Italian hubs of Chinese entrepreneurship.

All this is situated in a very lively context, with stretches of landscape of unique beauty and archaeological sites of extraordinary significance from the Greco-Roman and later periods. At the same time, statistics for this context often show record negative figures compared with almost all European cities, in terms of the rooting of criminal clans, prison population, unemployed and poor popu- lation, the number of individuals subjected to police telephone monitoring, and small and middle-scale tax evasion. The city is also inhabited by well-to-do social groups, as well as a wealthy but hardly propulsive upper class. These families live in high-income neighborhoods and good-quality apartment buildings, and frequent exclusive milieus based along the coasts, on the Bay of Naples islands and in Cilento. For all these reasons, Naples, which was once an ancient and important European capital, offers endless opportunities and materials for more or less rhetorical narratives crafted by scholars and operators of all the media.

In this chaotic and somehow unique urban region, a social magma on volcanic soil, the global forces and fluxes of change coagulate with pre-existing living conditions and with local questions that are deeply rooted in the geo-historical and cultural context, producing a remarkable variety of worlds and landscapes, almost never marked by tranquility. According to the methodology of analysis proposed by the OECD, both as a FUR (functional urban region) and as a "de facto city" (the most restrictive interpretations of a group of contiguous municipalities whose dependence from the regional capital is especially high), Naples is the fifth largest "de facto city" in Europe and the largest Italian city, along with Milan. Its gross internal product and unemployment rate, however, make it one of the most back- ward cities in Europe (Calafati, 2016, p. 224).

However, we need to adopt a cross-eyed gaze, one that is capable of shifting between microscopic and telescopic mode, and highlighting different qualitative dimensions in socioeconomic formations to capture the kaleidoscopic character of this city. In this context, there is a prevalence of highly heterogeneous local clusters, due to the living conditions, variety of incomers, and rooting and connections with national and international networks.

The socioeconomic perspective

A fragmented context in which serious unemployment coexists with dynamic sectors

If we examine manufacturing activities in the whole of the region, we will remark the highly fragmented character of the productive fabric, which is largely constituted of micro-businesses with no more than ten employees. Only in three towns in the region is the average size of local businesses significantly higher. These are areas that have historically housed well-known industries, namely, Ferrarelle at Riardo (Caserta), the Fiat plants at Pomigliano, and Alfa Romeo at Pratola Serra (Avellino).[4]

The various actors' capacity for cooperation and integration is very weak. Still, businesses with a substantial industrial tradition in the food, textile and transportation sectors manage to continue and sometimes even innovate. After the closure of the old industrial areas in the two peripheral districts – to the east and west – of the city of Naples between the 1970s and 1980s, most industrial development areas in the Provinces of Naples and Caserta are going through a crisis. All this is taking place in a context plagued by congestion-induced diseconomies, due to a population density of 2,600 inhabitants/km² (the highest among Italian provinces) and widespread anarchy in land use.

In the square under study, there are indications that: (a) the regional fabric is developing around pre-existing historical aggregates and configurations (the industrial development areas); (b) there is a diffuse presence of small companies that have sprung up spontaneously along certain development axes, intersecting specializations and neighboring towns, and that have given rise to peculiar spatial aggregations; (c) some new industrial zones have arisen in the logistically favored area of Nola.

For all the towns in the square, seven indicators[5] were used to calculate an index of manufacturing configuration. Based on the parameters of this index, the region can be subdivided into three large areas. In the first area, which encompasses all of the Province of Caserta and much of the Province of Benevento, all the way to the Samnite Apennines, there is a weak presence of manufacturing companies. The second area, situated within the Province of Caserta, has the lowest density of manufacturing activities. The third area, encompassing a zone extending inland from the coast between Naples and Salerno to the border with Puglia and Lucania, has the best manufacturing infrastructure, although with local differences.[6]

The distribution of wealth and poverty

Information derived from tax statements does not tell the whole story, but provides useful indications.[7] My breakdown of individual tax-statement data for 2010 highlights significant differences and a variegated areal distribution. The weight of employees – for example, in the service sector – is especially evident in the provincial capitals and in the innermost suburban towns. There is a correlation between demographic decline in some towns (e.g., in the Samnite Apennine) and low average incomes. On the other hand, many of the demographically more dynamic areas do not show high income levels.

My analysis of average incomes – not including the province capitals because of the particular conditions prevailing there – has highlighted some zones with higher average wages: the town of Cassino, whose average income is comparable with that of the larger towns thanks to the presence of the Fiat plant and the revenue it generates; the Sorrento peninsula and the islands of the Bay of Naples, where tourism is a significant source of income; and Telese Terme, a town in the Province of Benevento that is an important functional center for its whole district. Again, three areas with higher average income stand out. These areas coincide with those that emerge when other indicators are used. They extend along the following directions:

– from Caserta to Cassino;
– from Naples into the Nola district;
– from Salerno through Fisciano and Solofra to Avellino, and from there into the southernmost Province of Benevento.

A more distressed area also emerges, which extends fairly continuously from the coastal towns of the Province of Caserta to Afragola and Acerra, bypassing the cluster of the economically more vital towns of the Casertano. The lowest-income towns are concentrated in the corridor reaching out from Mondragone to Afragola. The central strip running from Napoli to Caserta, which shows a positive demographic trend, occupies the middle income bracket, although in some cases the lower classes show incomes comparable with the poorer towns in the Mondragone–Afragola corridor (Villa Literno, Casal di Principe and San Cipriano d'Aversa).

Data on bank deposits and use of bank funds up to 2011 also shed light on the distribution of wealth in the area. Their results are fairly consistent with the geography outlined by other indicators.

The cartograms based on these two indicators largely overlap. Of course, wealth is concentrated in the larger cities, but among the provincial capitals Caserta, Avellino and Salerno rank higher, while the average values for Napoli and Benevento, because of internal variability and the impact of urban poverty, lie one rung below, within the same range as those for smaller towns such as Cassino, Venafro, Vairano Patenora, Santa Maria Capua Vetere, Aversa, Fisciano and Battipaglia. For this as well as other indicators, Telese Terme shows especially high values. Two cases deserve special attention. One is that of Nola, which shows the highest values of the whole square, with per capita bank deposits that are almost double those of Naples and uses of bank funds much higher than those of any other town. This result reflects the vitality of the whole area economically centered around Nola, especially in terms of commerce. The second case of especially high bank deposits and bank fund use is that of the Sorrento-Amalfi peninsula, where wealth is more widespread, as the above data on income distribution also show. Along with Sorrento, which ranks high up in these statistics, Positano and Amalfi also show significant cash flows, mainly in connection with their thriving tourist industry.

The data on income are also fairly consistent with the above-discussed distribution of manufacturing activities.

In general, and allowing for occasional variability, the clusters of towns along the Salerno-Avellino axis appear to be especially dynamic and positive, as do the cluster extending from Naples into the Nola area and that extending from Caserta to Cassino. The positive dynamics of both the islands and the Sorrento coast are confirmed – or at least not contradicted – as are the weakness of the innermost Apennine centers and the special criticality of the polarity between Castel Volturno and Mondragone, which a strong demographic increase has partly made up for.

This socioeconomic geography of the urban region is confirmed by a further simple empirical indicator: the prevalent localization of food products under geographical designation protection. Of the 13 agricultural or dairy products granted a Protected Designation of Origin, only *Mozzarella di bufala* (buffalo mozzarella) is also produced in towns in the west area (Giugliano, Pozzuoli, Qualiano, Acerra, Arzano). And of the nine products under a Protected Geographical Indication, only the *Mela annurca campana* (a variety of apple) is also produced in the Giugliano and Aversa areas.[8] Of the 29 wines produced with grapes grown in the Campania Region and somehow placed under official control and protection, only three – two under a Controlled Designation of Origin and the other under a Typical Geographical Indication – are produced in the portion of the square encompassing the coastal towns in the Province of Caserta. This can be regarded as an indicator of a scarcity of especially valuable crops in this area, which presently includes several vast unbuilt spaces. It is worth remarking that over the last few years, when serious pollution of the air, the water table and the soil of the towns in the western Provinces of Naples and Caserta came to the attention of the media, a disinformation campaign was launched that cast a negative light on the agricultural products of these towns. Scientific tests of these products have revealed that the contamination of these products is actually minimal and spatially circumscribed, whereas air pollution is still a matter of serious concern (Palestino, 2015).[9]

The spatial perspective

The Neapolitan urban region shows evident traces of its geological and anthropological history. It is a land of more or less active volcanoes, which have formed craters and elevations that were subsequently occupied by buildings in various ways, constituting barriers and filters to urban expansion. As is well known, the coast and islands have environmental and landscape features of extraordinary value. The centuriation grids of the Roman period have played an important role in land parceling and have influenced the growth and stratification of fixed social capital. The existence of marshy areas (east and, above all, northwest of Naples) that were still being reclaimed in the 1940s significantly affected urbanization dynamics until the 1960s. Especially in the western area – the Giugliano plain and the coastal stretch of the Province of Caserta – until the last decades of the twentieth century the marshes prevented towns from forming. This resulted in unbuilt plain areas, but of low environmental quality. In the area of Campania Felix, the canal known as the *Regi lagni* has influenced soil use in the area at least since the 1700s. The building of the Napoli–Bari highway (opened in 1969), the only true modern transportation route, and the obsoleteness of the east–west railway, which up to this day provides a very slow connection between Naples and the interior towards Avellino and Puglia, bear witness to another constant, namely the Apennine barrier, which inhibits expansion in that direction.

In the 1700s, Naples was one of the capitals of Europe and played an international role, at least in certain ways. It was a large town, the capital of a kingdom, much visited, attractive and always crowded with people. It was marked by a cohabitation of social functions, classes and types in a spatial as well as functional proximity that still characterizes its urban landscape today.

Ever since the early 1900s, the urban region was marked by a certain polycentrism, as it houses settlements founded in ancient times.

The limited development of the area between Naples and Rome is partly due to the character of the areas of lower Latium, where, except for the coast or the strips of land running alongside the roads originally built by the Romans, the land is less blessed with growth factors than Campania. Several data indicate that the part of the Lazio Region bordering on the Campania Region, a partly depressed area, constitutes a filter of sorts. This has contributed to limit the expansion and densification of the Rome–Naples corridor. Since the advent of high-speed trains, which take passengers from the center of Naples to the center of Rome in 70 minutes, this middle ground is skipped rather than crossed.

A first very relevant datum is the population and urbanization trend over the last 60 years (see Table 8.2).

As Table 8.2 shows, over the last 30 years, while there has been a significant slowdown in population growth, unauthorized building and the expansion of settlement areas has entailed a dramatic increase in land use, especially in the towns of the northern and western areas. This dynamic has gone hand in hand with a change

Table 8.2 Population and urbanization trend in the Naples *square* over the last 60 years

	1951–1981	*1981–2011*
Population (% increment)	70%	21%
Urbanized land (% increment)	150%	195%

Source: data processing by Fabrizio Mangoni di Santo Stefano

in the average size of families, who today live in much more comfortable conditions of density compared with the overcrowding that was common in the 1960s.

We can suppose that there has been both a process of densification with tall residential buildings, residential parks or individual tall buildings, and a large number of low houses leaving little surface for public spaces. When considering land consumption, one should also take account of the infrastructure that has modernized the area in recent years, especially in terms of accessibility. These data should not be interpreted merely by assuming major urban sprawl. In the innermost suburban rings of Naples, and in other areas as well, increasing lotting out of land has led to the formation of residential aggregates destined for various social classes.

The geographies resulting from the analysis of the data

Any assessment of the expansive dynamics of the city, even over the last 100 years, must necessarily take into account the existence of early inhabited centers around Naples, between the first, second and third ring. Such centers are sparse in the west and northwest sectors of the quadrant. The concept of conurbation aptly characterizes the area's urban and demographic expansion and densification. Until the 1990s, maps still clearly showed the web of small towns interspersed with agricultural land that surrounded Naples. Over the last 20 years, in many areas densification has unified the fabric of the conurbation, which nevertheless still shows evident hierarchies.

The city is still complex and variegated, but the landscapes of the corridors leading out from the innermost suburbs to the most important suburban centers provide visual information about what was built, what functions found space and took root, who the inhabitants are – and to what extent they are immigrants – and what building approaches were adopted.

A recent analysis of these dynamics by concentric rings (Papa & Mazzeo, 2014), while highlighting certain aspects, does not fully account for the sociodemographic dynamics of the urban region. Evidently, analyses by concentric rings still suggest that the region is isotropic. In areas with especially variable geomorphology, the anisotropy of the built city is more evident.

Data on the density of population and buildings suggest that a more complete picture can be obtained by analyzing the expansion and densification axes along which the inner city merged with the ring towns.

Of course, at least part of the densification of this polycentric constellation has involved simultaneous population growth along several axes, as can be seen in aerial maps of the whole area. Index number analysis – not included here for the sake of brevity – is a simple method to trace the history of these expansions and highlight the main poles of demographic growth.[10]

At a scale of analysis providing the best compromise between different interpretive levels, a dozen corridors can be distinguished, which branch out from the provincial capitals – principally Naples, but also Caserta and Salerno – and extend around or through physical barriers. These corridors are the result of progressive densification, at different rates and intensities, of the urban region. They run through and merge together clusters of towns. Quite often, a town – or pair of towns – with a larger population, a higher residential attractiveness, or a stronger economic base stands out; in these cases, the cluster is named after it (or them).

The region is not an isotropic table. Path dependency is also evident in this region. Geo-historical matrices have guided these dynamics.[11] This is also true of the urban grid pattern, the localization of particular productive or service activities, and the nature of connections with other lower- or higher-ranking centers.

Naples is especially influential. It is worth reminding the reader that the town is bordered to the west and the east by two volcanic areas. These comprise a rather homogeneous zone (1; see Figure 8.1) constituted by the coasts of the Phlegraean Fields and the coast of the Vesuvius area, which are much denser in buildings and inhabitants than the interior. The towns at the foot of Vesuvius form a continuum with those of the Sorrento Coast. After Pompeii and Ercolano – which are highly attractive nodes for commuting tourists, who all use the same inter-town metropolitan railway line – having passed the town of Castellammare, one reaches the communes of the Sorrento peninsula. This is an area with a strong tourist economy, where many second homes have become first homes.

These coastal areas are closely connected with those of the three islands (2; see Figure 8.1), which boast extraordinary landscapes. For obvious reasons, Procida, Ischia and Capri cannot be regarded as specific contexts of a second homogeneous area. Overall, tourism has still been unable to break free of the limits of seasonality, which does not allow the area to express its full potential.

From the capital, corridors of urban and population expansion and consolidation branch out. These, too, are influenced by the corrugated nature of the space and by physiogeographical invariants. In these towns, the urban fabric of Naples has merged with the old farmhouses and a landscape that was predominantly agricultural until the first postwar period.

Going northwest from Naples, from the Astroni crater and the Pianura neighborhood, skirting the Phlegraean Fields, there is an expansion axis (3; see Figure 8.1) extending into the plain of the town of Giugliano and on to Castel Volturno and the Varcaturo building lots. It is dotted with unauthorized buildings, but still not very dense.

Another expansion axis (4; see Figure 8.1) extends outward from the lower-income neighborhoods of northern Naples, where there are many state-financed residential buildings. Here begins a continuum of housing that merges into the first-ring towns that formerly served as dormitory suburbs from Naples – Mugnano, Marano, Villaricca and the historical centers of Giugliano and Qualiano.

Yet another axis (5; see Figure 8.1) goes from northern Naples and the towns of Arzano, Casavatore and Casoria to the towns of Afragola and the Frattamaggiore area, crossing the border into the southern Province of Caserta. This cluster intersects another westward axis (6; see Figure 8.1), which joins the towns of southern Caserta to the mouth of the Volturno River.

Then there is the axis leading from Naples Airport, 15 minutes' drive from the historic city center, through the town of Acerra eastward (7; see Figure 8.1) to Pomigliano and Nola, with branches going out toward the Valle di Lauro and Avellino (7.1; see Figure 8.1), or the inland Vesuvian axis (7.2; see Figure 8.1) extending into the Agro Nocerino-Sarnese. Finally, there is an important south–north axis (8; see Figure 8.1) going from Salerno, Fisciano and Solofra toward Avellino and Benevento.

As one can see from the map, where these eight especially evident axes are shown, three areas – defined above as emergent urban areas – can be singled out, namely the area between Naples, Avellino and Salerno, the dense sprawl in the trapeze between Arzano, Aversa, Casoria and Acerra, and the land west of it, that is, the area between Giugliano and the Domizio littoral.

Although there is evidence of typically urban lifestyles outside of the city limits as they were defined until the mid-twentieth century, as a whole the conditions observable in this area still evoke the typical dynamics of a conurbation rather than a post-metropolitan model.

The institutional perspective

The public space between a weak State and exceptional status

Ever since the cholera outbreak of 1973 and the 1980 earthquake – and even earlier, with the extraordinary policies launched to make up for the gap between the north and south of Italy – severe problems in the Neapolitan area have been regularly addressed by proclaiming a state of emergency and appointing extraordinary government commissioners, and even granting the area a sort of "exceptional status" (Agamben, 2005), often with less than successful results (Laino, 2010, 2014).

The social history of the city and its interior has thus always been marked by the ambivalence of the state. The state was strong where, when and with whom it pleased, but left ample leeway to the self-regulation of local society (De Leo, 2011). This led to the formation of certain clearly distinguishable self-ruled areas, which in some cases were left at the mercy of informal dynamics or control by criminal organizations. This was already the case with the prostitution and contraband neighborhoods after World War II, but this model was then extended to the enclaves of criminal organizations, drug-dealing squares and whole zones where storekeepers and craftsmen are forced to pay protection to criminal organizations, and then again to neighborhoods with high concentrations of poor and outcast people and/or of immigrants living under conditions of extreme social duress. These neighborhoods are left to themselves, with no social security control and no building or street maintenance. These areas of waste and disorder sometimes clearly stand out from their surroundings, but in other cases they are embedded in the urban fabric.[12]

The Neapolitan region, like other regions in the Italian south, is notorious for its criminal organizations (the Camorra), which for several decades have proved capable of networking with similar organizations in other towns and even in other continents. This national and international scope[13] has not detracted from the strong local rooting of organized crime, which originated in the low-income neighborhoods of Naples and later expanded to the other centers of the conurbation and to the

Vesuvian and Caserta areas. Reliable sources speak of a vast and diverse network of about 80–100 clans operating in the provincial territories of Naples and Caserta. These groups often form alliances or are in conflict with one another. Unlike the Mafia, this vast aggregate does not answer to a single leading body. Their leaders, who are often very young and addicted to drugs, change rapidly. These crowded social networks are rooted at several scales, from microlocal through middle-size to international, and sometimes wield considerable financial power. These networks have accumulated and keep accumulating illegal money. They provide an income to tens of thousands of people, mostly from the poorest and most culturally and socially deprived strata of the population, but also including white-collar workers, professionals and entrepreneurs.

The geography of criminal organizations deserves separate treatment. In various periods, criminal activity in the city of Naples and in the municipalities of its hinterland have shown peaks and varying densities and, over the last few years, an extreme fragmentation of criminal organizations, which is partly the result of the state's counteractive strategies and of fierce struggles between some Camorra clans.

Land policies: between activism and ineptitude

The list of urban transformation programs for the city of Naples and its urban region that have not obtained satisfactory results is very long. Only in 2004 was a process of strategic urban planning set under way, but it failed to achieve its ends. In 2006, a strategic plan known only to personnel working inside the town administration was adopted. These were two different attempts to formulate a strategic plan, both only within the limits of the regional capital, and both of which failed (Belli, 2016). This, too, is possibly yet another sign – cause and effect – of the city's crisis of governance. In a nutshell, the central city, after being managed according to an urban plan developed between 1994 and 2004, today sees the general guidelines of that plan being contradicted. Aside from the intent to safeguard a vast pre-twentieth-century building heritage, the town plan launched in 1996 and definitively approved in 2004 envisaged the creation of two large urban parks in the western suburbs (Bagnoli) and the eastern suburbs, as well as the delocalization of the airport and the revitalization of the northern suburbs – all very important objectives that were never achieved.

In 2015, the procedure for the constitution of the new metropolitan city was completed. The metropolitan city is the institution that, under the provisions of a state act,[14] is to replace the provinces. This institution is to draw up a plan for the whole metropolitan area of Naples, but as of now, at the end of 2015, the process has essentially come to a stop.

If we look at planning and policies in the Naples area, the list of plans and programs that were abandoned or proved ineffective is fairly long. Most of the municipalities in the Province of Naples have a town plan with an average age of about 20 years. The environmental protection and recovery plans for the coastal area – such as the volcanic risk prevention plan for the Vesuvian area, or decontamination programs for polluted sites – have serious effectiveness issues. The same is true of programs for the conservation and promotion of the exceptional archaeological sites of the area (notably Pompeii, Herculaneum and Oplontis) or the legalization of informal settlements. The question is complex but, in general, local populations have developed a deep mistrust of planning by national and local institutions.

In the city of Naples, from the recovery of the suburbs to the relaunching of the port, from the regeneration of the historical center to the reconversion of large former industrial plants or the many buildings that have lost their original function, urban transformation programs have overall been plagued by serious inertia. Only the new subway line – which provided an extraordinary opportunity for the recovery of archaeological testimonies and the creation of a spread-out museum of modern art – can rank as an achievement of international standing, albeit an expensive one.[15] Over the last 20 years, the road network has been modernized. It now allows transit from the coast of Caserta to the towns north of Naples and those of the Vesuvian area in less than an hour by private car.

In the urban region, policies for the recovery and regularization of unauthorized areas and buildings have also proved ineffective, as have efforts to relaunch public and private building, regenerate public housing neighborhoods built in the zone-plan areas of the towns of the conurbation after the earthquake of 1980, and reuse land and buildings confiscated from criminal organizations. This makes for a long list of ideas and programs that were never fully worked out in detail and, above all, never carried out or completed.

Ever since the second half of the 1990s, the conurbation witnessed many cases of negotiated programming with mixed, interinstitutional (often prevalently public) partners. This led to a season of intense operative planning, a crowded and promising governance workshop that sparked many initiatives but, again, did not lead to satisfactory outcomes.[16] Under the momentum of the localism season, mayors and economic actors drew up and submitted thousands of projects, many of which were not carried out or did not reach their objectives. This outcome was partly due to institutional fragmentation. Many small towns and many other intervening actors often exercised veto powers. Another factor is that several social forces and some environmentalist movements view negatively any transformation of the urban space. These forces and movements are reluctant to accept new buildings, fearing they will spoil the landscape and attract speculators. Compared with other large and mid-sized Italian towns, the Neapolitan area is marked by an unwillingness to accept urban transformation and modern architectural planning.

Over the last 15 years, many towns in the conurbation have made up for a gap by approving urban plans. The provinces have drawn up and developed some good coordination plans, but the one for Naples has not been approved yet.[17] These plans, however, were unable to put a stop to widespread and usually pulverized unauthorized construction work involving tens of thousands of subjects, including entrepreneurs engaged in building high numbers of housing units.

All this has been taking place against the backdrop of the current institutional crisis, which has also witnessed a passage from the abolition of the provincial government level to the new government organ, the metropolitan city. The balance of the last 20 years of urban planning in the municipality of Naples and in the urban region as a whole is rather disappointing: a long string of sloweddown, stopped or never undertaken policy actions. This has fostered a general strong mistrust of planning, even in its strategic version. It is very unlikely that behind all this there are hidden non-institutional control centers, where hypothetical great speculators think up far-ranging programs to lay their hands on the city. Because of the climate of widespread mistrust in local institutions, between the end of 2013 and the beginning of 2014 the national government (once again!) entrusted some urban-scale policy actions to special commissioners, partly curtailing the powers of local authorities. This decision was a reaction to the inertia and overall ineffectiveness of local institutions. Thus, to unblock the transformation of the Bagnoli area, in September 2015 the prime minister appointed a new government commissioner.

The large population of Naples and the Campania Region grant them a significant weight in the election of the national parliament. Over the last few years (2010–15), both the Region and the Province of Naples have been governed by a center-right majority, mainly because of voter dissatisfaction with the left-wing governments of the first decade of the new century. Because of the serious crisis in the collection and disposal of urban solid waste, widespread corruption and a general inability to effectively address problems in the province or the region, after 15 years of center-left government (1994–2010) the right wing recovered voter consensus. The overall crisis of all the parties, however, is transversal and seems to be sweeping away all pre-existing organizations. Today, in 2015, the Campania Region again has a governor elected by the center-left, the former mayor of Salerno, who, however, is under political and media attack for having been found guilty in a trial for administrative misdoings.

The urban region of Naples combines a deeply rooted backwardness with typical dynamics of late modernity. This is why some researchers propose an approach that can be summarized in the slogan "Let's make Naples more like New York than like Calcutta!" – a paradigm of the crisis of suburbs in the globalized world.

When assessing urban and regional policies, it appears that, in spite of widespread collusion with irregular and informal ways of doing things, what emerges from the news reports of the last few years is not so much a corrupt political and administrative class bent on cutting illicit deals, or an active and predatory entrepreneurial class, but rather a public ruling class displaying serious inability to rule, address complex issues, and conceive and share visions, trust, hope and solutions for at least a part of the problems on the table. This public class is trapped into agendas dictated by emergency rather than programming. It no longer seems capable of combining knowledge and decision-making ability with an orientation toward the common good. This public class also includes university scholars, who rarely manage to come up with ideas that can actually be used to confront the problems plaguing civil cohabitation and development opportunities in the area.

Waste lands and the mapping of urban distress

My cartogram of the index of urban distress[18] confirms some evidence deduced from other indicators and from an empirical survey of the functions that more evidently point to the existence of a gap[19] (a significant presence of low-income housing units, a large percentage of poor people serving as a sort of resident reserve army, and the presence of landfills, abandoned quarries and waste pellet storage areas[20]).

Outside of the "volcanic" environment of the regional capital, which has essentially merged with the towns of the first ring – especially those of the Vesuvian coast and to the north – the quadrant can be divided into three large areas. To the east, there is a vast expanse we could characterize as an area of emergent urbanization. In this area, living conditions are generally better than elsewhere in the square under study, and there is more resilience (apart from serious pollution of the Sarno River). This area includes much of the Vesuvius district, the Agro Nocerino-Sarnese, and the whole less well-known area between Salerno and Avellino extending inland towards Benevento. Here an overall better standard of living seems to have taken hold, in spite of a relative distance from metropolitan-type services. Inside this part of the quadrant, there is a very evident corridor between Naples and Nola, connected by roads and railways, which shows especially high economic dynamism and a stronger and less vulnerable population.

A second area is constituted by the clusters of towns to the north, between Naples and Caserta, Arzano, Aversa, Casoria and Acerra. This can be defined as an area of densified urbanization. It is more heterogeneous and crowded, and several indicators point to a more variegated and contradictory reality, with a compresence of different conditions. Some towns or smaller socio-geographical enclaves show an overall trend to resilience and evolution. Other areas seem to be more affected by the crisis, often displaying high concentrations of critical factors. These areas are characterized by heterogeneity and a differentiation of the qualities of space and buildings, of living conditions, of the social and professional profiles of the inhabitants, often showing fragmentation even within a single municipality.

A third large area to the west is marked by outright fragility. It extends between Giugliano and the Litorale Domizio. Inside it, the area of Castel Volturno stands out as the largest and most evident area of widespread informality and waste landscape.[21] The map highlighting the distribution of urban sprawl indicates that until 1961 there were very few buildings in the area extending from the Phlegraean Fields and the Volturno all the way to the municipality of Castel Volturno. This was due to the area's marshy soil, its scarce agricultural value and, probably, the structure of land ownership.

From the Agro Aversano cluster, this vast area encompasses the whole plain of Giugliano and extends from there to include Casale di Principe, Villa Literno and Castel Volturno. According to a variety of indicators, the area is in a very critical condition. It was stigmatized in news stories as an extreme area, the reign of "Gomorrah," a land of irreparable lawlessness, with significant quotas of immigrants exposed to mistreatment by human flesh dealers and employed in precarious and underpaid slave labor. For years the town of Giugliano – the third most populous in Campania – was ruled by a prefect after the town government was dissolved. Here there are large open-air storage areas for waste pellets, as well as several major landfills, such as the one in the RESIT area,[22] a paradigm of illegality, with tons of toxic waste buried in it over the years. This area appears to oscillate between serious absenteeism on the part of the government, a significant capacity of criminal organizations to influence things, and the government's inclination to proclaim emergency measures to oppose the criminal organizations and their infiltration of public administrations.

Some investigations by our research group (De Leo, Lieto and Palestino) have put forward the interesting hypothesis that at least some areas in this part of Campania have served as waste dumps for towns in central and northern Italy. This hypothesis is not based only on the well-known scandal of the burying of noxious industrial waste, but also on other empirical evidence. Even the history of criminal organizations appears to indicate that the most powerful groups in the city of Naples are tending to branch out into the towns of the Province of Caserta.

In terms of a social division of space resulting in the formation of wastelands with socio-geographical enclaves where urban distress is especially severe, it is important to stress that the Naples area is highly heterogeneous. Like few other cities, the crowding together of bodies and buildings displays significant diversity, a remarkable spatial or even functional proximity of very different actors, social classes and practices. Homogeneous socio-geographical areas do exist, but are rarely vast, and lie right next to areas characterized by the same variety of buildings and people, down to a very small scale.

This is why the de facto city of Naples never appears as an area where functional and social division has taken on the Cartesian forms observable in other cities in northern Italy or in some European capitals. In the Neapolitan area, social hierarchies are apparently less steep than elsewhere and their geographical distribution appears confusing not only to the casual observer but also to the analyst. Even though socially peripheral zones are as evident in Naples as in other towns, its territory overall appears as an example of spatiality of compresence of social profiles and figures, living conditions and different types of buildings. This overlapping blurs but does not eliminate the social division of space. One of the peculiar characters both of local society and of the inhabited space is precisely the coexistence of values and lifestyles, practices and populations that are often rooted in different and sometimes polarized vital worlds or "operational landscapes." From the guts of the historical center to the most out-of-the-way locations in the towns of the conurbation, we observe forms of habitation and modes of space use and cohabitation rooted in the area's pre-capitalist history coexisting with the typical markers of contemporary globalization. There are indeed spaces resembling gated communities, but they are fairly small or embedded in contexts charged with confused and heterogeneous variety.

It will be interesting to investigate at least some significant forms of resistance and resilience thanks to which, although occurring in generally critical conditions or nearly extreme situations, these micro-sections of the socioeconomic fabric manage not only to survive, but also to enact processes of human promotion. They are usually well connected to some local dimensions and, at the same time, included in middle- and long-distance networks providing opportunities and allowing them to find new horizons of meaning and regenerate trust and hope. This is why this research work inevitably also relied on interviews and field investigations (see Laino & Manunza, 2014).

Conclusions: syntethic map

Soja and Brenner's theoretical analysis of the Naples area is stimulating. The present author has some reserves, however, regarding the applicability of the categories of these eminent scholars to southern Italian cities. Here different evolutionary dimensions of land transformation need to be highlighted. These dimensions, here as elsewhere, are multiscale and connected to global processes. We need to definitively go beyond an approach wholly based on development stage theory (Rostow, 1960) which construes the Italian South and its urban areas as a "not yet" compared with more advanced areas. There are good reasons to still regard the whole of southern Italy as essentially a periphery of the Rhine megalopolis. An invisible line extending from Lisbon through Barcelona and Naples to Sarajevo appears to mark the boundary between an objectively wealthier, more Westernized and modernized North from an equally globalized but less developed South. This satellite view highlights important dimensions and issues, but blurs other equally important aspects of life, social interaction and land transformation. An Olympic viewpoint opens the mind, but many important things elude us unless we frequent sewers, streets, homes and social webs.

Territorial analysts intending to develop truly useful models for the investigation of the relations between space and society, selecting the most significant dynamics to draw up maps, always run the risk of being confronted with the aerial photographer's dilemma[23] illustrated by the Lynds in the 1930s. Furthermore, at this scale, too, scholars should strive to make clear if their interpretations of the histories and specific conditions of Mediterranean welfare (Morlicchio et al., 2002; Maddaloni, 2015) have implications in terms of forms of reproduction and territorial dynamics. There are many clues and good arguments for trying to single out specific forms of evolution of southern cities. These forms need to be investigated by drawing up good maps, but not relying on these maps only.

If we accept the challenge of trying to draw up a zenithal map for this regional portrait, we can imagine a first layer highlighting the main geo-historical matrices of the Neapolitan region, which have been at work for thousands of years and have always played an essential role in the region. These conditions have determined a strong path dependency. The history of this area in the *longue durée*, the fertility of its soil and its geomorphology have imparted a very specific character to its territorial. Along with evident positive features, the territorial here still shows the signs of a certain harshness of living conditions determined by marshlands or high water-table areas that limited its use and had an impact not only on agriculture, but also on the forms of production and habitation, the functions and the practices of large socio-geographical districts.

As the present chapter has repeatedly stressed, this is a highly crowded area marked by the simultaneous presence of more or less polarized differences. More than elsewhere, this area produces an impression of disorder, of being a spatial and social melting pot rather than an ethnic one. This disorder is largely a result of the role of the state in Italian society, in general, and in the Italian South, in particular.

By intersecting different features, partly derived from the present author's analysis of socioeconomic data, some relatively more homogeneous intercommunal areas can be singled out, which are referred to repeatedly above. In some cases, these areas have a clear and deep-running territorial structure arising from years of evolution.

To overcome the aerial photographer's dilemma, we need to adopt a "cross-eyed", multifocal, trans-scalar, and multidimensional gaze, mistrusting overhastily traced boundary lines. We need to go back and forth between cartograms high-lighting statistical trends, observations made in the field and interviews with and life stories of individuals from different social strata inhabiting different districts in the study area.

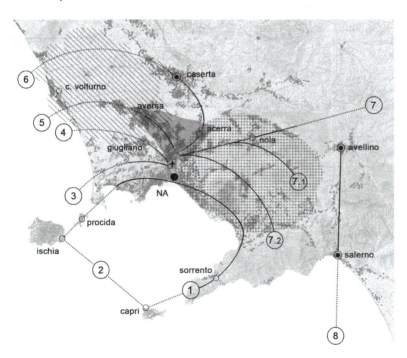

Figure 8.1 Synthetic map of the Naples *square*

Source: Author's elaboration

Besides highlighting homogeneous areas, it is useful to give at least a sense of the hubs of the main anthropic networks where, thanks to favorable local conditions, some nodes and segments of these networks – significantly connected at various scales, from local to regional, interregional and international – constitute operational networks.

A city is constituted by a number of hubs acting as pumps attracting and relaunching flows and exchanges of various kinds of resources. Examples of such hubs/pumps include universities, large hospitals, large market areas and even criminal clans with strong local roots, although capable of managing relations at other scales, from local to international. Other hubs include religious communities aggregating thousands of people in various towns in the conurbation, the plants of national or international businesses, banks and especially valuable territorial attractions drawing many visitors. The many places where social interaction occurs, deploying heterogeneous social contents and types reproducing the evolution of society, produce densely significant exchanges of goods, services, discourse fragments, cultural routines, and social selection and opportunity systems. The standards of living of the inhabitants – which do not depend merely on their income, but in which income plays an important role – are a result of relations between environmental quality, space conformation, the qualities of social fixed capital, soil uses, modes of habitation, the quality of buildings, and the anthropological, productive and socioeconomic dynamics generated by the "pumps" stimulating social interaction. In the Neapolitan area there are often critical problems in these dynamics. Here, as in other areas, the authorities' ability to manage public spaces and services is going through a serious crisis, marked by the absence of medium- or long-term strategies to govern ongoing change processes.

This research has investigated the presence and living conditions of immigrants (themselves witnesses of a world of worlds), and the geographical sedimentation of a lawlessness determined by criminal organizations, pollution and unauthorized building. It has also investigated significant social organizations and morphologies of resilience, from some productive sectors – agriculture, food, clothing, transportation and airplanes – to environmental justice movements and social groups that not only keep up resistance in areas affected by a serious crisis and a lack of opportunities, but sometimes manage to generate wealth, human promotion and virtuous circles of cohabitation. Some small groups try to produce quality crops and livestock products, which they trade over short or long supply chains.

At present, it is not easy to point out even the most evident among these hubs, which have sprung up in places where historical, social and environmental conditions and the strategies of groups – not only local ones – and webs of economic and social processes have significantly intersected with pre-existing local features, putting their stamp on the local landscape. My study on migrant presence has highlighted some concentrations showing what seem to be significant associations with local environmental and socioeconomic features.[24]

This relative functional distinction and social subdivision of the study quadrant is also apparently consistent with the localization of the most evident hubs of criminal organizations. Although part of national and international networks, over the last decades these organizations have rooted themselves strongly in the territory of the Province of Caserta as well as in several towns of the interior. They are less present, however, in more dynamic and less disorderly areas.

It is even more difficult to single out the (usually small) networks enacting resistance, resilience, activation and social mobilization practices. These include environmental movements and a myriad of organized groups, fragments of movements which, often relativizing expectations of state intervention, have been engaged for years in virtuous productive activities, social integration programs, environmental justice practices and the promotion of public heritage and cultural capital.

If we try to imagine the geographical distribution of these networks, a number of areas emerge where porous environmental conditions result in friction spaces connected to the characteristics of the urban area we have inherited from the twentieth century, with its load of contradictions.

Further investigation is needed, as well as a reflection on the possible contributions that other interpretive grids may offer. The study carried out in the framework of the PRIN Postmetropoli research confirms the need to build a different interpretive model, better suited to this specific social and geographical context.

Notes

1 On the emigration of young southern Italians to northern Italy, compare Svimez (2015, p. 20) and Istituto Giuseppe Toniolo (2016).
2 Campania is a region in southern Italy. It extends over 13,670.95 square kilometers and has a population of 5.8 million. It is the third most populous region in Italy, and the most dense. It has 550 municipalities, a metropolitan city (Naples) comprising 92 municipalities, and four more provinces with their respective capitals, namely Salerno, Caserta, Avellino and Benevento. Campania is one of the 20 regions in the country which have a governor elected directly by the people and a council which approves regional laws.
3 University studies in the South are going through a serious crisis. The percentage of university graduates in the Italian South is 18.2 percent of the population, less than that of Turkey (19.5 percent). The context is that of a nationwide negative trend in university enrollment.
4 See PRIN Postmetropoli (2015).
5 Paola De Vivo, belonging to our research group, has processed data on manufacturing activities according to the following indexes: entrepreneurship; activity; presence; density; employment; overall specialization; and average size of businesses.
6 This geography constitutes a first layer, which, superimposed with those obtained from the reading of other data - including environmental indicators and socioeconomic indicators, such as income – allows a synthetic interpretation of living conditions in different parts of the square.
7 Here, too, in assessing the data for the provincial capitals we must allow for their large populations; the single general value for the whole town blurs the strong differences between very polarized socio-geographical areas, including some very small ones.
8 Compare the official site of the Regione Campania (http://www.agricoltura.regione.campania.it/tipici/indice.htm).
9 The differentiation, s-regulation and resilience of these areas give a sense of the complexity of their economic, social and cultural dynamics. In general, several indicators appear to confirm the subdivision into three large areas outlined below.

10 For the present research, I investigated index numbers for the population from 1951 onward for six census periods in all the towns of the conurbation. I will be presenting the results of this analysis in a more extensive report.

11 These town clusters are quite consistent with the zones singled out by the experts of the Provincial Plans and the Regional Plans, and with the geographies outlined by several other analysts.

12 Over the last few decades, these dynamics have spilled over from Naples into some of the surrounding towns. The Vesuvian area (with the epic of Raffaele Cutolo) and later especially the areas north and west of Naples loom large in the public imagination. Media attention has been riveted particularly by the rooting of criminal clans, the burying of toxic waste and the large groups of immigrants, who contribute significantly to the economy in some areas and experience harsh living conditions in others.

    The areas used for many years as more or less illegal waste dumps or to bury toxic waste are typical drosscapes, tolerated off-limits areas, which according to some legal investigations in quite a few cases were even co-planned with exponents of the public administration.

13 The dramatization of this situation in recent popular books, films and TV series (notably *Gomorrah*) combining fiction with social and anthropological analysis of criminal organizations, would deserve a separate study.

14 Delrio Act (Act no.56 of 7 April 2014, "Disposizioni sulle città metropolitane, sulle province, sulle unioni e fusioni di comuni".

15 The stations of the new subway line were planned by renowned architects such as Gae Aulenti, Karim Rashid, Alessandro Mendini, Dominique Perrault, Óscar Tusquets Blanca, Massimiliano Fuksas, as well as some well-known Neapolitan architects. Works by famous contemporary artists were commissioned for several of these stations.

16 Some of the best known among these projects include the TESS for the Vesuvian coastal area, the Città del Fare for the towns northeast of Naples, the CIS in Nola, the Tarì, and the Città dell'Oro in Marcianise.

17 While waiting for the plan to be approved, the provincial government of Naples has adopted some guidelines to orient the decisions of the town planners.

18 See PRIN Postmetropoli (2015): "Indice di sofferenza urbana", § i.2.12. Interestingly, if we partly filter out the weight of the inactive population from this index, some disadvantaged areas emerge more sharply. The urban distress indicator is possibly distorted by the dependency index (number of elderly and minors). It is very likely that if we decreased the weight of this component certain polarities of serious social and environmental distress would stand out more distinctly.

19 Federica Palestino, a member of our research group, has specifically investigated this gap and summarized the results of her investigation in a paper (Palestino, 2015).

20 The so-called *ecoballe* are pellets of often undifferentiated RDF. They are regarded as special and non-transportable waste. Over 6 million tons of these pellets were produced between 2002 and 2008 and placed in numerous storage sites in the Province of Naples (4 million in Giugliano); each site is rented. The new president of the Campania Region has decided to use European funds to take the pellets to plants outside the Region of Atlante for appropriate treatment.

21 Aside from the above-mentioned geo-historical invariants, which could partly explain the present situation of these areas, there was an important phase in the history of the whole region when, because of the earthquake of November 1980, thousands of families were evacuated from buildings in the center of Naples that needed to be checked and repaired, and "deported" to second homes in the communes of Mondragone and Castel Volturno. This event marked a turning point in the degradation of this area.

22 The Resit area, which lies within the municipal limits of Giugliano, is highly polluted because it included quarries used as dumps for dangerous and toxic waste, partly from companies in northern Italy.

23 The Lynds introduced this definition in their methodological introduction to a case study to indicate the inevitable loss of detail that ensues when an observer raises their viewpoint high enough to take in a region in its entirety (1929, p. 56).

24 While at Mondragone, Castel Volturno and, in general, the coast of the Province of Caserta and the towns of the Giugliano area the presence of communities of exploited immigrants is more evident, in the inland Vesuvius area there seems to be a prevalence of immigrants working in manufacturing activities. On the islands, along the most dynamic coasts, and in some parts of the cities, some communities and groups of immigrants, although largely employed in ancillary jobs, have achieved better integration.

References

Agamben, G. (2005). *State of Exception*. Chicago: University of Chicago Press.

Belli, A. (2016). *Memory cache: Urbanistica e potere a Napoli*. Naples: Clean.

Calafati, A. (Ed.). (2014). *The Changing Italian Cities: Emerging Imbalances and Conflicts* (GSSI Urban Studies Working Paper No. 6). L'Aquila: Gran Sasso Science Institute.

Calafati, A. (2015). On the Economic Base of the European Cities. In C. Bianchetti, E. Cogato Lanza, A.E. Kercuku, A. Sampieri and A. Voghera (Eds.), *Territories in Crisis: Architecture and Urbanism Facing Changes in Europe* (pp. 49–62). Berlin: Jovis Verlag.

Calafati, A. (2016). Napoli la costruzione di una città strategica. In G. Punziano (Ed.), *Società, economia e spazio a Napoli: Esplorazioni e riflessioni* (Working Paper No. 28, pp. 223–233). L'Aquila: GSSI Social Sciences.

Castel, R. (2009). *La montée des incertitudes: Travail, protections, statut de l'individu*. Paris: Editions du Seuil.

Centro Studi Unione Industriali di Napoli. (2014). *Nuova perimetrazione e nuove funzioni per le Città metropolitan: Il caso di Napoli*. Napoli: Camera di Commercio di Napoli.

De Leo, D. (2011). Public Sphere and Illegal Settlements: A Case from the Naples Metro-region. In M. Cremaschi and F. Eckardt (Eds.), *Changing Places, Urbanity, Citizenship, and Ideology in the new European Neighbourhoods* (pp.199–220). Amsterdam: Tekne.

Dines, N. (2012). *Tuff City: Urban Change and Contested Space in Central Naples*. New York and Oxford: Berghahn Books.

Donolo, C. (2011). *Italia Sperduta: La sindrome del declino e le chiavi per uscirne*. Roma: Donzelli.

Gasparrini, C. (2015). *In the City, on the Cities. Nella città, sulla città*. Trento: List Lab.

Hughes, J., and Buongiovanni, C. (2015). *Remembering Parthenope: The Reception of Classical Naples from Antiquity to the Present*. Oxford: Oxford University Press.

Istituto Giuseppe Toniolo. (2016). *La condizione giovanile in Italia: Rapporto giovani 2016*. Bologna: il Mulino.

Kastani, C., and Schmid, C. (2015). Napoli, Italy. In ETH Studio Basel. (Ed.), *The Inevitable Specificity of Cities* (pp. 30–57). Baden: Lars Müller Publishers.

Laino, G. (1989). Flanery. In F. Ramondino and A. Muller (Eds.), *Dadapolis: Caleidoscopio napoletano* (pp. 383–386). Torino: Einaudi.

Laino, G. (2010). The Waste Crisis in Naples: The Need for a Rationality that is Pluralist, Hybrid and Contingent, as well as Responsible and Detailed. *DISP*, 180, 115–126.

Laino, G. (2014, 18–20 June). *Which Post-metropolis from the South?* Paper presented at the EURA Conference: Cities as Strategic Places and Players in a Globalized World. Paris.

Laino, G., and Manunza, L. (2014, 18–20 June). *Which Post-metropolis from the South?* [Video]. Presented at the EURA Conference: Cities as Strategic Places and Players in a Globalized World. Paris.

Maddaloni, D. (2015). Il modello mediterraneo di Welfare: Enrico Pugliese e la ricerca sullo Stato sociale in Italia. In S. Boffo, E. Morlicchio, G. Orientale Caputo and E. Rebeggiani (Eds.), *Mezzogiorno lavoro e società. Scritti in onore di Enrico Pugliese* (pp. 153–170). Napoli: Liguori.

Moe, N. (2002). *View from Vesuvius: Italian Culture and the Southern Question.* Berkeley: University of California Press.

Morlicchio, E., Pugliese, E., and Spinelli, E. (2002). Diminishing Welfare: The Italian Case. In G. Scaffner Goldberg and M. Rosenthal (Eds.), *Diminishing Welfare: A Cross National Study of Social Provision* (pp. 245–270). Westport, CT: Auburn House.

Palestino, M.F. (2015). How to Put Environmental Injustice on the Planner's Radical Agenda: Learning from the Land of Fires – Italy. In M. Macoun and K. Maier (Eds.), *Book of Proceedings AESOP Prague Annual Congress 2015: Definite Space – Fuzzy Responsibility* (pp. 2576–2586). Prague: Czech Technical University.

Papa, R., and Mazzeo, G. (2014). Characteristics of Sprawl in the Naples Metropolitan Area: Indications for Controlling and Monitoring Urban Transformations. In B. Murgante, S. Misra, A.M.A.C. Rocha, C. Torre, J.G. Rocha, M.I. Falcão, O. Gervasi et al. (Eds.), Computational Science and Its Applications – ICCSA 2014:14th International Conference, Guimarães, Portugal, June 30 – July 3, 2014, Proceedings, Part VI (pp. 520–531). *Lecture Notes in Computer Science,* 8580. Springer International Publishing Switzerland.

Peraldi, M. (2011). Città frontiere euromediterranee e capitalismo mercantile transnazionale. In S. Palidda (Ed.), *Città mediterranee e deriva liberista* (pp. 27–43). Messina: Mesogea Edizioni.

PRIN Postmetropoli. (2015). *Atlante web dei territori postmetropolitani* [Web Atlas]. Retrieved from www.postmetropoli.it/atlante

Rostow, W.W. (1960). *The Stages of Economic Growth: A Non-Communist Manifesto.* Cambridge: Cambridge University Press.

Sassen, S. (2014). *Expulsions: Brutality and Complexity in the Global Economy.* Cambridge, MA: Harvard University Press.

Svimez. (2015). *Rapporto Svimez 2015 sull'economia del Mezzogiorno, Introduzione e sintesi.* Retrieved from http://www.svimez.info/images/RAPPORTO/materiali2015/2015_10_27_linee.pdf

9 Palermo

An incomplete post-metropolitan area

Francesca Lotta, Marco Picone and
Filippo Schilleci[1]

On the threshold of the post-metropolis

Palermo is the most populated and important city of Sicily, and the fifth most populated city in Italy.[2] Although it is widely known for its marginality (Cannarozzo, 2000; Pinzello, 2003; Rossi Doria, 2003; Rossi Doria et al., 2005; Lo Piccolo, 2009) and the presence of criminal organizations (mafia), Palermo has long played a key role in the Mediterranean basin. One of the traditional clichés connected to Palermo and Sicily is that its people have developed a passive attitude as a consequence of the many foreign dominations of the island (starting from its foundation, Palermo has been ruled by the Carthaginians, the Romans, the Arabs, the Normans, the French and the Spanish). As for all clichés, this one is partly true, but cannot be considered the only reason that explains the complex situation of Palermo.

Most scholars point out that the city of Palermo has never been a metropolis (Giampino et al., 2014), and therefore there is no way it could be considered a post-metropolis, having almost entirely skipped the metropolitan phase. However, history should not be considered as a straight line connecting the past to the future through the same regular path: there are lots of twisted patterns and recurrences in the case of Sicily. Thus, even Palermo might show a few traits that characterize other post-metropolises. This does not mean that we are claiming Palermo's post-metropolitan nature as an easily acceptable status. However, the economic crisis has blurred the line between northern and southern Italy in many ways, and Palermo seems to undergo a new stage in the relationships with its hinterland and the other parts of Italy, as we will show here.

Given the marginality of its geographical position, we will present the Palermo region through its *area metropolitana* (metropolitan area), an administrative entity which was introduced in Sicily in 1986 and conceived to include 27 municipalities from Partinico (west) to Termini Imerese (east). These 27 municipalities include Ustica, a very small island northwest of Palermo, which arguably shows peculiar traits and cannot be related to the other municipalities (Piraino, 1988; Di Leo & Esposito, 1991; Grasso, 1994). The *area metropolitana*, although expectedly operative since 1995, has actually never played an active role in this region (Di Leo, 1997; Schilleci, 2005, 2008a, 2008b). Today, the *Regione Sicilia* (the administrative local authority) is working on a reform that should lead to the *città metropolitana* (metropolitan city) of Palermo (Lotta, 2015). We have chosen to consider the metropolitan area in order to take into account the relationships linking Palermo to its hinterland, but we have to stress that this condition is quite different from other cases in Italy, as western Sicily is largely surrounded by sea and has only minor relationships with the rest of Italy.

As a consequence of the geographical and historical conditions of western Sicily, considering a 100 × 100 km *square* for Palermo seemed an inconvenient solution, as the *square* would include both large sea areas and a few municipalities that do not have strong connections to Palermo. Therefore, in this regional portrait we never refer to a *square*, but rather to a *tessera*, a tile of a larger mosaic. We propose the word *tessera* for two main reasons: first, it breaks the overly rigid geometry which the *square* implies, and which seems hardly applicable to any part of Sicily; second, this Latin word recalls the ancient history of the island, suggesting that this particular geographical area, despite its long-lasting ties to the rest of Italy, still demands to be considered as a standalone case for its peculiar historical, geographical and cultural specificities. Our *tessera* is 40 × 100 km wide and embraces the metropolitan area of Palermo.

The two main points we want to highlight here revolve around the presence of foreign citizens (migrants) in Sicily and housing. Regarding migrants and migrations, the obvious starting point is that Sicily holds a strategic position in the Mediterranean area, and it is often used as an entranceway for those (sometimes illegal) migrants looking to reach northern Europe (we refer, for instance, to the famous case of Lampedusa). However, there are many more legal migrants moving to Sicily for other reasons in recent years, and we will try to discuss the reasons why.

Housing is also an important topic, considering the very high number of buildings that have been confiscated from mafia and other criminal organizations, along with the Sicilian incapability to facilitate the relationships between strong urbanization processes and the traditional presence of agricultural lands.

The following sections will present some data regarding the *tessera*. Data are divided into three sections: a socio-economic outlook describing the characteristics of demography, employment and income in western Sicily; a spatial analysis of housing and land use; and finally an institutional description of the administrative state of the art in Palermo and its surroundings. Each section describes the most consolidated trends in this area, but also discusses the most innovative changes and the challenges this area is facing in recent years. The final section points out some concluding remarks and puts the Palermo case within the theoretical framework of the post-metropolitan discourse in Italy.

Looking through the *tessera*

Socio-economic perspective

In order to evaluate the socio-economic outlook of Palermo and its *tessera*, we will analyze several data related to the following domains:

– **Demographics** – population and density; housing dispersion index; dependency ratio; foreign citizens; mobility index.
– **Economics** – unemployment rates; employees by industry sectors; average per capita income.

The generic outlook of Palermo has already been presented above, and is closely related to the cliché of a marginal condition, quite far from the standards of the high-income, high quality of life of northern Italy. Although it would be foolish to deny such a picture, which is historically rooted in the social, cultural and economic peculiarity of this Mediterranean island, it is also worth noticing that this area has been able to express several innovative tendencies in recent decades, and that more peculiar propensities have come out in recent years, as a consequence of the economic crisis and the general deterioration of the socio-economic status in Italy. It is true that the Palermo *tessera* still remains a deprived area if compared with most of the northern Italian regions, but the gap appears to be getting somehow smaller and, most importantly, suggests that Palermo might have some hidden resources (still to be fully developed) that could help it find a new place and role in post-metropolitan Italy.

The first set of data we are going to present is related to the demographic domain, and starts with the simplest numbers: the ones on population. The population trend in Palermo and its surrounding areas proves quite similar to most other major Italian cities, with the main city initially attracting population and then losing it to its surroundings. This may be considered a traditional case, as with most medium- or big-sized cities in Italy and western Europe.

Considering the whole Italian state, Palermo has long been the fifth city by population, surpassing Genoa in the 1981–1991 decade. The quick and steady growth of Palermo has faced a slowdown during the last four decades, but the city is still holding a leading position within its metropolitan area, with the second town (Bagheria) only counting a relatively small number of inhabitants, although the ratio between the inhabitants of Palermo and the inhabitants of Bagheria moves from 18:1 (1921) to 12:1 (2011). Looking at the population percentage variation from 1971 to 2011, most hinterland towns of the Palermo area show very high increases (Isola delle Femmine: +176 percent; Carini: +129 percent), while Palermo is stuck on a mere +2 percent (Figure 9.1).

The Palermo *tessera* seems to confirm, at least partially, Edward Soja's (2011) density convergence theory. Although the density of the main city has slightly increased over the 40 years between 1971 and 2011 (+91 per km^2), the surroundings have experienced a tremendous growth (Villabate: +2,490 per km^2,

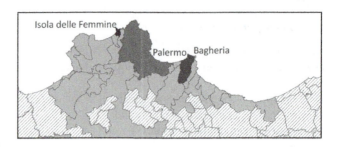

Figure 9.1 Percentage change of population between 1971 and 2011 in the Palermo
        tessera

Source: Authors' graphic based on PRIN Postmetropoli (2015)

effectively doubling its original density, to the point of surpassing Palermo as the
highest-density town of the area).

Looking at the population trends, therefore, Palermo is a clear example of centralization, with a traditional medium-sized city initially attracting population and
then stimulating a process of suburbanization, according to van den Berg's (1982)
urban lifecycle theory. Apparently, Palermo is only nowadays reaching a late disurbanization stage (Picone, 2006).

The analysis of the housing dispersion index (the ratio between the number of
scattered houses and the total of houses) in this area helps an understanding of
how Palermo and its surroundings are behaving in 2001, a transition year between
the metropolitan and the post-metropolitan phase. Moreover, the housing dispersion index is a good measure of how the socio-economic outlook is tightly
tied to the spatial one (we will discuss the latter in the following section). In the
coastal municipalities near the city, just like in Palermo, the dispersion index can
be considered low or medium, if compared with other Italian cities (the index
hits the 0.05 threshold in nine municipalities, and moves to 0.10 in most of the
others). The farther one moves from Palermo and its immediate surroundings,
the higher the indexes get, with a maximum value of 0.30. A single municipality,
Bolognetta (in addition to the island of Ustica, which, being an island, cannot be
easily compared with inland municipalities, and whose population is mainly tied
to the summer tourist presence), has a high dispersion index, greater than 0.40,
probably because of its strategic location, adjacent to a major road connecting
Palermo to Agrigento and Corleone.

This situation confirms the image of Palermo as a "strong" and compact city.
The population probably moves for working reasons, but there is also a hint to the
metropolitan phenomenon, which is not very vivid yet, having started in the 1990s
in the Palermo area. Recalling Soja's (2000) theories on the post-metropolis and
Bruegmann's (2005) reading of the sprawl, we claim that the area of Palermo is
quite closely abiding by these models, although the post-metropolitan phase and

the disurbanization phase are not fully developed yet, leaving the city to a late metropolitan and late suburbanization stage.

Continuing our description of the socio-economic outlook of Palermo and its surroundings, we consider the dependency ratio, that is, the ratio of the sum of the number of children (0–14 years old) and older persons (65 years or over) compared with the working-age population (15–64 years old), as a key factor to understand how this area is experiencing new trends that might question the legitimacy of some enduring clichés. The dependency ratio could be related to the productiveness and economic strength of the analyzed area, although, as a memento, we must not forget the dependency ratio only speculates that the productive part[3] of the population actually has an employment, but holds no certainties over this trait. Rather, the ratio highlights the presence of large clusters of young (0–14) or old (65+) people depending on the productive parts of society.

In 2011 Palermo has a lower dependency ratio (48) than Milan (60), Rome (58) and Naples (50). Twenty years before, this was exactly the opposite way round, with Milan (39), Rome (38) and Naples (45) all having a lower ratio than Palermo (48). This means that the demographic composition of Milan has changed a lot in those 20 years, while the composition of Palermo is still quite similar to 1991. One likely interpretation of this apparent paradox could lie within the consequences of the economic crisis, which struck the more productive parts of Italy and forced people to relocate to other countries. Sicily, considering its historically marginal role in the productive processes, did not experience a comparable change in its demographic composition. The metropolitan area of Palermo does not show any significant exception to the general trend so far described. In 2011, no single municipality has a particularly higher or lower ratio, and almost all are within the 40–60 range.

These data are even more significant if we compare the highest percentage variation of the dependency ratio from 1991 to 2011 for the municipalities in the Palermo area (Trappeto: +24 percent) with other Italian cases, such as the Milan area (San Donato Milanese: +124 percent) or the Venice area (Spinea: +87 percent). Once again, the demographic composition of Palermo appears steadier, although this is not necessarily a signal of a stable economic status.

Actually, if we move to more properly economic data and look at the unemployment rate, we must start by considering the general trend for that index in Italy (2001–2014). Generally, the rate was lower in 2011 than it was in 2001, but then it rose up and it is now (2014) higher than it was in 2001, because the economic crisis struck the Italian market a few years later than it did in the US or in other countries. According to the general Italian rate, in most Sicilian towns and cities there was a decrease in the unemployment rate over those ten years (Palermo moves from 29 percent in 2001 to 23 percent in 2011). The unemployment rates for Sicily in 2011 are thus lower than they were in 2001, but still quite high if compared with other Italian regions. In the Palermo area, unemployment is higher in those areas immediately surrounding the city, such as Capaci (31 percent) and Villabate (29 percent), and it seems that the farther one moves from Palermo, the better it gets (Termini Imerese shows a 22 percent rate, despite the recent crisis connected to the closing of the FIAT factories). Palermo itself has a 23 percent rate, which is very high if compared with northern Italian cities (Milan, Venice and Florence are all around 6 percent) but in line with other southern cities (Naples and Catania 26 percent, Cagliari 17 percent).

Considering the employees by industry sector, the Palermo region looks quite traditional. Fishing is still quite important in the economic outlook of some towns, but less and less relevant with each passing year (Santa Flavia moves from 40 percent employees in 2001 in sector A (agriculture and fishing) to a mere 26 percent in 2011), while agriculture *per se* is almost worthless and definitely less important, in a strategic sense, than it is elsewhere in Sicily. Even in sector I (which may be linked to tourism), most towns are experiencing negative trends, with very few exceptions. One of the few sectors that still seems quite alive and well is sector G (wholesale trade), but this does not appear to be a suggestion that the economic status of Palermo is particularly innovative.

If we refer to Allen J. Scott's (2008) ideas on the most relevant economic aspects in post-metropolises, it seems quite clear that Palermo and its surroundings are quite far from the general trends of global metropolises. Likewise, considering the average per capita income, in the region of Palermo there is a distinct difference between the capital city, where the income of taxpayers is one of the highest of all Sicily, and the rest of the municipalities. This is possibly due to the fact that those who reside in the municipality of Palermo have better-paid jobs, which allow them to live there. The remaining region, generally quite heterogeneous, is divided between coastal areas with a higher income and inland areas with lower incomes.

The average per capita incomes of the inhabitants, if compared with those of the taxpayers, are lower: Palermo has €11,073 income per inhabitant, compared with €19,867 per taxpayer. Things are different in northern Italy, because the difference between the two data is lower (e.g. Venice has a €17,207 income per inhabitant, compared with €22,223 income per taxpayer); this confirms the effects of the high Sicilian unemployment rates, as we have previously discussed.

All the data we have so far analyzed may apparently strengthen the idea of a marginal, deprived land. However, we have already pointed out that the dependency ratio is surprisingly hinting at a more promising – or at least less negative – situation than the one we would expect. Therefore, portraying Palermo and its *tessera* solely as a negative and hopeless area is at least restrictive. There are clear, if weak, signs of something evolving in Palermo, as slow as it may seem. In order to provide additional details, we now want to come back to some other demographic data, and discuss the growing presence of foreign citizens, which is affecting Sicily in unexpected ways (Attili, 2008; Lo Piccolo, 2013; D'Anneo, 2016).

In the 20 years between 1991 and 2011, the Palermo area shows a complex trend, with some municipalities facing negative values (Trabia) and others moving from positive to negative, or the other way round (Santa Flavia, Misilmeri, Villabate and so on). Within this area, most foreign citizens live in Palermo, which proves to be the most attractive city for its employment opportunities, although the percentage of foreign citizens in Palermo in 2011 (almost 3 percent) is still much lower than in northern or central Italian cities (Milan 14 percent, Prato 15 percent).

These trends lead to a few interesting considerations if we analyze the Index of Dispersion of the Foreign Population (IDFP), an index our research unit has proposed building upon the existing literature on migrants and foreign citizens (Caritas Migrantes, 2011; INEA, 2013; Giampino et al., 2014; Lo Piccolo & Todaro, 2015), and defined as the percentage of foreign population in a single municipality multiplied by 100 and divided by the percentage of foreign population in the most populous city of that region. In this case, the Palermo area is in line with most of the other Italian regions (e.g. the Lombardy region), with foreign people living mainly in the most populous city.

When we look at the data on migration flows in Sicily, we can point out a couple of significant points. The Palermo area is experiencing a slow but steady increase of incoming foreign people, most of them directed toward Palermo; at the same time, the suburbanization process is causing Italian people living in Palermo to relocate to the hinterland (mainly to Carini and Misilmeri), in search of cheaper accommodation. Anyway, the general outlook is quite similar to the trend we can see for Milan and Turin, although these cities show some polarization phenomena (since 1991 in the case of Turin, or 2011 in the case of Milan).

Another key point for our reasoning is the mobility index of commuters. Over the 2001–2011 decade, the residential mobility index is generally standardized and highlights how the inflows and outflows have increased. The high indexes of the largest city of the region, Palermo, have been achieved over the decade by other cities in the hinterland. Even in this case, data confirm the presence of a process of suburbanization caused by the labor market, but also by the cost of the leases and sales of properties. This suburbanization process is most evident if we analyze the mobility index that in 2001 showed high values only in Palermo; however, these indexes became more similar within a decade, with an average value of 0.80 (Torretta).

To summarize the evidence we have presented, we may consider the following:

–   The socio-economic long-term trends regarding Palermo are intimately related to a marginal condition and a deprived area, as correctly addressed by most scholars who focus on the influence of low employment rates and the destructive presence of criminal organizations (Cannarozzo, 2000, 2009; Rossi Doria, 2003); however, though these traits are not to be dismissed, there is a serious risk of overestimating them and ignoring the (weak) traces of something new growing in the background.
–   The economic crisis has somehow hit harder on the northern Italian regions in terms of the relative loss of employment and the worsening of economic parameters, leaving Palermo in a still hindered but possibly more competitive position if compared with other similar Italian cities, and opening new trends that are still uncertain but could prove innovative and unexpected.
–   The challenges that Palermo is now facing are first of all connected to the geographic position of Sicily in the center of the Mediterranean Sea: given

its location, Sicily is quickly turning from a reservoir of emigrants to a crossroads in the often desperate trajectories that lead immigrants to Europe (Guarrasi, 2011). In this very complex context, Palermo may act as a catalyst for promoting new policies of shelter and refuge for migrants: the local municipality is apparently supporting this approach in the last few years, trying to turn Palermo into not just a geographical, but also a cultural and political hub for those migrants that look at Europe as a promised land. These processes are strengthening the idea of a post-metropolitan role for the *tessera*.

Spatial perspective

In Sicily the phenomenon of soil consumption, which started in the 1960s, has strongly contributed to shape the regional territory both from the physical and from the functional point of view. Since then the soil consumption of the fragile island territory has never stopped entirely. The understanding of these processes cannot be separated from a close examination of the role that, historically, the building industry and housing revenue have played in the economy of the region. Although the building industry has played a leading role in the economic recovery of all of Italy since the 1950s, in Sicily, as in most parts of Southern Italy, this sector has taken on an exceptional importance, as a consequence of the fragility of the productive and social systems.

Since 1960, the data on soil consumption reflect the dispersive model that has characterized many other Italian areas. This model, which is well represented by low-density settlement sometimes supported by illegal practices, is common throughout the whole region.

Within the inner areas there are large and unused areas close to agricultural lands. On the contrary, from the 1950s to the 1990s, coastal areas have been characterized by a fully uncontrolled building growth, becoming a perfect representation of a continuous urbanization.

Another process, which started in the 1980s, has contributed to fill up the coastal area and increase the anthropized land percentage: the suburbanization phenomenon of the bigger cities on the coast inside the metropolitan areas. This growth headed towards middle cities according to a specific direction, related to the different geographical contexts, and with a bigger and bigger range.

The urban structure of the area known as the metropolitan area, even if the actual identification is linked only to legal characteristics, has taken the appearance of the urban sprawl model. Its principal peculiarities are: high soil consumption; high management costs; significant community flows related to the lack of facilities.

To complete the framework of the suburbanization that marks the metropolitan system, we must talk about the industrial areas, also known as ASI (in English, IDA – Industrial Development Areas), grown in the coastal area of Sicily, often localized near areas of natural interest. Moreover, the coastal parts which did not exhibit any industrial areas have been seized by beach establishments or seasonal settlements characterized by a very low density.

These are, therefore, the reasons why today the Metropolitan Area of Palermo[4] has such an elevated soil consumption. The analysis performed by the Soil Consumption Monitoring Network, commissioned by the Environmental Protection National System, highlighted that a big growth of soil consumption is present not only in the bigger cities and towns, but also in the marginal areas of metropolitan cities. In the case of Palermo, Isola delle Femmine is an illuminating case of this, with its actual value of 51.2 percent.

To analyze the phenomenon of the change of land use through the last 50 years, it's useful and necessary to thoroughly study two different sets of data: the growth of the settlements and the consequent transformation of agricultural territory.

The data on the settlements in Sicily reflect the dispersive model that has characterized many other Italian coastal areas (Indovina, 2003). The areas around Palermo were initially used for housing reasons, and later on for industrial uses. The coverage ratio of the Palermo region emphasizes that over the last decade the urbanization of Sicily has continued, especially in coastal areas and in those municipalities that are closer to the capital. This change in the land use has slowly jeopardized the identity of the so-called *agro* of Palermo.

This process is very different from that which has characterized the growth of the urban structure of the actual metropolitan area of Palermo. In fact, up to the second part of the eighteenth century, "the *agro* of Palermo, which means the entire coast from Alcamo to Termini Imerese, [. . .] is characterized by a different legal and institutional organization. The *agro* is a state property land, shared between Palermo and Termini Imerese; it means that there are no barons who have the power to found new cities. These cities, except Trabia, grew with no foundation rules" (Renda, 1984, p. 9).

In the twentieth century, after World War II, the causes of the growth are different and the rules change also as a consequence of new national and local laws. Particularly in the coastal territory, soil consumption is manifest through two different typologies. The first confirms a well-known phenomenon, consolidated over recent decades. The second shows a marked choice toward suburban areas. These phenomena show a metropolitan dimension, particularly for large-scale detail trade, for some manufacturing organizations and for particular types of facilities. Analyzing all the consolidated data of the municipalities, the socio-economic gap between Palermo and the other municipalities is ever present.

So, in the wide-area dimension and especially regarding the unfulfilled housing demand, all these considerations confirm the suburban role of the majority of the municipalities. At the same time it's possible to observe a new plural and post-metropolitan organization of lifestyle, housing and work (Giampino et al., 2014). Moreover, this recent organization has fragmented and restructured the traditional commuting relationship between housing and working, above all because of the still unaccomplished or incomplete metropolitan reality (de Spuches et al., 2002; Picone, 2006).

This is manifest for the case of Terrasini, whose coverage ratio was equal to 22 percent in 2001, and then 36 percent in 2011. Today, these same areas are affected by a strong increase in the presence of medium-sized and larger shopping malls.

As mentioned above, the second field of research to be considered is agricultural land use in the metropolitan area of Palermo. The focus of this analysis must be oriented to know the changes throughout recent decades and to understand the influence of the changes on the identity of the territory.

These data are tightly connected to the settlement data in Sicily and particularly in the analyzed area of Palermo. Comparing the two sets of data one can even understand the history of the territory. The transformation of the characters of land use in the metropolitan area – from agricultural to mainly urban – is a consequence of economic and political choices. Certainly this phenomenon begins in the middle of the twentieth century, but to understand its effective trend, it is sufficient to analyze events of the last 20 years.

Looking at the cartograms on agricultural lands between 2000 and 2010, in the region of Palermo there is a clear and pronounced distinction between the western and the eastern areas. From Palermo to Balestrate there is a significant increase of the utilized agricultural area (UAA), with the exception of Trappeto (–49 percent). On the contrary, in the eastern area, excluding Santa Flavia and Misilmeri (88 percent and 10 percent, respectively), there is a significant reduction of UAA. Over the years this change of use has been affected by coastal tourism, by new summer-houses with very low density (as we stated earlier), but also by a renewed interest toward agriculture (although this is not reflected in a consequential increase of employees in agriculture; Magnaghi, 2013), as many scholars have described on a local basis (Cannarozzo, 2000; Rossi Doria, 2007, 2009; Barbera et al., 2009).

These reflections are tied to the idea of scattered cities and sprawl, and explain these transformations through economic and political reasons rather than cultural outlooks.

To thoroughly understand the whole context of the transformations, it can be useful now to analyze some specific data. The research took into consideration many different elements that play an important role in the transformation of land use.

The first are the housing data. Many local studies, alongside constant monitoring, have for years projected an image of a region, Sicily, that suffers from a depopulation of the greater urban centers in favor of the smaller ones, where the population prefers to live mainly (but not only) for economic reasons (Picone, 2006).

This aspect could be related to a higher life quality satisfaction in small towns, especially if these are well connected to the main urban center (ISTAT, 2013). The data collected for Palermo, analyzed year by year and by comparing the whole series, confirm this idea.

As mentioned earlier, the *tessera* highlights a change, even if minimal, to the number of houses in the middle ranges, although Palermo obviously maintains a leading position over the remaining municipalities.

The difference is still very high. What matters is the confirmation of an increase of houses in neighboring municipalities, and this is paired with an increase of population in those municipalities, as a result of relocation for the reasons given above (see Figure 9.2).

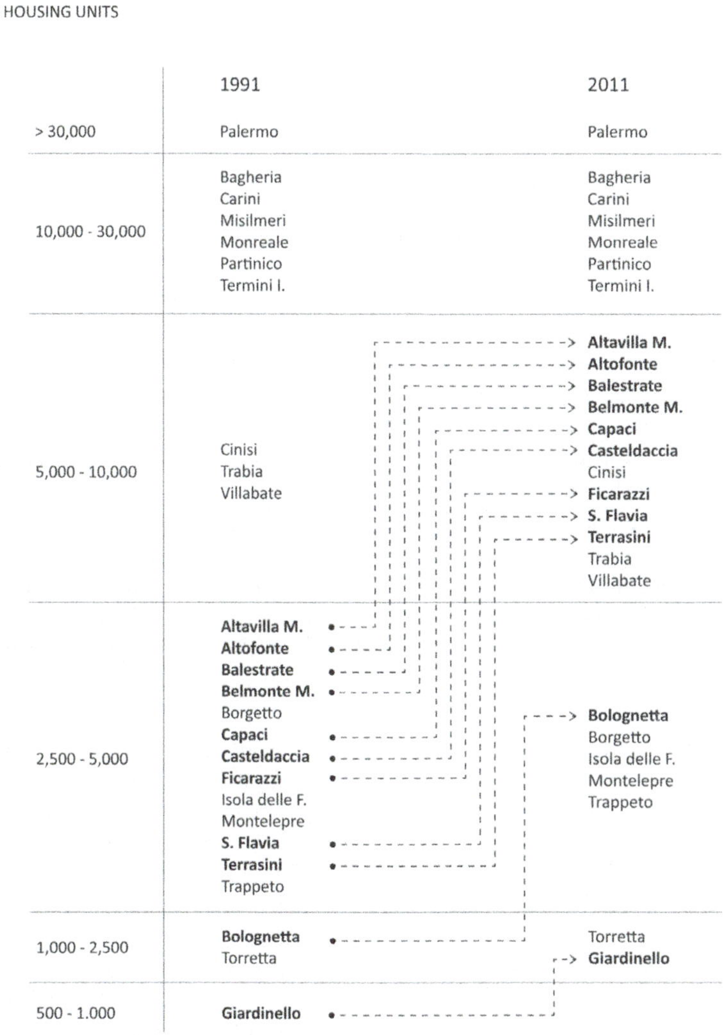

HOUSING UNITS

	1991	2011
> 30,000	Palermo	Palermo
10,000 - 30,000	Bagheria Carini Misilmeri Monreale Partinico Termini I.	Bagheria Carini Misilmeri Monreale Partinico Termini I.
5,000 - 10,000	Cinisi Trabia Villabate	**Altavilla M.** **Altofonte** **Balestrate** **Belmonte M.** **Capaci** **Casteldaccia** Cinisi **Ficarazzi** **S. Flavia** **Terrasini** Trabia Villabate
2,500 - 5,000	**Altavilla M.** **Altofonte** **Balestrate** **Belmonte M.** Borgetto **Capaci** **Casteldaccia** **Ficarazzi** Isola delle F. Montelepre **S. Flavia** **Terrasini** Trappeto	**Bolognetta** Borgetto Isola delle F. Montelepre Trappeto
1,000 - 2,500	**Bolognetta** Torretta	Torretta **Giardinello**
500 - 1.000	**Giardinello**	

Figure 9.2 Variation in housing units between 1991 and 2011 in the Palermo *tessera*

Source: Authors' calculation, based on data provided by ISTAT (Italian National Institute of Statistics) (Census data, 1991 and 2011)

The reflections on this indicator agree with what has already been asserted in the cases of the indicator on the residing population, on the housing dispersion index and on the unemployment rate.

A second interesting set of data, which has a close relationship with the first and with the history of the territory as highlighted before, is the accommodation capacity.

The data about accommodation capacity can be analyzed in several ways. First, we can look at them as absolute data, to be linked to the receptivity of each town. Second, we can analyze the data comparing all the towns in the *tessera*, estimating the whole accommodation capacity. Moreover, we can study the increase in the considered period. Finally, we can compare our areas with those outside of Sicily.

Matching all the analyses, the overall picture that emerges shows that in Sicily the largest city beats all the others. Palermo, in fact, offers a high accommodation capacity, and it is placed at the first level in the analysis.

Even if with a big difference at the same level we can find another town, Terrasini, probably for a large resort complex that hosts a large touristic flow, especially during the summer.

In the others towns, in the considered period, the accommodation capacity shows no significant variation. However, it's important to highlight that five small towns have no hotels, maybe because of their location or the low tourist attraction.

Another interesting piece of information is that Palermo is located among the top 20 Italian cities for its accommodation capacity.

In light of these considerations, it is necessary to analyze the real estate market.

The indicator of the average sales price of dwellings, warehouses, stores and offices, as well as the average lease price of dwellings, warehouses, stores and offices is interesting if it is related to the data on the resident population, the mobility index and the working issues. Therefore, the high cost of leases, such as those in sales in Palermo and in the coastal municipalities with a higher density, is justified by the decreases of the inner Sicilian areas. The highest ranked city for the average sales price of dwellings is Palermo, together with Cefalù, whose accommodation is related to seasonal tourism.

Bagheria and Santa Flavia, however, differ for the high price of shops and offices. In this last case an important role is played by the proximity with Bagheria and the functional railway link to other local municipalities and especially Palermo, which is only 17 kilometers away and part of the same urbanization.

With regard to industrial warehouses, the crisis of the FIAT factory has caused obvious consequences. The East Coast results, in 2012, are less expensive compared with the West Coast, where Carini and Palermo are the most expensive areas.

The last data considered concern a specific field that in Sicily, and particularly in the area of Palermo, in recent years plays an important role at the political level: the data on confiscated buildings, which must be considered as another aspect of the dis-regulation that characterizes corrupted political systems and hinders public action and the production of *commons* (Donolo, 2001; Cremaschi, 2009). In fact, the policies of confiscating buildings to criminal organizations represent a different approach to chaotic transformation practices, because it fuels new policies of territorial regulation.

The survey on confiscated buildings, even if it was carried out for only one year, is very interesting, both as an indicator for the region and in comparison with the other Italian areas.

This topic is closely linked to the areas where mafia, in its various forms, unfortunately has a long and established history. The data show a fair amount of residential and productive buildings that have been confiscated until now.

As in other cases, it's Palermo that heads the list, and the reason is easily explicable given the historical origins of the criminal phenomenon in Sicily (Cannarozzo, 2000, 2009). In the same high rank we can find such other towns as Monreale, Partinico and Bagheria.

Palermo heads the list even if we consider all the Italian cities, and the ratio between Palermo and Rome, or Palermo and Milan, is ten to one (Palermo has 2,481 confiscated buildings in 2012, whereas Rome has 241 and Milan 210). The reasons are very clear if we consider the history and the political relevance of criminal organizations in Sicily. At the same time, though, people started to realize the real weight of mafia in the 1990s with the killings of two judges, Falcone and Borsellino, and this gave way to a new awareness of the phenomenon, along with a stronger desire to fight it: this is why there are so many confiscated buildings in Palermo today.

In the second rank, always with interesting data, there are three towns. The number of towns without confiscated buildings is very low. It would be very interesting to know if the actual uses of these confiscated buildings are really a social use.

It's certain that mafia has regulated the processes of urbanization and the real estate market (Cannarozzo, 2009), and we must not forget these phenomena when we discuss the housing issues in Sicily today.

To summarize the issues we have presented, we may consider the following:

–   Undoubtedly in the initial phases the dispersive model that characterized the transformation of identity in the *tessera* of Palermo was the same model that affected other Italian metropolitan areas. However, in the most recent years the phenomenon developed to achieve different outcomes.
–   In order to truly understand the change of land use, we must consider two principal aspects: the buildings, including all of them and not housing only, and the agricultural land use. Certainly the two are strictly linked, since the consequence of the development of the first coincides with the decrease of the second.
–   The actual post-metropolitan vision of the Palermo *tessera* is to be connected to a new organization of lifestyle, housing and work as a consequence of the attempt to start institutionalized metropolitan processes at the beginning of the 1990s.

Institutional perspective

The institutional choices that have affected the island, along with its capital Palermo, reveal an ongoing, yet immature, process, a path which is often associated with existing administrative structures, in terms of aggregations and conservation of roles, positions and management tools.

Confirming that the institutional process has started but has not yet taken off, Sicily, even before other parts of Italy, has found a renewed interest in the Italian debate on redefining the institutional metropolitan city (Figures 9.3 and 9.4).

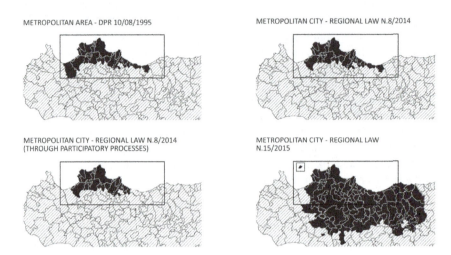

Figure 9.3 A comparison of the different ideas of the Palermo metropolitan area/city

Source: Original graphic by Francesca Lotta

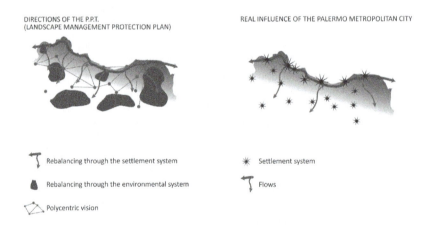

Figure 9.4 Ideogram of the main characteristics of the Landscape Management
Protection Plan and the metropolitan city of Palermo

Source: Original graphic by Riccardo Alongi and Francesca Lotta

In the 1960s, this interest already existed, when the issues of the city-region and regional planning were debated. The Region had expressed its will to establish a level of intermediate dimension and, with Regional Law[5] no. 9/1986, instituted the "Regional Provinces," aggregations of municipalities in consortia corresponding to the pre-existing Provinces.[6] The Region had also proposed the identification of "metropolitan areas" and had defined the criteria for their identification, delimitation, functions and objectives.[7] Since then, the new metropolis could hardly be mapped, because its boundaries began to be blurred (Picone, 2006). The difficulty at that time, like today, was aggravated by the local institutions ignoring the economic territorial features of the affected areas, the spatial and environmental implications, mobility, technological innovation, facility settlement, offer of services and finally the labor market (Di Leo, 1997; Schilleci, 2008b).[8]

Recently, the regional government has got back to the path of reform to establish the metropolitan cities, which include Palermo. With Regional Law no. 15/2015, the entire former Province of Palermo is identified as a single metropolitan city. No reasoning about the real dynamics in progress has been done. Once again the institutional model, revealed both in law and in practice, appears to be monocentric. Palermo still wants to maintain a central role because of its position as a political and administrative capital. The criteria to define the new administrative dimensions are not innovative: they are based on income position, in terms of functionality and concentration of certain service categories.

Also at the level of management of the new dimension there are not many innovations. The plan for the metropolitan area, dictated by Regional Law no. 71/1978, should have been managed at the municipal or provincial level, because the law did not require an administrative entity of metropolitan dimension. The result was an area with two overlapping plans.

In this way, the relationship between the different levels of planning became so confusing and unclear that the only result was the study for the General Directives of the Inter-municipal Plan for the Metropolitan Area of Palermo, presented in 2001 and including the General Guidelines, regarding cognitive analysis, the annexes, containing part of the information that were produced, and a commercial plan.

Despite the existence of some dynamism, this is not yet supported by actual implementation. Actually, the area of Palermo appears particularly active in promoting local projects.[9] These exceed the average of the largest Italian cities. However, most projects are limited to the Palermo municipality, which has proven unable to include the surrounding municipalities in its development programs (Giampino et al., 2010).

The partial data available show a strong engagement, but with few results. In fact, the hinterland of Palermo, headed by Monreale, counts two active pacts. With regard to GALs,[10] instead, part of the same municipalities belonging to the territorial pact is affected by this program and creates an exception in the entire Italian framework. Finally, considering the PRUSSTs, we have the same dynamic and Palermo has one PRUSST (against the Italian average score of 0.02). Actions for Agenda 21 instead are inactive in the Palermo region.

The absence of a coordination plan for large areas has a negative impact on the territory. Each municipality has planned its territory regardless of the surrounding areas. The largest absence has been and continues to be perceived in the adoption of some complex programs. These programs – aiming to enhance the partnership with private stakeholders, to devise new means of propulsion of urban regeneration, and so on – have only affected parts of the territory, with no systematic approach. The programs have established uncertain relationships within a potential scheme of Palermo's wider area, confirming what was already delineated by the relationships between municipal planning and complex programs (Lo Piccolo & Schilleci, 2005).

The case of complex programming initiatives that affected the eastern part of Palermo's former Province leads in fact to reflect about an incomplete or inconsistent dialectic between the projects expressed by the various tools and the complex programs. The latter sometimes show elements of a post-metropolitan innovation for the local territorial realities, looking for a difficult coordination with the municipal planning and with the (unrealized) wide-area planning.

With regard to the dynamics of post-metropolitan institutional prospects, the collected data and the elaborations of our research suggest some thoughts and directions. The area included in the *tessera* of Palermo has never been fully metropolitan either for its institutional structure and its government, or for socio-economic and territorial features.

In recent years, however, the data analyzed in the research show the will to propel the territory into a polynuclear dimension (which somehow characterizes the post-metropolitan dimension), with all ambiguities and contradictions of the path. Particularly, the components of change and innovation seem to emerge from some geographical areas which are less dependent on role, geography and functions from Palermo's municipality. They contrast and revolutionize the inertia of the centripetal administrative and hierarchically predominant dimension, which has so far prevented and delayed, in terms of choices and effectiveness, a real metropolitan governance characterizing the post-metropolis.

Indeed, Palermo as a metropolitan city continues to maintain its rank, its role, its attractiveness and innovation, but at the same time a few surrounding towns, albeit slowly, begin to structure a potential system of polynuclear city-region. In continuation of the paths taken in the 1990s,[11] some local governments have in fact had the power to promote a territorial coalition among the municipalities that fall between the valleys of Imera Settentrionale and Torto, the Madonie park authority, the former Province of Palermo and a public–private partnership.[12]

This coalition has created some forms of coordination.[13] These actions were coordinated only because of the will of the promoters and managers and are not included in a wider range of vision, but the most recent results, like the nullification of the public consultation[14] of Termini Imerese, are an indicator of an uphill process, characterized by a regional and introverted vision that basically ignores the flows and dynamics that cross it.

Some municipalities within the metropolitan city of Palermo, such as Termini Imerese, have expressed their intent to continue a difficult, but not unsubstantiated, path toward polycentrism, by working together with other nearby municipalities in a common framework. Under national influences, in 2013, the regional government got back to the idea of creating the metropolitan cities. Regional Law no. 8/2014 established three metropolitan cities, including Palermo, and despite the backwardness of the criteria they proposed (once again, these were territorial continuity and population) there is an element of innovation: Regional Law no. 15/2015, in article 45, paves the way for the establishment of new consortia.

In those places where we find the result of a decentralization or recentering, a deterritorialization or reterritorialization, a continuous extension or urban nucleation intensified, a growth of the homogeneity and heterogeneity, a socio-spatial integration and disintegration, there perhaps we can already talk about a new geography of post-metropolitan urbanization (Soja, 2000).

In this case, the institution of the metropolitan city of Palermo could provide an opportunity to delineate the creation of a strong and stable metropolitan government, able to perform functions already defined in the 1980s, while respecting processes undertaken by individual local realities.

Despite the absence of approved coordination plans, the draft plans, such as the *Schema di Massima* and the *QPS* (*Quadro Propositivo con Valenza Strategica*), reveal a polycentric territorial and organizational will.

The reasons for the great interest for polycentrism reside in at least two specific aspects: the transport system improvements and the introduction of new production methods and new lifestyles, previously concentrated only in the space of the capital city.

The planning of the metropolitan dimension of Palermo would be a great and necessary change of scale in the territorial organization of the entire coastline, where the greatest flows and exchanges of territory are concentrated.

A thorough planning which is aware of the residential issues, in a complex space like Palermo city, could define the relationship between the different functions and specific territories. Implementing initiatives of coordination, advocating and supporting local economic systems, could in fact start to densify the dynamic connections that are somehow reticular, in terms of interdependence and complementarity, and can structure and define the different parts of the metropolitan area being set up.

Another field of metropolitan area planning should also take environmental issues into account. In this regard, the draft of the Ecological Network could act as a focal point as well as the reorganization of the waste disposal system, too often oblivious of its territorial impact. Finally, the re-use in a new virtuous cycle of the buildings that are confiscated from mafia would represent an aspect that is not only civic and/or symbolic, but ultimately relevant, even in quantitative terms, within the territory under examination.

The metropolitan city, in any extension, should take into account the vocations and the characteristics of the different territories that compose it.

The new dimension should involve public and private actors and, through the compatibility and coherence between the different planning tools, should redefine and direct those balances necessary between the different parts of a territory and its inhabitants, with a conscious ability to analyze and guide the dynamics at play. Taking into account the studies of recent years and current research, however, we believe it is possible, starting from the legislative context, to propose some reflections on the real sphere of influence of the metropolitan city of Palermo and detect some overall addresses.

To summarize the issues we have presented, we may consider the following:

– The process of metropolization started in the 1990s but brought no effective consequences.
– The regional authority has been discussing metropolization processes for more than a year now, considering the input given by the national law on decentralization, but still is unable to introduce any new elements to the previously existing organization.
– The continuous reconsideration of the form and contents of the new metropolitan structure, fluctuating between the metropolitan city model and the consortia, suggests that these innovative elements can actually trigger a process of (post-)metropolization, in a territory that is actually quite suitable for these changes.

Conclusions

In this portrait, we have started discussing the metropolitan area of Palermo by recalling how important marginality and isolation are to understanding the Sicilian situation. Part of the data we have discussed so far implies that this marginality causes a lot of social, economic and political issues. For instance, the insufficient differentiated waste collection and the number of confiscated buildings are proof of the failure of the policies led by the national state and the local authorities, together with a sort of quiet resignation to an economic and social negative status that might seem to confirm the clichés we introduced at the beginning of our analysis.

However, other data suggest a different approach. We have discussed how the dependency ratio of Palermo is now unexpectedly lower than Milan's. This does not mean that finding a job in Palermo is easier than it is in Milan, of course, but it implies that Palermo and its region have some *potential energy* (given by the relatively high number of working-age population). This sort of energy may be the same that causes so many confiscated buildings to serve a renewed purpose, often for social and cultural goals. We could not discuss the use of confiscated buildings more thoroughly for a lack of data, and most reflections on that topic should use qualitative data instead of merely quantitative data; nonetheless, the number of social bottom–up proposals coming from young and unemployed people is definitely growing within the last decade in Palermo, and may be considered a sign of a slow but unyielding investment on social awareness and bottom–up policies.

Even if we consider all of these new trends and potentialities, there is still no simple answer to the question about the post-metropolitan status of this *tessera*. Is Palermo a post-metropolis? Not at all, if we compare it with Milan, Rome or Los Angeles. However, is Palermo showing a few post-metropolitan trends? Arguably so. If we consider the presence of foreign people or the density convergence theory, Palermo is behaving almost exactly like Milan or Rome, though the numbers are obviously lower in comparison. In our opinion, this means that a regional portrait of Palermo and its area must be carefully balanced on a tight line, hanging in the balance between the cliché of a marginal and deprived southern city and the acknowledgement of something new that might come in the future. In a sense, Palermo is on the threshold of the post-metropolitan discourse.

There remains the need to find tangible effects in identifying (post-)metropolitan planning strategies – not just institutional and administrative strategies, but those that have the determination and foresight to acquire a future overall vision. In this regard, the democratic construction of decisional processes and governance of the entire metropolitan area, along with the required instruments and acts of planning, would be desirable and necessary, albeit perhaps implausible, considering what we have described and analyzed in this chapter and in the research we have undertaken.

Notes

1 Although this chapter should be considered a result of the common work and reflection of the three authors, M. Picone took primary responsibility for the sections "On the threshold of the post-metropolis" and "Socio-economic perspective", F. Schilleci took primary responsibility for the section "Spatial perspective", and F. Lotta took primary responsibility for the section "Institutional perspective". The conclusions have been written by the three authors.
2 This regional portrait is strictly related to the other Sicilian portrait, which describes the south-eastern area of the island. The research group from the University of Palermo initially proposed to compare these two Sicilian cases (Palermo and the south-east) in order to appraise the similarities and differences between them, but most of all to prove how these two peculiar cases show some unexpected post-metropolitan traits. Therefore, even if we chose to present the two areas as separate portraits, we suggest that readers look for some shared characteristics. Within this portrait, there are several references to Sicily and the rest of Italy which can help the reader grasp the uniqueness and peculiarity of the island, as related to the Italian context.
3 The dependency ratio is actually just a demographic indicator; linking it to other economic elements (such as the unemployment rate or the inactivity rate) would actually require additional speculation.
4 We refer to the Metropolitan Area of Palermo as it was defined in 1995 by Regional Law no. 9/1986.
5 The Sicilian Region has a special status, approved by the constitutional law of 26 February 1948. This law has regulated the power to legislate on an exclusive basis about certain topics enumerated in the Statute, as local order authorities, urban planning, agriculture and forestry.
6 The law establishes that the Provinces must adopt the economic and social program. This will feed into a plan of economic development with social multiannual order to plan and articulate plans, sectoral and territorial projects.
7 The delimitation of the metropolitan system proposed, including Palermo, was based on administrative (belonging to the same Province) and demographic (a population of over 250,000 inhabitants) criteria.
8 The Metropolitan Area of Palermo which was proposed at that time included 27 municipalities. It was characterized by a core and by a ring made of thick and continuous urbanization along the coast, between the valleys of the Oreto and Eleuterio rivers. This was later extended from Termini Imerese to Partinico and had a land area of 906 km^2 and a population at 1991 of just over 1 million inhabitants (1,001,345), equal to 21.15 percent of the regional population.

9 Since the beginning of the 1990s, "the new instruments, known as local development partnership programmes, were conceived by the Ministry to support the development and implementation of specific projects through cooperation between the public and private sectors" (Lo Piccolo & Schilleci, 2005, p. 80). The scene quickly becomes much larger, with the introduction of the so-called complex urban programs as *Programmi Integrati di intervento (PII); Programmi di Recupero Urbano (PRU); Programmi di Riqualificazione Urbana (PRIU); Programmi di Riqualificazione Urbana e Sviluppo Sostenibile (PRUSST)*. These are consolidated in parallel with the experiences due within the framework of EU programs, like Agenda 21.

10 GAL is a local action group composed of public and private stakeholders to promote local development in a rural area. GALs are funded by the EU Initiative Program known as LEADER +.

11 At the time Termini Imerese, Terrasini, Trabia, Capaci and Palermo appealed to the TAR – Regional Administrative Court – asking for the revocation of the institutive decree. The reasons for this opposition were of a different kind, but all aimed at soliciting the Regional Government to revise Regional Law 9/86 so that better account was taken of the indications of the national law. One of the main demands considered the establishment of an elective organ of government for the metropolitan area (the metropolitan city) and the redefinition of the concept of metropolitan area more as a "system of cities," as configured in the national law, than as an area centered around a capital city, as suggested by the regional law. A short step to redefine the Metropolitan Area of Palermo was made, identifying not only administrative boundaries, but trying to work on local systems greatly consolidated and based on the elements and environmental reports as fundamental to this delimitation. The focus was also placed on the need for integration between the metropolitan system and regional territory, as well as on internal relations.
These reflections, however, never followed through and did not resolve either the problem of delimitation or, even less, the major issue of liaison with the provincial and municipal planning.

12 The latter is made up of the development company SOSVIMA (as technical coordinator) and ISMERA SVILUPPO, the GAL ISC Madonie, the *Banca di Credito Cooperativo "San Giuseppe"*, the *Banca di Credito Cooperativo "Mutuo Soccorso"*, *Confcooperative Unione Provinciale of Palermo, Fare ambiente coordinamento regionale Sicilia, Confederazione Italiana agricoltori Palermo* and *Confindustria Palermo*.

13 Distretto Culturale delle Madonie (2007), the Distretto delle carni bovine delle aree interne della Sicilia (2007), the GAL Madonie (2010), the Distretto turistico di Cefalù and of Parchi delle Madonie and of Himera (2011), the Gruppo Azione Costiera Golfo di Termini Imerese (2013) and the PIST (Piano Integrato Sviluppo Territoriale) Città a Rete Madonie-Termini (2009).

14 The aim was to request the separation from the metropolitan city of Palermo *in itinere* and then set about creating a consortium with the internal municipalities.

References

Attili, G. (2008). *Rappresentare la città dei migranti*. Milan: Jaca Book.

Barbera, G., La Mantia, T., and Rühl J. (2009). La Conca d'Oro: trasformazione di un paesaggio agrario e riflessi sulla sostenibilità. In M. Leone, F. Lo Piccolo, and F. Schilleci (Eds.), *Il paesaggio agricolo nella Conca d'Oro di Palermo* (pp. 69–95). Florence: Alinea.

Bruegmann, R. (2005). *Sprawl: A Compact History*. Chicago: University of Chicago Press.

Cannarozzo, T. (2000). Palermo: le trasformazioni di mezzo secolo. *Archivio di Studi Urbani e Regionali, 67*, 101–139.

Cannarozzo, T. (2009). La governance mafiosa e l'assalto al territorio. In M. Leone, F. Lo Piccolo, and F. Schilleci (Eds.), *Il paesaggio agricolo nella Conca d'Oro di Palermo* (pp. 39–51). Florence: Alinea.

Caritas Migrantes. (2011). *Dossier statistico immigrazione 2011.* XXI Rapporto. Rome: IDOS Edizioni.

Cremaschi, M. (2009). Il territorio delle organizzazioni criminali. *Territorio,* 49, 115–118.

D'Anneo, G. (2016). *Abbandonare o scegliere Palermo, dalla de-urbanizzazione alle nuove migrazioni.* Retrieved from: http://www.strumentires.com/index.php?option=com_cont ent&view=article&id=627:abbandonare-o-scegliere-palermo-dalla-de-urbanizzazione-alle-nuove-migrazioni&catid=16:immigrazione&Itemid=140.

de Spuches, G., Guarrasi, V., and Picone, M. (2002). *La città incompleta.* Palermo: Palumbo.

Di Leo, P. (1997). Area metropolitana di Palermo. *Città e Territorio, Bollettino del Dipartimento della Città e Territorio dell'Università di Palermo,* 3, 72–79.

Di Leo, P., and Esposito, G. (1991). *Palermo: Pianificazione urbana e Metropolitana. Due studi.* Atti del Seminario dell'INU, 28–29 gennaio, Palermo.

Donolo, C. (2001). *Disordine: l'economia criminale e le strategie della sfiducia.* Rome: Donzelli.

Giampino, A., Picone, M., and Todaro, V. (2014). Postmetropoli in contesti al 'margine'. *Planum,* 2(29), 1308–1316.

Giampino, A., Todaro, V., and Vinci, I. (2010). I piani strategici siciliani: interpretazioni di territorio ed orientamenti progettuali. In I. Vinci (Ed.), *Pianificazione strategica in contesti fragili* (pp. 43–93). Florence: Alinea.

Grasso, A. (1994). *Le Aree metropolitane siciliane. Funzioni, vincoli, strategie.* Bologna: Pàtron.

Guarrasi, V. (2011). *La città cosmopolita. Geografie dell'ascolto.* Palermo: Palumbo.

Indovina, F. (2003). È necessario 'diramare' la città diffusa? Le conseguenze sul governo del territorio di un chiarimento terminologico. In C.S. Bertuglia, A. Stanghellini, and L. Staricco (Eds.), *La diffusione urbana: tendenze attuali, scenari futuri* (pp. 116–131). Milan: FrancoAngeli.

INEA. (2013). *Indagine sull'impiego degli immigrati in agricoltura in Italia 2011.* Rome: INEA.

ISTAT. (2013). *Urbes. Il benessere equo e sostenibile nelle città,* http://www.istat.it/it/files/2013/06/Urbes_2013.pdf

Lo Piccolo, F. (2009). Territori agricoli a latitudini meridiane: residui marginali o risorse identitarie? In F. Lo Piccolo (Ed.), *Progettare le identità del territorio* (pp.11–42). Florence: Alinea.

Lo Piccolo, F. (2013). *Nuovi abitanti e diritto alla città: Un viaggio in Italia.* Florence: Altralinea.

Lo Piccolo, F., and Schilleci, F. (2005). Local Development Partnership Programmes in Sicily: Planning Cities without Plans. *Planning Practice and Research,* 20(1), 79–87.

Lo Piccolo, F., and Todaro, V. (2015). Concentración vs dispersión de los inmigrantes en Italia. Análisis comparativo de la distribución de la población extranjera en las regiones urbanas. *CyTET,* 47(184), 397–404.

Lo Piccolo, F., Picone, M., and Schilleci, F. (2013). Forme di territori post-metropolitani siciliani: un contesto al margine. *Planum, The Journal of Urbanism,* 27(2), 46–51.

Lotta, F. (2015). Palermo. In G. De Luca, and D. Moccia (Eds.), *Immagini di territori metropolitani* (pp. 114–119). Rome: INU Edizioni.

Magnaghi, A. (2013). Riterritorializzare il mondo. *Scienze del Territorio,* 1, 31–42.

Picone, M. (2006). Il ciclo di vita urbano in Sicilia. *Rivista Geografica Italiana*, 113, 129–146.

Pinzello, I. (Ed.). (2003). *Il ruolo delle aree metropolitane costiere del Mediterraneo.* Florence: Alinea.

Piraino, A. (1988). *Il sistema metropolitano di Palermo. Quale fisionomia.* Palermo: Celup.

PRIN Postmetropoli. (2015). *Atlante web dei territori postmetropolitani* [web atlas]. Retrieved from: http://www.postmetropoli.it/atlante.

Renda, F. (1984). Le borgate nella storia di Palermo. In C. Ajroldi (Ed.), *Le borgate di Palermo.* Caltanissetta – Rome: S. Sciascia Editore.

Rossi Doria, B. (2003). La Sicilia: da Regione del Mezzogiorno a periferia dell'Europa forte. In F. Lo Piccolo and F. Schilleci (Eds.), *A sud di Brobdingnag. L'identità dei luoghi: per uno sviluppo locale autosostenibile nella Sicilia Occidentale* (pp. 11–41). Milan: FrancoAngeli.

Rossi Doria, B. (2007). La Sicilia: una regione di città. In B. Rossi Doria (Ed.), *Sicilia terra di città.* Florence: IGM, (pp. 11–26).

Rossi Doria, B. (2009). La Conca d'Oro. I processi di urbanizzazione, le aree agricole, le politiche e i piani a Palermo. In M. Leone, F. Lo Piccolo, and F. Schilleci (Eds.), *Il paesaggio agricolo nella Conca d'Oro di Palermo* (pp. 25–38). Florence: Alinea.

Rossi Doria, B., Lo Piccolo, F., Schilleci, F., and Vinci, I. (2005). *Riconoscimento e rappresentazione di fenomeni territoriali inediti in Sicilia*, Paper presented at 'Terre d'Europa e fronti mediterranei', IX Conferenza nazionale SIU, Palermo 3–4 March (Vol. 1, pp. 263–273). Bagheria: Zangara Editore.

Schilleci, F. (2005). Il contesto normativo in Sicilia. Una difficile pianificazione tra ritardi e resistenze. In M. Savino (Ed.), *Pianificazione alla prova nel mezzogiorno* (pp. 189–208). Milan: FrancoAngeli.

Schilleci, F. (2008a). La dimensione metropolitana in Sicilia: un'occasione mancata? *Archivio di Studi Urbani e Regionali*, 91, 147–161.

Schilleci, F. (2008b). *Visioni metropolitane. Uno studio comparato tra l'Area Metropolitana di Palermo e la Comunidad de Madrid.* Florence: Alinea.

Scott, A.J. (2008). *Social Economy of the Metropolis: Cognitive-Cultural Capitalism and the Global Resurgence of Cities.* Oxford: Oxford University Press.

Soja, E.W. (2000). *Postmetropolis: Critical Studies of Cities and Regions.* Malden, MA: Blackwell.

Soja, E.W. (2011). Regional Urbanization and the End of the Metropolis Era. In G. Bridge and S. Watson (Eds.), *New Companion to the City* (pp. 679–689). Chichester: Wiley-Blackwell.

van den Berg, L., Drewett R., and Klaassen L.H. (1982). *Urban Europe: A Study of Growth and Decline.* Oxford: Pergamon.

10 South-eastern Sicily

A counterfactual post-metropolis

Francesco Lo Piccolo, Marco Picone and Vincenzo Todaro[1]

A counterfactual post-metropolitan region

When we refer to south-eastern Sicily (SES) we are considering an area that is apparently the opposite of any likely post-metropolitan case study.[2] This area holds no major city (with the partial exception of Syracuse and its 118,000 inhabitants) and appears like an island within an island, being one of the most marginal areas of all Sicily (Nobile, 1990; Schilirò, 2012). Media representations have contributed to strengthen this imagery, by portraying south-eastern Sicily as a land that is lost in the past, in the echoes of the baroque and traditional agriculture (Giampino et al., 2015; Azzolina et al., 2012; Abbate, 2011; Cannarozzo, 2010), with people hardly speaking Italian at all. However, this is far from the truth. South-eastern Sicily is probably one of the most dynamic areas of southern Italy (Asso & Trigilia, 2010), and shows some post-metropolitan traits that are definitely worth discussing. One might consider SES as a "counter-case" to the true post-metropolitan Italian cases of Milan and Turin; however, this counter-case has much to say on how the post-metropolitan nature is not necessarily tied to megacities or to a world-leading economy. Within this chapter, we will try to deconstruct the clichés related to south-eastern Sicily, and describe the most innovative trends one can find in this remote corner of Italy.

As a consequence of the geographical and historical situation of south-eastern Sicily, considering a 100 × 100 km *square* for this area seemed an inconvenient solution to us, because the *square* would include both sea areas and the city of Catania, with its industrial presence and a completely different outlook, if compared with Syracuse, Modica or Ragusa. Therefore, in this regional portrait we never refer to a 100 × 100 *square*, but rather to a *tessera*, a tile of a larger mosaic. We propose the word *tessera* for two main reasons: first, it breaks the overly rigid geometry which the *square* implies, and which seems hardly applicable to any part of Sicily; second, this Latin word recalls the ancient history of the island, suggesting that this particular geographical area, despite its long-lasting ties to the rest of Italy, still demands to be considered as a standalone case for its peculiar historical, geographical and cultural specificities. Our *tessera* is 60 × 100 km wide, and embraces 19 municipalities which are situated within the Provinces of Syracuse and Ragusa. All of the Province of Ragusa is included in the area, while only some parts of the Province of Syracuse are (see PRIN Postmetropoli, 2015).

The only city with a population of over 100,000 inhabitants is Syracuse, with three more towns over 50,000 (Ragusa, Vittoria, Modica) and seven under 10,000. These municipalities were chosen by applying the criteria of inter-local planning and programming initiatives, that is, by considering the connections between them in the light of their abilities to team up and play an active role in territorial planning.

The two main points we want to highlight here, considering their importance in the whole research project on Italian post-metropolises, revolve around the presence of foreign citizens (migrants) in Sicily and housing. Regarding migrants and migrations, the obvious starting point is that Sicily holds a strategic position in the Mediterranean area, and it is often used as a gateway for those (sometimes illegal) migrants looking to reach northern Europe (we refer, for instance, to the famous case of Lampedusa). However, there are many more legal migrants moving to Sicily for other reasons in recent years, especially in south-eastern Sicily, and we will try to point out the reasons why.

Housing is also an important topic, considering the Sicilian inability to facilitate the relationships between strong urbanization processes and the traditional presence of agricultural areas.

The following sections will present some data regarding south-eastern Sicily. The data are divided into three sections: a socio-economic outlook describing the characteristics of demography, employment and income in this part of Sicily; a spatial analysis of housing and land use; and finally an institutional description of the administrative state of the art in Syracuse, Ragusa and their surroundings. Each section describes the most consolidated trends in this area, but also discusses the most innovative changes and the challenges south-eastern Sicily has faced in recent years. The final section points out some concluding remarks and puts this Sicilian case within the theoretical framework of the post-metropolitan discourse in Italy.

Looking through the *tessera*

Socio-economic perspective

In order to evaluate the socio-economic outlook of south-eastern Sicily and its *tessera*, we will analyse several data related to the following domains.

- **Demographics** – population and density; housing dispersion index; dependency ratio; foreign citizens; mobility index.
- **Economics** – unemployment rates; employees by industry sectors; average per capita income.

Although the generic outlook of south-eastern Sicily might look quite similar to what we have already described in the Palermo case (see Chapter 9), things are a bit different here. According to some data (such as location, population and density), south-eastern Sicily (SES) is even more marginal and peripheral than Palermo, considering its distance from any significant economic centre (with the partial exclusion of Catania, about 60 kilometres north of Syracuse). However, the socio-economic data we will discuss here describe a richer area than Palermo, with some extremely innovative trends, making SES an exceptional case in all of Italy. Such a case might probably be compared with other marginal but resourceful areas in northern or central Italy, such as the so-called "Chiantishire" around Siena.

We will start by discussing the population trend, which shows a very unstable attitude here: Modica (the largest town in 1921) slowly yields its leading role to Syracuse, which almost doubles its population between 1951 and 1981. The secondary administrative centre, Ragusa, kept a marginal role in the development of the area (Figure 10.1). Looking at the population percentage variations from 1971 to 2011 and comparing them with other, more traditional cases such as Palermo, south-eastern Sicily shows low percentage increases (the highest being for the small town of Acate, +65%) and some significant decreases (such as Monterosso Almo, −21%). If depopulation can be evoked as an explanation for Monterosso Almo and similar cases, it is harder to explain Acate's growth. We will discuss later the reasons for this growth, but for now we will just point out that most of Acate's new citizens are foreign citizens.

When we try to adapt Edward Soja's (2011) density convergence theory to south-eastern Sicily, we get a surprising result. Unexpectedly, the densest town of SES is the small and only relatively relevant town of Pozzallo. Even in 1961, Pozzallo was at the top of the list, with a density of 797 inhabitants per km^2. In 2011, Pozzallo's density (1,231 inhabitants per km^2) is much higher than Syracuse's (570). Although this paradox is partially explained by the small size of the municipality of Pozzallo, if we try to apply Soja's density convergence diagram to SES, the results are utterly contradictory. This could probably be considered a hint to the polynuclear system that characterizes this region, with at least four greater core areas (Syracuse, Ragusa, Vittoria, Modica) and other lesser districts gravitating around them.

Looking at the population trends, the south-eastern *tessera* has long been a place to move away from, and thus does not comply with van den Berg's (1982) urban lifecycle theory. Arguably, most people moved to the nearby industrial cities of

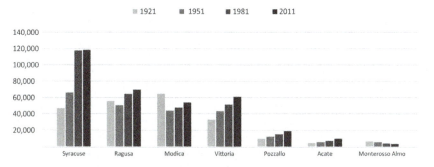

Figure 10.1 City population in south-eastern Sicily between 1921 and 2011

Source: Authors' graphic based on PRIN Postmetropoli (2015)

Catania and Gela, while others relocated outside of Sicily. These movements may be because of the rural nature of this area. Only Syracuse thrived, probably as a consequence of its close ties with Catania and the factories of nearby Augusta. In recent years, however, things have started to change, as SES now hosts several small or medium towns with increasing growth rates, most of them close to Ragusa. The reasons for this change must be explored within the domain of recent economic developments, involving a renewed role for agriculture, along with the tourism attractiveness of this region (Picone, 2006).

The analysis of the housing dispersion index (the ratio between the number of scattered houses and the total of the houses) in this area highlights a flattening of the values, with the lowest values found in Pozzallo and Comiso. This confirms that the traditional landscape is still quite intact in this area, because the low fragmentation is a result of cautious policies at the urban and the agricultural level.

In order to describe the socio-economic outlook of south-eastern Sicily, we have chosen to analyse the dependency ratio, that is, the ratio of the sum of the number of children (0–14 years old) and older persons (65 years or over) compared with the working-age population (15–64 years old). The dependency ratio could be related to the productiveness and economic strength of the analysed area, although one must not forget that it only speculates that the productive part[3] of the population actually has an employment, but holds no certainties over this trait. Rather, the ratio highlights the presence of large clusters of young (0–14) or old (65+) people depending on the productive sectors of the local population.

While the biggest towns of Syracuse and Ragusa have experienced an increase in their dependency ratio (Syracuse moves from 44 in 1991 to 49 in 2011, while Ragusa moves from 49 to 52 in the same period), small municipalities like Acate and Pozzallo have a significant drop in their values: Acate moves from 51 to 44, and Pozzallo from 53 to 46. This means that in 2011 we can find a larger working-age population in Acate than in Milan (60), and that this trend seems to be continuous in time. This phenomenon is linked to several factors: the opening and closing of demographic windows (Golini & Marini, 2006), the ageing population, and the incoming flows of foreign citizens working in the greenhouses.

These data are even more significant if we compare the highest percentage variation of the dependency ratio from 1991 to 2011 for the municipalities in SES (Portopalo di Capo Passero, +16%) with other Italian cases, such as the Milan area (San Donato Milanese, +124%) or the Venice area (Spinea, +87%). Moreover, most municipalities in SES have negative values in their percentage variation of the dependency ratio, meaning that in 2011 the working-age population is larger than in 1991. Most notable are the cases of Acate (−12%) and Pozzallo (−11%), but 12 out of 19 municipalities in the area have a similar profile.

More surprises come if we look at the unemployment rate, although in all of Italy this rate was lower in 2011 than in 2001, but then it rose up and it is now (2014) higher than in 2001. Accordingly, in most Sicilian towns and cities there was a strong decrease in the unemployment rate over those ten years (for instance, Palermo moves from 29% in 2001 to 23% in 2011). The unemployment rates for Sicily are lower in SES, with Syracuse staying around 17% in 2011, and Ragusa and Modica getting a respectable (by Sicilian standards) 13%, if we compare it with bigger southern cities such as Naples and Catania (both around 26%). Again, agriculture and tourism may be two leading fields dictating this more positive (or rather, less negative) trend.

These latter hypotheses are confirmed if we take a look at the employees by industry sector. SES proves to be one of the most interesting regions of all Italy, because its agriculture and fishing (sector A) percentages of employees are very close to the top of the list (Portopalo di Capo Passero has a remarkable 49%, but most towns in the area have greatly increased their employees in this sector). Acate, one of the smallest towns west of Ragusa, looks like a solid sample of this trend: the employees in agriculture moved from 1.1% in 2001 to 6.3% in 2011, and definitely contributed to the demographic growth of the whole municipality in recent years; much of this growth can be explained with the presence of greenhouses, where flowers, tomatoes and eggplants are grown and the increasing presence of foreign people, who are employed in the greenhouses, often as seasonal labourers. Moreover, vines play an important role given the growing importance of IGP (in English: Protected Geographical Indication, also known as PGI-quality) and DOC (in English: Controlled and Guaranteed Designation of Origin) wines, as the dairy industrial sector does for the same reasons. As for tourism (sector I), most towns in SES have experienced remarkable increases in this domain, particularly Portopalo di Capo Passero (6% in 2001, 13% in 2011) and Pozzallo (7% and 12% respectively). This may be mainly explained by beach tourism, but cultural tourism in the UNESCO cities of the baroque (Modica, Ragusa, Scicli) also plays a key role (Fusero & Simonetti, 2005).

Quality agriculture and tourism become then two strategic elements for understanding how SES is slowly but firmly shaping its outlook and changing its representations in the global arena: from a traditional, deprived and marginal periphery to a thriving economic driving force in Sicily, and one to be reckoned with in Italy. If we consider Allen J. Scott's (2008) ideas on the most relevant economic aspects in post-metropolises, SES – although incomparable with much bigger and different contexts like Los Angeles – unexpectedly shows some elements that may be defined as "post-metropolitan", such as a lower unemployment rate and a demographic increase for those small towns (like Acate) hosting a renewed agricultural attractiveness.

Considering the average per capita income per taxpayer, the city of Syracuse (€18,026) surpasses Ragusa, Modica, Noto and Avola with their slightly lower incomes (€14,200–16,000). Incomes are also high compared with the rest of Italy. Venice, for example, has an income of €17,207, lower than Syracuse and higher than Lucca (in Tuscany), where shop rents are more than twice as expensive. The average per capita incomes of inhabitants are lower than those per taxpayer, however: Syracuse has €11,356, compared with €18,026 per taxpayer. Things are different in northern Italy, because the variance between the two values is lower (for example Venice has a €17,207 income per inhabitant, compared with €22,223 income per taxpayer); this confirms the effects of the higher Sicilian unemployment rates previously discussed, and portrays a society with few, but rich, taxpayers.

As we will more thoroughly discuss later, the growing presence of foreign citizens is affecting Sicily in unexpected ways (Lo Piccolo, 2013). In the 20 years between 1991 and 2011, all the municipalities included in SES have experienced a steady increase of foreign citizens. Acate (19%) and Santa Croce Camerina (15%) have very high values, like most other towns west of Ragusa. Once again, this is tied to the presence of greenhouses and intensive agriculture, where foreign citizens are often employed in deprived work conditions, sometimes quite close to slavery and mistreatment. Most foreign citizens in SES traditionally come from North Africa, but recently some Eastern European migrants (for example from Romania) have overcome them.

These trends lead to a few interesting considerations if we analyse the Index of Dispersion of the Foreign Population (IDFP), an index we have proposed building upon the existing literature on migrants and foreign citizens (Caritas Migrantes, 2011; INEA, 2013; Giampino et al., 2014; Lo Piccolo & Todaro, 2015), and defined as the percentage of foreign population in a single municipality multiplied by 100 and divided by the percentage of foreign population in the most populous city of that region. In this case, Acate (717) and Santa Croce Camerina (581) have the highest IDFP of all Italy, given the relatively low presence of foreign citizens in the most populous city of SES (Syracuse; Figure 10.2). This is another hint to the peculiar, polynuclear, post-metropolitan configuration of this region. The Venetian area has some similarities, with a strong polarization comparable with the westernmost municipalities of SES.

When we look at the data on migration flows in Sicily, we can point out a couple of significant issues. Syracuse is experiencing a slow but steady increase of incoming foreign people, with Italian people moving out of the city and relocating elsewhere (probably because of the high cost of living), while some towns such as Ragusa, Modica and Noto all have positive values. At the same time, foreign people are moving

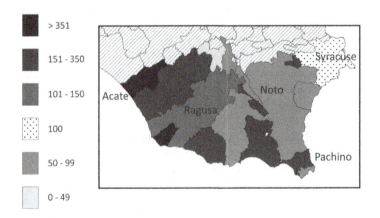

Figure 10.2 South-eastern Sicily: Index of Dispersion of the Foreign Population (IDFP) in 2011

Source: Authors' graphic based on PRIN Postmetropoli (2015)

to this region in very high numbers, if compared with the original population. This is especially true for Vittoria, Ragusa and Acate. There is also a strong increase of foreign people in Syracuse, but, given the high cost of living in that city, at least some of these people are likely able to afford that lifestyle, therefore suggesting different national origins (that is, Western Europeans looking for a historically and culturally attractive region to live in).

To summarize the evidence we have presented, we may consider the following:

1   South-eastern Sicily proves to be an exceptional case if compared with other parts of Sicily or southern Italy. This uniqueness is mainly due to a marginal, yet extremely resourceful, status that traces its roots to the baroque era and creates a space suitable for high-quality tourism and agriculture. In a sense, the most notable path dependence of SES is related to the role it has played within the island, and a somewhat wise exploitation of the traditional resources of the place, combined with a renewed interest for cultural and touristic relationships to other European countries.
2   The relatively small dimension of most cities and towns has likely reinforced the idea of a polynuclear urban region, with no capital centralizing functions and policies (as it happens, on the other hand, in the case of Palermo). The presence of foreign citizens, as we will more thoroughly discuss later, is an important piece of this puzzle. Therefore, the latest socio-economic developments are changing the traditional image of this apparently peripheral region, possibly turning it into a lesser, yet well-acknowledged cultural and economic polarity in Italy.
3   The challenges that SES is facing today lie mostly within the opportunity and ability to adapt to a quickly changing scenario, with Sicily no longer being a land of emigration but a place where incoming migrants could play a key socio-economic and cultural role. However, so far the situation does not comply with this, as migrants are often exploited, sometimes even abused and left to live and work in poor, inadequate conditions.

The controversial case of the immigrant population

With regard to the impact of globalization on urban spaces, Soja (2000), referring also to Chambers (1990), highlights the lack of conceptual and material limits of contemporaneous metropolis and the intensification of transnational flows of migrants, invoking the "turns toward cosmopolis" as resistance to the prevailing neoliberalism among other active approaches involved in the debate on post-metropolitan transition.

According to Soja, indeed, post-metropolis is the spatial – although transitory – result of new socio-spatial transformations of the cities; this is characterized by a high and new level of socio-economic fragmentation. In relation to these phenomena, social polarization of urban space, typical of the Fordist city, has given way to an "unstructured" and "dispersed" social geometry. This has called into question the traditional analytical models of the socio-spatial concentration geographies, and requires new interpretative categories.

These phenomena do not just occur in global cities, and they start to change the urban structure and scenario of even smaller (in terms of local population) urban areas or in extra-urban areas.

Over the last 50 years many European countries, considered areas of origin for international migratory flows in the twentieth century, became places of stable hospitality (King, 2000; Ambrosini, 2000).

More recently, the globalization processes and the deep socio-economic transformations, as well as the enlargement of the European Union to the countries of Eastern Europe, are at the heart of a complex system of interdependent factors that have changed the relationship between countries of origin and countries of destination for migratory flows (King, 2000).

Among the regions of Southern Europe, Sicily, in the last 30 years, has transformed itself from a land of emigrants into a land of immigrants, becoming the gateway to Europe, especially for the people arriving from North Africa.

With regard to the territorial distribution of foreign population in south-eastern Sicily, there is a clear phenomenon of socio-spatial polarization of immigrants, also in relation to the functional specialization of the territory. In effect, in south-eastern Sicily the immigrant population is mainly concentrated in rural areas and engaged in seasonal agricultural activities, especially in the summer–autumn period (Caritas Migrantes, 2011; Giampino et al., 2014).

With reference to the six discourses on the post-metropolis (Soja, 2000), these phenomena can be ascribed particularly to the discourse about "Exopolis", in which Soja describes the characteristics of a metropolitan dimension where in the area of south-eastern Sicily the traditional limits of settlements are exceeded. Moreover, the territorial distribution of the immigrant population in small municipalities shows a "restructured social mosaic" (Soja, 2000) that is at the same time, compared with a global scale, the result of the phenomena of de-territorialization and re-territorialization of capital, labour and culture ("Cosmopolis") and, in relation to the local scale, the outcome of hybridization, with increasingly evident impacts in injustice social terms and spatial marginalization and segregation ("Metropolarities") (Giampino et al., 2014).

Actually, south-eastern Sicily stands out as a polycentric structure of settlements; this structure, related to the quality agricultural production of the rural areas, promotes the dispersion of immigrant population, outlining a more distinctly post-metropolitan territorial profile in respect to other Sicilian areas.

However, the actual situation seems much more controversial if we analyse the rural context of south-eastern Sicily in greater depth, and in particular what is commonly called the "transformed strip" (municipalities of Vittoria, Acate, Ispica, Scicli, Pozzallo, Comiso, Santa Croce Camerina), along the coastal plain of Ragusa, which is characterized by intensive greenhouse production (fruit, vegetables, nurseries) (Todaro, 2014b).

In this area unofficial statistics (Caritas Migrantes, 2011; INEA, 2013) show a significant concentration of foreign workers employed in greenhouses; this allows a doubling of annual production of vegetables, but at the same time necessitates a greater number of workers.

Whereas the "greenhouse landscape", on the spatial front, has replaced the traditional dune-lined coastal landscape, from the eminently social point of view greenhouses also have determined a profound transformation in the "social landscape" of this area. This condition has led to a more complex "differentiated rurality" (Corrado, 2012), which is the result of the process of transformations in social and economic relations between the various ethnic groups; at the same time it has played an instrumental role in the success of the model of economic development of greenhouses. From this point of view the "social weakness" of immigrants is an essential component of the "greenhouses' landscape".

Behind this economic success, an extremely complex situation affects immigrants, often living and working in seriously demeaning conditions.[4]

The Ragusa area, in particular, apart from being a constant point of arrival for flows of illegal migrants from North Africa, already boasts a stable foreign presence; this is partly linked to historical immigration from the Maghreb, and partly to the temporary presence of workers (especially from Romania) on a cyclical basis, this being related to the shifting regional and inter-regional flows, which are, in turn, linked to the various production cycles (INEA, 2013). Most of these unskilled and low-cost manual workers are unregistered, and therefore are badly paid and unprotected; compared with these conditions, the various social, economic, sanitary and housing aspects are at some risk (Gertel & Sippel, 2014).

Examining living conditions in rural areas, they show a context of extreme difficulty: immigrants often live in small abandoned and unstable rural constructions, not far from the fields or greenhouses, and therefore a long way from inhabited neighbourhoods and services. The aforementioned living and working conditions, characterized by a vast spatial segregation, have serious repercussions on the immigrants' social and community situation. Working conditions in the greenhouses, the number of hours at work, the distance from towns and the unavailability of public transport that might render them "autonomous", constitute tangible limitations on their individual and collective freedom. Whereas, in the urban context, the "appropriation" of public space contributes significantly to the "construction" of a community or a group, with one's own spaces and one's own activities (Bonafede & Lo Piccolo, 2010; Lo Piccolo, 2013), for immigrants living and working in rural areas, and in particular in greenhouses, it is difficult to have access to these spaces and, consequently, to form a group, or, at the same time, to claim one's rights (Todaro, 2014a). For immigrants, claiming a "right to the city" (Lefebvre, 1968) often coincides with a demand for, and safeguard of, human rights (Bonafede & Lo Piccolo, 2010); therefore the difficulty of "access" to the city becomes a limitation on, or an actual denial of, these very fundamental rights.

Housing difficulties are linked, on the one hand, to forms of job exploitation and spatial segregation, and, on the other, to forms of social exclusion and isolation of individuals and small groups of immigrants; with regard to the aforementioned issues, they represent an extremely complex territorial profile, in which latent conditions of conflict find a niche (IRES, 2011).

The first condition of conflict to emerge principally involves clashes between different ethnic groups (in particular Northern Africans and Romanians) in the search for a job. Until the 2000s, the foreign workforce employed in the agricultural sector in the Province of Ragusa was made up almost entirely of Tunisians, and more generally, North Africans, arriving from the 1970s onwards. Over the years, these workers had acquired rights (fair wages, union rights, and so on) and a certain acknowledgement by society at large, which had put a few of them on the road to becoming entrepreneurs, and even, in some cases, to purchasing greenhouses. With the enlargement of the European Union to include Eastern Europe, a sort of "ethnic substitution" of immigrant workers took place in the Ragusa greenhouse belt (Colloca & Corrado, 2013); there was a sudden increase in fresh flows of immigrants, especially Romanians, seeking employment, and mostly taking the place of North Africans. These neo-Community workers came from countries characterized by serious socio-economic difficulties and were willing to accept very low wages (about 20 euros for a ten-hour working day), thus neutralizing the "social" gains achieved by the North Africans. For the whole immigrant manual workforce this was followed by a real loss of rights and a worsening of living and working conditions. Other critical conditions relate to the illegal status of immigrant greenhouse workers, with one part, in this case, moonlighting in the "black economy" and another in the "grey". Indeed, in the southern regions, the informal economy and irregular employment have even greater weight. These two aspects existed well before the arrival of immigrants (De Zulueta, 2003).

In respect to this condition, according to certain cautious estimates by Caritas Migrantes (2011), the former amounts to 10% (and in some periods of the year, up to 20%) of the total of "regular" workers. On the other hand, INEA (2013) suggests an estimate of 15,000–20,000 overall units of immigrant workers in agriculture and considers 50–60% of them to be "irregular"; in this case, immigrants are usually employed by small businesses, where there is a lower risk of controls.

In the light of the deliberations laid out above, it is clear that official statistics describe south-eastern Sicily as a dynamic, innovative (and post-modern) reality. At this point it would be useful to ask whether the conditions of the immigrant workers, which find little space in official reports, merely represent a factor that is instrumental in the success of this economic system (Berlan, 2008), or, on the contrary, if they call the whole system into question, highlighting a part of this story yet to surface.

Spatial perspective

Spatial phenomena and particularly those linked to the dynamics of the settlement system and other variations of utilizing the land, taken in parallel with demographic dynamics and those relating to population distribution, restore a polycentric distribution to SES, in contrast with the accentuated monocentrism of the greater metropolitan area of Palermo. The *tessera* comprises the whole Province of Ragusa and the southern part of the Province of Syracuse (including its administrative centre), where Syracuse, with it 122,503 inhabitants, against the 73,030 inhabitants of Ragusa (ISTAT, 2014), is instrumentally considered the main centre; however, the whole urban area is characterized by a polycentric settlement structure, in which small and medium-sized towns are interdependent with respect to the provision of facilities and services (Giampino et al., 2014).

The settlement model is quite common in the rest of Italy, with a network of small or medium-sized towns, which have traditionally followed lines of development based on the sharing of higher-ranking services and specialization. The advantages for territorial development that emerge in these forms of reticular territories are numerous. They range from economic growth (together with differentiation and specialization of production, promotion of district dynamics between small and medium-sized businesses often with evident results with regard to development of research and technical growth) to a raising of the quality of life (with reference to the improvement of the variety and specialization of services). In all cases mentioned these contexts have, as a precondition, the development of an adequate infrastructure system, which, in the case under examination, might be represented by the completion of the Catania–Syracuse–Ragusa motorway and the reinforcing of Comiso airport, but especially the overcoming of specific, traditionally individualistic, logical ideas that characterize, in particular, the public policies of certain municipalities, all of which renders the potential effects of "building a network" ineffective.

In this case, the small- and medium-sized urban areas are strongly linked to the historic events that assigned to each of them specific functions (also related to productive activities), establishing interdependent relations among them and with larger urban areas. In particular, in the region of Ragusa, agriculture constitutes the first sector of productive specialization with relevant results in relation to the innovation of the production, which is recognized at national and international level (Asmundo et al., 2011; Giampino et al., 2014).

Specifically in the region of Ragusa, the morphology of the territory contributed to the creation of a complex and polycentric settlement scheme where small- and medium-sized urban areas are scattered on the edge of calcarenitic terraces opening up towards the coast and creating breath-taking landscapes. Direct relationships can be observed between several settlements in the hills and their equivalent along the coastal strip: Vittoria with Scoglitti; Comiso with Punta Secca (suburb of Santa Croce Camerina); Ragusa with Marina di Ragusa. In these coastal areas most of the residential seasonal growth extends.

Generally, the areas around the largest towns were used initially for housing, and later on for industrial uses and coastal tourism. The settlements' coverage ratio in south-eastern Sicily is very low (although it has a strong impact on the landscape because of settlement dispersion), with the highest percentage being in Pozzallo (22%), and the rest having an average of less than 10%. In 2011, the situation is almost unchanged. The lowest peak is found in the municipalities of Noto and Rosolini, which respectively have a coverage ratio of 1% and 5%, while Syracuse and Ispica exceed the 10% threshold and the rest remains below.

These strong increases, along with the diffusion of greenhouses and an economy gravitating towards agriculture, prove very interesting and meaningful consequences (Magnaghi, 2013; Fusero & Simonetti, 2005).

As mentioned earlier, the number of houses remains quite steady in south-eastern Sicily. Acate, Santa Croce Camerina and Vittoria, however, have all experienced an increase in their number of houses, and this can be tied (at least for the first two cases) to the demographic growth and the inflow of foreign citizens.

Reflections on this indicator agree with what has already been asserted in the cases of the indicator on the resident population, on the housing dispersion index and on the unemployment rate.

In relation to the price of buildings, in south-eastern Sicily the sales price of dwellings, warehouses, stores and offices is strongly influenced by the peculiarities of the territory and the economic activities related to them. Syracuse, Modica, Scicli and Ragusa were declared UNESCO sites and affected by rehabilitation programmes of the historic town, and therefore are the most expensive areas. Regarding shops, the rents exceed the prices of Palermo, close to the €2,000 per square meter threshold, and still remain low when compared with many popular tourist destinations of the Italian coast. Just like the region of Palermo, south-eastern prices decrease as one moves inland.

Finally, in relation to the accommodation capacity, the analysed data show a significant increase of the tourist offering. Field research and scholarly literature explain the phenomenon with the more organized and better tourist offering, also aimed at the international level, which characterized the area in the last decade. All of this must certainly be related to the baroque architecture, growing seaside tourism and the aforementioned imagery of historical landscape that characterizes the area. These are elements that the municipalities have enhanced, turning them into a driving force for the economy of the whole area.

However, taking a closer look at the phenomena analysed, a few interesting and controversial aspects need to be underlined.

The current offering, actually, is based on a short and fragmented cultural chain, weak in terms of system services and innovative contents if compared with the central role of cultural heritage, and colliding with a strong national and international competitiveness in the market of tourist destinations of cultural interest.

The Province of Syracuse in Sicily is second only to that of Messina for the number and level of hotels. In 2012 it counts 4 five-star hotels (in 2005, the year of introduction of Syracuse in the WHL, it was one), 34 four-star hotels (in 2005 they were 14), 48 three-star hotels (in 2005 they were 43), 16 two-star hotels (in 2005 they were 17), 9 one-star hotels (in 2005 they were 16). The four five-star hotels are all in Syracuse – two of them in Ortygia. However, a significant increase of tourists does not correspond to the increase of the four- and five-star hotels. In 2012, for number of tourists, the province of Syracuse (1,249,936) comes after those of Messina (3,464,271), Palermo (3,057,733), Trapani (2,084,475), Catania (1,871,849) and Agrigento (1,300,906) (Tourism Observatory data, Department of Tourism, Sport and Entertainment, Regione Siciliana, 2014).

The increase of the tourist offering is also certainly related to the inscription of the "Syracuse and the Rocky Necropolis of Pantalica" site in the UNESCO World Heritage List in 2005.

This popular acknowledgement at the local and at the global level is generally considered a contributing factor to the rise in popularity of the site, in its "appeal" and consequently in promoting tourism. In the case of Syracuse, the growing tourist offering, together with directly or indirectly linked forms of speculation (mainly related to a distorted vision of promoting tourism development, with serious effects on high-quality soil consumption, especially in coastal areas and agricultural landscape), could impair the value of cultural heritage for which the site has been included in the WHL. The real risk does not imply a significant increase in tourism flows and economy. On the contrary, the process of replacement of traditional handicraft and commercial activities in Ortygia, together with the process of construction of coastal strip and internal or close interventions to the UNESCO site, shows how the presence of the UNESCO site has been an accelerator of the forms of pressure without the effective promotion of development actions, or – even less – the implementation of safeguarding actions (Lo Piccolo & Todaro, 2014).

In relation to the Ragusa region, if we look at the products, services and facilities for tourists, the region has significantly changed its territorial profile over the last 20 years. Namely two main trends have been recorded: new accommodation facilities have been developed, from hotels and holiday villages to a wide range of large-, medium- and small-sized facilities, and they are now evenly spread throughout the territory, while in the past they were exclusively located along the coast. Over the last decade, accommodation facilities other than hotels, mainly rural accommodations and B&Bs, had a consistent and significant positive trend: in the 2012–13 period, 206 new facilities came into operation (Giampino et al., 2015).

Concerning tourist flows, a few surveys carried out in this field (Mantovani, 2010; Magazzino & Mantovani, 2012) and crossing various basic data, clearly show that in the 2000–08 period, tourist arrivals and overnight stays in the Province of Ragusa, if compared with Sicily, increased by 5.0% and 5.8% with respect to the period 1990–99, when they were 4.5% and 5.2% respectively.

Moreover, given the broader scenario of the international crisis that is also affecting tourism, in general south-eastern Sicily seems to maintain positive figures.

According to some scholars, the Italian RAI TV series *Inspector Montalbano*[5] (put on the air in Italy and in 18 other countries from 1999–2013) significantly contributed to this success. *Inspector Montalbano*, protagonist of the stories of Camilleri, played its part in limiting the crisis of the tourism sector in the 2007–13 period, in a comparison with regional trends of Sicily (Mantovani, 2010).

Furthermore, although we cannot argue that *Inspector Montalbano* is directly responsible for the steady performance of tourist flows, it is undeniable that the TV series showed the territory and the landscapes of south-eastern Sicily successfully and made them known to the world.

Over the last few years, many tourists went to see the so-called "places of Montalbano". The Inspector's house located on the beach of Punta Secca, in the territory of Santa Croce Camerina, has been transformed into "La casa di Montalbano" B&B. The town hall of Scicli, which in the TV series is home to the police station, has been moved to a different venue in order to be visited as one of the most popular sites.

Although the "Montalbano effect" has helped the world familiarize itself with this area and has contributed to maintaining high levels of tourism, the actual, relative policies have not been capable of transforming and modernizing the quality of tourist facilities and bringing them into line with international standards (Giampino et al., 2015).

In fact, there is a very weak, or sometimes even non-existent, system strategy aimed at directing tourist flows and the tourist demand towards a more sustainable, responsible and innovative tourism. In particular, the current offer relies on a short and fragmented supply chain featuring extremely poor innovation with respect to the key role of cultural heritage and system services. Nonetheless, a very strong national and international competitiveness does exist in the market of cultural destinations for tourists.

To summarize the evidence we have presented, we may consider the following:

1   From the spatial point of view, the whole urban area is characterized by a polycentric settlement structure, in which small- and medium-sized towns are interdependent with respect to the provision of facilities and services. This settlement development is based on the sharing of higher-ranking services and specialization of towns.
2   More recently pressure of the settlements increased, especially along the coasts. This is largely because of the international attractiveness of this area, which increased because of the following two factors: marketing activities related to the cultural and gastronomic offer (those related to the establishment of UNESCO sites, *Inspector Montalbano*, and so on) for international tourism; and the opportunity to easily find unskilled work in the field of greenhouses for immigrant workers coming first from North Africa and more recently from Eastern Europe.
3   The settlement growth determined an increase of the impact on the environment and landscape, as well as the increase in the price of buildings in the most attractive centres (Syracuse, Ragusa, Modica, Scicli, Noto). On the other hand, local policies have not been able to transform and modernize the quality of tourist facilities, bringing them into line with international standards. While, in relation to the immigrant workers, major problems are noted with regard to the lack of houses and services, as well as the forms of abuse and labour exploitation.

Institutional perspective

The data analysed below highlight that south-eastern Sicily has a high level of local and inter-local planning and programming initiatives. From the planning point of view, the Provinces of Ragusa and Syracuse are traditionally characterized by a greater number of planning instruments than the other provinces in Sicily, dealing with aspects of both territorial planning and environmental and landscape safeguarding.

Furthermore, more recently the *tessera* is characterized by inter-institutional cooperation practices in order to promote new socio-economic development programmes (Progetti Integrati Territoriali, Patti Territoriali, Progetti Integrati d'Area, Programmi di Riqualificazione Urbana e Sviluppo Sostenibile del Territorio, Programmi di Recupero Urbano, Programmi di Iniziativa Comunitaria, Piani strategici, Piani Integrati di Sviluppo Urbano, Piani Integrati di Sviluppo Territoriale). However, these tools establish controversial relationships with respect to the traditional urban planning instruments and policies (Lo Piccolo & Todaro, 2014).

The new instruments have considerable financial resources at their disposal. In contrast, town planning policies are essentially perceived as regulative or, even worse, as restrictive. In many cases a real clash between the former and the latter can be perceived. On the one hand, local development policies have distributed considerable financial resources in a context of fiscal crisis and serious economic deficiency in local administrations, and have therefore imposed themselves with the "supremacy of money". On the other hand, traditional town planning policies have not been understood by local communities and authorities as real opportunities for guiding and stimulating local development and have often been put into practice in a bureaucratic way (Lo Piccolo & Schilleci, 2005; Lo Piccolo & Todaro, 2014).

However, the results emerging from the new instruments often prove to be short-lived and incapable of activating effective and long-lasting processes of socio-economic development. The general absence of any link-up with town planning should also be emphasized. In fact, in cases in which the new instruments are administratively handled by the town planning sector of the same municipality, they assume the form of isolated projects in most cases, with the result of generalized town planning provisions, which are generally weak.

Moreover, the paradoxical result is that the new instruments, rather than playing a leading role in promoting innovative strategies and actions, become a collection of goals and actions deriving from other pre-existing programming instruments.

With regard to the topics examined, the principal elements of continuity with the recent past seem to consist in singling out tourism as a lever in activating processes of local development and enhancement. It has to be said that these objectives have already been widely associated with integrated territorial planning (which has incorporated many of the new instruments), but these new instruments tend to be more specialized with regard to the sub-sections of cultural tourism.

Although these instruments are characterized by a bottom–up approach, typical of a post-metropolitan reality, the result is an inverse, and totally inefficient conformity, which is that of the new instruments compared with the other existing local programmes (Lo Piccolo et al., 2012).

With reference to partnerships and territorial aggregations regarding these local policies, the need to build networks, usually encouraged by national and regional guidelines, finds an atypical variant in south-eastern Sicily.

We can identify two main territorial nodes: the urban area of Syracuse and the territory of Ragusa. In the first case, although active programmes have aggregated several municipalities (Augusta, Noto, Avola, Syracuse) in different forms from time to time, territorial coordination processes were activated (for example Piani Strategici) to bring individual projects to common strategies. However, the attempt to establish a coalition proves a formal aggregation of municipalities, unable to work for common aims. Anyway, Syracuse remains a reference city for local development policies and tends to activate autonomous programmes.

In the second case, local development strategies describe two main areas of territorial aggregation of municipalities: the mountainous area of the system of Hyblaean Mounts (Giarratana, Monterosso Almo, Comiso, Modica, Ragusa) and the coastal system (Acate, Vittoria, Santa Croce Camerina, Scicli, Pozzallo) (Giampino et al., 2010).

Also in this case the aggregations of municipalities often produce weak alliances geared towards competitiveness in the accumulation of partners, in order to obtain public funding (especially structural funds), rather than effectiveness of strategy for territorial growth and development. This status appears evident from the fitful commitment of mayors and town councillors in launching new programmes (strategic plans).

In some cases the role of programme coordination is entrusted to territorial development agencies, which were set up during the running of previous programmes, such as, for example, offices (urban centres, civic centres, and so on) for "EU policies" or "European projects" spawned in the larger cities.

We can observe a tangible example of this situation in Ortygia, Syracuse's old town. Looking specifically at the outcomes of these instruments in the case of Ortygia, an urban context significantly affected by changes in physical, economic, social and environmental components emerges. However, some critical issues can be observed (Lo Piccolo & Todaro, 2014).

In these years, several projects of urban regeneration were enabled, with incentives for creating renovation and economic revitalization initiatives. Ortygia peninsula was then involved in a process of renewal that, even through the localization of key administrative functions, has reinstated centrality to the peninsula that has returned to be inhabited by the Syracusans (Liistro, 2008). This process resulted in the reactivation of the housing market – also boosted by the significant presence of foreign investments – significantly increasing real estate values (Cannarozzo, 2006).

Although in the last 20 years the peninsula of Ortygia has attracted the interest of planning and programming, the activated instruments have resulted in the realization of (sometimes only partial) punctual interventions that did not follow a unitary and organic project (Lo Piccolo & Schilleci, 2005; Lo Piccolo, 2007). It shows, in fact, the evident imbalance between the localization of recovery interventions carried out in the proximity of archaeological and historic monumental interest areas or the seafront and inland areas, which are still characterized by serious physical and social degradation. Added to this is the growing investment by individuals and real estate companies, not governed by public action, which determines the progressive replacement of traditional socio-economic networks with commercial and tourism activities. This phenomenon, accompanied by the progressive disappearance of neighbourhood services (especially for children and the elderly), is causing the loss of the minimum requirements to ensure habitability (Lo Piccolo & Todaro, 2014).

Furthermore, as regards policies for enhancing the cultural heritage in south-eastern Sicily, a specific phenomenon has been observed, with particular importance for the significant and often controversial effects it produced.

This phenomenon stems from a process promoted by the Agencies for Cultural and Environmental Heritage of Syracuse and Catania, later joined by the city of Ragusa, and consists in the "construction" of the unitary territorial image of the "late baroque cities". This image of the territory, based on the recognition of baroque architecture and urban planning as a unifying identity value attracting tourists and visitors, inspired the cultural enhancement policies that were implemented in the 1990–2000 period. Among them, in 2002, the "Late Baroque Cities of Val di Noto" (Noto, Scicli, Ragusa, Militello Val di Catania, Caltagirone, Palazzolo Acreide, Catania, Modica) were listed as UNESCO World Heritage sites, and the Southeast Cultural District "Late Baroque Cities of Val di Noto" (financed in 2009 by the Regional Operational Plan of Sicily 2000–06, Measure 2.02.d) was established with the purpose of implementing the management plan of the UNESCO site (Giampino et al., 2015).

Moreover, the image of this area produced by the TV series *Inspector Montalbano* (see the section on tourism) also contributed to the construction of this phenomenon.

In the light of this phenomenon, and of the misrepresentation that inevitably comes with it, it should, however, be pointed out that tourism is a recently emerged opportunity for the territory of Ragusa, which needs well-structured strategies and enhanced consolidation (Trigilia, 2012; Azzolina et al., 2012). In this territory, the tourist districts were initially established with a spirit of cooperation and they are currently nothing but an aggregation of municipalities unable to express a "unitary vision of the territory of the Southeast" (Azzolina et al., 2012, p. 161). Moreover, the supply of tourist services is based on a traditional model of tourism, which is fully focused on accommodation facilities and catering services. Such a model features extremely poor innovation with respect to the key role of cultural heritage, despite a very strong national and international competitiveness in the market of cultural destinations for tourists. In particular, services and infrastructure (including technological ones) prove to be inadequate both in the private and public sector (Giampino et al., 2015).

To summarize the evidence we have presented, we may consider the following:

1   South-eastern Sicily shows a high level of local and inter-local planning tools. From the planning point of view, the Provinces of Ragusa and Syracuse are traditionally characterized by a greater number of planning instruments than the other Provinces in Sicily, dealing with aspects of both territorial planning and environmental and landscape safeguarding.

2   More recently the area shows a marked tendency to inter-institutional cooperation, by activating new territorial development programmes. These recent experiences are interesting for two reasons: the capability to build networks of inter-institutional cooperation, usually encouraged by national and regional guidelines, and the presumed "flexibility" of these programmes with respect to the "rigidity" of the traditional planning instruments.

3   New instruments often become a collection of goals and actions deriving from other pre-existing programming instruments rather than playing a leading role in promoting innovative strategies and actions; new programmes also establish controversial relationships with respect to the traditional urban planning instruments. Furthermore, the networks of inter-institutional cooperation often produce weak alliances geared towards competitiveness in the accumulation of partners, in order to obtain public funding, rather than effectiveness of strategy for territorial growth and development.

Conclusions

Even temporarily neglecting any social, urban or economic analysis, it is enough to take a simple look at the demographic profile of Los Angeles, on the one hand, and of Palermo, on the other hand, to understand how those scales cannot be superimposed at all – even worse if we take into account the area between Syracuse and Ragusa. And yet, Soja argues:

> the grounding of the post-metropolitan transition in Los Angeles is not meant to constrict interpretation of the post-metropolis just to this singular and often highly exceptional city-region. Rather, it is guided by an attempt to emphasize what might be called its generalizable particularities, the degree to which one can use the specific case of Los Angeles to learn more about the new urbanization processes that are affecting, with varying degrees of intensity, all other cityspaces in the world (Soja, 2000, p. 154).

In other words, if we want to "test" the existence and the possible functioning of post-metropolitan systems, we have to play along with Soja: it is not a matter of adapting the Los Angeles model to the world, but of extrapolating from the particular Californian case those "lessons" that can be valid for all the world.

It is a paradoxical game, of course, based on the "what if" rule, as "counterfactual history" suggests (Ferguson, 1999): in that kind of history, every essential question begins with "what if . . . ?" We believe that in addition to the counterfactual history we might think in terms of a counterfactual geography. Instead of asking ourselves, like historians would do, what would have happened if Hitler had won the war, we will ask what would happen if south-eastern Sicily were a post-metropolitan land. Our goal is to ascertain whether, with Soja's words, there are lessons that Los Angeles can teach to the Sicilian urban studies. Or rather, in a more provocative key, but basically as a logical consequence of these premises, if the south-east of the island can show to the world, including Los Angeles, some variations to the standard model in California, used to explain the operation of the cities of the future.

There are two basic reasons that can help us further this reasoning: if we look at the number of employees by industry sectors, within the boundaries imposed by the ongoing crisis, there are interesting variations that help us to outline a more post-metropolitan territorial profile than the one of Palermo, where the traditional leading sectors, such as building manufactures, remain the same.

Second, if we look at the effects that the economic transition raises on spatial structures, we can detect in south-eastern Sicily a polynuclear localization process of productive, industrial and non-industrial activities, which follows the historic polycentric settlement pattern, compared with a conversion of the industries to commercial activities already affected by a process of delocalization of the centre of Palermo. Similarly, in reference to the internationalization of the agricultural products of south-eastern Sicily, this area proves capable of innovating its productive district (Asmundo et al., 2011).

If the area of Palermo, from a normative and conceptual point of view, can at least be considered a metropolitan city, south-eastern Sicily, traditionally considered a non-metropolitan context, shows a more dynamic, innovative and post-modern situation. What if, as a consequence, south-eastern Sicily were a new reality able to provide useful insights on possible future alternative post-metropolises? And what if, paradoxically, south-eastern Sicily were even more post-metropolitan, in some respects, than Los Angeles?

One of the topics that seems particularly innovative in SES is the way planning has affected these areas, because most municipalities in the Provinces of Ragusa and Syracuse, as we recalled earlier, produced lots of urban and territorial plans, many more than the other Provinces in Sicily. These tools, however, should interact with the socio-economic policies starting from the challenges that we have described (migrants, cultural tourism, quality agriculture, and so on). If these two domains (planning and socio-economic policies) were capable of properly interacting, SES might launch development processes that are more efficient than the average of southern Italy, once again proving to be a leading region in this part of the country.

Notes

1 Although this chapter should be considered a result of the common work and reflection of the three authors, M. Picone took primary responsibility for the sections "A counterfactual post-metropolitan region" and "Socio-economic perspective", F. Lo Piccolo took primary responsibility for the sections "The controversial case of the immigrant population" and "Conclusions", and V. Todaro took primary responsibility for the sections "Spatial perspective" and "Institutional perspective". Maps and tables have been developed by Riccardo Alongi and Giovanna Ceno.

2 This regional portrait is strictly related to the other Sicilian portrait, which describes the metropolitan area of Palermo (see Chapter 9). Our research group from the University of Palermo initially proposed to compare these two Sicilian cases (Palermo and the south-east) in order to appraise the similarities and differences between them, but most of all to prove how these two peculiar cases show some unexpected post-metropolitan traits. Therefore, even if we chose to present the two areas as separate portraits, we suggest that readers look for some shared characteristics. Within this portrait, there are several references to Sicily and the rest of Italy which can help the reader grasp the uniqueness and peculiarity of the island, as related to the Italian context.

3 The dependency ratio is actually just a demographic indicator; linking it to other economic elements (such as the unemployment rate or the inactivity rate) would require additional speculation.
4 Data on this topic are provided not only by the official enquiries made by the Italian Institute of Statistics (ISTAT) but also by parallel reports, such as those from Caritas Migrantes (2011), IRES (2011) and INEA (2013).
5 At present (12 episodes from 2012–15) *The Young Montalbano* is being broadcast, which deals with the events of the Inspector at a young age.

References

Abbate, G. (2011). La valorizzazione dei centri minori come elemento strategico dello sviluppo del territorio. In F. Toppetti (Ed.), *Paesaggi e città storica. Teorie e politiche del progetto* (pp. 141–144). Firenze: Alinea.

Ambrosini, M. (2000). Migrazioni internazionali, reti etniche e mercato del lavoro: per una revisione degli approcci teorici e delle letture correnti. In G. Scidà (Ed.), *I sociologi italiani e le dinamiche dei processi migratori* (pp. 46–57). Milano: FrancoAngeli.

Asmundo, A., Asso, P.F., and Pitti, G. (2011). Innovare in Sicilia durante la crisi: un aggiornamento di Remare controcorrente. *StrumentiRes*, 3(4), 1–7.

Asso, P.F., and Trigilia, C. (Eds.). (2010). *Remare controcorrente. Imprese e territori dell'innovazione in Sicilia*. Roma: Donzelli.

Azzolina, L., Biagiotti, A., Colloca, C., Giambalvo, M., Giunta, R., Lucido, S., Manzo, C., and Rizza, S. (2012). I beni culturali e ambientali. Ragusa. In P. Casavola and C. Trigilia (Eds.), *La nuova occasione. Città e valorizzazione delle risorse locali* (pp. 203–212). Roma: Donzelli Editore.

Berlan, J.P. (2008). L'immigré agricole comme modèle sociétal? *Études rurales*, 182, 219–226.

Bonafede, G., and Lo Piccolo, F. (2010). Spazi di soglia e diritto alla cittadinanza: esperienze e riflessioni per la riconquista dello spazio pubblico. In G. Berruti, V. D'Ambrosio, C. Orfeo, and P. Scala (Eds.), *Abitare il futuro . . . dopo Copenhagen* (pp. 1671–1685). Napoli: CLEAN edizioni.

Cannarozzo, T. (2006). Dal piano ai progetti. Due interventi pubblici di recepero residenziale a Ortigia. In F. Trapani (Ed.), *Urbacost. Un progetto pilota per la Sicilia centrale* (pp. 194–201). Milano: FrancoAngeli.

Cannarozzo, T. (2010). Centri storici e città contemporanea: dinamiche e politiche. In G. Abbate, T. Cannarozzo, and G. Trombino (Eds.), *Centri storici e territorio. Il caso di Scicli* (pp. 9–22). Firenze: Alinea.

Caritas Migrantes. (2011). *Dossier statistico immigrazione 2011. XXI Rapporto*. Roma: IDOS Edizioni.

Chambers, I. (1990). *Border Dialogues: Journeys in Postmodernity*. London and New York: Routledge.

Colloca, C., and Corrado, A. (2013). Trasformazioni meridionali: migranti e aree rurali. In C. Colloca and A. Corrado (Eds.), *La globalizzazione delle campagne. Migranti e società rurali nel Sud Italia* (pp. 13–29). Milano: FrancoAngeli.

Corrado, A. (2012). Ruralità differenziate e migrazioni nel Sud Italia. *Agriregionieuropa*, 28(8), 72–75.

De Zulueta, T. (2003). *Migrants in Irregular Employment in the Agricultural Sector of Southern European Countries: Report for the Debate in the Standing Committee*. Strasbourg: Council of Europe.

Ferguson, N. (1999). Virtual History: Towards a 'Chaotic' Theory of the Past. In N. Ferguson (Ed.), *Virtual History* (pp. 1–90). London: Basic Books.

Fusero, P., and Simonetti, F. (Eds.). (2005). *Il sistema ibleo. Interventi e strategie.* Modica: Idealprint.

Gertel, J., and Sippel, S.R. (2014). Epilogue: The Social Costs of Eating Fresh. In J. Gertel and S.R. Sippel (Eds.), *Seasonal Workers in Mediterranean Agriculture: The Social Costs of Eating Fresh* (pp. 246–252). London: Routledge.

Giampino, A., Lo Piccolo, F., and Todaro, V. (2015). The Power of Fiction in Times of Crisis: Movie-Tourism and Heritage Planning in Montalbano's Places. In A. Gospodini (Ed.), *Proceedings of the International Conference on Changing Cities II: Spatial, Design, Landscape & Socioeconomic Dimensions.* Porto Heli, Peloponnese, Greece, June 22–26 (pp. 283–292). Thessaloniki: Grafima Publ.

Giampino, A., Picone, M., and Todaro, V. (2014). Postmetropoli in contesti al 'margine'. *Planum,* 2(29), 1308–1316.

Giampino, A., Todaro, V., and Vinci, I. (2010). I piani strategici siciliani: interpretazioni di territorio ed orientamenti progettuali. In I. Vinci (Ed.), *Pianificazione strategica in contesti fragili* (pp. 43–93). Firenze: Alinea.

Golini, A., and Marini, C. (2006). Aspetti nazionali ed internazionali delle popolazioni considerate da una finestra demografica, *Quaderni di ricerca. Serie speciale. Convergenze e divergenze nell'area euro-mediterranea,* 2, Università Politecnica delle Marche.

INEA. (2013). *Indagine sull'impiego degli immigrati in agricoltura in Italia 2011,* Roma: INEA.

IRES, Istituto Ricerche Economiche e Sociali. (2011). *Immigrazione, sfruttamento e conflitto sociale. Una mappatura delle aree a rischio e quattro studi di caso territoriali, Rapporto 1/2011.* Retrieved from http://www.ires.it/contenuti/immigrazione-sfrutta-mento-e-conflitto-sociale-mappatura-delle-aree-rischio-e-quattro-studi.

ISTAT. (2014). *Popolazione residente al 31 dicembre 2014* [data file]. Retrieved from: http://demo.istat.it/pop2014/index3.html.

King, R. (2000). Southern Europe in the Changing Global Map of Migration. In R. King, G. Lazaridis and C. Tsardanidis (Eds.), *Eldorado or Fortress? Migration in Southern Europe* (pp. 1–26). Basingstoke: Macmillan.

Liistro, M. (2008). *Ortigia: memoria e futuro.* Roma: Edizioni Kappa.

Lefebvre, H. (1968). *Le droit à la ville.* Paris: Anthropos.

Lo Piccolo, F. (2007). Siracusa: misconoscimento e potenzialità dell'identità locale. In B. Rossi Doria (Ed.), *Sicilia terra di città* (pp. 150–175). Firenze: Istituto Geografico Militare.

Lo Piccolo, F. (2013). Nuovi abitanti e diritto alla città: riposizionamenti teorici e responsabilità operative della disciplina urbanistica. In F. Lo Piccolo (Ed.), *Nuovi abitanti e diritto alla città. Un viaggio in Italia* (pp. 15–32). Firenze: Altralinea.

Lo Piccolo, F., and Schilleci, F. (2005). Local Development Partnership Programmes in Sicily: Planning Cities without Plans. *Planning Practice and Research,* 20(1), 79–87.

Lo Piccolo, F., and Todaro, V. (2014). From Planning to Management of Cultural Heritage Sites: Controversies and Conflicts between UNESCO WHL Management Plans and Local Spatial Planning in South-eastern Sicily. *European Spatial Research and Policy,* 21(2), 47–76.

Lo Piccolo, F., and Todaro, V. (2015). Concentración vs dispersión de los inmigrantes en Italia. Análisis comparativo de la distribución de la población extranjera en las regiones urbanas, *CyTET,* 47(184), 397–404.

Lo Piccolo, F., Leone, D., and Pizzuto, P. (2012). The (Controversial) Role of the UNESCO WHL Management Plans in Promoting Sustainable Tourism Development. *Journal of Policy Research in Tourism, Leisure and Events*, 4(3), 249–276.

Magazzino, M., and Mantovani, M. (2012). L'impatto delle produzioni cinematografiche sul turismo. Il caso de il Commissario Montalbano per la Provincia di Ragusa. *Rivista di Scienze del Turismo*, 1, 29–42.

Magnaghi, A. (2013). Riterritorializzare il mondo. *Scienze del Territorio*, 1, 47–58.

Mantovani, M. (2010). Produzioni cinematografiche e turismo: le politiche pubbliche per la localizzazione cinematografica. *Rivista di Scienze del Turismo*, 3, 8–103.

Nobile, M.R. (1990). *Architettura religiosa negli Iblei. Dal Rinascimento al Barocco*. Siracusa: Ediprint.

Picone, M. (2006). Il ciclo di vita urbano in Sicilia. *Rivista Geografica Italiana*, 113, 129–146.

PRIN Postmetropoli. (2015). *Atlante web dei territori postmetropolitani* [web atlas]. Retrieved from: http://www.postmetropoli.it/atlante.

Schilirò, D. (2012). Industria e distretti produttivi in Sicilia fra incentivi e sviluppo, *StrumentiRes*, 4(1), 1–10.

Scott, A.J. (2008). *Social Economy of the Metropolis: Cognitive-Cultural Capitalism and the Global Resurgence of Cities*. Oxford: Oxford University Press.

Soja, E.W. (2000). *Postmetropolis: Critical Studies of Cities and Regions*. Malden, MA: Blackwell.

Soja, E.W. (2011). Regional Urbanization and the End of the Metropolis Era. In G. Bridge and S. Watson (Eds.), *New Companion to the City* (pp. 679–89). Chichester: Wiley-Blackwell.

Todaro, V. (2014a). *Immigrants and Post-metropolitan Territories: Some Case Studies from Marginal Contexts*. AESOP Conference, 9–12 July 2014: From control to co-evolution, Utrecht.

Todaro, V. (2014b). Immigrati in contesti fragili, tra conflitti latenti e limiti delle politiche locali di accoglienza. *Urbanistica Informazioni*, 257, 42–45.

Trigilia, C. (2012). *Non c'è Nord senza Sud. Perché la crescita dell'Italia si decide nel Mezzogiorno*. Bologna: il Mulino.

van den Berg, L., Drewett R., and Klaassen L.H. (1982). *Urban Europe: A Study of Growth and Decline*. Oxford: Pergamon.

11 The territory of the Sardinian Province of Olbia-Tempio on the post-metropolitan horizon

From edge area to node of a new city-world

Lidia Decandia[1]

Introduction

This chapter focuses on a territory performing extremely unusual features: the province of Olbia-Tempio, an area situated in the north of Sardinia which, in recent decades, compared with the other urban contexts of the island, has taken on highly dynamic traits. This part of the region, where no classically outlined urban reality existed before the 1960s, shows the emerging features of an authentic post-metropolitan territory: the invention of a particular simulacrum city – the holiday city – together with the effects produced by the introduction of television, IT communication and globalisation, generated this profound transformation.

Because of this variety of factors, this corner of the world, which had remained for centuries in basic isolation – thanks indeed to its unusual environmental-historic character being reinterpreted and used within a nascent consumer economy – entered into a network of flows and a mediatised aesthetic space, becoming an integral part of that city-world and world-city that now embraces the entire world (Lefebvre, 1968/1970; Choay, 1994; Amin & Thrift, 2002; Soja, 2000/2007; Brenner, 2014).

The section entirely frames the area of the province that is an environmental-historic and geographical unit particularly involved in this powerful transformation. It contains the whole of the old region of Gallura, dominated by the presence of Mount Limbara, which acts as a watershed with the old region of Mount Acuto, a portion of which – the area on the other side of the mountain – is situated within the said provincial confines and hence within the section. It is in fact the Oschiri-Monti environmental corridor, separating the Gallura Mountains from the highlands of the central-north sector that identifies the border to the south. The choice of this portion of territory enabled us to analyse the interaction between: on one side, the phenomena that took place in developing the coastal city, which has its driving force in the towns of Olbia and Arzachena; on the other, the effects this development has produced on the settlement framework of the internal areas, which up until the 1950s were the centre of activity for this territory.

To account for the effects produced and provide the key to interpreting the data that have arisen from the *Atlante* (PRIN Postmetropoli, 2015), we use a narrative perspective for this chapter. Starting with a general background and summarised reading of the environmental features characterising this territory, the regional portrait attempts to outline those processes of de-territorialisation and re-territorialisation by means of which this unprecedented urban reality is emerging – a reality that is taking on decidedly unusual features, which make it perhaps unique in the panorama of Italian urban regions. Rather than being characterised by extension and density of built-up territories, it stands out for the vastness of its "empty", silent lands. In these areas where, as some suggestions present in the data supplied by the *Atlante* show, the contemporary period is rediscovering in innovative forms, archaic elements and evidence of possible futures appears to be under way, highlighting how these areas "discarded by modernity", if reinterpreted in a project-oriented form, could turn into "cornerstones" for the construction of a new idea of city.

Areas discarded by modernity on the post-metropolitan horizon

From the industrial society to the consumer society: marginal territories as integral parts of post-industrial production

"I shall begin with the following hypothesis: society has been completely urbanised" (Lefebvre, 1970/1973, p. 7). This was how in 1970 Lefebvre, recently taken up by Brenner (2014, p. 17), announced a revolution, which at the time he saw in a virtual state, but which would lead in just a few decades to transforming the whole world into a completely urbanised reality. Departing from this hypothesis, in its ever-topical, interesting text, Lefebvre showed how the effects produced by the Industrial Revolution would reach such a critical point as to produce authentic socio-spatial restructuring on a planetary scale, determined by a process of reorganisation of capital[2] – reorganisation that would weave into a single "urban fibre [. . .] different places, territories and scales", including those zones "situated very far from the traditional centres of the agglomerations, urbanism and metropolitan life" (Lefebvre, 1970/1973, p. 10).

In this sense, Lefebvre did not intend, however, to refer to a process of expansion of the "kingdom of built-up city zones", which would result in a single, unending urbanised area but, rather, to assert the predominance of "an unprecedented urban reality" (Lefebvre, 1970/1973, p. 10)[3] over the country. "An urban reality simultaneously enlarged and unleashed that" – as he himself stated – "would lose in this shift the features the previous epoch had attributed to it: organic totality, competence, exciting image, measured space, dominated by the splendour of monuments. It would be populated by signs of the urban in the disintegration of urbanity", becoming "stipulation, repressive order through signals, summary code of circulation (routes) and recognition" (Lefebvre, 1970/1973, p. 20).

Soja's book *Postmetropolis* also opens with the image of a world "becoming very similar to a city", taken up from Mumford (1961) after a gap of 30 years (Soja, 2000/2007, p. 33). The author invented this concept precisely to attempt to redefine what he himself called the Fourth Urban Revolution (Soja, 2000/2007, p. 174) – a revolution under way that, by a simultaneous process of de-territorialisation and re-territorialisation, was determining the "creation of new forms and recombinations of social spatiality and territorial identities" (Soja, 2000/2007, p. 177), very different and considerably more complex than the preceding ones. These are difficult forms to map out following sharp lines of demarcation between city and country, urban and non-urban, real and imaginary.

Soja himself highlights how, within this reorganisation process, more marginal spaces indeed are absorbed into this new urban world.

"The new executive class" – in fact, as Castells, whom he quotes, also shrewdly remarks – "is actually colonising entire spatial segments that link up with one another across cities, the countryside and the world; they isolate themselves from the fragments of local societies which consequently become destructured in the process of selective reorganisation of work and residence", defining a "variable geometry of production and consumption" (Castells, 1989, p. 348). In this wider context also the "wild zones that do not appear to be urban according to a conventional canon" (Soja, 2000/2007, p. 49) become urban, as they are influenced by a particular urban way of life. Within this system some places are abandoned, being obsolete monuments of a previous modern era, while other places are reconstituted as a simulated, aesthetised urban landscape (Soja, 2000/2007, p. 173).

These marginal territories, moreover, not only become part of the new urban horizon, but are instrumentalised to become themselves "integral parts of post-industrial production and financial speculation", capable of corroding "constantly the residual elements of agrarian life", and of eating "greedily anything, anywhere, first and foremost to increase wealth and accumulate capital" (Merrifield, 2014, p. 125).

As Lefebvre himself had announced, this process of spatial recombination is made possible by the process of economic reorganisation that takes place through the passage from the industrial society to the "bureaucratic society of manoeuvred consumerism" (Lefebvre, 1970/1973, p. 10).

Not by chance, in fact, the industrial economy – which already back in the 1960s reached an authentic critical point – began to understand that, by using the possibilities of sensorial and symbolic hyperstimulation offered by new media, it would be able to make a profit, not just from the production of manufactured goods and objects but, above all, from inactivity and non-work. However, this inactivity was not liberated by, but strictly dependent on and, indeed, aimed at hyperconsumption. It was continually fed, as various authors have admirably observed, on the capacity to administer and exploit desire, turning it into pleasure, so that it would become productive and therefore profitable (Recalcati, 2011; Magatti, 2012).[4]

Offering surrogates for the desire for festivity and admiration for wild nature

The economic system latched onto different desires in order to create new goods to which the said form of organisation of the territory determined by industrialisation processes no longer managed to give an answer. These desires included: on the one hand, the desire for festivity that constituted one of the cardinal elements of the life of the pre-industrial city, reduced to minimum terms by rationalisation processes, production engineering and reorganisation of time operated by the new production machine; on the other, admiration for that nature which the industrial civilisation itself, precisely through its advent, had destructured – with the implosion of the city, depopulation and exploitation of the country (Lefebvre, 1968/1970).

To respond to these desires, the production system began to offer surrogates: spectacular environments in which the places to live and experience were substituted by backgrounds to gaze at (Debord, 1967/2002).

In particular the desire for festivity, which was one of the fundamental elements of the right to the city, considered a "moment of participation of the community in the lavish expense of life" (Debord, 1967/2002, p. 128) in which to dissipate so as to construct relational goods, be turned into pleasure by means of the invention of the holiday (Bandinu, 1980).[5] To respond to this desire, the legal space of modern festivity has been rigorously delimited by inventing the right to free time. At the same time, once it is established which desires should become needs, trivialised environments are created to offer images for consumption and to channel – gaining obvious profits – some of that energy and symbolic capital (expressed by the desire for festivity which, with the disappearance of traditional societies, no longer found expression in the consolidated city) (Bandinu, 1980). While in the city the *ordinary time* of work and production persisted, with the overall account of its costs and its conflictive adhesion to a historical praxis, the *mythical time* of festivity, packaged up in the holiday as an entirely predetermined halt in time, was transferred somewhere else: it left the city and was accommodated by the territory, which began to be populated by "signs of the urban in the dissolution of urbanity itself" (Lefebvre, 1968/1970, p. 20).

In the same way, the desire for nature that the industrial society had contributed to devastating was dealt with by conserving ancient pictures of landscapes, artificially maintained to answer the needs of urban man, who was searching for archetypal images of a past that no longer existed and that, in these forms, perhaps never did.[6]

It is precisely to respond to this desire for a lost fairy-tale world – the manifestation of an artificial model created at a desk – that environments are created where the spaces of nature are transformed in backdrops and these are no longer spaces of experience of production and life. These are no longer spaces to live in but to look at, like a sort of film of the territory in which to spectacularise history and "de-realise" reality. It was in this new production that the "extensive and intensive trivialisation" process started (Debord, 1967/2002, p. 132) of territories that simultaneously cancelled the two opposing terms city/country and substituted them with an "eclectic mix of what they decompose into" (Debord, 1967/2002, p. 136).

Within this process the different qualities of places, though emptied of their meaning, take on an important role. These qualities – which were the outcomes of the relations human beings had established with their life environments – become autonomous and detached from the life that had produced them and – like the skin peeled from the fruit - become exactly the backdrops in which urban man, jumping between various dimensions, may find a trivial response to what he no longer finds in the city or in the country. Once they have been transformed into images (Baudrillard, 1976/1990), these different realities, packaged like goods to be sold to the highest bidder, are in fact put into a new aesthetic circuit conveyed by the media and used as precious sources in this new economy in a nascent state.

The case of the Province of Olbia-Tempio

It is within this framework that it is possible to grasp the great transformation that has taken place on that portion of territory of North Sardinia that we have framed in our section. The *square* we have chosen to use delimits, in fact, a portion of territory consisting of the environmental-historic sub-region of Gallura and a portion of that of Monte Acuto, which together form the current (though being abandoned) administrative territory of the Province of Olbia-Tempio.

This part of the territory, where no urban reality was present until the 1960s, today shows the features of an authentic post-metropolitan reality (Soja, 2000/2007). This profound transformation was generated by the invention of a simulacrum city – the holiday city – and the effects produced by the introduction of television, multiplied by the effects of the IT revolution and globalisation.

This variety of factors has meant that this corner of the world, which had remained for centuries in basic isolation – thanks indeed to its unusual environmental-historic character being reinterpreted and used within a nascent consumer economy – has entered into a network of flows and a mediatised aesthetic space, becoming an integral part of that city-world and world-city that now embraces the entire world (Lefebvre, 1970/1973; Choay, 1994 ; Amin & Thrift 2002; Soja, 2000/2007; Brenner, 2014).

The environmental and historic features of a territory

The territory we have framed in a jigsaw *square* appears markedly characterised by the pervasiveness taken on by the environmental dimension. On this territory nature is present in "overpowering", dramatic forms, in some respects full of tension, conveying strong sensations. The morphological structure itself gives rise to mighty landscapes, full of solitude: vast stretches, fascinating, mighty rock formations, perforated by the elementary forces of nature, by imperious knocking wrought by wind and atmosphere. Man had to cope with the dramatic power of these natural forms to build, over time, his own settlement structure.

Mount Limbara, with its rugged relief, is the dominant element, the intrinsic structure, marking the character of this region both from an environmental point of view and in terms of cultural history. From this mountain streams spring that flow through the whole territory, forming ramifications like a spider's web on the surface – the matrix of the life environment and the settlement. The main streams, with their source embedded between granite walls, mark out great valleys and plains as they take a more winding course to reach the sea, where they carve out deep coastal inlets called *rias*. Apart from being a precious chest of animal and vegetable species, Mount Limbara, situated in the central part of the *square*, was the hub of the settlement structure around which the organisation of the entire territory of Gallura unfolded. A territory characterised since the nineteenth century by a framework of small villages linked with each other by a web of paths that, if we exclude Terranova, Longone (nowadays Olbia and Santa Teresa di Gallura) and La Maddalena, were largely set out like a crown around the mountain.[7] These nuclei were the pivots of vast, silent territories, stretching almost always to the sea, populated solely by the white, rarefied presence of the cottages: the dwellings of shepherd-farmers and the pivots of a sparsely populated, large-grid farming system[8] (Le Lannou, 1941/1979). It was precisely one of these territories close to the sea that, just at the end of the nineteenth century, saw the small community of Arzachena appear, which would enter the orbit in the 1960s of Italian industrial capitalism and, above all, that of international finance.

From the world of villages to post-metropolitan reality: economic development, spatial processes, social dynamics and institutional perspective

The invention of the Costa Smeralda: the simulacrum generates a new reality

In 1962 with the arrival of Karim al-Husayni, Aga Khan IV – a 25-year-old Ishmaelite prince who had just graduated from Harvard – the construction of an unprecedented territorial reality began with the support of some other important actors of international capitalism. Thanks to a massive injection of private foreign capital, but also to significant state and regional public funding (making infrastructure development possible in this territory) (Gelsomino, 2012; Piga, 2012), the Costa Smeralda was "founded" on the coast in the north-eastern part of the *square*, and in particular in Arzachena Municipality. It is a holiday city that took on the appearance of a simulacrum city, completely detached from the territory and real life, but perfectly included in a network of global flows[9] – a city not produced over time through the relations between man and space but designed by the hand of important international architects who wisely inserted it among the stones and lentisk bushes of those arid, inhospitable coasts, so as to create a new landscape which, as Bandinu observes, has become "a picture drawn on purpose" where "the villas and hotels are houses with gentle shapes. Fairy-tale architecture and furniture have created a style" (Bandinu, 1980).

Figure 11.1 Costa Smeralda: Porto Cervo Village

Source: Photo by Leonardo Lutzoni

In creating this very unusual holiday city, as Bandinu keenly observes, "the experiment of late capitalism struck an archaic, pre-agricultural domestic economy" (Bandinu, 1980). The landscape and its signs, from natural objects that were the product of agricultural and pastoral life, were emptied of life and adopted as an ahistoric scenario, primeval and timeless, to respond to the desires of urban man seeking to recuperate precisely that image of wild nature. It was not a case of simple exploitation of an existing situation but, rather, the creation of a work of art, a nature-product. What was needed was to "invent a scene, a market display which would embody the heaven of desires [. . .] to package up a bit of sea, espouse a villa with a bush or a rock is a syntactic operation of a higher civilisation, the refined interpreter of all writing [. . .] it's not an easy business to crumble up a place and make it the dwelling of a desire" (Bandinu, 1980, p. 79).

Thanks to an extraordinary marketing operation, which promoted its image all over the world, and to the building of an international airport (Gelsomino, 2012; Piga, 2012), this particular "invented settlement", in becoming a tourist resort for the international elite, led this part of Sardinia into the particular urban world that was taking shape in those years.

The Costa Smeralda invention turned into a molecule generating a new hyper-real reality[10] – an authentic work of urban fertilisation of territories that, until a short time ago, were "empty and silent" in which, as Baudrillard was to say: "the 'real' is produced from miniaturised cells, matrices and memories, control models – and from this can be reproduced an infinite number of times" (Baudrillard, 1978/2008, p. 60, own translation). Modelled on the villages invented by the Ishmaelite prince's architects, myriad villages multiplied, still on the coast side situated in the north-eastern part of the *square*, made up of second homes[11] and hotels destined to accommodate a seasonal population[12] using this stock of housing just for a few months a year, and leading to exponential growth in the building industry.[13] A sort of linear coastal city took shape that produced extremely high land consumption,[14] invented to offer accommodation to a notable tourist flow.[15]

The creation of this holiday city, and the contemporary intensification of global interdependencies and interconnections, together with a general improvement in infrastructure systems, reorganisation of the harbour and the building of an international airport, profoundly modified, in the whole of the Gallura region, the relations woven by the people with their life environments and acted powerfully on local cultures and imagination.[16]

Discontinuity: the break-up of the ancient relations between men and environments

First of all, the relations woven over the centuries between communities and their life environments began to break up. For whereas in the past each nucleus forming the framework of the settlement base lived in close contact with the country because its subsistence was based on it, from this moment onwards the introduction of this reality into the economic and cultural flows that were overriding the local dimension prompted depopulation of the cottages and a substantial relinquishment of the traditional activities linked with the countryside, as shown by the variation in agricultural land use between 1982 and 2010.[17]

With the disappearance of the world of cottages and the transformation of the peasant and pastoral society – understood in a wide sense as a cultural and productive reality that had maintained a close tie with its own territorial sphere for centuries, intimately shaping its systems – a decisive, progressive detachment was thus determined between environmental-landscape fabric and social fabric. The environment, from space of production and life, began to turn into a background, a panoramic view in which production, even if it continued, was certainly no longer related to the direct needs of the community (Decandia, 2008).

New departures and re-territorialisation: the success of the coastal city

This phase of detachment was followed by a thorough readjustment of the relations between man and space, causing a new settlement model to gain ground.

The foundation of the city of tourism and holidays, which had its reference bases on land belonging to Arzachena Municipality and the Olbia area – also situated on the east coast in the central part of the *square* – generated new business worlds by attracting capital and investments, and this led to a considerable increase in the population of the entire Gallura[18] region that tended to be concentrated in the coastal nuclei; these took on a driving role for the hinterland (Cannaos, 2015).[19]

Olbia, in particular, which was a small nucleus of little more than 3,000 inhabitants ravaged by malaria at the end of the nineteenth century, and which had only begun to emerge in the first half of the twentieth century as a small trading town, began to attract large flows of population and Italian and foreign capital. As Cannaos observes: "in 50 years the town population trebled, growing from around 18,000 inhabitants to almost 54,000,[20] and still today, even though some of the more general dynamics seem to be slowing down, it is growing by around 1,000 inhabitants a year" (Cannaos, 2014).

The migratory flows that encounter each other in the town are varied. To the flows coming from the villages of central Gallura and from the Monteacuto and Nuoro areas, together with those coming from areas outside the island context (Murineddu, 1997), an important non-European component was added between 1991 and 2011, reaching 7% of the population in 2011, as can be seen from the *Atlante* data.[21]

In this sense the town has taken on the outline of an authentic border town able to welcome the variety of arrivals. In a few decades it has turned into one of the most dynamic realities, not just at a regional level but also in Italy – a dynamism that has taken on ambivalent and contradictory features, as shown also by the arrival of organised crime[22] and the decrease in the number of employees in the educational field between 2001 and 2011.[23]

In a few years the town has become established as an important production centre, specialising above all in the tourist sector; the creation of the industrial zone where industries are situated that are prevalently linked with the field of construction, harbour improvement, the building of a new airport and the creation of new infrastructures has impressively changed the face and structure of the town, making it a full-blown gateway to the island – a gateway that in recent decades, in spite of the crisis already evident in 2011 with a rise in the unemployment rate from 16.85% to 17.74%,[24] has increasingly enhanced its tourist rating. Whereas industrial production has diminished, there has been a rise in those employed in the building sector; not only have the hotel and restaurant sectors grown, but also those concerned with film production, financial and insurance business and, above all, accountancy, company management and management consultancy.[25]

The exponential increment in the construction sector generated – in a vicious circle linking the economy to land consumption – an exponential increase in built areas. Suffice it to think that from the *Atlante* data[26] it emerges that the percentage of sealed soil in Olbia has reached almost half the natural soil. In this rush to build, the very high percentage of property for residential use but not declared shows, moreover, another extremely worrying fact: the massive spread of the phenomenon of illegal building.[27]

The city has equipped itself with services – schools, hospitals, shopping malls and, not least, a university campus – that have become a reference point not only for town

214   *Lidia Decandia*

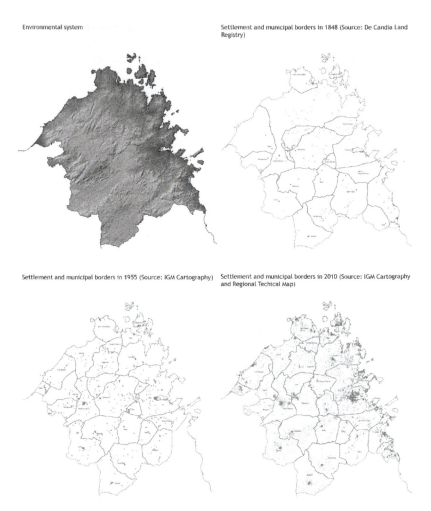

Figure 11.2 Sardinian Province of Olbia-Tempio: from the world of villages to urban
reality

Source: Processing by Leonardo Lutzoni

residents, but for the entire population of Gallura and other zones.[28] The recent purchase
of the San Raffaele Hospital by Qatar, not yet finalised but which will be concluded
within a few years, will create a research and care centre on an international scale.

If this nucleus largely constitutes a sort of gateway to the island, in other ways it
is also maintaining its close ties with the inland towns, ties that are inscribed in the
DNA of its history. As Murineddu (1997) has shown, it is actually the immigrant
population coming from the High Gallura and Monte Acuto villages that maintain
relations, not just social but also economic and cultural, with the hinterlands.

Of course it is not only the Olbia agglomeration that is growing in such a clamorous way; all the coastal centres are showing high rates of population growth. Arzachena, just to give one example, has trebled its number of inhabitants in the last 50 years, rising from 4,618 to 11,447 inhabitants, but the same is taking place in many other coastal towns. Between 2001 and 2011 alone, Loiri, Porto San Paolo and San Teodoro, small municipalities gravitating around Olbia, have seen their populations almost double.[29] On the Gallura coast the building rate between 1991 and 2001 was among the highest in Italy.[30]

The dynamic nature of the coastal areas is also testified by: an influx of foreign population that in 2011 reached peaks of 8% in Santa Teresa di Gallura and 9% in the municipality of Palau,[31] two municipalities of the north coast, in the top part of the *square*, and by the social dynamics themselves. The working-age population in the coastal municipalities amounts to 71.5%. The youthful age of the population[32] and the average number of single-member families bear witness to a greater generational turnover and family composition that shows an increase in single young people. The coast clearly seems to offer greater opportunities, as the data on wealth levels achieved compared with the inland municipalities also show.[33] From the point of view of education, too, the number of graduates and those with high school diplomas is greater along the coast than in the hinterland municipalities, if we exclude the municipalities of Tempio and Calangianus. In the same way, per capita production of waste appears greater, as does energy consumption, though there has been a drop in recent years in investment in renewable energies, with the coast proving more enterprising than the interior, which is proceeding slowly.[34] The dichotomous behaviour of the coast and hinterland is also evident from the electoral point of view: for whereas stability prevails along the coast with a centre-right wing tendency, inland the left is predominant.[35]

Broadening the use of the territory: redirecting territorial relations

If it is true that the concentration of many services and economic activities in the coastal towns has created a centripetal effect towards the coast,[36] nevertheless the clear improvement in road communications achieved over the last 30 years has contributed to generating an increasingly wide-ranging use of the territory.

For if in the past the geographical conditions linked with the bad state of the roads, together with an almost total dependence of the economy on its own territorial bases, meant that each community constituted an anthropologically determined cultural unit, recognisable and strongly anchored to its own life environment, from the 1960s onwards the improvement in infrastructure and the introduction of cars, as well as localisation of services and emerging new economies linked with the holiday industry, caused a change in the trend of territorial relations.

The territory of the Province of Olbia-Tempio began to be used more and more as though it were a single settlement context. It has become increasingly common to no longer live in a single village but between different places: people live in a village in winter and at their house by the sea in summer (Cannaos, 2013); students attend school in one village while they live in a different one (high schools

Figure 11.3 International Festival "Isole che Parlano", 17th edition, "Ai Giganti" concert
        by Hamid Drake (USA), Tomba dei giganti by "Li Mizzani", Monticanu,
        Palau

Source: Photo by Nanni Angeli

are almost completely concentrated in Tempio and Olbia, and what is more, the
decrease in population in the internal municipalities is creating the need to unite
the lower schools in some nuclei, too); people go to the coast for shopping and for
entertainment (see in *Atlante*[37] the localisation of shopping malls and amusement
parks); they go for a walk, collect mushrooms or go jogging in the mountains and
listen to music and go to concerts in the countryside.[38] A strange kind of reality
seems to be emerging in which some towns, especially Olbia and Arzachena,
distinctly have a driving role. From a model of use that was poorly hierarchised,
revolving around a complex, minute system of settlement nuclei and cottages scattered throughout the countryside, we have proceeded to a highly "striped" system.
A sort of "matted" territory where the coastal town, like a kind of magnet, attracts
the "dust blown" over the territory, leaving in the internal areas "gaps" of silence,
rich in nature and history, silhouetted on a background of polycentric settlement
structure which continues, nevertheless, though in a weak way, to constitute the
framework of an off-balance territory-city all to be understood and decoded.[39]

The polycentric articulation of the settlement framework: the internal villages

Within this unusual territory-city the small villages situated in inland areas (in the
central and lower part of the *square*), though characterised by depopulation and

ageing population phenomena, have continued to maintain an important role and to represent a strong territorial identity in territorial organisation (the localisation of libraries and cultural places, as arose during the course of the research, is extremely significant in this respect). Each of them continues to be an important identity resource, in which to live and participate, often maintaining a special productive fabric, too. This is the case, for example, of Calangianus, anchored to the ever-present cork industry in spite of the serious crisis that has hit the sector,[40] and of Buddusò, the centre of the granite district, but also Luras, characterised by agricultural work, as well as for being a basin of small industries linked with the construction sector.[41] The situation is different for the villages located between the mountain and the sea that have begun to show new, emerging phenomena within this polycentric settlement framework. For if it is true that the internal nuclei seem to be showing a decrease and an ageing population,[42] the phenomenon is gradually taking on different features closer to the coast: more recently built nuclei, generated by the joining up of cottages and situated in an intermediate position between the sea and the mountain, such as S. Antonio and Telti, are resisting depopulation. Others, namely Luogosanto and Monti, even seem to show hints of vitality. A particularly interesting fact in this respect is the increase in foreign population that has taken place in very recent years. In the village of Monti, especially, an increase of 21% was recorded between 2010 and 2011 and in the Berchidda community a surprising 26% increase was recorded.[43]

We are speaking of course of small but interesting traces able to disclose possible "proof of future". The emergence is interesting in this respect of new cooperative project-based forms linked with local development, much more frequently found in the interior than along the coast.[44] The continuous increase in recent years in cooperative projects reveals first of all that in these internal areas fertile developmental co-learning is under way, and it is leading the various communities, in the past withdrawn and not used to working together, to cooperate on projects. This is interesting proof of "synechism", as Soja would call it (Soja, 2000/2007), which might show itself to be a winner in the years ahead in building the future of this post-metropolitan territory.

In many ways we could say that in these internal municipalities the contemporary is rediscovering the archaic in innovative forms (Didi-Huberman, 2009). Not by chance there are many cooperative projects devoted to themes of rural development, tourism, the environment, the landscape, great events, culture and innovation. For it is in these areas that new intermittent cultural centralities are becoming established, tied to unique events that revive ancient places of worship and sites with exceptional environmental quality (such as "Time in Jazz" at Berchidda, the festival coordinated by Paolo Fresu, one of the most important jazz musicians on the international scene, which involves many of the municipalities around Mount Limbara, especially those on the southern slope, in the lower part of the *square*). New forms of common territorial projects are emerging that rediscover, by reinventing them in a contemporary key, professions connected with agriculture and land use; sectors such as viticulture and the consequent production of wine are being developed, but so is the rearing of prized cattle. The potential of the environmental and landscape dimension is being rediscovered with the purpose of inventing new forms of historic and cultural tourism; work has begun to upgrade settlement nuclei (see projects on urban regeneration) and also, as normally occurs, the cottages spread throughout the countryside. In some cases – such as Luogosanto, but also Arzachena and Sant'Antonio – return-to-the-land processes are being triggered, often started by new inhabitants, who leave the towns and metropolises of the mainland to go and live in the country, and these are beginning to generate the production of new economies (Lutzoni, 2013, 2014, 2015). In a dimension that is no longer local, but is interweaving different kinds of scale, a particular urban condition is taking root, in which empty areas, too, seem to acquire an important meaning.

Among the different towns of the settlement framework of Gallura a special role has been taken by Tempio, the ancient "capital" of the region, though its central role in the territory appears to have decreased in favour of Olbia; it nevertheless continues because of the constant presence of important services (schools, hospitals, the tribunal, and so on) to be a vital node, as data on population show,[45] with an increase of 20%, and for economic activities: an important nucleus of the settlement structure.

Within this polycentric organisation, though the identity role taken by these historic nuclei still persists, their figurative image and physical structure are, however, undergoing deep transformations. For the increase in individual well-being – due to greater economic possibilities and the establishment of new values and ideas introduced by the consumer economy – has determined an exponential increase in housing, built following logics remote from the contexts. Even though the population of the internal nuclei decreases, these are surrounded by suburbs often doubling the size of the inhabited area.[46] Up until the 1950s a large number of families lived in a single room;[47] today the ratio between population and number of rooms is very low. The "peripheral zones" have begun to be dotted with single-family homes. In a game of mirrors, it is often the Costa Smeralda villas, which aimed to interpret an actually non-existent tradition, that have provided the typological model for new expansion. Even if, compared with the coast, condominium structures prevail, it is no longer the micro-units of the neighbourhood, the relations between families, and the complexity of relations between public and private that are building up organic fabrics, but the social success of individuals that is dictating the rules for a form of urban expansion highly focused on the single-family home.

This logic of urban fabric organisation clearly responds to the success of new social values. A weakening of the traditional forms of the family is witnessed. Although, compared with the world of the coast, single-unit families are fewer, the number of components of families has decreased; everywhere there is a tendency towards increased fragility of individuals and communities (suffice it to think of the increase in the number of drug addicts) and a relaxation of those forms of social cooperation and alliances that were the outcome of traditional culture (neighbourhood relations, *manialia* (reciprocal help among neighbours), cork workshops), but also a fragmentation of the consolidated cultural heritage and knowledge.

Looking through the square from a specific perspective

World connections

This settlement structure that has determined a particular territorial-urban reality, difficult to harness under the classical categories with which we are used to giving order to the world – apart from being characterised by an extended use of the territory and a complex system of relations linking the different settlement nuclei with each other – appears to be closely connected with the world and perfectly integrated into the global economy circuits. It is not a case just of virtual connections, but real ones that enable easy physical transfers. For instance, during the summer at Olbia harbour, the first Italian port for passenger traffic,[48] 14 ships dock each day and the prominent Olbia-Costa Smeralda international airport links this terminal with all the most important cities of Northern Europe – from Moscow to London, to Taliesin and Frankfurt, just to mention a few examples. The data provided by the statistics show Olbia in the summer season as one of the most important airports in terms of influx of passengers.

A world of darkness and silence in the centre of the city

And yet, in spite of its belonging to an urban world, this micro-region of the island maintains some of the distinctive features that make it perhaps unique in the panorama of Italian urban regions. The element that most distinguishes it is the vastness of the empty, silent lands. In this portion of territory the outstanding environmental components take on a significant role in configuring its uniqueness.

The vast stretches of territory due to low-density settlement and the extensive municipal territories spread around the small villages[49] are the figures upon which the sense of belonging is built: the "environmental dominants" which, as Maciocco observes, still constitute the elements the settled population identifies with (Maciocco, 2011). These are the figurative and educational images (Serreli, 2011) around which a strange city is taking shape, in which gaps prevail over full areas.

For in this unusual urban reality there are no cathedrals or bell-towers, as symbolic places around which significant relations are built with one's life environment, but instead reference points linked with the particular mountain morphology or the sinuous valleys. Everyone, including children, get their bearings from these characteristic figures: Monti di Deu, Monte Limbara, Monti Pinu, Sarra di Monti, Monti di La Signora, and so on. The special value the environmental dimension has taken on is enhanced in some respects by the straightforward communications that have made relations easier, not only between the various nuclei but also with the rest of the world. Even if man no longer lives immersed in this landscape, does not manipulate it or establish an intimate relationship with it as used to occur in the past, the landscape still nevertheless constitutes the background to this new, extended fruition of the territory. Precisely because travelling from one village to another is very simple and people live, as we have said, between various places, the vastness of the horizons and the exceptional environmental quality of these silent voids are an integral part of this extraordinary urban landscape.

The lands of the internal areas dominated by the presence of Mount Limbara are above all those where depopulation has reached the greatest dimensions and become a genuine resource of emptiness and silence in this strange territory-city. On the immense horizons, as a consequence of the processes of depopulation of the countryside when people abandoned the cottages, nature seems to have over-whelmed man's life more than ever.

Looking at a night satellite view shows how, within the European nebula, the darkness of these territories represents a really remarkable space – a reserve of immense silence, a deposit of naturalness in the heart of this so densely urbanised ancient continent.

In this silent, empty expanse, the concept of land consumption is absent. Behind this overriding nature, stone walls, scattered houses – sometimes abandoned – and small country churches reveal the traces of a life that is over. We need to resort to names, stories and tales that still live in the memory of the elderly to perceive those worlds of meaning by which this territory was shaped and made significant in the minute operations of "belonging" that the inhabitants of these lands used to carry out in their daily work and life. It is a void that is only apparent, which cherishes an unlimited reserve of meaning and which, if one is not content with just a glance, can reveal worlds.

Yet these spaces do not constitute a different reality from the city: here there is not an archaic culture, a peasant and pastoral world, a rural culture countering a far-off urban culture but, if anything, a countryside that is going back to being part of the city and a city that is reciprocally returning to being part of the country.

For the farmers and shepherds linked with the economy and culture of cottages no longer live in these natural, quiet places. If you were to encounter one you would need to be wary, as he would most probably be an imitation at the disposal of distracted tourists seeking emotions on Sardinian land – idyllic images pre-served to respond to man who escapes the city looking for a past that no longer exists and perhaps, in these terms, never did exist.

In actual fact, the farmers who live here, including those very few cases where they continue to live in the country, do not wear corduroy trousers or dance the "*scottis*", an ancient dance of Gallura, but move about with great ease between Sardinia, Italy and Europe, showing their animals and their products at the main international fairs. They do so without travelling for days and nights but by tak-ing very short trips. If only a few decades ago, still in the memory of men, those who lived in cottages situated in the foothills of Mount Limbara in the territory of Calangianus took at least two hours to reach the village on foot, nowadays in the same length of time it is possible to actually be in the centre of London, Berlin, Frankfurt or Paris, just to give a few examples, and vice versa of course. And paradoxically it has become easier to reach Rome or Berlin than a small village of Ogliastra, another historic sub-region of the island, situated on the east coast.

We are faced with radical changes that are completely upsetting the geographi-cal and spatial categories according to which this territory was organised and people lived for thousands of years. Whereas in the past a cottage inhabitant existed thanks to a simple subsistence economy, today, with the electrification of country areas and the ability to connect to the internet (in the whole province the share of population without broadband access is low) from almost any part of the territory, a cottage inhabitant can live speculating on the stock exchange or working with the most important art galleries of London and New York. The example of Fabrizio De André – one of the most famous songwriters in the history of Italian folk music, who chose to live for years in a cottage in the municipality of Tempio, situated in the eastern part of the *square*, producing some of his most inspiring songs there for the world – makes us realise how much this territory really has become an integral part of an unprecedented urban dimension that undoubtedly goes far beyond the horizons of the ancient city.

Notes

1 Research Unit of the Sapienza University of Rome coordinated by Professor Carlo Cellamare, Department of Civil, Constructional and Environmental Engineering (DICEA). Working Team of the University of Sassari led by Lidia Decandia (Team Coordinator), Department of Architecture and Urban Design, Alghero. Team members: Cristian Cannaos, Leonardo Lutzoni.
2 According to Lefebvre (1970/1973) the industrialisation process, having reached its critical point, would cause such a process of implosion-explosion that, as he himself stated, "the non-city and the anti-city will take over the city, penetrate it, cause it to explode and consequently spread enormously, flowing into the urbanisation of society, into the urban fibre that covers the remains of the city prior to industry" (Lefebvre, 1970/1973, p. 20).
3 Rather than conceive of the urban as a specific spatial layout in contrast with the outskirts, the country and other presumed non-urban areas, Lefebvre (1970/1973) actually maintained that capitalist urbanisation would "form an irregular grid of varying densities, thicknesses and activities" (Lefebvre, 1970/1973, p. 1), which would spread all over the surface of the world.
4 As Recalcati observes, commenting on Lacan's thought on the capitalist argument: after the experience had weakened of the limit that had the task of articulating the desire present in traditional societies to achieve something unachievable, a void impossible to reach, embodied by a God or the actual figure of the father, the capitalist argument exploits man's bewilderment, without a compass or symbolic anchorage, to offer him, by means of the production of consumer objects, the immediate possibility of pleasure. "The belief that animates the capitalist's argument is twofold: it is the belief that the subject is free, with no limits or ties, moved only by his desire for pleasure, and intoxicated by his will to consume, but it is also the belief that it is the object that causes the desire [. . .] it may be confused with a simple presence, with a Thing, or a mountain of things [. . .]. The dazzle maintained by the capitalist argument consists of making the object deceptively shine, not to make satisfaction possible, but to show the grasping nature, impossible to satisfy, of the urge to enjoy [. . .] the capitalist argument is supported by the idolatrous and fetishist faith in the object of enjoyment. It is a case of faith in the object as a remedy for the pain of existing [. . .] the faith in the object the capitalist argument cleverly nurtures defines the artificially salvific character of hyper-consumerism" (Recalcati, 2011, pp. 43–45).
5 As Bandinu maintains, "tourism has become one of the great semiotic machines by which power administers festivity and through which it models the collective imagination" (Bandinu, 1980, p. 39).
6 As Lefebvre observes (1968/1970), the country is put at the service of the city: "the city poisons nature; it devours it, to then recreate it in the imagination so that this illusion of activity will last" (Lefebvre, 1968/1970, p. 104).

7 Gallura – as Angius wrote in 1841 – "was composed of one city, three hamlets and five villages. The only city is Tempio, thanks to the recent privilege of municipality conferred on it by Carlo Alberto. The hamlets are Terranova, which retained the title of city up until halfway through the 17th Century, Longone, restored around 1810 by many different peoples, and La Maddalena, which around 1780 began to have a population, then grew rapidly above that number enabling subsistence on its territory. The villages were Calangianos, Aggius, Bortigiadas, Luras and Nuches, very old in the Gemini, as is Tempio" (Angius, 1841/2006a, p. 503, own translation). Though Angius acknowledged city status for Tempio, granted by Carlo Alberto, we should not think this term is the equivalent of the classical meaning we give to it. For Tempio only had 4,500 residents (Angius, 1841/2006b, p. 1661): rather than a city, therefore, a village slightly larger than the others.

8 This form of sparse population, a specific form belonging to the Gallura territory, originated in the seventeenth century when peasants and shepherds, living up until then in the communities of High Gallura, moved towards the coast in an attempt to exploit the vast empty spaces of the coastal territories. These shepherds, who originally practised semi-nomadic sheep-farming, using seasonal settlements, slowly began to settle in these areas and create stable settlement structures: the cottages that were to become the hub of management deriving from the individual acquisition of land. Within these vast properties the outcome of this process of appropriation of collective lands of the Salti (as the undivided lands destined as pasture were called), this hybrid figure of the peasant-shepherd began to practise purely subsistence agriculture and sheep-farming. On the populating of the cottages see, in particular, Le Lannou (1941/1979).

9 It was in fact in the interweaving and overlapping of various spatial economic orders – local, regional, state and international – that this new land emerged. A new land that right from the start did not have the features of a static entity anchored to a geographical, solely land-based space, a container of presumed local social facts (Bolocan Goldstein, 2014) but, rather, was configured as the knot of a skein formed of tangled trans-scalar networks that caused various hierarchies of power to coagulate in that place (Brenner, 2000).

10 On the role simulacra have in generating hyper-real territories and on how they change the actual concept of reality by generating new forms of use of post-metropolitan territories, see Soja (2000/2007), in particular Chapter 9, Simcity: reorganising urban imagination, pp. 315–345.

11 Just to give a few examples, in 2001 in Arzachena the empty houses were 66% of the total, in Santa Teresa 69% and in San Teodoro 86%. The number of second homes is shown in the first place by a very low "crowding" index. See PRIN Postmetropoli (2015): "Percentuale di abitazioni vuote 2001", § c.5.1.2.

12 "In 2011 the Province of Olbia-Tempio was the Sardinian province with the largest number of homes not occupied by residents (over 45%), against an average for the other Sardinian provinces of around 20%. If compared with the other metropolitan areas considered in the *Atlante*, the numbers for the Gallura coast show us that from this point of view this territory belongs to the class with the most homes empty in Italy (over 63%). Only the small and very small villages of the Alpine arch reach the same percentages. Olbia and Arzachena are in the same class as Venice," Cannaos (2015). See PRIN Postmetropoli (2015): "Dimensioni e affollamento delle abitazioni", § c.5.

13 "The high rates of property values bear witness to the value taken on by the construction industry in the coastal areas, comparable with the centres of the large Italian cities. As appears from the data mapped in the *Atlante*, in these areas prices are reached like those we find in the centre of Rome or Milan. Arzachena (namely the Costa Smeralda) is the municipality where the highest average price of housing is recorded at over 5,000 euro per sq. m. Inexpensive leases do not exist along the coast, while they are the rule inland. Commercial businesses also reach property values similar to those of the large Italian cities" Cannaos (2015). See PRIN Postmetropoli (2015): "Prezzi medi di compravendita di abitazioni 2012", § d.1.1.

14 Just to give a few examples, in Arzachena the soil-sealing percentage in 2012 was 5.32, but the maximum peak reached was for Palau, at 8.34%, against the 3.86% of the municipality of Santa Teresa di Gallura. See PRIN Postmetropoli (2015): "Percentuale di suolo impermeabilizzato 2009", § b.1.2.

15 "As the data referring to tourism show, the number of beds per municipality shows us how the relatively small towns on the Gallura coast (Arzachena has less than 15,000 inhabitants) are comparable to cities like Turin, Naples and Palermo" Cannaos (2015). See PRIN Postmetropoli (2015): "Numero di posti letto negli esercizi alberghieri e complementari", § d.3.1.2.

"The accommodation level of the Gallura coast is very high. Only the small towns of the Alpine arch reach these percentages (though they have just a few hundred residents), together with three municipalities of the coast of Tuscany and two beneath Venice. This bears further witness to the degree of tourist specialisation, which is very high. Even if we make a comparison with the compounded accommodation function (i.e. we put as denominator as well as inhabitants also the sq. km. of territory, which in the case of Gallura are many), the Gallura coast still remains one of the most (perhaps the most) specialised places of Italy" Cannaos (2015). See PRIN Postmetropoli (2015): "Tasso di funzione ricettiva composto", § d.3.5.

16 The arrival on the island of a particular kind of elite tourism, characterised by a system of signs and values perfectly included in a luxury consumer system, conveyed new cultural urban models that deeply disrupted the traditional cultural reference codes. As Bandinu observes, "the archaic models of tradition clash with those of festivity and consumption promoted by the practice and principles of elite tourism" (Bandinu, 1980, p. 136). The effect of this transformation was enhanced by the introduction of the new television medium, which from the 1960s onwards built up a media-based aesthetic space that overrode the boundaries of ancient local homelands to create an authentic circuit of world communication, strengthened by further developments in digital communication. Within this system, as Adorno had already observed, "products studied for mass consumption are packed in a more or less massified way and to a large extent determine this consumption themselves" (Adorno, 1967/2011, p. 113, own translation). The "new means of communication and messaging" (Bandinu, 1996), as well as the invasion, also in the island context, of the said "sign-objects" of the world market, contribute, as many authors have highlighted (Bandinu, 1996; Pira, 1978; Cherchi, 1999 and 2013), to conveying new behaviour codes – codes obviously produced to respond to the prompting of the consumer industry, putting desire to work to transform it into profit, but having nothing to do with the life horizons and values produced in local universes. This flood of "objects-signs-messages" arriving from outside shattered the universe of traditions and produced very powerful standardisation of cultures and behaviours (Pasolini, 1975), multiplied over the last decades by the effects produced by IT communication and globalisation.

17 See on the subject the data on the index of coverage of agricultural areas and natural areas and the percentage of agricultural surface used compared with the total natural surface. See PRIN Postmetropoli (2015), "Suolo agricolo", § b.2.

18 "In 1961 nearly 100,000 people lived in the province of Olbia-Tempio, in 2011 over 153,000. If we consider that in the same period the population of Sardinia rose from 1,420,000 to 1,644,000, it is easy to understand that the increase in the inhabitants of Gallura was really exceptional" (Cannaos, 2015).

19 "As transpires from the data in the *Atlante*, the growth in population has involved above all the coastal municipalities, often indeed to the detriment of the nearby internal ones. Of the 26 municipalities of the province 12 lost inhabitants between 1961 and 2011 (all inland municipalities, with the exception of La Maddalena municipality, which remained basically unchanged, however). Of these 12 municipalities, six lost more than 20% of their population. Bortigiadas has the most negative record, losing half its inhabitants in 50 years. If half the municipalities lose inhabitants and diminish significantly,

it is obvious that the ones that have grown have done so in a considerable way. Of 14 municipalities that in these 50 years have increased their population, two have shown minimal variations and are, obiously, internal (Monti and S. Antonio di Gallura). Of the remaining 12 only Tempio and Telti are internal municipalities (+20% population), while all the others are coastal. Six of these municipalities recorded an increase of over 100% in 50 years (i.e. have more than doubled their popoulation). To demonstrate this suffice it to say that Olbia-Tempio was the top province in the south for demographic variation between 2001 and 2011, and at 15th place among the 110 Italian provinces for growth, with an increase of 8.8% in the population. The second Sardinian province for growth in this decade was Sassari (+1.8%), in 70th place" Cannaos (2015). See PRIN Postmetropoli (2015): "Densità di popolazione", § a.1.

20 Between 2001 and 2011 alone, almost 8,000 people transferred their residence to the city. PRIN Postmetropoli (2015): "Popolazione residente dal 1971 al 2011", § a.1.1.

21 See Trend in foreign population 1991–2001–2011. PRIN Postmetropoli (2015): "Percentuale di popolazione straniera sulla popolazione totale 1991–2001-2011", § c.3.1.

22 As highlighted in the *Atlante*, the cases of confiscation of property from organised crime rings are almost all concentrated in the municipalities of the east coast. PRIN Postmetropoli (2015): "Beni immobili confiscati 2013", § c.6.1.

23 PRIN Postmetropoli (2015): "Percentuale di addetti per settore sul totale degli addetti – 2001 e 2011_ Settore P-istruzione", § d.4.2 e § d.4.2.

24 PRIN Postmetropoli (2015): "Tasso di disoccupazione – 2004–2012", § d.5.1.

25 Ibid, "Percentuale di addetti per settore sul totale degli addetti – 2001 e 2011", § d.4.2 e § d.4.2.

26 PRIN Postmetropoli (2015): "Percentuale di suolo impermeabilizzato 2009", § b.1.2.

27 There is a vast amount of property not declared for residential use; if we look at the details, only the case of Palermo is similar but not so widespread. PRIN Postmetropoli (2015): "Percentuale di immobili ad uso residenziale non dichiarati e accatastati – 2011", § c.6.3.

28 PRIN Postmetropoli (2015): "Poli e strutture attrattive", § e.2.

29 PRIN Postmetropoli (2015): "Popolazione residente dal 1971 al 2011", § a.1.1.

30 PRIN Postmetropoli (2015): "Variazione percentuale delle abitazioni totali tra 1991, 2001 e 2011", § a.2.2.

31 The presence of a new foreign population is also confirmed by the increase in the high ratio of foreign pupils present in schools (as is taking place in the intermediate towns, Monti and S. Antonio, too). It should be pointed out that the new Italians grow as a percentage, in Gallura as in no other part of Sardinia. PRIN Postmetropoli (2015): "Percentuale di popolazione straniera sulla popolazione totale 1991–2001–2011", § c.3.1.

32 "The old-age index of all coastal municipalities is low and the indices for structure dependency and turnover of the active population also show that the population of these municipalities is younger than that of the hinterland, as is confirmed by the calculation of the percentage of elderly population" (Cannaos, 2015). See PRIN Postmetropoli (2015): "Composizione demografica", § c.1.

33 In the coastal municipalities incomes are on average greater compared with the inland ones. In fact, it is here that we find fewer poor people (low income under €10,000) and more rich (more incomes above €120,000). PRIN Postmetropoli (2015): "Reddito medio pro capite di residenti e contribuenti – 2012", § d.2.1.

34 PRIN Postmetropoli (2015): "Produzione di energia rinnovabile", § g.2 e "Rifiuti urbani", § g.4.

35 PRIN Postmetropoli (2015): "Numero di vittorie delle coalizioni di Centrodestra o Centrosinistra", § h.2.2.

36 Commuter levels are higher in the internal municipalities than the coastal ones, and are greater around Olbia, as the areas of affluence show. PRIN Postmetropoli (2015): "Flussi pendolari - 2011", § f.2.1.2.

37 PRIN Postmetropoli (2015): "Grande commercio", § e.2.7 e "Parchi di divertimento", § e.2.10.
38 Events are more and more widespread, including ones of a high cultural level in the rural regions: among them all we recall "Time in Jazz", arranged by Paolo Fresu, and the "Islands that Speak", organised by Paolo and Giovanni Angeli.
39 The concentration index, which is very high precisely in the more internal municipalities, as are the data on population density and coverage ratios, shows that in the internal areas the population is now highly concentrated in the historic centres which constituted the focal points of the ancient settlement framework. On this subject see also the map on density gradients. Cf. PRIN Postmetropoli (2015).
40 A notable increase in the unemployment rate bears witness to the crisis. Calangianus, which in 2001, thanks indeed to the presence of the cork industry, had the lowest rate of unemployment in the whole of Gallura, at 9.7%, saw it rise by 17.33% over ten years. See PRIN Postmetropoli (2015): "Tasso di disoccupazione", § d.5.1.
41 Cf. PRIN Postmetropoli (2015): "Percentuale addetti per settore", § d.4.2 e § d.4.3.
42 PRIN Postmetropoli (2015): "Composizione demografica", § c.1.
43 See PRIN Postmetropoli (2015): "Tasso di crescita medio della popolazione straniera 2010–2013", § c.3.2.
44 "The project cooperation considered generally concerns programmes with an 'integrated' nature (coalitions and partnerships between public and private actors – often the expression of a local partnership – but also the integration of policies and sectors for intervention), which have as their more or less clear aim (but not always actually pursued) the enhancement of endogenous resources (material and immaterial) for the local development of territories with an inter-municipal dimension." See in particular the work done by the Turin Research Unit, DIST, Turin Polytechnic, Italy, Umberto Janin Rivolin (Scientific Coordinator).
45 See PRIN Postmetropoli (2015), op. cit., "Composizione demografica", § c.1.
46 See PRIN Postmetropoli (2015): "Variazione percentuale delle abitazioni totali tra 1991, 2001 e 2011", § a.2.2.
47 See PRIN Postmetropoli (2015): "Densità di abitazioni – 1991, 2001, 2011", § a.2.3.
48 If ports with short-distance traffic, that is, Naples and Messina, are excluded.
49 In the past the territory that is currently Olbia-Tempio Province, as can be seen in the first census (1861), was the least densely populated territory of Italy, up until the census of 1981, the moment when the record passed to Ogliastra. The municipalities of Gallura have the largest average area, 130 sq. km., in Italy. See Cannaos (2013). Still in 2011 (PRIN Postmetropoli (2015): "Densità demografica", § a.1.4), the population density is very low: see the various concentration indices and coverage ratios. The map for soil-sealing (PRIN Postmetropoli (2015): "Percentuale di suolo impermeabilizzato-2009", § b.1.2) also shows that, if the territories of the coastal municipalities of Olbia and Arzachena are excluded, the soil-sealing index is really quite insignificant.

References

Adorno, T.W. (2011). *Parva aesthetica. Saggi 1958–1967* (R. Masiero, It. Trans.). Milano: Mimesis. (Original work published 1967 as *Ohne Leitbild Aesthetica*. Frankfurt: Suhrkamp Verlag.)
Amin, A., and Thrift, N. (2002). *Cities: Reimagining the Urban*. Cambridge: Polity Press.
Angius, V. (2006a). Gallura. In Carta L. (Ed.), *Città e villaggi nella Sardegna dell'Ottocento* (Vol. 1, pp. 470–528). Nuoro: Ilisso. (Original work published 1841.)
Angius, V. (2006b). Tempio. In Carta L. (Ed.), *Città e villaggi nella Sardegna dell'Ottocento* (Vol. 3, pp. 1657–1677). Nuoro: Ilisso. (Original work published 1841.)
Bandinu, B. (1980). *Costa Smeralda: Come nasce una favola turistica*. Milan: Rizzoli.

Bandinu, B. (1996). *Lettera a un giovane sardo*. Cagliari: Edizioni della Torre.

Baudrillard, J. (1990). *Lo scambio simbolico e la morte* (G. Mancuso, It. Trans.). Milan: Feltrinelli. (Original work published 1976 as *L'Échange symbolique et la mort*. Paris: Editions Gallimard.)

Baudrillard, J. (2008). *Simulacri e impostura: Bestie Beaubourg, apparenze e altri oggetti* (M.G. Brega, Ed. and Italian trans.). Milan: Pgreco Edizioni. (Original works published 1977 and 1978.)

Bolocan Goldstein, M. (2014). Scala geografica/Spazialità urbana: Ripensare il mondo attraverso le città. In P. Perulli (Ed.), *Terra mobile: Atlante della società globale*. Turin: Einaudi.

Brenner, N. (2000). The Urban Question: Reflections on Henri Lefebvre, Urban Theory and the Politics of Scale. *International Journal of Urban and Regional Research*, 24(2), 361–378.

Brenner, N. (2014). Introduction: Urban Theory without an Outside. In N. Brenner (Ed.), *Implosions/Explosions: Towards a Study of Planetary Urbanization*. Berlin: Jovis Verlag GmbH.

Cannaos, C. (2013). L'insediamento e la rete di città in Sardegna. In E. Bonacucina, S. Borsato, F. Bua, C. Cannaos, A. Cappai, P. Idini, V. Talu et al. (Eds.), *Sardegna. L'antica e la nuova felicità*. Milan: FrancoAngeli.

Cannaos, C. (2014). Verso la costa. Il ruolo del turismo nella litoralizzazione della Sardegna. *Preliminary Proceedings: Touristic Territories: Touristic Imagery and the Construction of Contemporary Landscape*, Girona. 23–25 January 2014, pp. 669–680.

Cannaos, C. (2015). Misurare il cambiamento. In L. Decandia, C. Cannaos, and L. Lutzoni (Eds.), *Oltre la città e la metropoli: il territorio della provincia di Olbia-Tempio nell'ambito dell'orizzonte postmetropolitano*. Torino: Guerini.

Castells, M. (1989). *The Informational City: Information, Technology, Economic Restructuring and the Urban Regional Process*. Cambridge, MA and Oxford, UK: Blackwell.

Cherchi, P. (1999). *Etnos e apocalisse. Mutamento e crisi nella cultura sarda e in altre culture periferiche*. Cagliari: Zonza.

Cherchi, P. (2013). *Per un'identità critica. Alcune incursioni autoanalitiche nel mondo identitario dei sardi*. Cagliari: Arcadia.

Choay, F. (1994). Le règne de l'urbain et la mort de la ville. In J. Dethier, and G. Alain (Ed.), *La ville. Art et Architecture en Europe 1870–1993* (pp. 26–35). Paris: Centre Georges Pompidou.

Debord, G. (2002). *La società dello spettacolo* (P. Stanziale, It. Trans.). Bolsena: Massari Editore. (Original work published 1967)

Decandia, L. (2008). *Polifonie urbane. Oltre i confini della visione prospettica*. Rome: Meltemi.

Didi-Huberman, G. (2009). *Survivance des lucioles*. Paris: Édition de Minuit.

Gelsomino, G. (2012). *Costa Smeralda 1962–2012. Storia. Cronaca, Mito. Almanacco Gallurese*. Sassari: Iniziative Editoriali.

Lefebvre, H. (1970). *Il diritto alla città* (It. Trans). Padova: Marsilio Editori. (Original work published 1968 as *Le droit à la ville*. Paris: Anthropos.)

Lefebvre, H. (1973). *La rivoluzione urbana* (It. Trans). Rome: Armando. (Original work published 1970 as *La révolution urbaine*. Gallimard: Paris.)

Le Lannou, M. (1979). *Pastori e contadini di Sardegna* (It. Trans.). Cagliari: Della Torre. (Original work published 1941 as *Pâtres et paysans de la Sardaigne*. Tours: Arrault.)

Lutzoni, L. (2013). Empty Territory: Diversity as a Perspective for New Territorial and Local Dimensions of the Project. In C. Perrone (Ed.), *Living Landscape – Landscape for Living: Policies, Practices, Images.* Conference Proceedings (Florence, February–June 2012), *Planum,* 27(2), 15–20.

Lutzoni, L. (2014). *Tra vuoto e movimento: una nuova occasione di sviluppo per le aree interne. Nuove prospettive per il territorio-città del Monte Limbara* (unpublished doctoral dissertation). Università La Sapienza, Rome.

Lutzoni, L. (2015). Paesaggi in divenire. La territorialità attiva dei nuovi abitanti: il caso di Luogosanto in Alta Gallura. In *Città e Territorio Virtuale – Città Memoria Gente, Libro degli Atti del 9° Congresso Città e Territorio Virtuale* (pp. 576–583). Rome: RomaTre-Press.

Maciocco, G. (2011). Orizzonti della città ambientale. La pianificazione strategica della provincia di Sassari. In G. Maciocco, M. Balestrieri, and T. Congiu (Eds.), *Il progetto urbano del territorio. Il piano strategico della provincia di Sassari.* Milan: FrancoAngeli.

Magatti, M. (2012). *La grande contrazione. I fallimenti della libertà e le vie del suo riscatto.* Milan: Feltrinelli Editore.

Merrifield, A. (2014). The Right to the City and Beyond: Notes on a Lefebvrian Reconceptualization. In N. Brenner (Ed.), *Implosions/Explosions: Towards a Study of Planetary Urbanization* (pp. 523–533). Berlin: Jovis Verlag GmbH.

Mumford, L. (1961). *The City in History: Its Origins, Its Transformations, and Its Prospects.* New York: Harcourt, Brace and World.

Murineddu, G. (1997). Immigrati e partecipazione sociale: tempiesi e calangianesi in Olbia. In B. Bandinu, G. Murineddu, and E. Tognotti (Eds.), *Olbia città multietnica* (pp. 61–94). Cagliari: AM&D Edizioni.

Pasolini, P. (1975). Il vero fascismo e quindi il vero antifascismo. *Scritti Corsari,* 45–50. Milan: Garzanti.

Piga, G. (2012). *La Principessa. Storia della Costa Smeralda 1959–2013.* Olbia: Servizi Didattici srl.

Pira, M. (1978). *La rivolta dell'oggetto. Antropologia in Sardegna.* Milan: Editore Giuffrè.

PRIN Postmetropoli. (2015). *Atlante web dei territori postmetropolitani* [web atlas]. Retrieved from http://www.postmetropoli.it/atlante.

Recalcati, M. (2011). *Cosa resta del padre? La paternità nell'epoca ipermoderna.* Milan: Raffaello Cortina.

Serreli, S. (2011). External territories and environmental city project. In G. Maciocco, G. Sanna, and S. Serreli (Eds.), *The Urban Potential of External Territories* (pp. 80–141). Milan: FrancoAngeli.

Soja, E.W. (2007). *Dopo la metropoli. Per una critica della geografia urbana e* regionale (E. Frixia, Ed. and It. Trans.). Bologna: Patron Editore. (Original work published 2000 as *Postmetropolis. Critical Studies of Cities and Regions.* Oxford: Blackwell.)

PART III

Post-metropolis

Looking across the *squares*

12 Corridors as post-metropolitan connectors

The Italian case

Paolo Perulli, Laura Lieto, Luca Garavaglia and Daniele Pennati[1]

Introduction

In current literature on planetary urbanization, a new emphasis is given to new forms assumed by urban growth following non-standard models of physical and social density, dimension and heterogeneity. In such an emerging framework, new forms of extended urbanization linking and forming connections among territories (various forms of networks, borders and differences) and urban–rural continuum (such as the town-country Asian extended urbanization) are considered (Brenner, 2014).

Cities are seen as part of a planetary process in which "the city is everywhere and in everything," as Neil Brenner puts it, or, as Jean-Luc Nancy wrote 15 years earlier, "the centre is everywhere and the circumference nowhere, or the other way around" (Nancy, 1999). The city becomes circulation, transport, mobility, oscillation and vibration, according to Nancy. Hence, new forms of extended value chain in the production of space have to be taken into account.

In the Italian case we can find support to (and evidence of) the critical theorization of cities, especially as far as new territorial corridors emerge in the geography of spaces. Corridor is a polysemic word used in many other contexts: for example, in Japan corridors are an interpretative frame to explain the sprawling urbanization patterns of the Tokyo region. Corridor is a word often used (for example by the European Commission) to show a transport axis, but it can be seen as an urban-territorial axis as well, pointing to many different functions and characteristics. In everyday speech, the word "corridor" is used for a linear space designed to connect different places, highlighting interconnection capacity. A second meaning strategically identifies corridor as a safe "passage" inside a hostile environment: it is a space isolated from the context, linking two places far from each other. It is a bridge, and bridging is a key word in current planetary urbanization made of diverse, often divided places. Moreover, the Latin etymology evokes an idea of speed: the corridor is a space that "runs" from one place to another. However, all these different meanings are related to three key concepts: crossing, interconnection and linearity. It is a space of flows, defined (following Lefebvre) by practices more than by conventions (Lefebvre, 2014, p. 50).

In the international literature, the urbanization process of Italy has been labelled "Urb-Italy". Scholars such as Florida (2006) and Soja and Kanai

(2007) have written that the focus on cities is wrong, as growth and innovation come from new urban corridors. This is correct. However, according to them, "Urb-Italy" is a mega-city-region including Milan-Rome-Turin, with 46.9 million inhabitants. This is not correct at all. It is a functionalist fallacy: given the need to represent "the urban" as expansive mega-city-regions, defining a super-conurbation including Milan-Rome-Turin follows as a consequence. Our work on corridors presented here shows more complicated patterns. Corridors are shown as linking big cities and networks of cities, but also excluding other cities. It is the case of Milan-Turin: a tunnel effect has been created due to the high-speed trains connecting the two cities. In between, a void has been produced. Territorial corridors are strongly related to locational patterns of firms and services, particularly upper-level functional urban services. The geography of corridors is then led by a constellation of factors: infrastructural and (more often through global value chains and supply chains) logistic, economic and social factors. And geographical, physical factors are also included, such as the streams and levees explored by the Tuscany research unit in our research project.

Indeed, the same methodological mistake is made applying conceptual tools such as "global city-region" to Asia. The concept elaborated in a Western cultural setting is not easily transferable to another setting like Asia, where cities as autonomous subjects never existed, nor did the urban–rural duality. We need more diversified conceptual toolboxes, avoiding the totality of a process such as urbanization, accepting the plurality of the world also in its foundational and explanatory terms.

A second key aspect to be considered in these preliminary remarks regards urban governance. This is an interpretative paradigm in some sense competitive, in some other sense integrative towards the planetary urbanization paradigm. The urban governance paradigm emerged in urban studies, particularly in the last ten years following a neo-Weberian approach. Cities are seen here as political and economic plastically dualistic structures, able to experiment collective action (cities as actors) and produce forms of governance in the production of local goods (local collective competition goods) at various territorial layers (Le Galès, 2002; Crouch et al., 2004). Their dimension is not necessarily local, as far as widespread global–local interplay is at work.

The local production and governance of goods, and its influence on territorial systems, is a matter of fact mostly ignored by the planetary urbanization literature. Instead, local forms of policy-making, negotiation and assemblage of social actors are differentiated modes of interaction to be considered in the comparative urban research. A critical point raised by some urban scholars, particularly in Asia, is that simply applying to their countries the Lefebvrian paradigm of planetary urbanization and complete subordination of the agrarian to the urban makes it impossible to take local contexts into consideration. In countries such as China, in which the Weberian autonomy of the city never existed, we cannot apply the global city-region Western category as such. A more complex paradigm is needed, taking into account phenomena which are long-lasting and rooted in historical contexts. The argument is developed by Tang (2014) in a text aimed at criticizing the direct translation of Western concepts in the Eastern urban world. 'Where Lefebvre meets the East', as in Hong Kong and Mainland China, new categories of interpretation are asked for in order to understand the coexistence of rural and urban, the peculiar system of land property rights, and the cultural, political and economic differences of the East.

While the Weberian thinking – seeing the Western city as a unique phenomenon joining market forces with political citizenship – remains unchallenged,[2] there is a need for a new insight into the hybridization of political-economic forms in the globalized urbanity of the twenty-first century.

Since its origin, the city has been a mutual, reciprocal exchange and recognition among different micro-systems: synekism is the original union of dwellings to form a city.

More recently, the increasing mobility of capital, people and information has changed the spatial relations of urban societies. The city has always been a myriad of contracts, both immediate and long-lasting, formal and informal. Their nature is the same of the city itself: endless bargaining among, and combination of "diverse" populations of inhabitants, users and occasional travellers, immigrants (including political refugees and illegal migration and unauthorized trafficking of labour). Today the rationalization impressed to social life has increased calculative-contractual relations in every field of social life, not only in the economic field, but also in the political, creative, technical and scientific areas. Although strong informal, biotic linkages survive in cities (often associated with kinship and ethnic relations) as a remainder of the Chicago school of the twentieth century, the "contract city" is an emerging dominant form. Contracts involve both local and global actors: states and "their" cities, multinational organizations and international institutions, corporate firms (in transport and logistics supply chains as well as in finance) and national and local governments, unions of states (such as the European Union) and "their" regions and cities. All these overlapping networks of contracts revolve around the city: in some cases public institutions, the private sector and civil society participate in the governance. For global, "worlding" cities[3] today, supra-national and global contractual relations are perhaps more important than the relations they have "within" their own, locally bounded nation-states. Hence the importance of (and the need for) studying the interconnected urbanity represented by emerging territorial corridors across the world: their frontiers, borders and thresholds represent a new geography of capitalism and power.

Territorial corridors and their governance and conflicts (today governance structures for such important "extended urban systems" are not given at all) are part of these new developments of the old Lefebvrian urban question revisited. Supra-local and supra-national as they often are, territorial corridors are an emerging extended urban form still looking for scientific and political representation.

On the nature and functions of corridors

Sciences studying and organizing corridors give slightly different operative meanings to the term: in transport and logistic disciplines, the corridor is an ensemble of parallel infrastructures, as linear as possible, crossing the land to connect two poles (the in-between environment being a mere support for the infrastructural axis).

Geographical studies rather emphasize the accessibility aspect: proximity to corridors produces benefits for regional economies and urban development. Despite the fact that every definition depends on the specific approach of each discipline, scientific meanings of the term "corridor" can be abridged to three main interpretations (Priemus, 2000; Priemus & Zonneveld, 2003): (1) corridor as infrastructural axis; (2) corridor as axis of economic development; (3) corridor as urbanization axis. These three definitions do not exclude each other: indeed, it is difficult to imagine a linear metropolitan system not supported by a well-developed mobility system, or to think of urban growth and investments in mobility infrastructures without an adequate rate of economic development.

Nevertheless, during the last two decades, a reductive definition of the concept of "corridor" hegemonized the Italian political and media debate. According to this approach, corridors are just infrastructural axes linking major Italian cities. Consequently, corridor development programmes are mostly aimed at the improvement of mobility infrastructures. Apart from research projects led by universities (Fubini, 2008; Busi & Pezzagno, 2011), there are no traces of concern for territorial and economic aspects of corridor development. National strategies and investments dedicated to corridor development have been focused on Priority Projects identified in the Trans-European Transport Networks (TEN-T) programme, which has been criticized by many scholars for being blind to issues related to regional development along corridors (Albrechts & Coppens, 2003; Priemus & Zonneveld, 2003; Pain, 2010). Such a partial approach seems to be responsible for the scarce concern for intra-corridor cooperation and coordination effects on economic and social development at local and regional scale in Italian policies (Dematteis & Governa, 2001; Boitani & Ponti, 2006; Pennati, 2013).

Furthermore, the EU approach to corridors focuses on the needs of the main metropolitan areas, which are to be interconnected by the high-speed "core network corridors" (CNC[4]) of the TEN-T, mostly ignoring in-between social and economic environments. The attention of policy-makers and the greatest part of investments in mobility infrastructures are concentrated in the more densely populated and richer areas (on the other hand, it should be considered that only in major metropolitan areas is the demand for mobility big enough to justify the enormous investments required for the development of the trans-continental networks designed by TEN-T Priority Projects). Other urban and local administrations along CNC infrastructural axes are not included in corridor planning, if not at later stages, when strategic decisions regarding "where" and "how" have already been taken, and only to negotiate compensations for the negative impacts generated by new or empowered infrastructures bypassing their own territories.

What happens if we change the point of view on the corridor, observing it as a linear open-ended whole instead of looking only at its poles (Graham & Marvin, 2001)? What if we consider it as a constituent form of post-metropolitan formations at different scales? If the issue is no longer to go from Rome to Milan or from Milan to Turin in the shortest travel time, but to understand how social and economic dynamics are organized along CNC (or other non-CNC corridors) in Italy, an approach focused on infrastructures might not suffice: we also need to look at social and economic processes taking place in all local systems involved. In many Italian regions, dense clusters of small cities and local production systems are present along corridors, and their roles could be important in corridor development. A local-focused perspective could be useful to identify emerging territorial assemblages and value chains extended along corridors, and might allow for a better production and evaluation of public initiatives for the development of these systems at all scales.

In order to understand if corridors are emerging territorial systems in the Italian context, and to gain some hints about their trans-scalar organization and dynamics, we will now examine three different aspects of corridor dynamics: demographic and urban dynamics regarding the growth of Italian urban and local systems in the last century (see "Demographic dynamics and urbanization in Italian corridors" below); daily commuting flows connecting metropolitan areas, medium-sized cities and rural areas (see "The dynamics of everyday life" below); and economic specializations in advanced tertiary activities in cities along corridors (see "The spatial organization of economic networks in Italian corridors" below).

Demographic dynamics and urbanization in Italian corridors

Data on population distribution and density allow an alternative approach on corridors, since they provide information about urban growth dynamics taking place in linear systems along mobility infrastructures – one of the main conditions of the existence of effective "territorial corridors".

The map of population density in 2011 highlights the presence of major metropolitan areas (Rome, Milan, Turin, Naples) and great metropolitan regions in Lombardy and Veneto.[5] Other densely populated areas are not as extended: the Ligurian arch, the Tuscany region (Firenze-Prato-Pistoia-Pisa-Lucca-Livorno-La Spezia), the "Via Emilia" (Piacenza-Parma-Reggio Emilia-Modena-Bologna), the Adriatic coast. Most of these areas are innervated by at least a CNC (in Lombardy, along the Via Emilia, along the Adriatic coast), but corridors cannot be easily discerned in this map. However, in a diachronic analysis they become evident: demographic evolution in the last 20 years marked a population loss for metropolitan core areas, which favoured densification in metropolitan hinterlands and along some linear axes, mostly along main highways and railroads. After a century of steady densification of the same areas (those which were already dense – mostly, major metropolises), in the last two decades the stronger densification also interested less dense regions, located along some development axes. This led to relevant transformations, increasing land use, sprawl or regionalization (depending on local and regional context: Lanzani, 2003, 2011). An example is Trentino-Alto Adige, along the Brennero axis (northern part of the Italian segment of Scandinavian–Mediterranean CNC), where strong densification dynamics appear in action: these alpine areas are not densely populated, if compared with the nearby Po Valley, but their density grows with the same intensity of the other corridor areas in the macro-region of northern Italy.

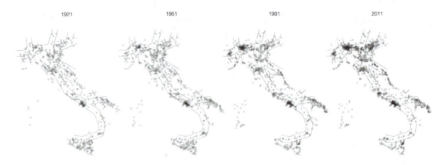

Figure 12.1 Evolution of Italian small-sized cities (10,000–50,000 inhabitants): spatial
distribution

Source: Authors' calculation, based on data provided by ISTAT (Italian National Institute of Statistics)
(Census data 1921, 1951, 1981, 2011)

Demographic data regarding urban growth are useful to gain a closer looks
at development dynamics in these areas, searching for traces of the assemblage
of territorial corridor systems. In the last century, the most radical transformations interested small and medium-sized cities: in 1921 only 36% of the Italian
population belonged to a municipality with 10,000–250,000 inhabitants. In 2011,
that value reached 54%. Moreover, the number of small and medium-sized cities
almost doubled in the last 90 years, rising from 603 to 1,192.[6]

Spatial distribution of these fast-growing cities also changed, highlighting some
axes of territorial development in which urban growth has been decidedly stronger.
These changes can be better observed by focusing on two classes of cities: small
cities ranging from 10,000–50,000 inhabitants (Figure 12.1), and medium-sized
cities with a population of 50,001–250,000 inhabitants (Figure 12.2). While the
spatial distribution of medium-sized cities only shows moderate changes in the
observed period, small cities appear more dynamic, passing from a homogeneous

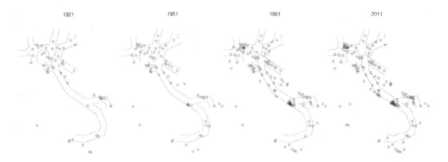

Figure 12.2 Evolution of Italian medium-sized cities (50,001–250,000 inhabitants):
spatial distribution

Source: Authors' calculation, based on data provided by ISTAT (Italian National Institute of Statistics)
(Census data 1921, 1951, 1981, 2011)

dispersion in space to a strong concentration in a few areas: some big clusters of cities (based on spatial proximity) can be identified, in particular in metropolitan regions and, starting from the last quarter of the twentieth century, also along main infrastructural axes (following the development of the Italian highway network). Small cities in these areas seem to have been the main beneficiaries of the population losses experienced by major cities after 1970.

The growth of small and medium-sized cities along main mobility axes is blatant in the representation provided in Figures 12.1 and 12.2, which compares their spatial distribution with the paths of CNCs, allowing for some considerations about the presence of territorial corridors:

- Along the Mediterranean CNC, the axis connecting Milan–Verona–Venice is quite self-evident, while the link between Milan and Turin does not converge with the areas of urban growth. In that region, clusters of small and medium-sized cities are not positioned along main mobility infrastructures: instead, they follow the alpine arch, where many industrial districts (Biella, Valsesia, Omegna) and industrial areas (Ivrea, home to Olivetti computer factories) are located. This seems a strong hint that mobility infrastructures aren't the only factor determining urban growth.
- In central Italy, between the metropolitan areas of Florence and Rome, urban growth and densification processes are stronger in the linear urban cluster of Umbria (Perugia, Spoleto, Terni), and does not follow the parallel, straight path of the Scandinavian–Mediterranean CNC (along Arezzo and Orvieto), marked by the A1-E35 highway and by the high-speed railway.
- In southern Italy, the path of the Scandinavian–Mediterranean CNC between Naples and Bari or between Naples and Palermo seems to be purely arbitrary: in these areas, the CNC is more a "project" than an effective territorial system.
- In Apulia, densification processes appear to be scarcely influenced by corridor dynamics. In this rural region, small and medium-sized cities, although numerous and relatively close to each other, do not show significant spatial growth, and there are no discernible signs of regionalization processes: most densification concentrates inside municipal boundaries, or the immediate hinterland of main cities (Bari, Taranto), and does not concern rural areas or infrastructural axes. Similar dynamics seem to affect other clusters of small and medium-sized cities in southern Italy (i.e. in south-western Sicily).
- Some of the main linear clusters of medium-sized cities growing along mobility infrastructures (the region between Milan and Bologna, the Ligurian arch, the southern part of the Adriatic Corridor,) are not part of any CNC: these territorial corridors are thus "invisible" to Italian policies for corridor development.

These findings emphasize the role of small and medium-sized cities in post-metropolitan dynamics in Italy. In the last 30 years, these cities have been protagonists of relevant processes of territorial development, comparable with the ones taking place at the same time in main metropolitan areas. Along the most important mobility infrastructures, in particular in the densely populated regions of northern and central Italy, corridor dynamics seem to constitute one of the main factors influencing densification (while in most regions of central and southern Italy other factors seem to be in action, and no traces of territorial corridors can be discerned), and brought to a steady growth in population of small and medium-sized cities (significantly, cities located at the intersection of corridors

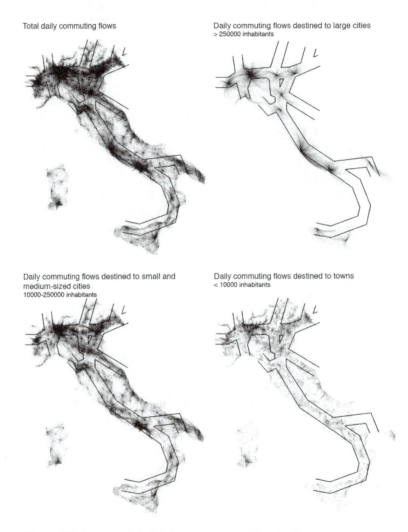

Figure 12.3 Inter-municipal daily commuting patterns in Italy

Arcs represent commuting flows between two municipalities. Flows consisting of less than five commuters (amounting to 5% of all inter-municipal commuting movements) are not shown.

Source: Authors' calculation, based on data provided by ISTAT (Italian National Institute of Statistics) (Census data 2011)

show the highest gains). In those regions, corridors appear as complex trans-scalar territorial systems where growing metropolitan areas melt with "chains" of small and medium-sized cities, sharing common dynamics regarding urban growth and densification. Recent research based on the same demographic data (Feltrin et al., 2010) identified 22 emerging metropolitan areas in the regions of central and northern Italy, all of them located along main mobility infrastructures, generated by the growth of medium-sized cities (Piacenza, Perugia, Brescia, Trento, and so on) or by the welding of clusters of small cities (around Verona, along the "Via Emilia", along the Adriatic coastline in Romagna, and so on).

The dynamics of everyday life

The diachronic analysis of urban growth along main mobility axes provided us with some preliminary hints that territorial corridor dynamics might be present in some Italian regions. Obviously, to verify the presence of corridors and their organization, "short run" flows must also be considered: the analysis of commuting data between municipalities[7] (and, in the next chapter, the analysis of local specializations in advanced tertiary activities) will provide some elements for a better identification of the interconnection capacity of corridors (in terms of social and economic impact).

Data on commuting movements provide useful information to describe the relationships linking municipalities, and to identify urban hierarchies or polycentric post-metropolitan systems. In Figure 12.3, four different elaborations of commuting flows[8] are given: in addition to the map representing the whole of the flows, flows destined to major cities (over 250,000 inhabitants), to small and medium-sized cities, to towns (under 10,000 inhabitants) have been singled out. Each disaggregation expresses different patterns: towns attract only short-range commuting movements (27.4% of all commuting movements: only a few towns located in main metropolitan areas show a better-than-average capacity to attract flows); at the opposite end of our urban spectrum, flows destined to major cities (15.5% of all commuting movements) are for the most part long-ranged. In northern Italy, catchment areas of major cities frequently overlap each other – a hint of the presence of post-metropolitan dynamics in those regions (Perulli, 2012).

However, apart from this evidence, the most interesting findings can be deducted from the analysis of flows destined to small and medium-sized cities. Flows towards these cities are 57.1% of all commuting flows. Their patterns not only highlight the polycentric nature of most metropolitan areas (notably, Milan, Turin, and Naples), in which medium-sized cities collect dense commuting flows, bypassing the metropolitan centre, but also detect high densities of flows inside clusters of cities along some corridors. In these spaces, catchment areas of all small and medium-sized cities are almost coincident, denoting the presence of polycentric systems in which urban hierarchies are weak, and interdependences between these cities (and between them and metropolitan centres) seem to be very strong:

- the corridor extended from the metropolitan area of Milan to Brescia, Verona, Padua, Venice, Trieste;
- the pre-alpine arch of Piedmont, centred on Turin and spreading from Biella to Cuneo;
- the Via Emilia and the Adriatic coastline, with its uninterrupted line of small and medium-sized cities elongated from Pescara to Milan;
- the cluster including Florence, Prato, Pistoia, Pisa, Livorno, Massa-Carrara in Tuscany, reaching the eastern area of the Ligurian arch (La Spezia);
- the axis between Rome and Naples;
- the Salento area and the metropolitan area of Taranto in Apulia;
- less evident traces of corridor dynamics can also be spotted in the areas between Florence, Perugia and Rome and, in southern Italy, between south-eastern Sicily and Calabria.

These dynamics also interest small cities and towns (fewer than 50,000 inhabitants). Around 75% of all commuting movements between cities with fewer than 250,000 inhabitants are destined to small cities: in particular, along territorial corridors minor centres are not only generators but also recipients of a relevant part of commuting movements, including long-range (trans-provincial) flows. In these areas, small cities actively contribute to the assemblage of dense polycentric networks of commuting flows, where urban hierarchies are weak and constantly changing: high accessibility provides even smaller cities with a large "geographical reach" (Beauregard, 1995), inducing urban specialization to attract inhabitants, commuters and city-users (Martinotti, 1993).

Diachronic analysis highlights a relevant and constant growth of commuting movements. Every day over 11 million commuters travel to another municipality to reach their place of work or their school. In the last recorded decade (2001–2011), commuting destined to major cities increased by 13% (+195,721), while commuting destined to towns grew over 20% (+523,837) and medium-sized cities attracted almost 1 million new commuters (+17%).

The growth of commuting flows destined to medium-sized cities and towns does not correspond to a growth of short-range commuting. On the contrary, commuting movements between adjoining municipalities show a slight decrease (from 48.4% of all commuting movements in 2001 to 46.5% in 2011), while long-range commuting is strongly increasing: +34% for movements over 50 km, and +97% for movements over 100 km. Many factors contributed to the swelling of long-range commuting: one of them is the persisting effects of the economic crisis on many local economies, which forced workers to seek a job farther away from home. The improvement of mobility infrastructures and service also had a role in these dynamics: where high-speed train connections have been activated (between the cities of Turin, Milan, Bologna, Florence, Rome and Naples), long-range commuting flows showed a relevant growth. But medium-sized cities and towns are only marginally influenced by the impact of those infrastructures, which are only available to metropolitan centres. Most likely, their attractiveness depends on the capacity to maintain a lively economic system even in times of crisis.

The spatial organization of economic networks in Italian corridors

According to many scholars, high levels of wealth, development and innovation are distinctive traits of corridors (Whebell, 1969, Priemus, 2001; Priemus & Zonneveld, 2003). The European Union approach on corridors seems to be based on this same prospective: enforce accessibility in order to stimulate growth and development along main trans-national and trans-regional connection axes (Pain, 2007).

In order to verify this assertion, we analysed territorial information about economic achievements and wealth distribution in Italian municipalities (Figure 12.4 shows an example of these elaborations), focusing on the analysis of the spatial organization of trans-territorial value chains along main corridors. The findings we obtained are not straightforward: in northern Italy, corridors constitute one of the main axes of economic growth, with higher-than-average performances (compared with national and regional average values) recorded not only in metropolitan areas but also in medium-sized and small cities, and in most industrial districts. Conversely, in southern Italy and in the islands of Sardinia and Sicily, there are no traces of a better performance of corridors, and the drivers of growth are to be found elsewhere (that is, in the activation of available local resources and knowledge: Casavola & Trigilia, 2012).

These variances seem to be caused not only by the well-known economic gap between northern and southern Italy (Sereni, 1961; Barca, 1999) or by the lack of mobility infrastructures in those regions (Garavaglia, 2012), but also from historical

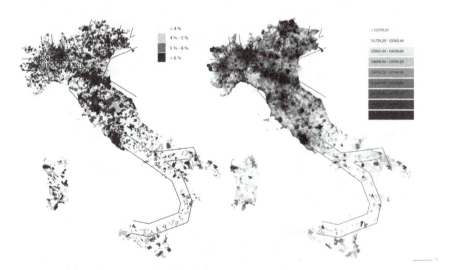

Figure 12.4 Innovative firms and distribution of wealth in Italian municipalities

Left map shows the percentage of local firms operating in innovative sectors (as identified by ISTAT); right map shows the distribution of average pro-capita income.

Source: Authors' calculation, based on data provided by ISTAT (Italian National Institute of Statistics) (Census data 2011) and MEF (Italian Ministry of Economy and Finance) (2012)

differences in the role of cities in social and economic development processes, dating back to the Norman invasion in the eleventh century, when the conquerors restored a strong, centralized feudal power that strangled municipal authorities, while in the same years in northern Italy cities began to grow as political and economic subjects (Cattaneo, 1972). Since then, urban centres in southern Italy lost most of their vivacity and became consumer cities (Weber, 1985), lacking control over their hinterland and scarcely interconnected between each other, thus unable to act as "engines" for local and regional economic development (Trigilia, 2014). This situation has lasted until the present day, and represents a threat to the capacity of the new infrastructural projects for the assemblage of corridors organized by the European and Italian governments to sustain a faster rate of development in southern Italy, without further interventions to revitalize identities and roles of cities in economic networks both at regional and global scale.

In the areas where territorial corridor dynamics can be identified using economic indicators (and in particular in the macro-region of northern Italy, whose metropolitan centre is Milan: Turri, 2000; Perulli & Pichierri, 2010; Perulli, 2012), cities seem to play a relevant role in the regional economy. In order to explore in more detail this scenario, we focused on the availability of advanced business services (since most literature on spatial organization of economic networks in the information society points out the pivotal role of cities as providers of business services required to access and compete in the global market: Sassen, 1991; Scott, 1998; Castells, 2000; Taylor, 2004, Cohen, 2006; Perulli, 2010; Moretti, 2013).

Data on business services in the cities and local systems[9] along corridors in northern Italy highlights the role of Milan as first supplier of business services to the entire macro-region: the presence of those activities in Milan is substantially larger, both in absolute terms and in relative density, than in all other metropolitan and urban centres. Milan is a hub for most of the crucial functions needed to access global markets (financial services, management consulting, ICT, advertising, design, and so on). Concentration of banking and financial services is very high, compared with other urban centres, making Milan the only city in northern Italy to boast a significant availability of back-office activities (such as monetary intermediation, management of mutual funds, administration of financial markets and holding activities of financial groups[10]).

This is a confirmation of the role of Milan as a world-city and as the main globalization platform for the whole macro-region (Taylor, 2004; Magatti et al., 2005; Perulli & Pichierri, 2010; Bonomi, 2012; Taylor, 2012). All production chains operating in northern Italy look to Milan when they have to find and organize the rare services needed to enter and compete in international markets, organizing city-region dynamics (Scott, 1998). But while Milan is the strongest provider of business services in northern Italy, it is not the only one: business services of a more standardized type (computer services, accounting and management, legal services, entertainment activities, cultural services) are widely spread in all urban centres and in some industrial districts. More significantly, many cities, even small ones, have high degrees of specializations in one or more "rare" services embodying high contents of knowledge and/or creativity (design, financial assets, trade fairs, advertising, market research, ICT, but also activities related to leisure, culture, welfare). The high degree of differentiation in urban availability of advanced business services seems to compose a cohesive mosaic in which local service ranges tend to be integrated, rather than redundant: duplications in local business services between cities in the same area are very rare. The coordination is pronounced in metropolitan areas (that is, the ones identified by Feltrin et al., 2010) and in main territorial corridors. Along the Mediterranean Corridor (Figure 12.5), Turin shows specializations in services related to innovation and research, Novara and Verona in logistic activities, Vicenza in fair and events management, Padua in education and ICT, Venice in design, Trieste in research activities. On the axis of the "Via Emilia" (Figure 12.6), the integration of tertiary functions is less evident, in particular around the metropolitan area of Bologna; nevertheless, local peaks of density in some advanced services are emerging, counterbalanced by low densities in other cities nearby: Piacenza has a strong density of logistics activities, Reggio Emilia is specialized in accounting and management services (strictly connected to the industrial districts nearby), Modena in design, Parma in cultural activities, Bologna (a larger city, with a wider range of services) in rarer services such as ICT, education and research, Rimini in fair and events management.

On the other hand, cities of similar size and history, but located outside main corridors and metropolitan areas, show higher levels of duplication in the availability of business services: it is the case of southern Piedmont, where the cities of Cuneo, Asti, Alessandria (and also the smallest cities of Fossano, Mondovì, Alba, and so on) compete with each other in the offer of services for the same value chains (agri-food, logistics, tourism).

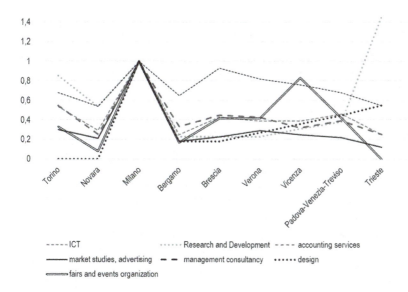

Figure 12.5 Density of advanced tertiary activities in the Italian cities along the
Mediterranean Corridor

Milan = 1

Source: Authors' calculation, based on data provided by ISTAT (Italian National Institute of Statistics) (2009)

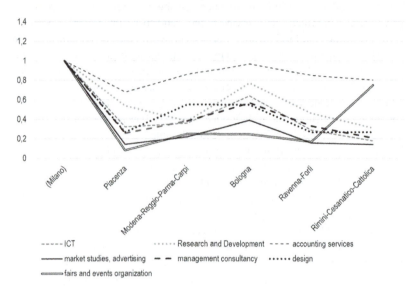

Figure 12.6 Density of advanced tertiary activities in the Italian cities of the "Via Emilia" Milan = 1

Source: Authors' calculation, based on data provided by ISTAT (Italian National Institute of Statistics) (2009)

Italian corridors as polycentric systems

The exploration of social and economic dynamics organized along CNC corridors highlighted a complex scenario: in some regions of northern and central Italy, territorial corridors can be identified, while along other CNC corridors there are no signs of corridor dynamics. Different performances do not depend solely on the characteristics of available infrastructures for mobility, although these infrastructures are crucial in the assemblage of corridor systems. High density of flows (of people, goods, information) is obviously a relevant factor, but best-performing corridors also show increasing integrations between cities, influencing urban growth dynamics and economic specializations. In these areas, corridors are not only fast connections between main metropolitan areas: they are polycentric systems where new spaces for social and economic activities are organized. Such territorial corridors are functionally integrated with major metropolitan areas, sharing polycentric metropolis dynamics (Hall & Pain, 2006, 2008): smaller centres are not required to provide rare services, which business networks can already find in the major metropolitan areas, and tend to specialize instead in a limited number of business services. The great variety in urban packages of business services favours the development of agglomeration economies (Scott, 1998). In territorial corridors, small and medium-sized cities are main actors of social and economic development. The importance of cities seems to proceed from at least two major factors. One of them resides in the characteristics of the world-cities of Milan and Rome, relatively too small to play a hegemonic role as platforms for the globalization of the Italian economy (Magatti et al., 2005; Taylor, 2012). The second factor can be traced back to the role historically played since the Middle Ages by small and medium-sized cities in the spatial organization of the economy in Lombardy, Veneto, Emilia-Romagna and Tuscany. More recently, in these same regions, medium-sized cities had an important role in the birth and development of industrial districts (Bagnasco, 1988), acting as providers of education services (secondary education, and in particular technical schools) and business services (accountancy, financial services, logistic services, ICT, and so on). The golden age of industrial districts is now over, surpassed by new production forms organized in long value chains (Gereffi & Korzeniewicz, 1994; Gereffi & Bair, 2001) extended at trans-local and trans-national scale (Corò & Micelli, 2006), but the polycentric *milieu* in which they were generated did not lose all of its competitive advantages, and might be breeding new functional systems organized at a larger scale, capable of sustaining a good rate of economic development (although even in these areas the current global economic crisis is exacting a heavy toll on many industrial and tertiary activities, with a dramatic impact on small-sized firms).

Concentration of post-metropolitan dynamics in some regions of northern and central Italy is not to say that Urb-Italy (Florida, 2006; Soja & Kanai, 2007), including Turin, Milan and Rome, actually exists as a system: instead, a number of smaller territorial systems, elongated along corridors, seem to constitute the main axes of growth and development, each one with its own socio-economic peculiarities and its own forms of "territorial added value" (Dematteis & Governa, 2005). TEN-T infrastructural projects do not consider those dynamics, exposing themselves to the threat of generating distortions and inefficiencies in economic development: in order to appreciate these complex polycentric systems, and to gain better control of ongoing territorialization processes (Reffestin, 1984; Turco, 1988; Dematteis & Governa, 2001), a "place-based" approach to the regulation of territorial corridors could be useful.

Emerging governance issues

The organization of social and economic dynamics at the scale of corridors generates a strong demand for governance that cannot be fully satisfied by the scalar and territorial frames currently available in Italy. Polycentric corridor systems are difficult to regulate, as they are: (1) organized in trans-territorial networks trespassing administrative boundaries between cities and between regions; and (2) fed by flows. Therefore their spatial extension and their territorial hierarchies are much more the results of the aggregation of individual behaviours by private actors (residents, students, workers, firms, value chains, and so on: Scott, 1998; Hall & Pain, 2006) than the outcome of public planning. Nevertheless, they seem to constitute a relevant dimension for the organization of value chains and knowledge systems, as they provide specific forms of competitive advantage (mostly agglomeration economies: Scott,

1998). Territorial corridors are also breeding pits for emerging problems of spatial regulation (Brenner, 2004), connected to land use (Turri, 2000), environmental protection, traffic congestion, and for new social inequalities (wealth inequalities, income inequalities, educational inequalities, social stratification inequalities, and so on: Scott, 1998). These issues need to be addressed by place-based policies (Barca, 2009), different for each corridor system. Public intervention on corridors cannot concern only mobility infrastructures: its concern must also be the regulation of interdependences between local systems and the reduction of territorial competition (Brosio, 1999), both responsible for diseconomies, spillovers, waste of resources. To achieve such results, trans-scalar and scale-making policies are needed: responsibilities and powers required for an efficient regulation of a corridors area still fragmented on the vertical axis between regions, provinces, municipalities, state and the EU. The administrative framework in which transscalar cooperation/coordination among and within corridors could be organized is still lacking in Italy: public intervention on corridors only concerns mobility infrastructures, and there are no traces of *state scalar strategies* (Brenner, 1999; Brenner, 2004) which are required to enforce the competitiveness of corridors in global economies (in particular, in most areas of southern Italy, where corridors are not an effective dimension of organization for value chains and knowledge systems, specific programmes to stimulate flows and to foster trans-territorial cooperation should be administered). Also, despite the rich toolkit available (that is, pacts, "conferenze di servizi", ad hoc agencies, and so on), horizontal cooperation between regions and provinces involved in corridor governance seems very limited, due to the lack of economic incentives and political enforcement.

Fast answers to these problems are not likely to be produced by the Italian Parliament, because of the lack of national strategies on corridors development and also because of recurring conflicts between national and local administrators over scalar distribution of public powers: similar questions concerning the governance of metropolitan areas took 25 years to find an institutional solution (metropolitan cities, first established by law no. 142/1990, were only activated on 1 January 2015). In the absence of national or regional strategies and agencies dedicated to corridors, cities might play an important role in regulation: in the last decade, many cities along main corridors organized coalitions in order to define new development paths for economic actors, to strengthen and coordinate their supply of advanced business services, to rationalize the efforts for the production of local collective competition goods. This happened between metropolitan nodes (an example is the MI-TO programme, intended to enhance coordination between Milan and Turin for many functions, starting from tertiary education and research), but also between small and medium-sized cities along dense territorial corridors: Padova-Venice-Treviso on the Mediterranean CNC, Trento-Verona-Mantova along the Scandinavian–Mediterranean CNC, and so on (Carbognin et al., 2004, Perulli & Garavaglia, 2006; Perulli, 2010). These coalitions are often weakly structured: lacking dedicated resources or governing powers, they are heavily dependent on political choices. In most cases, they have rarely been able to generate and sustain long-lasting strategies and interventions. However, these alliances experimented with new models of trans-institutional coordination and new *organizing logics* (Sassen, 2008) that have sometimes proven successful in regulating complex polycentric systems where the scalar power of the state was unable to reduce spatial conflicts.

Hopefully, the new powers and resources allocated to local governments by the recent reform of the Italian Constitution (including most of the responsibilities concerning welfare and economic development), the new instruments for inter-municipal collaboration introduced by the "Delrio law" (law no.156/2014), and the availability of national funding programmes for innovation of urban areas (that is, the "Smart Cities" national initiative, resources dedicated to metropolitan cities, and so on) will allow cities to enforce those "bottom–up" networks for the governance of corridor issues.

Conclusive remarks

In this chapter corridors are considered as emerging territorial assemblages; as such, we have investigated them in the Italian context, to unsettle conventional definitions of capital, labour and resources mobilization over different territorial partitions.

We have grounded our investigation and findings on emerging strands of urban theory addressing post-metropolitan phenomena as highly variable connections, and have worked them out on a practical terrain, in the stickiness and contingency of corridor-like urbanization processes observable at a closer distance in the Italian context. In these conclusive remarks, some theoretical considerations are offered, as feedback "from the ground" to the post-metropolitan debate.

Corridors as strategic figures and political constructs

Corridors emerge as connectivity devices of a complex nature: they simultaneously work as infrastructure, ecological and landscape patterns, as well as strategic configurations of capital flows. As such, these networking vectors are a powerful metaphor of an overflowing urbanity crossing different scales and dragging different processes – urban, natural, social, economic, political.

Challenging the mainstreamed figure of Urb-Italy, through corridor analysis we have highlighted how these formations work as including/excluding devices, producing "voids" where locational patterns of firms and services are not present.

This strategic and political nature of corridors makes room for a different understanding of traditional categories of urban analysis: for example, a new kind of "periphery" seems relevant, no longer measured in terms of distance from the urban centre, but rather in terms of those "voids" substantially bypassed by capital flows. It would be a mistake, though, to understand such voids as forms of socio-spatial segregation, as their relations with corridors are not just based on spatial criteria such as proximity or distance from some centrality. The core–periphery distinction is here more a matter of unequal distribution of rewards among different activities (that is, transformation, production, distribution), than just a physical issue (Arrighi & Drangel, 1986; Bair, 2005). Furthermore, the "voids" bypassed by logistics corridors (as those we have highlighted in our investigation) can be entangled with other networks: for example, they can be part of land mosaics and ecological corridors (Forman, 1995), and thus be in play at a different scale, according to different constitutive processes.

This observation helps understanding the multiple logics in play when it comes to corridors: no longer regarded just as infrastructure, they can be conceptualized, more broadly, as complex *chains* straddling over disparate regions and performing different roles at once, not just related to the economy, but also to the environment, society and politics.

In such a perspective, corridors can be conveniently placed within global value chains (Gereffi et al., 2001; Bair, 2005), in which they work as networking devices of urbanization, deeply embedded in the materiality of urban processes and thus susceptible to differences and frictions.

On global value chains, scale-making and bigness

Stemmed from world-system theory (Hopkins & Wallerstein, 1977), the literature on global value chains represents a next-generation theoretical effort to understand not just how commodity chains work (from raw materials to final goods), but, most importantly, how such chains can facilitate upgrading of firms wishing to access the world economy, and how such firm-upgrading affects national economies and local societies (Gereffi et al., 2001). Chains scholars have increasingly focused, in recent years, on the "spatially dispersed and organizationally complex production networks that are an important part of economic globalization" and, in these terms, have acknowledged the need to understand global capitalism, to "illuminate how [. . .] discrete locations and activities are connected to each other as constituent links that collectively comprise the commodity chain" (Bair, 2005, p. 158). Furthermore, they have pointed out how matters of power and domination arising from chain analysis are not just related to traditional patterns of ownership – basically acknowledging the role of lead corporate firms – but also to finer-grain networks of subcontracting firms. The micro and meso level of chain analysis thus comes to the fore, beyond the holistic perspective of world-system theory, and thus contexts matter much more than in the early stage of chain research.

In this perspective, scholars have shifted their focus from social implications of firms upgrading, to issues of exclusion as well as path dependency illuminated by context analysis. Such a critical turning point has given rise to a different understanding of global capitalism, and opened new lines of inquiry more sensitive to differences and contexts.

Among them, supply-chain capitalism (one of the current versions of the broader discourse on global value chains) is a model to understand "both the *continent-crossing scale* and the *constitutive diversity* of contemporary global capitalism" (Lowenhaupt-Tsing, 2009, p. 148 – emphasis added) in contrast with theories mainly acknowledging capitalist homogeneity.

In such a perspective, multiple scales are in play simultaneously, and this has consequences for how we understand metropolitan formations.

The "critical scale" to observe and eventually govern metropolitan formations has been progressively stretching out, and not just in dimensional terms: there is no critical scale once and for all – as big as it might be – but the scale itself is under question, as it cannot be predetermined but "must be brought into being: proposed, practiced, and evaded, as well as taken for granted" (Lowenhaupt-Tsing, 2005, p. 58).

Scales, in the post-metropolitan horizon, are politically contested: different practices, projects, programmes bring different scales into being, from the scale of the region to that of the planet. Bigness is thus not a matter of widening the angle of satellite mapping tools: bigness is a matter of associations, occurring at different scales, bringing about different commitments, often conflicting, radically contingent and heterogeneous, entangled with materiality. In these terms, it can be understood as "a *revolution without a program*" (Koolhaas, 2006), an ideology independent from a specific will: it is an ever-shifting representation of flows and territorialization patterns, drifting cascades of information and transformations, where what's visible is constitutively unstable, threatened by the rising of new trajectories and uneven associations.

Such an idea of bigness contradicts the optimistic, popular accounts of the spread of market economy and liberal democracy (Fukuyama, 1992; Friedman, 2000) in the advance of a global era. These stories were committed to a coordinated and homogeneous vision of global integration that have then been replaced by discontinuity, heterogeneity and instability of urbanization processes.

We argue that this notion of bigness should be included into the theoretical frame addressing research on contemporary urbanization processes, currently mainstreamed – especially in the geographical discourse – by the idea that global capitalism is a homogenous formation, aimed at erasing differences according to the Marxist notion of creative destruction as the main strategy of the capital.

It is worth noticing that, to some extent, the world urbanization theory (a branch of critical urban theory as purported by scholars in the legacy of the Frankfurt School – Brenner, Marcuse, and others) has been stretched to its own limits, and places always considered *outside* the urban condition are now included *within* the same, big picture. The Amazon, the Arctic, the Himalayas, the atmosphere are progressively becoming "urban" (see "Extreme territories of urbanization", research project of the Urban Theory Lab at Harvard, coordinated by Neil Brenner). The world would have become "one", according to the idea that capitalism has shaped an urban world *without an outside* (Brenner & Katsikis, 2013). We do not fully agree with this idea. As urban scholars, we are constitutively sensitive to contexts and differences, and thus need a different theoretical lever to work out such concerns.

The notion of supply-chain capitalism acknowledges the structural role of difference in the mobilization of labour, resources and capital: based on outsourcing – that is, shifting work to third parties in order to reduce labour costs and enhance efficiency of corporate business – it allows thinking of capitalism as both a global enterprise aimed at standardization, and a device for the formation of different niches of labour and production, where segregation and creativity are intertwined.

Supply-chain capitalism escapes homogeneity and abstraction, as diversity is the constituent form of its scale-making process: different enterprises, scattered throughout the globe and linked together within the same supply chain, reflect very different conditions as responses to the need of corporate business to cut labour costs and discipline the workforce. In such a perspective, supply chains are much harder to govern than state bureaucracies or corporations, as a large part of them is formed out of legal grey zones and, most importantly, "within the constant flux of boom-and-bust opportunities" (Lowenhaupt-Tsing, 2009, p.150).

In these terms, the notion of supply-chain capitalism enriches the general frame provided by critical urban theory, as it allows a different, more effective appreciation of bigness: not just a matter of uneven connections between territories for productive and exploitation motives, but also, and foremost, a matter of dynamic scale-making throughout diversities. Such an approach looks suitable for planning as a political endeavour dealing with the materiality of the world, open to its heterogeneity and differences, attentive to associations more than predefined models of how stability and change occur (Lieto & Beauregard, 2013). In such a perspective, the idea of scale-making is crucial, as it poses the concept of scale as an outcome and not as a predefined metric standard to watch the real world from.

Corridors as trans-scalar territorial assemblages offer a new lens to investigate and describe post-metropolitan processes otherwise opaque, but relevant to acknowledge the strength and pervasiveness of the current urbanization of capital. From this standpoint, it is clear that conventional modes of representation are no longer suitable to catch the emerging, critical features of such phenomena, and consequently traditional governance frames need to be deeply revised.

This poses relevant problems not just in analytical terms, but rather in terms of governmentality. Issues at the top of regional planners' agendas – environmental and landscape preservation, climate change effects mitigation, demographic redistribution due to migrations and other major problems (poverty, wars, political inequalities, and so on) – are all relevant here. And it is clear they are all mutually dependent, no matter how highly or loosely connected they can be, and each phenomenon can be viewed as the specific grip of a "global aspiration", as the "encounter across difference" (Lowenhaupt-Tsing, 2005, p.3) of networks of power, trade and meaning.

From a regional planning standpoint, the overlapping connections of heterogeneous projects of space and scale-making framed by such a bigness is critical, and deserves investigation. The figurations that Edward Soja, in his work, has offered as a new inquiry on post-metropolitan formations speak on this behalf: exopolis, fractal city, and other images (Soja, 2000), all suggest a change of pace in how we frame urban phenomena, in a back-and-forth movement straddling over different scales, distances, connections.

The key concept – to figure out a different analytical and political approach to post-metropolitan formations – is difference. It allows us to acknowledge "the constitutive diversity of contemporary global capitalism" (Lowenhaupt-Tsing,

2009, p.148) in contrast with theories of homogeneity and replication; it also allows us to understand processes and patterns of capital, labour and resources mobilization within a common frame of global standardization unfolding through networks linking niches of diversity, of irreducible specificity. Global is local knowledge "in the sense [it] cannot be understood without the benefit of historically specific cultural assumptions" (Lowenhaupt-Tsing, 2005, p.7).

In this chapter, we do not provide solutions; rather we aim to support, through issues and findings from our field investigations on Italian corridors, a new research agenda addressing a post-metropolitan line of inquiry, and its inherently global aspirations, towards differences and frictions arising from a specific socio-territorial context.

Italy's transition from a bounded urbanization phase to a post-metropolitan one is a story still to be told. But a remarkable contribution can come from this locale to understand how traveling ideas of global urbanization matter, how they become practical, thus contested and forged by difference.

As unbounded figures of current urbanization processes, corridors help understanding of how the universal aspirations of global value chains crossing the globe become enmeshed in space, are contested, reshaped and recharged with new implications and differences.

They are unbounded in nature, but also frictional, as dragging-effect devices traveling through cities, regions and societies, thus changing their role and functions as long as their trajectory unfolds in space.

Notes

1 This chapter grew out of a common work of the authors in the field of post-metropolitan research. However, P. Perulli took primary responsibility for the introduction, D. Pennati took primary responsibility for the sections entitled "On the nature and functions of corridors", "Demographic dynamics and urbanization in Italian corridors" and "The dynamics of everyday life", L. Garavaglia took primary responsibility for the sections entitled "The spatial organization of economic networks in Italian corridors", "Italian corridors as polycentric systems" and "Emerging governance issues", and L. Lieto took primary responsibility for the conclusive remarks.

2 Criticism towards Weber expressed by authors such as A. Appadurai and P.J. Taylor does not take into consideration the inherently dialectic Weberian approach to economy and society.

3 S. Sassen, N. Brenner, A. Ong and A. Roy are among the authors to be considered here.

4 In the 2013 revision of the TEN-T programme (EU Regulation No. 1316), "core network corridors" (CNC) were introduced to facilitate the implementation of Priority Projects. Nine core network corridors have been identified, four of them crossing Italy: Mediterranean Corridor (France – Turin – Milan – Venice – Trieste – Slovenia); Baltic–Adriatic corridor (Austria – Trieste – Venice – Bologna – Ravenna); Scandinavian–Mediterranean corridor (Austria–Trento–Verona–Bologna–Florence–Rome – Naples – Palermo); North Sea–Mediterranean corridor (Switzerland – Novara/Milan – Genoa).

5 See PRIN Postmetropoli (2015): "Popolazione residente dal 1971 al 2011", § a.1.1.

6 The demographic dynamics of the Italian municipalities have been reconstructed from national census data between 1861 and 2011.

7 2001, 2011 census, ISTAT data.

8 Only daily commuting flows for work and study between different municipalities have been considered.
9 The territorial unit chosen for this analysis is the *Sistema Locale del Lavoro* (Local Labour System), defined by ISTAT (Italian National Statistical Institute) in order to encompass most of the commuter flows generated by local systems. This layer ignores administrative (provincial or regional) boundaries and gives prominence to the extension of flows of people, knowledge and creativity, allowing researchers to accurately identify the area of direct influence of an urban centre on its hinterland. In our analysis, based on ISTAT data, we examined 34 tertiary activities in all 266 Local Labour Systems of northern Italy (Garavaglia, 2014).
10 Milan is one of the five financial markets in Europe, home to the Italian *Borsa Valori* (Stock Exchange). The city hosts the offices of 125 banks, of which 55 represent international groups (ABI data, 2012) and a much greater number of companies engaged in financial activities (data for year 2009 count 1,883 local units of firms in banking activities, and 3,995 local units of other financial services – without counting insurance activities). Recently, mergers of some of the greatest Italian banks (it is worth mentioning at least Unicredit Group and Intesa San Paolo) led to an even greater concentration of banking functions in Milan.

References

Albrechts, L., and Coppens, T. (2003). Megacorridors: striking a balance between the space of flows and the space of places. *Journal of Transport Geography*, 11, 215–224.
Arrighi, G., and Drangel, J. (1986). The stratification of the world economy. *Review*, 10(1), 9–74.
Bagnasco, A. (1988). *La costruzione sociale del mercato*. Bologna: il Mulino.
Bair, J. (2005). Global capitalism and commodity chains: Looking back, going forward. *Competition & Change*, 9(2), 153–180.
Barca, F. (1999). *Il capitalismo italiano. Storia di un compromesso senza riforme*. Roma: Donzelli.
Barca, F. (2009). *An agenda for a reformed cohesion policy: A place-based approach to meeting European Union challenges and expectations*. European Commission (independent report).
Beauregard, R. (1995). Theorizing the global–local connection. In P.L. Knox and P.J. Taylor (Eds.), *World cities in a world system* (pp. 232–248). Cambridge: Cambridge University Press.
Boitani, A., and Ponti, M. (2006). Infrastrutture e politica dei trasporti. *Il Mulino*, 1, 102–112.
Bonomi, A. (Ed.). (2012). *Milano: Le tre città che stanno in una*. Milano: Bruno Mondadori.
Brenner, N. (1999). *Global cities, glocal states: State re-scaling and the remarking of urban governance in the European Union* (Doctoral dissertation). Chicago: University of Chicago.
Brenner, N. (2004). *New state spaces: Urban governance and the rescaling of statehood*. New York: Oxford University Press.
Brenner, N. (Ed.) (2014). *Implosions/explosions: Towards a study of planetary urbanization*. Berlin: Jovis Verlag GmbH.
Brenner, N., and Katsikis, N. (2013). Is the Mediterranean urban? *New Geographies*, 5, 215–234.
Brosio, G. (1999). Modelli di concorrenza fra governi locali. In G. Martinotti (Ed.), *La dimensione metropolitana. Sviluppo e governo della nuova città*. Bologna: il Mulino.
Busi, R., and Pezzagno, M. (2011). *Una città di 500 Km. Letture del territorio padano*. Roma: Gangemi.

Carbognin, M., Turri, E., and Varanini, G.M. (Eds.) (2004). *Una Rete di Città. Verona e l'area metropolitana Adige-Garda.* Verona: Cierre Edizioni.

Casavola, P., and Trigilia, C. (Eds.) (2012). *La nuova occasione. Città e valorizzazione delle risorse locali.* Roma: Donzelli.

Castells, M. (2000). *The rise of the network society* (2nd ed.). Oxford: Blackwell.

Cattaneo, C. (1972). La città considerata come principio ideale delle istorie italiane. In D. Castelnuovo Frigessi (Ed.) *Carlo Cattaneo, Opere scelte, Volume IV: Scritti 1852–1864: Storia universale e ideologia delle genti.* Torino: Einaudi.

Cohen, R.B. (2006). The new international division of labor, multinational corporations and urban hierarchy. In N. Brenner and R. Keil (Eds.), *The global cities reader.* New York: Routledge.

Corò, G., and Micelli, S. (2006). *I nuovi distretti produttivi. Innovazione, internazionalizzazione e competitività dei territori.* Venezia: Marsilio.

Crouch, C., Le Galès, P., Trigilia, C., and Voelzkow, H. (Eds.) (2004). *Changing governance of local economies: Responses of European local production systems.* Oxford: Oxford University Press.

Dematteis, G., and Governa, F. (Eds.) (2001). *Contesti locali e grandi infrastrutture. Politiche e progetti in Italia e in Europa.* Milano: Franco Angeli.

Dematteis, G., and Governa, F. (Eds.) (2005). *Territorialità, sviluppo locale, sostenibilità: il modello SLoT.* Milano: Franco Angeli.

Feltrin, P., Maset, S., Dalla Torre, R., and Valentini, M. (2010). Crescita economica, infrastrutture e mobilità: la scala sovra regionale e quella regionale. In P. Perulli (Ed.), *Nord Regione Globale. Il Veneto.* Milano: Bruno Mondadori.

Florida, R. (2006, July 3–10). The new megalopolis: Our focus on cities is wrong, growth and innovation came from new urban corridors. *Newsweek International Edition.* Retrieved from http://www.msnbc.msn.com/id/13528839/site/newsweek/

Forman, T.T. (1995). *Land mosaics.* Cambridge: Cambridge University Press.

Friedman, T. (2000). *The lexus and the olive tree: Understanding globalization.* New York: Anchor Books.

Fubini, A. (2008). *Corridor policies and territorial development: Main infrastructure and urban nodes within Corridor V.* Milano: Franco Angeli.

Fukuyama, F. (1992). *The end of history and the last man.* New York: Free Press.

Garavaglia, L. (Ed.) (2012). *Rappresentare l'Italia. Gli scenari dello sviluppo urbano a 150 anni dall'Unità.* Firenze: ReCS.

Garavaglia, L. (2014). The distribution of advanced business services in Northern Italy: towards a polycentric metropolis model? *Mètropoles,* 14, 1957–7788.

Gereffi, G., and Bair, J. (2001). Local clusters in global chains: The causes and consequences of export dynamism in Torreon's blue jeans industry. *World Development,* 29, 1885–1903.

Gereffi, G., and Korzeniewicz, M. (1994). *Commodity chains and global capitalism.* Westport: Greenwood Press.

Gereffi, G., Humphrey, J., Kaplinsky, R., and Sturgeon, T.J. (2001). Globalization, value chains and development. *IDS Bulletin,* 32(3), 1–8.

Graham, L., and Marvin, S. (2001). *Splintering urbanism: Networked infrastructures, technological mobilities and the urban condition.* London: Routledge.

Hall, P., and Pain, K. (2006). *The polycentric metropolis: Learning from mega-city regions in Europe.* London: Earthscan.

Hall, P., and Pain, K. (2008). Informational quantity versus informational quality: The perils of navigating the space of flows. *Regional Studies,* 42(8), 1065–1077.

Hopkins, T., and Wallerstein, I. (1977). Patterns of development of the modern world-system. *Review,* 1(2), 11–145.

Koolhaas, R. (2006). *Bigness*. Macerata: Quodlibet.

Lanzani, A. (2003). *I paesaggi italiani*. Roma: Meltemi.

Lanzani, A. (2011). *In cammino nel paesaggio. Questioni di geografia e urbanistica.* Rome: Carocci.

Le Galès, P. (2002). *European cities*. Oxford: Oxford University Press.

Lefebvre, H. (2014, or. 1970). From the City to Urban Society. In N. Brenner (ed.), *Implosions/Explosions. Towards a Study of Planetary Urbanization*. Berlin: Jovis.

Lieto, L., and Beauregard, R. (2013). Planning for a material world. *CRIOS*, 6, 11–20.

Lowenhaupt-Tsing, A. (2005). *Friction: An ethnography of global connection*. Princeton: Princeton University Press.

Lowenhaupt-Tsing, A. (2009). Supply chains and the human condition. *Rethinking Marxism*, 21(2), 148–176.

Magatti, M. et al. (Eds.) (2005). *Milano, nodo della rete globale. Un itinerario di analisi e proposte*. Milano: Bruno Mondadori.

Martinotti, G. (1993). *Metropoli. La nuova morfologia sociale della città*. Bologna: il Mulino.

Moretti, E. (2013). *La nuova geografia del lavoro*. Milano: Mondadori.

Nancy, J. (1999). *La ville au loin*. Paris: Fayard.

Pain, K. (2007). *Gateways and corridors in globalisation: Planning sustainable infra-structures for transcontinental spaces of flows*. Paper presented at the 1st International Conference on Gateways and Corridors, Vancouver, Canada.

Pain, K. (2010). New worlds for old? Twenty-first-century gateways and corridors: Reflections on a European spatial perspective. *International Journal of Urban and Regional Research*. doi: 10.1111/j.1468–2427.2010.01005.x

Pennati, D. (2013). *Sul Corridoio, territori alla prova dell'alta velocità* (Unpublished doctoral dissertation). IUAV University, Venice.

Perulli, P. (Ed.) (2010). *Nord Regione Globale. Il Veneto*. Milano: Bruno Mondadori.

Perulli, P. (Ed.) (2012). *Nord. Una città-regione globale*. Bologna: il Mulino.

Perulli, P., and Garavaglia, L. (2006). La pianificazione strategica e le reti di città. *Studi Organizzativi*, 2.

Perulli, P., and Pichierri, A. (Eds.) (2010). *La crisi italiana nel mondo globale. Economia e società del Nord*. Torino: Einaudi.

Priemus, H. (2001). Corridors in the Netherlands: Apple of discord in spatial planning. *Tijdschrift voor Economische en Sociale Geografie*, 92(1), 100–107.

Priemus, H., and Zonneveld, W. (2003). What are corridors and what are the issues? Introduction to special issue: the governance of corridors. *Journal of Transport Geography*, 11, 167–177.

Reffestin, C. (1984). Territorializzazione, deterritorializzazione, riterritorializzazione. In A. Turco (Ed.), *Regione e regionalizzazione*. Milano: Franco Angeli.

Sassen, S. (1991). *The global city*. Princeton: Princeton University Press.

Sassen, S. (2008). *Territory, authority, rights: From medieval to global assemblages*. Princeton: Princeton University Press.

Scott, A.J. (1998). *Regions and the world economy: The coming shape of global production, competition and political order*. Oxford: Oxford University Press.

Sereni, E. (1961). *Storia del paesaggio agrario italiano*. Roma: Laterza.

Soja, E.W. (2000). *Postmetropolis: Critical studies of cities and regions*. Oxford: Basil Blackwell.

Soja, E.W., and Kanai, M. (2007). The urbanization of the world. In R. Burdett and D. Sudjic (Eds.), *The endless city*. London: Phaidon.

Tang, W.S. (2014). Where Lefebvre Meets the East: Urbanization in Hong Kong. In L. Stanek, C. Schmid, and A. Moravànszky (eds.), *Urban Revolution Now. Henry Lefebvre in Social Research and Architecture.* Furnham: Ashgate.

Taylor, P.J. (2004). *World city network.* London: Routledge.

Taylor, P.J. (2012). Milano città leader dell'Italia nel World City Network d'inizio ventunesimo secolo. In P. Perulli (Ed.), *La città-regione globale.* Bologna: il Mulino.

Trigilia, C. (2014, November). *Le città medie al Nord e al Sud. Una frattura di lunga durata.* Paper presented at the National School of Local Development 'Sebastiano Brusco', Asti. Retrieved from: http://masl.digspes.unipmn.it/files/fall/trigilia.pdf

Turco, A. (1988). *Verso una teoria geografica della complessità.* Milano: Unicopli.

Turri, E. (2000). *La megalopoli padana.* Venezia: Marsilio.

Weber, M. (1985). *Wirtschaft und Gesellschaft. Grundriss der verstehenden Soziologie.* Tübingen: Mohr.

Whebell, C.F.J. (1969). Corridors: A theory of urban system. *Annals of the Association of American Geographers*, 59, 1–26.

13 Place matters

Spatial implications of post-metropolitan transition

Giancarlo Paba and Camilla Perrone[1]

Introduction

This contribution analyses two assumptions discussed in the literature on post-metropolitan transition and regional planning, taking some representations of the city in contemporary art and architecture as suggestion (that is, Malevich, Le Corbusier, Webber, Latour). The first assumption states the power of globalization processes to overcome the resistance of places and territories. In this view, the world is finally considered flat, homogeneous and indistinct. Territorial policies thus take an isotropic nature, "one-size-fits-all", blind to urban and regional specificities.

The second assumption develops a place-based approach: the territory is regarded as rough, anisotropic, unpredictable, "hilly". Accordingly, urban and territorial policies take a diversified nature that recognizes spatial, social and cultural differences.

Building on some recent research contributions on post-metropolitan transition within an economic and socio-spatial changing environment (Soja, Storper, McCann, Sassen), this contribution interprets the regional urbanization processes as an interplay between "streams and levees" (borrowing Benton MacKaye's definition), and "fixity and motion" (following a line of research going from David Harvey to Christian Schmid). This interpretation is suggested as a new way to supersede the dualistic nature of the aforementioned assumptions.

Finally, some spatial implications on the design of regional policies are briefly analysed.

Black Square ("nothing to see, not even nothing")

In his latest sophisticated book, entitled *Abysmal: A critique of cartographic reason*, the great Swedish geographer Gunnar Olsson dwells on a picture by Kasimir Malevich. The picture in question is *Black Square*, oil on canvas, painted in 1914–1915, depicting "a geometric figure centrally placed within a white area that extends to the edges of the non-framed and perfectly quadratic canvas of 18 × 18 *vershok* or 80.01 × 80.01 centimeters" (Olsson, 2007, p. 128).

The central square is black, and indeed it is Malevich's desire to go beyond every form of figuration, to represent an undifferentiated and uniform nothingness (and "not even nothing"): "to surpass representational form"; "to escape from the objective identity of the image"; to create "non-representational presentations of the non-representable"; to show "the zero to which everything is reduced and from which everything evolves" (Olsson, 2007).

Nevertheless, works of art live, they have their own agency (Gell, 1998), an autonomous existence, independent from their creators; therefore Malevich's *Black Square* also lives and transforms in time. Made to represent nothing, the picture ends up representing something, showing a figure, putting across a meaning. Olsson sees *Black Square*'s transformation as an accident: "Since the experimenting artist could not afford the best quality paint, the surface of the picture is now badly cracked, the underlying canvas shining through in its scarred and partly overpainted nakedness, an unintentional baring of the projection screen without which there would be nothing to see not even nothing" (Olsson, 2007, p. 181). The same consideration has been made by other critics, for example Philip Shaw: "Time has not been kind to Kasimir Malevich's painting, *Black Square*. In 1915 when the work was first displayed the surface of the square was pristine and pure; now the black paint has cracked revealing the white ground like mortar in crazy paving" (Shaw, 2013, p. 1)[2].

We will come back later to the meaning of the square's transformation, one which we deem important for our research. In the following lines we will dwell on some aspects of the artistic and intellectual context that *Black Square* was created in, which are profoundly linked to the modern movement in architecture and planning.

Malevich was very interested in aviation and aerial photography, a passion shared by Le Corbusier and other exponents of art and modern architecture (Le Corbusier, 1935; Boyer, 2003; Lampe, 2013).

As is known, the ambition to look at the earth from the sky is a constant in human history, from Icarus to Nadar, Leonardo Da Vinci to Duchamp, Geddes to Le Corbusier (Lampe, 2013). The view from above enables us to build a single image of the city and landscape, to read the relationships between city and territory, to perceive plots, organizations, structures.

Nevertheless, it is only with tall constructions and the concrete possibility to distance ourselves from the earth that the depth of our gaze changes. Roland Barthes dedicated a book to the role that the Eiffel Tower has had in changing the idea of Paris, and therefore the very idea of city: the "bird's-eye view [. . .] and the birth of aviation, permits us to transcend sensation and see things in their *structure*"; "[the] euphoria of aerial vision [. . .] recognises nothing other than a nicely connected space" (Barthes, 1997, pp. 9–10). Vision is freed from the restrictions of sensation, the senses, the body of the observer, the very corporeity of the city: from the top of the Eiffel Tower, Paris appears "like an abstract canvas in which *dark oblongs* (derived from a very old past) are contiguous with the *white rectangles* of modern architecture" (Barthes, 1997, p. 12, our italics). In the end, the greater the verticality, the more horizontal the vision, the territory translated into a two-dimensional and abstract surface (as De Certeau argued, recalling the views from the Twin Towers in New York).

Malevich's *Black Square* and *White on White* therefore constitute the finale of an abstraction process (the levelling of the territory, victory of surfaces, conquest of a complete flatness) that began with aerial photos and the first geometrical landscapes taken from those photos.

Nevertheless, it is only with Le Corbusier that the view of the earth from an aeroplane upturns the traditional concept of city and territory. In 1935 Le Corbusier was asked to write a book on the invention of the aeroplane. Upon accepting the task, Le Corbusier did not restrict himself to writing about the invention itself. Instead, he saw the aeroplane as a viewing device, an instrument of "miraculous emancipation", a (conceptual and visual) weapon to criticize and destroy the traditional city: "The airplane is an indictment. It indicts the city. It indicts those who control the city. By means of the airplane, we now have proof, recorded on the photographic plate, of the rightness of our desire to alter methods of architecture and town-planning. With its eagle eye the airplane looks at the city. It looks at London, Paris, Berlin, New York, Barcelona, Algiers, Buenos Aires, São Paulo. Alas, what a sorry account! [. . .]. The airplane instills, above all, a new conscience, the modern conscience. Cities, with their misery, must be torn down. They must be largely destroyed and fresh cities rebuilt" (Le Corbusier, 1935, pp. 11–12; Boyer, 2003).

Another invention that Le Corbusier would have thought a further "miraculous emancipation" from the city's coarseness and resistance is digital representation. Depicted on a computer screen, every dimension of the city can be investigated: there is no dimension that cannot be reached by playing with the zoom, no detail that cannot be explored, exploded, dismantled, dissected. The panopticon seems to have become complete, and democratic, within everyone's reach.

Bruno Latour underlines the power of the new means of representation and at the same time highlights the illusion of the unlimited visibility that would derive from them: "The most complete panopticon, the most integrated software, is never more than a peep show" (Latour, 2012, p. 91). The deep sense of Paris remains invisible: it escapes both traditional walking (which instead would suffice for De Certeau), and the digital device's game of Russian dolls. To enter what Latour calls the plasma of the city, the invisible and fluid secret of the city, a strategy of plural and articulated knowledge is needed; the zoom, the traditional scalarity, the Russian dolls slotting into each other need to be abandoned. It means we have to go beyond maps, be they paper or digital:

> we suggest maps should be considered as dashboards of a calculation interface that allows one to pinpoint successive signposts while moving through the world, the famous multiverse of William James. This distinction, we argue, might, on the one hand, help geography to grasp the very idea of risks and, on the other, help to free geography from its fascination with the base map by allowing a whole set of new features, such as anticipation, participation, reflexivity, and feedback (November et al., 2010, p. 581).

Now we can finally come back to *Black Square*: why is the transformation that the picture undergoes in time important? What bond exists between the life of *Black Square* and the urban and territorial metabolism? The picture's transformation is important because it represents the matter's rebellion, the emersion of traces, the plots' resistance, the depth and three-dimensionality of the things of the world (material layouts, places, cities, urban filaments). The picture's transformation – if *Black Square*'s agency can be used as an example of the territory's agency – represents the resilience of territories, the persistence of matrices and textures, the obduracy of technologies and infrastructures, the thickness and stratification of the territorial palimpsests. For us, the square that we used in the research on the post-metropolitan transformations in Italy does not have the function of "blackening" the territory, reducing it to a two-dimensional and abstract surface. Instead, it is the point of departure for a multidimensional investigation into the territory's depth and the dialectic between transformations and permanencies.

Flatness vs. steepness

In recent decades the debate around the urban question has been characterized by the awareness that contemporary urbanization processes caused a profound crisis in the relations between space and community, sociality and proximity, placed-based and place-neutral activities, the fixedness of places and fluidity of communication. This awareness is accompanied by the assertion that the metabolism of the city and metropolis has changed, both in functional and morphological terms.

In the 1960s Melvin Webber provided the most effective reconstruction of these changes, in particular for an image – which we will come back to later – that still seems to perfectly sum up the meaning of these processes.

This is how Webber sums up the main aspects of his critical analysis:

> Contrary to the *vertical* division of territory that accords with place conceptions of region, I view the functional processes [. . .] as *horizontally* stratified. [. . .] We thus find no Euclidean territorial divisions – only continuous variations, spatial discontinuity, persisting disparity, complex pluralism, and dynamic ambiguity. Seen in a communication context then, the urban settlement is far from being a unitary place. Its composition and its spatial dimensions are relative to the observations of participants in different realms at different instants of time (Webber, 1964, pp. 119–120).

No human settlement can today be considered as a unitary place, instead it is "a part of a whole array of shifting and interpenetrating realmspaces" (Webber, 1964, p. 118). Therefore, what are important are the *realmspaces*, the places of interaction, and these can be nodal, linked to a place, or non-nodal, released from one place in particular and connected to several places scattered in space. Webber made a sort of map of the horizontal extension of the realmspaces, the domains relating to the different levels of activity specialization, and we can say that the deriving image portrays the extended and flat geographical space of the contemporary city in disembodiment from the cities and territories. The urban space is seen as a space of relations, "for it is interaction, not place, that is the essence of the city and of city life" (Webber, 1964, p. 147).

In his 1960s essays, Webber therefore very effectively pinpointed the image of the dissolution of places, the assertion of "community without propinquity", the city's disappearance (*The Post-City Age*), the domination of individual means of transport (*The Joy of the Automobile*), the joyful triumph of the sprawling metropolis (*The Joy of Spread-City*).

Nonetheless, towards the end of the 1990s Melvin Webber published an article with an interesting and surprising title, *Tenacious Cities*. Webber does not renege his vision of the city, in particular his positive judgement of the spread of settlements in space. Instead, he underlines how the importance of places and inertia of cities have not disappeared. In particular, physical proximity, face-to-face relations, asserts Webber, continue to play an important role in the contemporary city too:

> Surely the social dynamics of interpersonal relations must be contributing to the tenacity of the agglomerated urban pattern as well. It's no doubt true that many people enjoy the sheer psychological and cultural stimulation that accompanies urban life lived at rather high densities. [. . .] For all of us, some portion of our lives is delimited to our local environs. Daily life is largely local, even as our vocational and avocational activities may engage us in affairs of the larger world (Webber, 1996, p. 3).

In the contemporary debate on city and territory, the flatness of the world and disappearance of proximity are once more being called into question. "The world is curved, not flat," writes Philip McCann for example, one of the exponents of the *New Economic Geography* (McCann, 2008). The world is not only curved and wrinkled in the physical sense (geomorphology matters, as we will see later), but it is curved in the economic and social sense too. McCann disputes the "flat world hypothesis" by Thomas Friedman (2005), according to which globalization processes have flattened the planet's surface, lowered communication and transaction costs, decreed the end of geography, abolished distances, eliminated the reasons that drove towards the spatial concentration of activities and resources in the past.

The world's surface is coarse and corrugated: the globalization processes which, according to the "flat world hypothesis", tend to flatten the territory (Friedman, 2005), are contrasted by new processes of localization and concentration: "the global economy appears to be simultaneously characterized both by global flattening and local steepening" (McCann, 2008, p. 361).

Therefore, the world is increasingly becoming convex, asserts McCann once more, the convexities nestling in the global flatness: some (old and) new economies of agglomeration are (re)gaining strength; certain transaction costs are once again tending to increase ("spatial transactions costs associated with the high knowledge inputs required for high value-added outputs have increased"; McCann, 2008, pp. 361–362); the resources linked to the distribution of human capital are tending to maintain, or re-assume, a localized character. And it is precisely the more sophisticated and innovative activities that require a suitable physical and social environment to carry out constant and top-level interactions.

Localized interaction, and tacit and contextual knowledge ("the local buzz") are therefore regaining importance in the organization of settlement systems (Rodrìguez-Pose & Crescenzi, 2008; Bathelt et al., 2004; Becattini, 2009). Cities, dense and urbanized regions, are like "mountains in a flat world", namely convexities, "buzz cities" (Storper & Venables, 2004), in which the different forms of proximity (cognitive, organizational, social and institutional – Boschma, 2005) act as a real and proper "tectonic force", capable of corrugating the world's surface (Rodrìguez-Pose & Crescenzi, 2008, p. 382).

Later we shall see how the curve/convexity of world geography involves not only large metropolitan formations, but also medium and small towns and cities, the city networks, minor urban systems, regions and regional cities. We will also see how a tectonic force, this time in the true sense of the word, still works on the physical geography of territories (and historical geography), how material (and symbolic) places still count, orienting the layout and configuration of the urbanization processes (Batty, 2008).

The very forms and dimensions of the urban settlements therefore count more than ever: *size, scale, shape*:

> imply different geographical advantages, and this again casts doubt on the question of what the ideal size of city should be. [. . .] The impacts of climate change, the quest for better economic performance, and the seemingly intractable problems of ethnic segregation and deprivation due to failures in job and housing markets can all be informed by a science that links size to scale and shape through information, material, and social networks that constitute the essential functioning of cities (Batty, 2008, p. 771).

To sum up, it is therefore possible to say (or at least to put forward as a work hypothesis, or a research topic) that today the world is more anisotropic than ever. A multidimensional anisotropy, inherited and together (re)produced in the dynamics of globalization/localization: each time local differences/specificities being opportunities or reclusion, shared wealth or (new) poverty, capacity to self-govern one's trajectory towards transformation or entrapment in decline and poverty.

Place-based vs. place-neutral

Government policies must be aware of this anisotropy, of the irreducible specificity of places, and not set them down as a limit, but as a necessity and a resource. Both in his theoretical contributions (Barca et al., 2012), and in the well-known report to the European Union on territorial cohesion in 2009, Fabrizio Barca puts forward the reasons for a place-based approach to regional/territorial development, in contrast to a place-neutral approach:

The importance of aspects such as human capital and innovation (endogenous growth theory), agglomeration and distance (new economic geography), and institutions (institutional economics) has been brought to the fore. As importantly, globalization has also drawn attention to the often neglected role of space. Globalization has made localities and their interaction more important for economic growth and prosperity [...]. Space is becoming increasingly "slippery," in the sense that capital, goods, people, and ideas travel more easily [...], but, at the same time, increasingly "sticky" and "thick" because capital, goods, people, and ideas, despite being constantly on the move, tend to remain stuck in large agglomerations [...]. Consequently, globalization has made space and place more rather than less important (Barca et al., 2012, p. 136).

The consequences on policy design are evident: corresponding to a space conceived as isotropic is the elaboration of "isomorphic policies", everywhere equal ("one-size-fits-all'", prevalently infrastructural, "top-down, supply-side, spatially blind" policies (Barca et al., 2012, p. 137). Vice versa, in a place-based approach, "space matters and shapes the potential for development not only of territories, but, through externalities, of the individuals who live in them. Consequently, development strategies should not be space-neutral, but, [...] placed-based and highly contingent on context" (Barca et al., 2012, p. 139).

Space and places therefore count in the processes to redefine the urban "mountains" that dot and organize the surface of the world: space meant in a multidimensional and complex sense, seen as "dynamic, problematic, developmental, ideologically charged, and filled with action, dialectics, process, and social causality, rather than as fixed, dead background, container, stage, extra-social environment" (Soja, 2011, p. 687).

Therefore, our research took the placed-based approach described above, nevertheless making a further breakdown and analysis in particular in those directions indicated in some recent research papers (Batty, 2001, 2008; Bathelt et al., 2004). In defining "polynucleated urban landscapes", Batty underlines the phenomena of "persistence and resilience" that can be rediscovered in urban expansion and transformation processes, and how it has been precisely this resistance of places and territories that in time has kept the polycentric or "polynucleated" urban structures alive (Batty, 2001, 2008). The research sets out to verify this settlement model in northern Tuscany (in other areas in central Italy). In particular, it aims to verify the hypothesis that effective forms of resistance/persistence/resilience of biophysical and geo-historical patterns exist in polynucleated urban landscapes.

Spatial implications of post-metropolitan transition: streams and levees, fixity and motion, path dependency

We started from the story of the *Black Square*, the painting by Malevich, taking it as a symbol of the modern project to blackening and cancel the territory. However, to us its independent life instead seemed to indicate the resilience of territories, urban plots and the material signs resulting from the interweaving between geosphere, biosphere and anthroposphere (Soja, 2010; De Landa, 2000; Sassen & Dotan, 2011; Paba, 2011).

At the end of these observations, we would like to use another suggestion, from the history of planning, one that seems particularly suited to circumscribing the conceptual and operational frame of our research. Benton MacKaye, the great *geotect* of the Regional Planning Association of America, has devoted many reflections to the meaning that geophysical features take on in the emerging theory of regional planning (MacKaye, 1928, 1968).

The attention towards the watersheds and physical features (attention which is a significant bridge between the regional planning of the early twentieth century and the contemporary bio-regionalism) led MacKaye to develop a theory of flows and containments, connections and levees, which would be applied in many planning experiences (from the Appalachian Trail to the Tennessee Valley Authority, from the New York Regional Plan to the Boston Super By-Pass).

In some design scenarios – for example for the region of Boston – MacKaye summarizes the model under the definition of "streams and levees". The evolution of the major regional units is seen as a interplay between structured and complex flows (water, natural resources, people and goods) on one hand and levees (geophysical, environmental, cultural) on the other hand. Precisely that, "streams and levees". Post-metropolitan territories, in our view, are characterized by this interplay between "distensive forces" that connect, unite and link, and "tectonic forces" which corrugate, delimit and protect the places of urban and social life.

Recently, Cristian Schmid addressed the question of specificity as the constitutive feature of cities while exploring its meaning for urbanization. He investigates "how specificity is produced and reproduced, what role it plays in the production of urban spaces, and how it influences the planetary trajectory of urbanization" (Schmid, 2015, p. 286). In his work, Schmid describes the interplay between *distensive* and *tectonic* forces as interaction between *facilitation* and *limitation*: whatever is the territorial material pattern (whether monocentric, polycentric, extensive, densely interconnected or whatever), it incorporates a dual dimension: "it facilitates processes of interaction, but it also channels them thus hampers alternative possibilities of development" (Schmid, 2015, p. 294). The author sees this conceptual couple as part of the dialectic of *fixity* and *motion* introduced by David Harvey to explain the constitutive and permanent contradiction inherent in the production of the built environment (Harvey, 1985).

In Schmid's words, the process of facilitation and limitation is then described as:

> the dialectics of fixity and motion, the contradiction between the dynamics of urbanization and the permanence, the persistence of the spatial structures it produces [. . .]. This also explains why urbanization manifests such a high degree of path dependency: the built environment cannot be changed overnight, or at least not without causing massive destruction and devaluation of existing investments. Thus an urban fabric arises that can often barely be fundamentally changed and can only be adjusted with considerable efforts (Schmid, 2015, pp. 294–295).

During the process of physical transformation of the territories (urbanization), nature is both destroyed and recreated as a second nature through the society's appropriation and transformation. Despite this, the natural spaces do not disappear but can reappear at any time in a dialectical contraposition that involves two antagonistic "modes" of path dependency: the resistance of geo-historical matrices and the persistency of the urbanization (as a result of the immobility and rigidity of the built environment that cannot be changed overnight unless you produce destruction and impairment of investments). Within this conceptual frame, "the city, as a second nature, is caught between fixity and motion. Every urban development creates new possibilities, but at the same time also establishes fixed structures, thus limiting the potential for later corrections or changes to the course of development" (Schmid, 2015, p. 295). The dialectics between *streams* and *levees*, *facilitation* and *limitation*, *fixity* and *motion*, is therefore recognized as a distinctive character of the process of urbanization, as well as an emerging issue of the post-metropolitan transition.

In our view this dialectics also anticipates and explains the spatial implications of the tendency towards a regional urbanization theorized by Soja (2011, 2015). In particular, these implications contribute to depict a multifaceted portrait of Italy. It is then possible to say that the Italian post-metropolitan transition takes a variegated nature. Such nature shows some dominant tendencies (multi-scalar regional urbanization, planetary urbanization), while revealing the role of path dependency and the resistance of geo-historical background, in creating the specificity of Italian urban landscapes.

Notes

1 Although this chapter should be considered a result of the common work and reflection of the two authors, G. Paba took primary responsibility for the sections entitled "*Black Square* ("nothing to see, not even nothing")" and "Flatness vs. steepness" and C. Perrone took primary responsibility for the sections entitled "Place-based vs. place-neutral" and "Spatial implications of post-metropolitan transition".
2 Malevich would repaint the black square other times, seeking an absolute and unassailable blackness (for example see the 1923 version). In addition he would also paint squares of other colours, and even a white square on a white background, as if in the end the goal were to represent nothing on nothing.

References

Barca, F. (2009). *An Agenda for a Reformed Cohesion Policy: A place-based approach to meeting European Union challenges and expectations*. Independent report prepared at the request of Danuta Hübner, Commissioner for Regional Policy, April.

Barca, F., McCann, P., and Rodrìguez-Pose, A. (2012). The Case for Regional Development Intervention: Place-based versus place-neutral approaches. *Journal of Regional Science*, 52 (1), 134–152.

Barthes R. (1997). *The Eiffel Tower and Other Mythologies*. Berkeley: University of California Press.

Bathelt, H., Malmberg, A., and Maskell, P. (2004). Clusters and Knowledge: Local buzz, global pipelines and the process of knowledge creation. *Progress in Human Geography*, 28, 31–56.

Batty, M. (2001). Polynucleated Urban Landscapes. *Urban Studies*, 38 (4), 635–655.

Batty, M. (2008). The Size, Scale, and Shape of Cities. *Science*, 319, 769–771.

Becattini, G. (2009). *Ritorno al territorio*. Bologna: il Mulino.

Boschma, R.A. (2005). Proximity and Innovation: A critical assessment. *Regional Studies*, 39 (1), 61–74.

Boyer, M.C. (2003). Aviation and the Aerial View: Le Corbusier's spatial transformations in the 1930s and 1940s. *Diacritics*, 33 (3/4), 93–116.

De Landa, M. (2000). *A Thousand Years of Nonlinear History*. New York: Swerve Edition.

Friedman, T.L. (2005). *The World is Flat: A brief history of the twenty-first century*. New York: Farrar, Straus and Giroux.

Gell, A. (1998). *Art and Agency: An anthropological theory*. Oxford: Clarendon.

Harvey, D. (1985). The Geopolitics of Capitalism. In D. Gregory and J. Urry (Eds.), *Social Relations and Spatial Structures* (pp. 128–163). London: Macmillan.

Lampe, A. (2013). *Vues d'en haut*. Metz: Editions du Centre Pompidou-Metz.

Latour, B. (2012). Paris, Invisible City: The plasma. *City, Culture and Society*, 3, 91–93.

Le Corbusier. (1935). *Aircraft*. New York: The Studio Publications.

MacKaye, B. (1928). *The New Exploration: A philosophy of regional planning*. New York: Harcourt, Brace and Company.

MacKaye, B. (1968). *From Geography to Geotechnics*. Urbana: University of Illinois Press.

McCann, P. (2008). Globalization and Economic Geography: The world is curved, not flat. *Cambridge Journal of Regions, Economy and Society*, 1, 351–370.

November, V., Camacho-Hubner, E., and Latour, B. (2010). Entering a Risky Territory: Space in the age of digital navigation. *Environment and Planning D: Society and Space*, 28, 581–599.

Olsson, G. (2007). *Abysmal: A critique of cartographic reason*. Chicago: University of Chicago Press.

Paba, G. (2011). Le cose (che) contano: nuovi orizzonti di agency nella pianificazione del territorio. *CRIOS*, 1, 67–78.

Rodríguez-Pose, A., and Crescenzi, R. (2008). Mountains in a Flat World: Why proximity still matters for the location of economic activity. *Cambridge Journal of Regions, Economy and Society*, 1, 371–388.

Sassen, S., and Dotan, N. (2011). Delegating, not Returning, to the Biosphere: How to use the multi-scalar and ecological properties of cities. *Global Environmental Change*, 21, 823–834.

Schmid, C. (2015). Specificity and Urbanization: A theoretical outlook. In R. Diener et al. (Eds.), *The Inevitable Specificity of Cities*. Zürich: Lars Muller Publishers.

Shaw, P. (2013). Modernism and the Sublime. In N. Llewellyn and C. Riding (Eds.), *The Art of the Sublime* (www.tate.org.uk/art/research-publications/the-sublime/philip-shaw-modernism-and-the-sublime-r1109219, accessed 10 June 2016).Soja, E. (2010). Cities and State in Geohistory. *Theory and Society*, 39 (3), 361–376.

Soja, E. (2011). Regional Urbanization and the End of the Metropolis Era. In G. Bridge and S. Watson, (Eds.), *New Companion to the City*. Chichester: Wiley-Blackwell.

Soja, E. (2015). Accentuate the Regional. *International Journal of Urban and Regional Research*, 39 (2), 372–381.

Storper, M., and Venables, A.J. (2004). Buzz: Face-to-face contact and the urban economy. *Journal of Economic Geography*, 4, 351–370.

Webber, M. (1964). The Urban Place and the Non-Place Urban Realm. In M. Webber et al. (Eds.), *Explorations into Urban Structure*. Philadelphia: Pennsylvania University Press.

Webber, M. (1996). Tenacious Cities. In *Proceedings of the NCGIA Sponsored Research Conference on Spatial Technologies, Geographic Information, and the City*, Baltimore, 214–218.

14 Institutions matter

Governance and citizenship in a post-metropolitan perspective

Valeria Fedeli

Post-metropolis: fragmentation, cooperation and new governance models

If mayors ruled the world – the title of Benjamin Barber's work (2014) could introduce the reflection on governance in the time of post-metropolis. According to the author, in fact, the municipal model could be seen as an answer to governance problems, both in terms of effectiveness and legitimacy. Mayors are seen as a resource for a new democratic era, a possible remedy against the current political and institutional crisis, with their pragmatic willingness to address and solve problems. In particular, when they are able to cooperate and network, since problems exceed their operational boundaries: "Cities have little choice: to survive and flourish they must remain hospitable to pragmatism, to problem-solving, to networking, to creativity and innovation, and to cooperation" (Barber, 2014, p. 13). Cities are regarded as the last possible hope, able to succeed where nation-states have failed; able to cross boundaries and deal with interdependence and transcalarity of processes, allowing people to participate locally and cooperate globally. In this perspective, cities are seen not as isolated in their municipal boundaries, but as able to build innovative alliances to address problems, alliances that cannot be predefined at state level. In a world that is more and more urban, such a hypothesis could sound at the same time challenging and tricky – challenging because it questions every traditional solution of a new institutional level able to deal with the new scale and dimension of the urban; tricky because it proposes a fuzzy boundaries logic (Allmendinger et al., 2015) which, in our understanding, deserves more critical discussion before the final capitulation of other non-municipal solutions.

Actually, the post-metropolitan Italy that we have observed during our research presents relevant hints in this perspective. Highly fragmented on the one hand, highly cooperative on the other, the urban regions we have studied have shown evidence of both institutional fragmentation and new geographies of cooperation (institutionalized or not). In fact, the analysis of voluntary cooperative relations generated in the last 20 years by Italian municipalities shows pluralistic, variable, fragmented spatial patterns. In general terms, the post-metropolitan condition seems to be characterized by a sort of "explosion-implosion" (Brenner, 2014) of the relationship between administrative boundaries and the geographies of social-economic-environmental and political processes that the urban is experiencing.

On the one hand, all the forms of government discussed so far, set up to deal with such processes, have exploded or imploded. Temporary associations between municipalities have multiplied but often remain weak and fragile; consortia, namely in the field of public facilities, have flourished even more but without a clear relationship between functional reasons and political accountability. Functional areas defined on the basis of different laws with their own rationales have generated a dense network of technical geographies, which are not able to express a vision. The province, the second-level institutional tier, in charge of promoting coordination in decision-making between municipalities since the 1990s, has never reached a significant legitimacy and capacity of action. Inter-municipal cooperation has developed only in the context in which it has been promoted and supported by regions with monetary or non-monetary incentives. In other words, most of the forms developed in the last century by the nation-state to deal with the regional scale of the urban have multiplied and somehow failed, not being able to deliver any stable, efficient or powerful institutional solution.

On the other hand, the explosion of forms of voluntary cooperation, based on single strategies or projects, sometimes on forms of locally organized opposition to regionally and nationally led projects, has produced a plethora of temporary assemblages (Sassen, 2006; Latour, 2005), which unfortunately also seem unable to produce efficient and legitimate governance solutions. The European Union has added some additional reasons to cooperate on a non-urban scale, but with limited support in comparison with other principles for action. Hard spaces and soft spaces coexist as "'in-between' spaces of governance that exist outside, alongside or in-between the formal statutory scales of government, from area masterplans to multiregional growth strategies" (Allmendinger & Haughton, 2013) trying to deal with the complexity of government and governance in an urban world.

Finally, drawing from research results, central cities seem to reproduce, but for a few exceptions, a condition of self-referentialism and solitude, having remained outside any single form of horizontal and voluntary cooperation. Traditional metropolitan first rings, which have never really reached a condition of political and institutional constituency as such, are experiencing a new crisis of identity. Once dominated by the central city, now bypassed by the suburban world extending next door, they are experiencing competition with both the central cities and other regional territories, trying to attract decentralizing and recentralizing functions. The other traditional regional cities have kept their autonomy and relationship with the surrounding areas, but have not constituted all together a political and institutional alternative to both the central city and the regional power. The same can be said for the in-between spaces of the "urbanoid galaxy" described by Fregolent and Vettoretto (with Bottaro and Curci) in Chapter 16 of this book, suspended between the metropolitan rings and the regional cities: they have been protagonist of a convulsed and fragmented era of cooperation, generated by a number of assemblages of different natures, meanings and roles, switching on and off in an intermittent, asynchronic, discontinuous rhythm, and producing instable configurations, with, unfortunately, limited impact on the long term. Assemblages with karstic or short life ratios, which are not able to settle in time, have accumulated over spaces, as our discussions show. These assemblages are necessarily partial, based on simple policy issues: sometimes efficient at dealing with urgent problems, but often not able to feed long-term strategies or produce new forms of leadership or political subjects. Sometimes they are able to produce "strategy-making episodes, where strategic spatial planning moves beyond formal planning arenas in attempts to destabilize existing practices and structures" (Allmendinger et al., 2015, p. 27). And they are able to produce new spatial imaginaries, not based on institutional boundaries, but based on boundaries in relation to projects. All in all, a sort of doping process has emerged – sometimes generated by law – that has produced contradictory and paradoxical implosions and explosions: on the one hand, coop-eration has been a way to guarantee facilities essential for citizens; on the other hand, centralizing facilities for cooperation has created new marginalities and distance between the administration and its constituency, the citizens. Ultimately, the post-metropolitan space looks like "a multiplicity of co-existing spaces, each involving differing assemblages of interests, materialities and actors in a complex set of political mobilisations [. . .] defined by its practices, not by some predeter-mined scalar arrangements of power" (Allmendinger et al., 2015, p. 35).

Actually, during 2015, because of the implementation of a new law, a form of metropolitan government, the so-called "città metropolitan," has been taking shape: 25 years after the original introduction in Italy of metropolitan areas ("aree metropolitane", in 1990), the law, passed in 2014, has finally imposed a historical turn on the Italian institutional framework. Approved in order to reduce public expenditures through the elimination of provincial institutions, considered weak and useless, the law has tried to overcome the political and institutional obstacles to metropolitan reform in Italy. As a result of the new compulsory framework, almost all the areas included in our research project have become metropolitan cit-ies, which means essentially that a new institution has been constituted, assuming the previous provincial boundaries and in the form of a non-directly elected body. Despite the fact that the process of implementation of the law has just started and much will depend on the local chart (since the law allows differentiated interpreta-tion on the basis of local charts – in Italian, Statuto), the rationale of the law seems to still be based on a municipal coordination model (Tubertini, 2015). The new "città metropolitana" in fact almost inherits the previous province competences: its president is not directly elected, the metropolitan conference is a conference of mayors and it has no taxes of its own. Notwithstanding expectations raised by more active local implementation contexts, the reform does not seem to provide a consistent shift in the institutional vision. In fact, the mayor is the mayor of the central city and competences run by the metropolitan city are not supported by a real capacity of action; transcalarity and boundaries are not really questioned, and there is not even space for the construction of a political arena capable of including economic and social actors. What is more is that the political investment, both at the national and local level, has so far not been what's needed by such an endeavor as the construction of a new regional scale of government/governance. As a final conclusion, the research highlights not only the persisting distance between the *de facto* city and the *de jure* city (Calafati, 2014a), but also between a municipal and metropolitan vision (Calafati, 2014b) and a post-metropolitan or regional one, in need of a non-traditional government/governance solution, in relation to boundaries, competences and roles.

Post-metropolis: new urban question and a new idea of citizenship

All in all, the fragmentation of institutional boundaries together with the high number of cooperation networks highlights the necessity of a new regional constituency that is able to give voice and representation to the new urban world and its problems. There is no, nor has there been until now, space for expression of the new translocal needs of people: mobility policies together with environmental ones, in particular, have shown the limits of traditional jurisdictions based on municipal boundaries, but also those associated with an idea of metropolis, still based on the power and roles of the central city and on a logic of stock, rather than flows. How can we invent solutions that give voice to the needs of itinerant populations, users and inhabitants of a urbanized world? How can we build, for example, a housing policy that takes care of the processes of re-localization of families caused by the mismatch between affordability and real estate values in the large urban region? There is a high risk of encouraging an under-representation of a new demand of citizenship, which no longer corresponds with both the traditional urban one and the metropolitan one. Of course, it is quite complicated to invent institutions for a not-yet city or for a no-more city: but in fact, we are still anchored to an idea of citizenship based on the nineteenth-century city, and this can become a relevant social question.

In 2009, Jacques Donzelot put forward the hypothesis formulated by Thomas Humphrey Marshall in 1950, according to which the idea of citizenship has been profoundly changing in the last two centuries, as it has become associated with different attributes (Donzelot, 2009). *Civil citizenship*, as a first form of citizenship, in this sense, was related to the general acknowledgment of the notion of equality of all individuals towards justice, property rights and freedom of exchange. *Political citizenship* enlarged the rights to freedom of thought and opinion, including all those for whom it is possible to obtain respect, and this was based on a wider notion of sovereignty and autonomy of all individuals. *Social citizenship*, as a further formulation, was an answer to the material limits of political citizenship, aimed at granting to all individuals the ability to support their own needs. When, at the end of the nineteenth century, the social question gets a more typical urban dimension, *citizenship becomes urban*: the city, with all its problems, becomes the scene and the social question becomes an urban question. The right to claim is the "right to the city," as a promise of rights and opportunities. The results of our research project show that this idea of *urban citizenship* is probably not enough to deal with the new regional dimension of the urban.

Edward Soja, discussing the post-metropolis conceptualization, described the crisis of traditional governance models:

> Among the many effects of this extended form of regional urbanization and its associated scalar restructuring has been an aggravated crisis of urban and regional governance (Brenner, 2005). The old administrative and political geography of national governments around the world have been among the slowest geographies to change over the past four decades, especially when compared to economic and cultural reorganizations of space. This governance crisis is also evident at the national and global scales, where there has been an explosion of what is called supranational regionalism, as nation-states form larger coalitions to deal with the impact of globalization, the new economy, and the IT revolution (Soja, 2011b, p.463).

In different recent contributions, Roger Keil and Douglas Young reflect on the notion of *in-betweenness*, proposed by Sieverts in 2003, which aims to stress the negative prejudice against the suburban, seen as the place of disorder. Sieverts' position – elaborated within the experience in Ruhr in post-unification Germany, during which he introduced the idea of *Zwischenstadt* (Sieverts, 2003) – conceptualized a fragmented urban landscape, young and often hated by planners, since it is the outcome of multiple rationalities of individual actors producing a non-rational landscape (Sieverts, 2003, p. 21). In a society that does not recognize a clear role and status to this kind of landscape, these places become in Sieverts' proposal, in contrast, places of possible, new spaces of freedom and experimentation, complex open systems that are open to disorder as a precondition for complexity and multiplicity. Keil and Young (2010), adopting the notion of in-between, are interested in the emergence of new landscapes, where the dichotomy between the urban and the rural is completely redefined and innovation seems more destined to take place in areas once conceived as peripheral. The in-between city of Sievert is just an apparently unplanned city that lives in hybridation, between legality and illegality – a space for vulnerability, invisibility and impotence. It expresses a series of dynamic relationships between the urban and the new socio-spatial relationship in a globalized urban world: at first sight a forgotten space, or a residual one, if compared with the central creative city or the rich suburb, it becomes the outcome of the redistribution of global investments (Sieverts, 2003, p. 254). It is a space often forgotten by politics and policies, being the outcome of new interactions between novel rationalities not often represented by politics: strategies of growth, practices of collective consumption, residential expansion, preservation of environment and landscape. The suburban is therefore, *per se*, not just the field of rescaling traditional social and environmental questions, but the heart of a new political tension; it is not just the space for excellence of accumulation of tensions as well as the one in which the theoretical framework that we have used to describe the city in terms of urban politics – as for example the *growth machine theory* (Moloch, 1976) but also the *urban regime theory* (Stone, 1989) – but show their difficulty in stepping back from an idea of the city as the outcome of stabilized *governance patterns.*

In a similar direction, in his introduction to *Implosions/Explosions: Towards the study of a planetary urbanization*, Neil Brenner reminds us that the traditionally urban question is related to the idea of the "city" as a specific form of settlement, characterized by dimension, density and social diversity that clearly distinguishes it from a "non-city social world" (Brenner, 2014, p. 15), located outside or beyond the urban.

Brenner's book questions the effects of this on the political and institutional dimension and on the possibility of conceptualizing a new citizenship in this condition, meant as a condition of "empowerment" for those who live in those contexts. In particular, referring to Lefebvre, in 1989, stating the necessity to give space to a revolutionary notion of *citizenship*, Andy Merrifield's contribution in the book reminds us about the persistent lack of conceptualization of the issue of citizenship in a transcalar perspective "offline somewhere local, online somewhere planetary" (Merrifield, 2014a, p. 174). While in a traditional definition of the right to the city, there is still a strong material claim, a planetary urbanization perspective seems to leave behind the simultaneity and place-based of the right to be claimed. The fight for local commons, in other words, goes together with the "broader politics of the global commons" (Merrifield, 2014a, p. 174), where the exclusion from the new urban rights has to take into account a planetary urban condition:

> Right to what city? If urbanization is planetary, if the urban – or urban society – is everywhere, is this right to the city the right to the metropolitan region, right to the whole urban agglomeration? Or does it just mean the right to a certain neighborhood, to the city's downtown, the right to centrality? And if there are centers everywhere, just as there are multiple peripheries, does that mean the right of these peripheries to occupy, take back, the centers? (Merrifield, 2014b, p. 525).

Merrifield points out a paradoxical conclusion in this perspective. If the urban is everywhere, the question of citizenship cannot be linked to a traditional model of the city, place-based and local. This has strong implications for the idea of being rooted to a place, with a fixed boundary. Following this line of reasoning, Merrifield proposes to reflect upon citizenship as a "politics of encounter" enabling us to "experiment with reality": "a politics of encounter forces us to encounter ourselves, concretely, alongside others; it doesn't make a facile, abstract claim for something that's all around us and which is already ours" (Merrifield, 2014b, p. 532). In this sense, the issue of citizenship seems to be redefined in a transcalar and relational condition, in which the city as a traditional fact has just a partial role.

These briefly synthesized positions present different inputs to the debate. In the first one it's the new spatial scale of urban processes that should be investigated to shape the new elements of contemporary citizenship and urban question. The second proposes to look at the condition of in-betweenness as the space to explore the same issues and give voice to it. The third seems to dissolve the issue of citizenship in a transcalar dimension. In all three perspectives, we could conclude that we have the urgency to give voice and expression to questions and expectations, needs and problems that do not have voice or expression in the traditional citizenship idea that supports our understanding and our policy and governance design. Who supports the demands of a commuter travelling in a large urban region? Which access to public mobility is granted to people in the suburban? What are the problems, for example, of young people or older people in the in-between? What are the specific peculiarities of gender issues in this condition? Which is the political space of representation of those new citizens? These are just examples of the questions raised, not far from those proposed recently by Pierre Rosanvallon in his challenging research project, "Le parlement des invisibles", where he points out the necessity to give voice to new citizenship claims in order to support a new democratic phase:

> through the book and the website, new forms of direct representation of society will emerge to restore a democratic life capable of withstanding the worrying trends that are emerging today (Rosanvallon, 2013, p. 62, editors' translation from French).

As a matter of fact, as this chapter has tried to argue, the relationship between government/governance and citizenship in a post-metropolitan condition remains open and unsolved. The failure of traditional institutional solutions, together with the frailty of soft spaces/assemblages we can see in the cases we have studied, encourage the design of non-ordinary and post-Euclidean solutions, looking at processes of regional urbanization as processes that also deeply challenge our ideas of (local) democracy.

References

Allmendinger, P., and Haughton, G. (2013). Spaces of neoliberal experimentation: soft spaces, postpolitics, and neoliberal governmentality, *Environment and Planning A*, 45, 217–234.

Allmendinger, P., Haughton, G., Knieling, J., and Othengrafen, F. (2015). *Soft spaces in Europe: Re-negotiating governance, boundaries and borders*. London: Routledge.

Barber, B.R. (2014). *If mayors ruled the world: Dysfunctional nations, rising cities*. New Haven, CT: Yale University Press.

Brenner, N. (Ed.). (2014). *Implosions/explosions: Towards a study of planetary urbanization*. Berlin: Jovis Verlag GmbH.

Calafati, A. (2014a). *Città e aree metropolitane in Italia* (GSSI Urban Studies Working Paper No. 1). L'Aquila: Gran Sasso Science Institute. Retrieved from http://ssrn.com/abstract=2369323.

Calafati, A. (2014b). *Città metropolitane: le ragioni economiche* [online]. Retrieved from GSSI: http://www.studi-urbani-gssi.eu/?p=150.

Donzelot, J. (2009). *Vers une citoyenneté urbaine*. Paris: Rue d'Ulm.

Haughton, G., Allmendinger, P., Counsell, D., and Vigar, G. (2010). *The new spatial planning: Territorial management with soft spaces and fuzzy boundaries*. London: Routledge.

Keil, R., and Young, D. (2010). Reconnecting the disconnected: The politics of infrastructure in the in-between city. *Cities*, 27, 87–95.

Latour, B. (2005). *Reassembling the social: An introduction to actor-network theory.* Oxford: Oxford University Press.

Merrifield, A. (2014a). The urban question under planetary urbanisation. In N. Brenner (Ed.), *Implosions/explosions: Towards a study of planetary urbanization* (pp. 164–180). Berlin: Jovis Verlag GmbH.

Merrifield, A. (2014b). The right to the city and beyond: Notes on a Lefebvrian reconceptualization. In N. Brenner (Ed.), *Implosions/explosions: Towards a study of planetary urbanization* (pp. 523–533). Berlin: Jovis Verlag GmbH.

Molotch, H. (1976). The city as a growth machine: Toward a political economy of place. *American Journal of Sociology*, 82(2), 309–332.

Rosanvallon, P. (2013). *Le parlament des invisibles. Raconteur la vie*. Paris: Seuil.

Sassen, S. (2006). *Territory, authority, rights: From medieval to global assemblages.* Princeton, NJ: Princeton University Press.

Sieverts, T. (2003). *Cities without cities: An interpretation of the Zwischenstadt*. London: Routledge.

Soja, E.W. (2000). *Postmetropolis: Critical studies of cities and regions*. Oxford: Blackwell.

Soja, E.W. (2011a). Regional urbanization and the end of the metropolis era. In G. Bridge, and S. Watson (Eds.), *New companion to the city* (pp. 679–689). Chichester: Wiley-Blackwell.

Soja, E.W. (2011b). Beyond postmetropolis. *Urban Geography*, 32(4), 451–469. DOI: 10.2747/0272-3638.32.4.451

Stone, C.N. (1989). *Regime politics: Governing Atlanta, 1946–1988*. Lawrence, KS: University Press of Kansas.

Tubertini, C. (2015). Le Regioni e le politiche di riordino territoriale locale: Province e Città Metropolitane. *Astrid Rassegna*, 234(19).

15 S-regulation matters

Daniela De Leo and Maria Federica Palestino[1]

This chapter briefly reports our investigation about *s-regulation*, a neologism introduced by the sociologist Donolo (2001), which refers to the ambiguous relation between Italian society and system of rules. According to Donolo, in our research perspective s-regulation matters because the combination of weak territorial control and inadequate regulations and laws by government, together with the deep rooted presence of criminal organizations, facilitates exploitation, abuses and illicit businesses.

Today s-regulation matters even more because the effects of informal/illegal/criminal powers, increasingly widespread all over the peninsula, are also triggering relevant socio-ecological vulnerability through the interplay between what we call the 'Italian anomaly' and the 'waste metabolics'. Therefore the point is not only to read s-regulation as a 'crime' to be prosecuted and punished, but also as a 'weakness' to be addressed by requiring those who govern to interact with communities and cultures so as to create a strategy for recovery.

The Italian anomaly

This part of the research focuses on the understanding of where s-regulation is located and what role it plays in post-metropolitan territories. The aim was to define comparable representations of this issue at the national level that could be useful for scholars, policy-designers and policy-makers, for better understanding and for dealing with it.

In fact, until now, Italian s-regulation phenomena have not been defined as relevant issues, and no analysis of their dimensions has been made. Here, some hypotheses have been developed by selecting available data for each *square*.

Our investigation was based on Elster's approach to Italian society (1989): delays, lack of civic conscience, disaffection in respect of the rules, which does not depend so much on a poor modernization and economic rationality, but on "an excess of individual rationality that, faced with the rules, always calculates whether it is more convenient to follow or to break them, with disastrous collective effects." Elster called it the "Italian anomaly," and it seems a useful key to find indicators for investigating some s-regulated behavior types that become extremely problematic according with their concentration and localization.

The research goal was to understand if this anomaly (of causes, effects, inter-dependencies, and so on) is related to specific s-regulation phenomena, such as the process of illegal building development, the substitution of municipalities with extraordinary commissions, the "confiscated assets" (residential and not) of the criminal organizations in the country.

From north to south, the Atlas shows areas of concentration and overlapping of phenomena strongly correlating to the peculiar relationship with the system of rules, and regarding *individual choices* (illegal buildings), the *fragility of public institutions* (commissioned municipalities), and *former Mafia properties* (criminal affairs locations and investments): these could signal target areas for more specific policies.

In this perspective, illegal building development is considered a key fac-tor because it also reflects an individual attitude against "respect of the rules" whereas it is indissolubly linked to the "black economy," a structural element of the so-called "Italy system." This *"abusivismo"* is a social, cultural and economic phenomenon that involves a variety of factors connected with permanent or transitory conditions, such as the state of the building trade, economic cycles and political trends. But in general, the overall picture does not consider informal buildings created by organized crime (De Leo, 2011): this is not a residual phe-nomenon if we consider that approximately 55 percent of recent illegal buildings are concentrated in four regions (Campania, Puglia, Calabria and Sicily), where the rate of organized crime is traditionally higher.

This underlines the significant connection between s-regulation related to illegal building and the spread of criminal phenomena. Nevertheless, forms of complementarity between weak institutions, informality and organized crime confirm the porous boundary between legal and illegal practices, as well as the strong interdependencies between regulation and s-regulation and between local cultures and informal sectors of the economy.

In the last 30 years, urban development in Italy has shown a quite strong urban-ization, most of which has been done without any urban regulations and plans in significant areas of the country (in southern Italy but also in the Veneto and Lazio Region). The North has seen new settlements of medium and large dimensions, such as forms of sprawl and of productive urbanized countryside; the South has seen the spread of medium-sized lotting for first and second houses.

Despite all this, the whole question of *abusivismo* seems to have gone out of fashion, and the political drift is basically toward deregulation. Recently, the subject was taken up again, but more of the focus has been on the important dimensions of "transgression" and "necessity," and illegality is narrowly inter-preted as a departure from existing urban regulations.

The general lack of attention has produced an absence of reliable data, also related to the fact that the parties responsible for the detection of abuses (the municipalities) are the same that have responsibility for ensuring demolitions: an expensive practice with a very low rate of public consensus. Therefore, the (very few) data provided by the municipalities are more connected with their promises to intervene to right the abuses than to self-declarations of their own incapacity.

With the lack of reliable data on illegal buildings, it has been possible, as an alternative, to look at the collection of national data related to so-called "ghost buildings" (Casaburi & Troiano, 2013). This latter is a journalistic expression for those properties that were not in any way registered by the national tax authorities. The data – collected (from 2007) at the nationwide level by the Inland Revenue by using a sophisticated detection system – showed in detail the spread of individuals' convenience "for breaching of the rules" (as Elster said) for housing and productive buildings. These data depict behavior and the individual choices (but choices with complex spatial and urban effects) as possible telltale signs of the spread of this specific form of s-regulation, of clear evasion of the system of rules, all over the country.

The point is that informal and illegal satisfaction of social demands reduces the value that people attach to respect for the rules, with knock-on effects on the processes of urban and social development. For instance, if the demand for housing is satisfied by the organized crime (by providing, for example, dwellings at lower prices), systematically followed by a steady stream of "amnesties" on the part of the national government, the ongoing production of new areas of illegality appears legitimate, and the boundaries between legality and legitimacy gradually blur, even within sectors hitherto extraneous to criminal processes.

In an overall framework of urban and social s-regulation as an effect of regulation that is directly or indirectly criminal, an unusual setting is produced in the form of illegal settlements, and this has effects on the "weak link" between people and public institutions. It favors the emergence of more individualist and particularistic behavior at the expense of compliance with the rules.

Summarizing, the Italian situation appears complex because the deep-rooted criminal organizations spread, and insert themselves with little effort, into a faulty mechanism, by adding more s-regulation to all the other present and visible forms of s-regulation.

In this sense, s-regulation has to be read not only as "crime" (to prosecute and punish) but also as "weakness" (which needs to be addressed), and allows us to highlight how some phenomena clarify the question, "Why do some regions govern themselves better than others?" (Storper, 2013, p. 15), even in the same country.

By showing the link between discretion and corruption, s-regulation can be described and interpreted as a changing relationship between what is legal and illegal, legitimate and illegitimate, authorized or not: when there is more ample discretion, the levels of corruption are higher. In fact, in a general context of s-regulation, corruption of the entire technical and political staff is often a structural element, while discretion and unequal treatments are the result of individual behavior. All of these aspects have a high price within a system of rules in which the evaluation of the public good that the rule protects is, in itself, discretionary. Discretion continuously generates inequalities instead of reducing them. In fact, in the absence of alternatives, the progressive extension of s-regulation generates a deregulated regime altogether favorable to opportunistic actors, which seems to deteriorate the relationship between citizens and institutions and to worsen the lives of the weakest people.

With this concern, on the basis of data available at the municipal level, the overlapping of the three different indicators ("ghost buildings," municipalities replaced by an extraordinary commission, and confiscated assets of organized crime) clearly shows concentration areas that are in much more urgent need of attention, and that Milan is not so far away from Napoli or Palermo, or Torino from Rome and the southwest of Sicily.[2]

Waste metabolics

In present-day Italy, unprecedented forms of conflict and cohabitation are emerging, setting the stage for the rise of a new urban question (Castells, 1972), which is connected to waste metabolics. The demand for justice to contrast the related socio-ecological vulnerabilities calls upon public actors to address the social inequities they produce. In supporting the shift from the "right to the city" to the "right to urban environments" (Kaika & Swyngedouw, 2011), public institutions are notably hard put to deal with the issues at hand.

Looking at this phenomenon on a "planetary urbanization" scale, we must add that traditional forms of elitist environmentalism are gradually being replaced – from the south of the world to the heart of Europe – by what scholars of urban political ecology define as "environmentalism of the poor" (Martinez-Alier, 2002). This shift is due to increasing awareness of the connections between nature and human beings and their impact on everyday life, work and health issues.

Going back to the US of the 1980s, the rise of the first environmental justice movements was triggered by cynical political decisions based on the "path of least resistance," whereby activities with noxious effects on health were located next to areas inhabited by poor people, also discriminated by race and class. Leaving aside racial factors, which play a minor role in Italian society, similar social conditions are threatening waste metabolics in Italy: that is, the set of wasted places, things and people which are, according to Lynch (1990), part of a universal wasting stream and represent the dark side of change.

The Italian infrastructure for waste-disposal is shaping segments of the so-called "operational landscapes" (Brenner, 2014), which are made of incinerators, landfills, waste-recycling plants, waste-water processing plants and even former industrial areas waiting for reclamation by the state. Although these public facilities and neglected spaces are less "noble" than the schools, parks and theaters of the core centers, they are equally important for the balance of urban ecosystems because the new spatial orderings of extended urban regions in Italy will depend on them.

The environmental dilemmas that threaten the frail equilibrium of the Italian metabolism, shaping collective imagination through the internal contradictions of waste, can be exemplified by the case of the poisoning of the northern Campania Region: an area between the Provinces of Naples and Caserta once known as "Campania Felix" and now stigmatized as the "Land of Fires."

The public institutions' inadequate regulation of local waste treatment and disposal plants, also due to the opaque management of the Regional Plan for Urban Solid Waste

(Iacuelli, 2008), gave rise to a decline of the sociocultural capital that was a driver for improper land use. The consequence was the concealing of waste or its accumulation and burning in open spaces and rural areas.

The process of "slow violence" (Nixon, 2011) inflicted on the area (with a population of over 3 million) has placed a heavy load of disease and sorrow on common people, deeply undermining their lifestyles and their relationship with the local environment. Media stigmatization has also amplified the deterioration of traditional land maintenance and controls, causing a loss of competitiveness, mostly in the agro-alimentary sector, and further de-territorialization.

Narratives produced and circulated in Campania over the last few years highlight how issues of environmental vulnerability are being addressed in a discussion which draws on technical-scientific, legal, economic and populist rhetoric and, depending on the target, takes a more or less conflicting stance, or one of outright struggle against institutional planning models. This confused reasoning has manipulated public opinion, destabilized decisional processes and even transformed environmental policies and laws into mere symbols (Palestino, 2015).

In dealing with national demands for environmental justice, images (and stigma) have become so powerful to have pushed Italian institutions to simulate regulation through symbolic strategies, not only in the case at hand, but also in other environmental conflicts: such as the digging of the tunnel for the high-speed railway in Val di Susa (Piedmont Region), or the damage caused by the former Ilva ironworks in Taranto (Puglia Region).

This is the reason why, on the boundary between legality and illegality, the clash between images of Campania Felix and stigma of the Land of Fires can be taken as a symbol of a more general disruption of space and society and, hence, as a metaphor of the national incapability to fight criminal entrepreneurialism, arbitrate in matters of public health and, more generally, deal with environmental justice issues and socio-ecological vulnerabilities.

As for the environmental side of the "Italian anomaly," this seems to follow the metaphor of *simcity*, that is: "a different and more subtle form of social and spatial regulation, one that [. . .] plays with the mind, manipulating civic consciousness and popular images of city space and urban life to maintain order" (Soja, 2000, p. 324).

Being a representative example of how images and stigma affect the urban metabolism – both in replacing the public responsibilities of the institutions and in creating knock-on effects on the production of wasted things, places and lives – the case of the Land of Fires asks for reflection on the permeability to further vulnerabilities. To avoid their flourishing in the "less resistant" interstices of the peninsula and placing the whole national metabolism at risk, such vulnerabilities need to be analyzed and deconstructed in depth.

The implosion-explosion of northern Campanian cities and towns through regionalization processes of the urban has also set in motion a sort of "differential urbanization" (Brenner & Schmid, 2015) based on liquid identities, sometimes temporary ones, that are as recognizable as those that were once founded on administrative boundaries, art-historical heritage or natural features.

Because the mechanisms of control and defense activated to shed light on the disaster and to react against it have been determining the cultural growth of a section of inhabitants, the only opportunity to bounce back toward Campania Felix seems to lie in community resilience.

In fact, the urban region at hand is inhabited by communities which, in the transition from the "not in my backyard" approach of the 1990s to the "not in anyone's backyard" one of recent years, have gradually become sensitive to collective values such as health, rights and participation. Scholars in the field of local activism have pointed out the emergence of increasingly sophisticated movements. By combining "street science" (Corburn, 2005), alternative forms of production and creative ways of defending rights (Caggiano & De Rosa, 2015), they are behaving as in situ environmental justice organizations (Armiero, 2014).

In generalizing what we can learn from the Land of Fires, I would suggest that similar socio-ecological dynamics show the insurgent demand for new profiles of local administration and for radical experiments in governance. A smart infrastructure of waste, to be connected with participative reclamation processes, could offer the opportunity to share innovative planning and design of new spatial orderings.

The shift from using images as a strategy to "maintain order" to using them as narratives for community resilience could help the recovery of urban regions. In applying the metaphor of the "creative destruction" of panarchy (Holling & Gunderson, 2002) to the many Lands of Fires that are still hidden on the Italian peninsula and elsewhere, we would be investing in the "potential" of communities to open a window of opportunity for change.

Notes

1 This contribution is the outcome of a joint effort by the authors. In particular, "The Italian anomaly" is authored by D. De Leo and "Waste metabolics" is authored by M.F. Palestino.
2 See PRIN Postmetropoli (2015): "Beni immobili confiscati – 2013", § c.6.1; "Immobili non dichiarati e accatastati – 2011", § c.6.2.

References

Armiero, M. (2014). Garbage under the Volcano: The Waste Crisis in Campania and the Struggles for Environmental Justice. In M. Armiero, and L. Sedrez (Eds.), *A History of Environmentalism*. London-New York: Bloomsbury.

Brenner, N. (2014). Introduction: Urban Theory without an Outside. In N. Brenner (Ed.), *Towards a Study of Planetary Urbanization* (pp. 14–27). Berlin: Jovis Verlag GmbH.

Brenner, N., and Schmid, C. (2015).Towards a New Epistemology of the Urban? *City*, 19(2–3), 151–182.

Caggiano, M., and De Rosa, P.S. (2015). Social Economy as antidote to Criminal Economy: How Social Cooperation is Reclaiming Commons in the Contests of Campania's Environmental Conflicts. *PACO-The Open Journal of Sociopolitical Studies*, 8(2), 530–554.

Casaburi, L., and Troiano, U. (2013). Ghost-House Busters: The Electoral Response to a Large Anti Tax Evasion Program. *Social Science Research Network*, 1–50.

Castells, M. (1972). *La Question urbaine*. Paris: Maspero.

Corburn, J. (2005). *Street Science: Community Knowledge and Environmental Health Justice*. Cambridge, MA: MIT.

De Leo, D. (2011). Public Sphere and Illegal Settlements: A Case from the Naples Metro-region. In M. Cremaschi, and F. Eckardt (Eds.), *Changing Places: Urbanity, Citizenship, and Ideology in the New European Neighbourhoods* (pp. 199–220). Amsterdam: Tekne.

Donolo, C. (2001). *Disordine*. Roma: Donzelli.

Elster, J. (1989). *The Cement of Society*. Cambridge: Cambridge University Press.

Holling, C.S., and Gunderson, L.H. (2002). *Panarchy: Understanding Transformations in Human and Natural Systems*. Washington: Island Press.

Iacuelli, A. (2008). *Le vie infinite dei rifiuti. Il sistema campano*. Roma: Rinascita edizioni.

Kaika, M., and Swyngedouw, E. (2011). The Urbanization of Nature: Great Promises, Impasse, and New Beginnings. In G. Bridge, and S. Watson (Eds.), *The New Blackwell Companion to the City* (pp. 96–107). Chichester: Wiley-Blackwell.

Lynch, K. (1990). *Wasting Away*. San Francisco: Sierra Club.

Martinez-Alier, J. (2002). *The Environmentalism of the Poor: A Study of Ecological Conflicts and Valuation*. Cheltenham: Edward Elgar Publishing.

Nixon, R. (2011). *Slow Violence and the Environmentalism of the Poor*. Cambridge, MA –London: Harvard University Press.

Palestino, M.F. (2015). How to Put Environmental Injustice on the Planner's Radical Agenda: Learning from the Land of Fires – Italy. In M. Macoun, and K. Maier (Eds.), *Book of Proceedings AESOP Prague Annual Congress 2015: Definite Space – Fuzzy Responsibility* (pp. 2576–2586). Prague: Czech Technical University.

PRIN Postmetropoli. (2015). *Atlante web dei territori postmetropolitani* [web atlas]. Retrieved from http://www.postmetropoli.it/atlante.

Soja, E.W. (2000). *Postmetropolis: Critical Studies of Cities and Regions*. Oxford: Blackwell.

Storper, M. (2013). *Governing the Large Metropolis* (Working papers du Programme Cities are Back in Town). Retrieved from http://blogs.sciences-po.fr/recherche-villes/files/2013/11/WPStorper2.pdf.

16 Urban typologies within contemporary Italian urbanization

Laura Fregolent and Luciano Vettoretto, with Marco Bottaro and Francesco Curci

The *Atlante dei territori postmetropolitani* (PRIN Postmetropoli, 2015) shows the geographical distribution of a wide variety of social, economic and physical indicators describing recent urbanization processes and enabling the interpretation of the phenomenology of post-metropolis and planetary urbanization in the Italian case. In this short chapter, macro and synthetic representations will be provided, through a multivariate analysis of selected sets of variables.

Obviously, official statistical data have many limitations. Indicators describe amounts of population and economic activities rather than flows (apart from the traditional house–workplace commuting). However, spatial unities are defined by their political-administrative borders, which are often of little significance for exploring key dimensions of contemporary urbanization (networks, borders, differences) (Schmid, 2014a).

Nonetheless, it is possible to select a few sets of variables that can be considered sufficiently adequate proxies, particularly in order to recognize different morphologies of *concentrated* and *extended urbanization* (Brenner & Katsikis, 2014). A multivariate analysis was applied to the following sets of indicators: population distribution, density and dynamics, including inhabitants and commuters; economic activities and their dynamics; social features such as rate of migrants, social status, per capita income, Gini coefficient. The analysis produced a fairly large variety of concentrated and extended urbanization phenomenologies (twelve typologies, which will be described, for sake of brevity, in six aggregated clusters with their main internal varieties). Quantitative results were compared with a large amount of empirical information, including economic and social reports, local development programs, case studies on social practices and local conflicts, spatial projects and megaprojects, policy evaluation reports, and so on.

Urban Italy: a short historical framing

Italy has been, during its long urban history, a densely urbanized territory, with many large (some, until the forming of the Italian state, were capitals), medium and small cities, each with their peculiar urbanity. Particularly in central and northern Italy, the relationship between cities and the countryside was very complex: often élites, as well as financial capital invested in the first phases of modern industrialization and ideas for development, came from the countryside. Initially, industrial activities were not located in cities, but rather in the country-side (particularly in some valleys such as the Valdarno in Tuscany or the Valle dell'Agno in Veneto) or even in new cities (Bagnasco, 1977; Lanaro, 1989). The old historical cities and their topography and urban fabric could not face modern plant locations, and were for a long time non-industrial cities, sites for exchange, trade, leisure and production of culture.

Italy's massive industrialization occurred notably after the Second World War. Particularly between 1959 and 1962, the industrial production in advanced Fordist sectors increased more than 300 percent and salaries more than 6 percent on aver-age. More than 9 million people migrated from southern Italy to northern industrial centers (among which Turin, Milan and Genoa), but also from the countryside to nearby cities of every dimension, and from hilly and mountainous areas to plains and valleys. The urban structure grew very fast, and urbanization was a massive phenomenon not only from a physical point of view, but also social and cultural. The rise in revenues and the availability of mass consumption goods (particu-larly low-price cars and television sets) radically changed everyday life (mobility patterns, holidays, consumption patterns, culture and leisure, even language, with the weakening of the very widespread use of local dialects) with a substantial dif-fusion of (variegated) urban lifestyles. More than the phenomenon of industrial cities, Italy experienced the rise of an industrial society, which impacted not only cities, but also almost all settlement typologies and social situations.

The crisis of the Fordist phase and the well-known emergence of Marshallian "industrial districts" triggered a new urbanization phase, particularly in some regions (such as Veneto, Toscana and Emilia) marked by a significant popula-tion diffusion. Moreover, economic activities grew on ancient settlements and infrastructures, often named "*città diffusa*," and pretty peculiar lifestyles which hybridized in a kind of *bricolage*, with traditional and innovative social and cul-tural features (for a typology of this urban Italy see: Vettoretto, 1996; Fregolent & Vettoretto, *infra*). From this point of view, in some way and with strong differ-ences, all of Italy became urban.

Globalization, with the crisis of traditional industrial districts and the new roles of networked urban economies, once again changed urbanization patterns. The regional portraits in this volume show such transformations, and, in some cases, the emergence of post-metropolitan features (with particular regard to the rela-tionships between urban and metropolitan cores and their surrounding spaces; the transformation of previously monocentric structures in polycentric ones as in the Milan case; or the new social practices of multiple populations in supposedly non-urban, sometimes remote, areas such as the Sardinian Gallura).

The urban typologies presented hereafter describe this emerging situation.

Concentrated and concentrating urbanizations

According to Brenner and Katsikis, *concentrated urbanization* "refers to the perpetual and crisis-induced restructuring of densely concentrated agglomerations"

(Brenner & Katsikis, 2014, p. 434). It includes a wide variety of situations: metropolis, metropolitan regions, city-regions, cities, dense suburban developments, edge cities, and so on. Concentrated urbanization refers to processes rather than spatial facts clearly identifiable. Its main character, over time, is the quantitative and qualitative changing concentration of physical, social, cultural and economic features, affecting the production of borders, networks and differences. In Italy – and more generally in some European countries such as Switzerland or Germany – concentrated urbanization has its basis in the ancient high-density urban network of large, medium and even small cities and their close surroundings. On the other hand, *concentrating urbanization* describes recent processes of implosion along the most important infrastructure corridors, and, at the same time, the explosion of the pre-existing ancient sets of villages and small towns supported by ancient road networks. Such processes produce a new kind of urban medium-density space with a variety of lifestyles. In both cases, there is a significant relationship between urbanization and topography (almost all Italian plains and valleys are urbanized).

The analysis shows that 64 percent of the Italian population live in such situations (about 29 million inhabitants), covering 24 percent of the total surface (50 percent live in concentrated and 14 percent in concentrating situations). Figures 16.1 and 16.2 show the distribution of this kind of urban situation, which concerns almost all Italian lowlands, and, particularly, the Po Valley.

Concentrated urbanization shows a large variety of phenomenologies. *Metropolitan and large urban polarities* mostly refer to the new socioeconomic and physical consequences of globalization. Processes are well-known: de-industrialization, steep growth of advanced services (knowledge intensive business services – KIBS), high infrastructure density and accessibility (international airports, highways, high-speed rail networks, regional transit, very low levels of digital divide), highest per capita incomes, valuable human resources. This macro-cluster aggregates three groups, which show marked differences among northern and central and southern areas, with urban structures and fabric deeply different, in particular from a social and economic perspective. Milan and Rome clearly appear as major metropolitan centers, included in international networks for different reasons and histories (Rome because it is a capital city). This morphology shares main economic features with other central-northern cities (Turin, Bologna, Florence), mainly because of economic bases and population dynamics, but with different weight, quality and intensity. Looking at traditional urban ranking indicators, Milan and Rome appear at the top. Obviously, rankings depend on cognitive frames by which indicators are selected. Adopting a plural perspective on urbanity, many (overlapping and fuzzy) borders and hierarchies are recognizable. For example, in terms of cultural heritage and resources, cultural events or international tourist mobility (and the consequences of the spatial and temporal compresence of many populations) other geographies can emerge, where, for example, Rome, Florence and Venice stand out. However, it is quite clear that Milan is the most important Italian global node. It is probably for this reason that Milan is a metropolitan core with a very high level of social inequalities (measured through the Gini coefficient), and per capita income, much more than

Rome, Turin, Florence and Bologna. Apparently, globalization has produced new rich social groups (linked to "global" professions), and new servile strata (in which the foreign population plays an important role). At the same time, population is increasingly aging (aging produces many consequences on urbanity, with regard to the demand of low-wage caretaking, lifestyles, mobility, welfare, uses of space, social practices, and so on).

This morphology changes significantly in the southern situation, with Naples (which can be considered a metropolitan center as well), Palermo, Bari and a few other cities (Figure 16.2). While a city like Naples does not have particular infrastructural disadvantages, its social situation is very different. In fact, it presents a younger population, much lower per capita incomes, unemployment, social risks and poverty, smaller presence of KIBS. At the same time, though, it shows a lower level of inequalities, probably because of the socially porous character of the city that allows for a more blended and less polarized urban society, with limited processes of gentrification (see the regional portrait). Clearly, this model of urbanization and of urbanity is very different from the previous one: systems of differences, networks, life-worlds seem in some way peculiar.

Such territories have fuzzy boundaries. The external areas – often made of ancient little settlements, and, more recently, of industrial low-class housing (periphery) – are more and more integrated with the city. For example, the Milan case shows how the urban fringe, with its high level of infrastructure facilities and accessibility, is by now the localization of core economic metropolitan activities, in a situation of medium to high per capita incomes, younger and growing population and fast densification. Through commuting patterns and density dynamics (see the *Atlante*), it is possible to recognize some of Soja's post-metropolitan features (see the regional portraits).

The metropolitan development does not seem to erase the traditional old dense city, which is still one of the most widespread Italian urban phenomenologies. A set of *medium and small cities and consolidated fringe developments* (Figure 16.1) is visible, often located along the Venice–Milan and Milan–Bologna corridors (such as Venice, Treviso, Padua, Verona, Parma, Piacenza and their integrated fringes) with welds between Padua and Bologna and Verona–Trento–Modena along highways and railways, alongside smaller but vibrant cities of ancient foundation, that continue to exist and thrive. These are situations of high accessibility, per capita incomes, amount of KIBS, but also of some substantial inequalities, higher turnouts, with models of urbanity sometimes peculiar in terms of old and new ways of living in the urban space. Often regional centers (but sometimes displaying national or international characters, such as Padua for its huge and attractive university, Venice for its cultural heritage, Verona as an international logistics and transportation node, and so on) retain an urbanity made of strong social and cultural activities, bottom–up organizations, still vibrant public spaces, high quality of life, seemingly social integration capabilities.

Metropolitan nodes and cities are connected by a kind of *urbanoid galaxy*. Urbanoid refers to a process of population concentration and advanced economic activities, in a situation of high accessibility. At the same time, though, it is different from traditional cities (with regard to public spaces, urban fabric, housing and urban typologies and elements, public facilities, social practices, and so on). In brief: a basically quasi-concentrated urban pattern quite different from both city and suburbs, emerging from the growth of historical villages (not from suburbs or peripheries) invested, in time, by the industrialization of society, the development of transport networks, the closeness to transportation facilities (railways stations, tollbooths, minor airports), the rise of industrial districts and revenues, the impacts of globalization on the manufacturing industry and the expansion of service industries. These processes produced a variety of lifestyles, from the strictly local individual-private one to the cosmopolitan one. In the urbanoid – often site of deeply restructuring industrial districts – manufacturing is still dominant. However, the economic base appears particularly diversified because of the presence of all ranges of tertiary activities, from tourism (particularly the new forms of farmhouses), to large and medium shopping centers and KIBS, while the agricultural land is still a substantial landscape marker. This very dynamic urbanoid – populated by young families coming from cities and

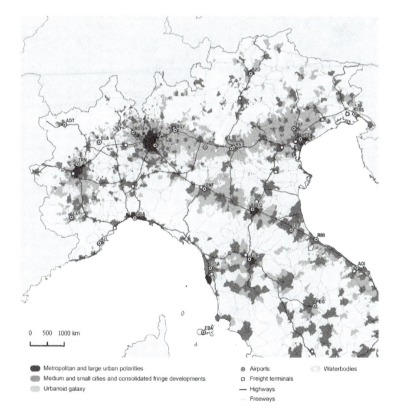

Figure 16.1 Concentrated and concentrating urbanizations: northern and central Italy

Source: Authors' elaboration based on data from PRIN Postmetropoli (2015)

metropolitan centers and/or attracted by more distant and less accessible spaces – is apparently very rich, with high per capita income associated to very low inequalities, probably because of the absence of situations of great wealth and extreme poverty (despite the large amount of migrants), with a very high turnout. The urbanoid is a world made of differences in landscape, social and economic practices, mobility patterns, lifestyles, housing models. In some respects, it appears as one of the most significant post-metropolitan spaces.

Finally, these areas indicate the emergence of wide and differentiated polycentric regions such as the northern urban region articulated in two main urban corridors (Milan–Venice and Milan–Rimini), the Adriatic linear city, or the corridors emerging among Florence, Rome and Naples. Such situations include a very large variety of urban situations, ranging from global/European areas, integrated surrounding spaces (of post-metropolitan kind), sets of both autonomous/networked traditional medium and small cities, with many borders, networks and differences.

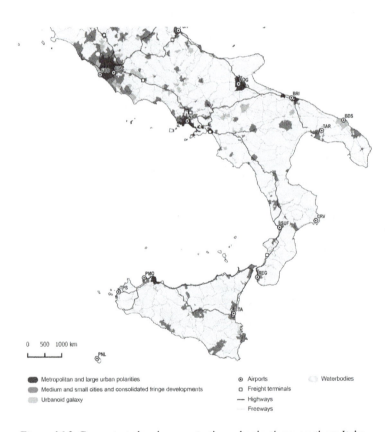

Figure 16.2 Concentrated and concentrating urbanizations: southern Italy

Source: Authors' elaboration based on PRIN Postmetropoli (2015)

Extensive urbanizations: spaces of agricultural and industrial production

These spaces (6 million inhabitants and a quarter of the surface) cover the farthest territories from most of the infrastructure networks, and can be divided into two main situations: the area between the Milan–Venice and Milan–Bologna corridors (*agricultural and industrial lowland between concentrated urbanizations*) and the hilly areas in central Italy (*mountainous and hilly areas with diversified economic bases*) (Figure 16.3). These situations share a substantial rural landscape devoted both to extensive and intensive agro-industry (sometimes advanced), a slowly declining manufacturing base, appreciable development of tourist activities, a steady population, low density, and a significant proportion of migrants, attracted by housing availability, lower real estate prices, a relative accessibility to concentrated urbanizations, and labor demand (agriculture, manufacturing, caretaking and other low-wage jobs). The per capita income is above average, and inequalities, because of the absence of very rich or very poor people, are less important than in more touristic similar areas.

These areas are subject to changes because of the restructuring of industrial districts, innovation in agriculture and agro-industry (more entrepreneurial practices, young entrepreneurs and advanced market strategies than in the past), and the important rise of tourism, particularly farmhouses and similar. Changes are quite significant, and the previous development model (traditional manufacturing and agriculture) is changing pretty quickly. Such territories are quite differentiated: the proximity of traditional economy and social life is more and more overlapped with increasingly important flows of goods (particularly niche agricultural high-value-added products and specialized traditional handicrafts), people (migrants, national and international tourists often attracted and informed through apps, Internet tools and so on) and the presence of a young population sometimes graduated from metropolitan universities that create innovative activities, in a situation of high facility density (ethnographical museums, a diffuse network of local public libraries, sports facilities, bike and pedestrian trails that link cultural and natural places, many local events) and of a re-invented tradition for the purpose of local development, often promoted bottom–up. In such situations, not only practices and events are pretty differentiated, but temporalities and processes also have different speeds: the slow and quite steady demographic change interacts with the faster change in local development practices (sometimes supported by EU programs) with an increase in the variety of "place users," which, using the space interactively, are "space-makers" as well. Borders and networks are multiple and overlapping, differences divide deeply-rooted lifestyles from re-invented traditions, with social and economic consequences. These situations are quite interesting because of their capability to attract and develop different urban lifestyles mainly through the invention of traditions, a conscious (post-modern?) production of a simulacrum of a (probably never existed) rural-communitarian world.

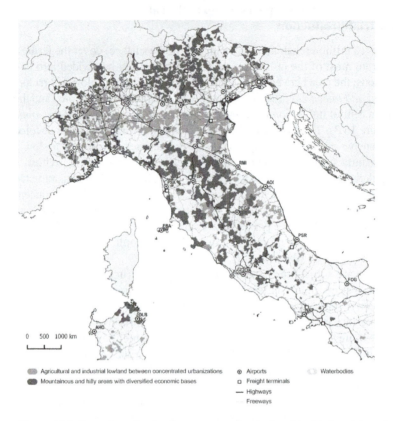

Figure 16.3 Extensive urbanizations: spaces of agricultural and industrial production

Source: Authors' elaboration based on PRIN Postmetropoli (2015)

Dynamic coastal and internal hybrid intensive–extensive urbanization

This very hybrid situation, located mainly in the southern plains (particularly in Apulia), counts a population of more than 11 million and almost 20 percent of the surface (Figure 16.4). The physical urbanization differs significantly, compared with the northern one, for historical reasons, at least partially to be referred to the ancient regulations of agricultural-landed property such as the latifundium. In many parts of these areas it is still possible to recognize a fairly clear distinction between small and medium cities and the countryside. Even for farmers it is still customary to live in concentrated settlements, and work in the countryside. This territory does not have particular accessibility disadvantages, being served by highways, railway networks and top-level stations, local and national airports, industrial, commercial, fishing and leisure ports, and a limited digital divide.

This situation is often marked by critical social conditions because of high unemployment and illiteracy rates, lower per capita income, social risks (but the number of graduates is average). At the same time, demography is vital because of the presence of young people, higher birth rates and larger families. Lower real estate values match lower incomes, despite an increasing demand for holiday housing, often from metropolitan populations. For the mentioned historical reasons, the rural landscape is still very important, in a frame of an often weak economy (trade, construction, real estate, public sector) with a significant development of tourist activities, linked to agro-industrial excellences (olive oil, wine, vegetables, and so on), mainly developed through farmhouses and holiday houses located almost everywhere (historical centers, countryside, costal development). Economic activities are often performed in informal ways, outside public regulations (for example the weight of illegal buildings lacking any planning permission is significant). The mix of agriculture, food, beaches and cultural heritage is very

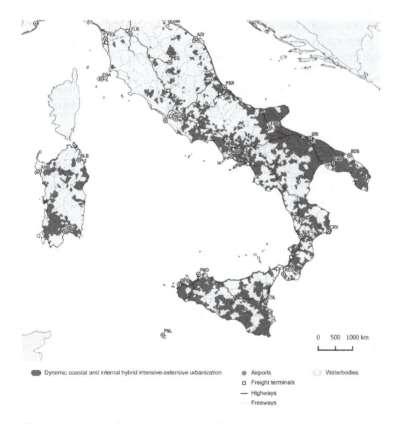

Figure 16.4 Dynamic coastal and internal hybrid intensive–extensive urbanization

Source: Authors' elaboration based on PRIN Postmetropoli (2015)

important in order to abandon the stereotype of a rural and backward area. The representation of this space is furthermore rapidly changing, and, particularly, Apulia has become the preferred location of an increasing number of national and international movies. The interaction between dynamism and stagnancy, formal and informal, old and new, local and international, is a key for interpreting the various models of urbanity in this area.

Other extended urbanization situations

Mountains and sea traditional resorts (half a million of inhabitants, 6 percent of the surface), mainly located in Alpine territories, have many similarities with the "Alpine resorts" described by Schmid (2014b, pp. 420–422) for the Swiss case (Figure 16.5). As in the previous typology, these places (with high per capita income, elderly population, high property values and levels of inequality, and increasing tourist activities) are becoming more and more connoted by urban features (shopping centers, high-end boutiques and stores, important cultural facilities and events, spas, sport facilities, and so on). Here, with intermittence, metropolitan and urban populations live in hotels, holiday houses and farmhouses. Social practices of temporary populations are in significant part similar to the typical ones of urban leisure. Internal differences are remarkable, and sometimes conflicts among groups linked to tourism activities, realtors, local groups mobilized on environmental or cultural heritage issues and external users are clearly perceivable as a significant clue of resistance to unwanted uses of space and urbanity models.

Backstage declining low-density areas (2 million inhabitants, 20 percent of the surface) are quite differentiated but share some basic features: low accessibility, remoteness from concentrated urbanizations and from transport network nodes, high level of digital divide, elderly people, demographic decline, low density and turnout, and a mountainous landscape (Figure 16.6). Quite unexpectedly, levels of inequality are above average, probably because of the diffusion of low retirement provisions alongside medium–high revenues. These backstage areas can be differentiated in *quiet rural and touristic depopulating areas* mainly located in northern and central mountainous areas, at the edges of *concentrated and concentrating urbanizations, spaces of agricultural and industrial production,* and in *fallow lands.* In the first case, the economic base is a mix of traditional and sometimes innovative agriculture and various forms of tourism (with a significant weight of holiday homes). Generally speaking, such a situation is not as negative as the official statistical data depict, at least partially because of the vitality of these places in cultural and tourist actions and policy, and the capability to re-invent and sell their traditions in local development policies. Actually, such places can be recognized at least in part as a kind of "theme park" for many external metropolitan users: bikers, walkers, nature lovers, traditional food hunters, people looking for peace and quiet, explorers or amateur anthropologists looking for "authentic" past life-worlds, or even new inhabitants searching for a new "urban remote" lifestyle. Therefore, such areas are a complex stratification of differences, urbanity models and overlapping of multiple networks.

The situation of the *fallow lands* is quite different, and very similar to those described by Schmid (2014b, pp. 422–425) in his study on urban Switzerland (reason for which his denomination was used). These *fallow lands* are mainly located in the southern mountainous territories, at the edge of the *dynamic coastal and internal hybrid intensive–extensive urbanizations.* In such a case, social conditions are very critical because of high unemployment and illiteracy rates, social risks, the lowest per capita income. Turnout is minimal. Here, even tourism appears very weak, and the relationship with the other concentrated or extended urbanizations appears to be very weak. The main kind of relationship seems to be migrations toward wealthier areas. The urban seems not only far away, but absent.

Figure 16.5 Mountains and traditional sea resorts

Source: Authors' elaboration based on PRIN Postmetropoli (2015)

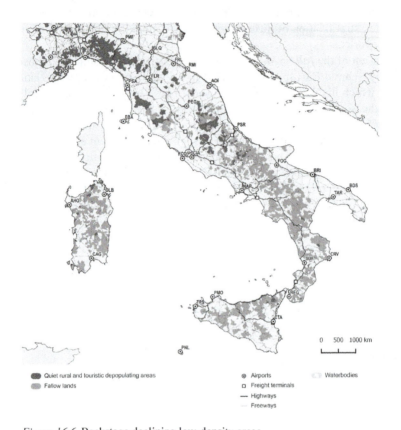

Figure 16.6 Backstage declining low-density areas

Source: Authors' elaboration based on PRIN Postmetropoli (2015)

Over binary urban representations

This short chapter depicts a complex urbanized Italy highlighting several clues of post-metropolitan features. The representation, obviously non-neutral like others, calls for cognitive frames and policies that should abandon traditional binary categories: metropolitan–non-metropolitan, urban–non-urban, city–countryside, concentrated–diffuse, high–low density, developed–awkward. It is necessary to consider the plurality of urbanization and urbanity patterns and their problematical interactions as a public policy issue.

References

Bagnasco, A. (1977). *Tre Italie. La problematica territoriale dello sviluppo italiano.* Bologna: il Mulino.

Brenner, N. (Ed.). (2014). *Implosions/Explosions: Towards a Study of Planetary Urbanization.* Berlin: Jovis Verlag GmbH.

Brenner, N., and Katsikis, N. (2014). Is the Mediterranean Urban? In N. Brenner (Ed.), *Implosions/Explosions: Towards a Study of Planetary Urbanization* (pp. 428–459). Berlin: Jovis Verlag GmbH.

Lanaro, S. (1989). La campagna organizza la città?. *Meridiana*, 5, 49–60.

PRIN Postmetropoli. (2015). *Atlante web dei territori postmetropolitani* [web atlas]. Retrieved from: http://www.postmetropoli.it/atlante.

Schmid, C. (2014a). Network, Borders, Differences: Towards a Theory of the Urban. In N. Brenner (Ed.), *Implosions/Explosions: Towards a Study of Planetary Urbanization* (pp. 67–80). Berlin: Jovis Verlag GmbH.

Schmid, C. (2014b). A Typology of Urban Switzerland. In N. Brenner (Ed.), *Implosions/Explosions: Towards a Study of Planetary Urbanization* (pp. 398–427). Berlin: Jovis Verlag GmbH.

Vettoretto, L. (1996). Morfologie sociali territoriali. In A. Clementi, G. Dematteis, and P.C. Palermo (Eds.), *Le forme del territorio italiano* (Vol. 2, pp. 617–635). Bari: Laterza.

17 Is Italy still special?

Conceptual and empirical remarks on urbanization in the era of globalization

Carlo Cellamare and Luciano Vettoretto

Many scholars have argued, over time, about Italy's social, economic, political and cultural peculiarities. Its urbanization too has always been studied as fairly distinctive: many historic cities with singular settings, often held up as models of an appealing way of life.

How has globalization changed the Italian city and its *image*? Is Italian urbanization just a part of an overall global flattening? Do Italian cities, and their social and spatial settings and practices, show a radical break with the past? Do its greater metropolitan city-regions show patterns and transformations like those of post-metropolitan situations around the world?

In this chapter, we will try to frame these issues through a discussion of some concepts which seem of basic importance for the understanding of Italian urbanization. Such concepts are mostly related to the influence of time (and space, place, territory, also as a legacy from the past) in the urban persistence and transformation (not only physical, but also social and economic), which appears much more powerful than in other realities, such as the US or Asia.

First remark: the (supposed) flatness of the world and Italy's peaks and valleys

The effect of globalization has not been to "flatten the world." Friedman's interpretation of the world as a level playing field, as a process of equalizing power, capacity, opportunities of more and more connected people, seems more wishful thinking than reality (Friedman, 2005). As many scholars argue, the world is instead fairly spiky (see, among others, Rodriguez-Posé & Crescenzi, 2008; Florida et al., 2008). Economic and social opportunities are differentiated in their dispersion around the world, and even across countries and regions. Such supposed equality/flatness of opportunities seems more and more selective with regards to geography, history, and so on.

Economic as well as social and cultural globalization are producing – or reproducing – far more differences than similarities among territories. As the neoclassical economic theory failed in predicting convergences among countries in the long run, globalization produces, at the same time, homogenization and differentiation. How much differentiation and how much homogenization depends, at least in part, on the historical, geographical and institutional legacy of each territory.

Italy is a case of strong differences, inside the national borders and in comparison with other territories, even when globalization produces major economic, social and urban transformation.

Italy's population is about 59 million. Shanghai has 24 million inhabitants, Beijing almost 20 million. These two megacities account for 44 million inhabitants, 75 percent of all of Italy. The urban dimension in Italy is totally different. The Italian territory is densely punctuated by more-or-less ancient urban nodes, with a strong sense of identity and often a fairly vibrant civic life. About 30 percent of the population lives in 105 cities with populations of more than 60,000 inhabitants. Twenty-two percent live in small cities with populations of between 20,000 and 60,000 inhabitants. Economy and society are hosted in (and produce) a variety of different models of urbanity.

Such small cities are cities in the full sense of the term: they provide services, they usually boast a large amount of cultural capital, a deep sense of identity and civic engagement, and a lively environment. The metropolitan phenomenon has been quite limited in its quantitative terms (compared with the USA, Northern Europe or the recent Asian megacities). Generally speaking, its territory has maintained, in the long run, a (morphologically) polycentric structure which dates from the Middle Ages or even earlier, with roots in Greek and Roman colonization.

Both larger and smaller cities have developed connections and forms of embedment into their regional spaces, so that we can recognize a large variety of situations: urban corridors as open systems of relatively integrated places and regions, historically polycentric city-regions (or regions of cities) diversely affected by and/or reactive with the globalization process, large, monocentric agglomerations in rapid transformation toward a more diffuse and regionalized grid of centralities (leisure, jobs, facilities, and so on), local systems with diversified economies and strong identities but nevertheless open to change, urban simulacra (such as some "new cities" in Sardinia) together with previously marginal areas revived by attracting new (often globalized) inhabitants. Often, such different spatialities are simultaneously present, impacting each other and, consequently, effecting social and urban configurations, and producing very complex territorialities (see the regional portraits).

Even if the nighttime satellite images of light-studded Italy seem to depict a giant mega-city which covers almost the whole country (connecting Milan, Turin and Rome), a country which would be the third wealthiest in Europe and the seventh in the world (Florida et al., 2008; see also Soja & Kanai, 2007 for the concept of URB-Italy), the analysis of flows of people, goods and information (see Chapter 12 in this volume) show the persistence of regional patterns, more or less connecting each other, in some case forming corridors (particularly, from Venice to Milan and Milan to Bologna), in a transcalar game of lifeworlds, territories of circulation, spheres of daily life, urban and metropolitan networks, local production systems alongside the global ones, and so on. If every place is influenced by (economic, social, cultural) globalization, at the same time the Italian patterns seem often capable of combining the hypermodernity of globalization with a constant re-invention (starting from the legacy) of territories and places, sometimes simulacra, sometimes original spatialities (as in the case of Sardinia).

Globalization is a game of de-territorialization and re-territorialization (Cacciari, 2008; Madden, 2012), of often creative invention and production of places across the wrinkled crust of the earth (and, at the same time, practices of resistance and effects in terms of resilience). The Lefebvrian "urban" is everywhere, but at the same time the (changing) cities continue to exist.

Second remark: concerning what is "urban"

As previously illustrated (see Chapter 3 in this volume), the idea of "post-metropolis" (Soja, 1999), which somehow inspired the work of the national research group, was conceived for the Los Angeles area and therefore can hardly be applied to the Italian context. For this reason, this research has addressed regional processes of urbanization. In many cases, with the exception of that of Milan, it is difficult to speak of true metropolitan areas in Italy. Rome itself, though Italy's capital, can barely be considered a metropolis.

What can be gleaned from the work of Soja, however, is the multidimensional quality that characterizes the urban, in particular those immaterial qualities, be they financial flows or symbolic systems, that refer back to the notion of "third space" already developed in previous years (1996). In truth, even with regard to this idea, Lefebvre's work (1970, 1974) was seminal and well ahead of its time, and most authors (Harvey, 2006; Harrison, 2007; Jessop et al., 2008; Schmid, 2012; Goonewardena et al., 2008; Brenner, 2014) begin with it and continue to build upon these dimensions, although in some cases with differing interpretations.

These ideas are widely adopted by Brenner (2014), in reasoning about "planetary urbanization." In this case, however, in the concrete work of interpretation, it seems to disappear entirely. While the work of Brenner's research group shows great intelligence in dealing with a great many methodological and data collection problems (Brenner & Katsikis, 2014), they seem in the end to forget this dimension and focus more on those aspects of urbanization, and more generally forms of "human activity" (including such uses of resources), which are physically detectable by treating such uses of land, or infrastructure networks and connections, or more recently the environmental aspects, remaining dependent on the availability of comparable information at a global scale. The research work on Italy has allowed us, instead, to address a complexity of problems and synergies lacking in global research. It has overcome (erroneous) macroscopic visions (as in the above-mentioned interpretation of the Turin–Milan–Rome system) and been capable of greater degrees of depth even compared with other regional portrait experiences (Diener et al., 2006). Rather than simply look to the "scope" of the phenomenon of urbanization, the national research was instead forced to look at the different "forms (and processes) of urbanization," as indeed Brenner and his group had suggested.

This is not just an apparent problem of scale. It is also a problem of the interpretative categories that are used, and it is useful here to return to the multiplicity of dimensions introduced by Soja, and later by various others. Although there is still significant progress to be made, research has taken into account, in some cases, the characters of urban metabolism (how, for example, energy and waste flows characterize urban form), or in other cases the flows, in particular, of people (see the research developed by the Milan unit), or the relations between systems (see the reflection on "corridors" developed by Perulli and others, but also the reasoning on relations by the Venetian territorial unit). Furthermore, there is the study of environmental conflicts (as in the Veneto region) as indicators of the processes of an ongoing "planetary urbanization." The Sardinian study showed, instead, that the areas of this island, with very low density and strong natural and environmental components, can instead be considered "post-metropolitan" or subject to "planetary urbanization" if you look not only at the tourist flows (extremely relevant in this context), but also at the concentration of capital flows, on the one hand, and the changing nature of the places, on the other, with a crucial role played by the development and promotion of image perception, in this case due to the market.

Similarly, the question also arises, for example, with respect to agricultural or rural areas (however one prefers to call them), which have so profoundly changed the nature not so much in relation to the products of urban systems, but to their functions and to the people who live there and the cultures they bring. These cultures, even if cloaked in an "anti-urban" logic, are ever more urban in the perception that characterizes them. Furthermore, the Roman unit has studied the forms of dwelling, taking into account a multi-dimensionality that goes from the physicality of the house, property market trends, flows of movement, the organization of daily life, to the cultures of dwelling, and so on. The urban question is based on the question of how the city is inhabited and very often changes can be recognized not only in the physical structures of settlements, but in the very way of living and interpreting what we call urban.

The "implosion/explosion" dichotomy, to make a radical distinction, while certainly helping to fuel the debate, does not explain all the processes and does not help to clarify matters. We should talk instead about different forms of stratification of the urban, the co-existence of different ways to inhabit the city. It is, first and foremost, a stratification brought about through historical development, which means the co-existence today of various different structures that have emerged over time. It regards the hierarchy of city centers, now well-established distributions of urban functions, the local living arrangements and the reach of everyday life, the system of local and supra-local relations that has emerged over time (see Chapter 5 in this volume), and so on. But it also means layering different ways of life and different dimensions of urbanity all in the same physical context. The research has tried to read these dynamics through the processes of transformation of urban regions, and the role of mediation played by the territory. For Lefebvre, the city was the mediator between the great supra-local socio-economic processes and the effects on people's daily lives. Today this mediating role is played by the territory and the socio-economic processes have become global.

Third remark: path/space dependence

In the very long run, starting in some cases, like Milan with ancient Roman colonization, or even earlier, as in the case of the Greek Naples, or from the more
"recent" medieval cities, urban persistence still supports the contemporary city
and metropolis. Perhaps no other country has a similar legacy (New York and
Boston were founded around 1630: Reps, 1965), apart from the urban Asia (China,
Japan, India, and so on), whose trajectories of transition to a quasi-Western modern urbanization are pretty recent.

Urban persistence is linked primarily to physical factors. In particular, the
case of Tuscany demonstrates that the primeval influence of physical geography
(topography, water, soil, and so on) has been the basic determinant of settlements
(differently from other situations, where the "physical" has been "tamed," like
the levelling of Manhattan around 1815 or the recent levelling of hills to produce
suitable room for the new Chinese urbanization).

Urban history has been, in some sense, a long history of urbanization on a
single track, and the inertia presented by the physical artifacts of previous urban
cultures has significantly influenced subsequent urban growth. Perhaps for this
reason Italian urbanization seems more dependent on its past even with respect
to other European countries. This "path dependence" is not only the trivial
acknowledgment that preceding events influence successive ones. Particularly in
evolutionary economics, the concept has been profoundly explored and critiqued
(see, among others: Martin & Sunley, 2006; Martin, 2010; Simmie & Martin,
2010). Such reflections focus on important issues not only for the (regional)
economic analysis, but also for studying the process of urbanization. They not
only explain the self-reinforcing character of path dependence, which is in some
way linked to successful events, and why it is so difficult to deviate from an
established route, particularly in the presence of "sunk costs" (such as the huge
investments involved in the building of an inhabitable territory). Such reinforcing
dynamics, starting from an urbanization mainly determined at its very beginning
by physical-geographic factors, demonstrate why, particularly in Italy, urbanization is mainly constructed on itself, even in the case of sprawl. The Veneto
case, for example, depicts a situation where the contemporary urban corridor follows a sort of "secular cycle" (Braudel, 1992), starting from the flows of capitals,
merchants, goods and ideas between Milan and Venice, reinforced during the
"proto-industrial" formation, remaining latent during the Industrial Revolution
and now returning, as a complex and transcalar connection of a variety of events,
places, spatialities and actors.

Path dependence may lock in territories, systems of companies and firms,
alongside cognitive frames. In some cases, this lock-in reinforces habits, trust,
inter-connections and generates increasing returns. It creates an "atmosphere"
which facilitates learning and the circulation of (particularly tacit) knowledge
through proximity and interaction, as in the case of Marshallian industrial districts. The process of formation of specialized, concentrated industrial areas is
quite similar to the description of urban growth we have suggested, particularly

in the cases of Tuscany and Veneto. According to Marshall, at the beginning the physical factors determine a firm location, and, in case of increasing return, a district is constituted forming a "region" in which

> ideals of life and [. . .] religious, political and economic thread of the [. . .] history are interwoven. [. . .] When an industry has thus chosen a locality for itself, it is likely to stay there long: so great are the advantages which people following the same skilled trade get from near neighborhood to one another. The mysteries of the trade become no mysteries; but are as it were in the air, and children learn many of them unconsciously (Marshall, 1890, p. 165).

So, the lock-in, as the main feature of path dependence, involves both time and space. Outcomes (and antecedents) of path dependence are quite local in character, and path dependence (as outcome and as process) is a local and contingent phenomenon, and hence to a high degree place-dependent. As in path dependence, spatial (dependence) forms have consequences on events, in such a way that spatiality is closely integrated to the production of history (Massey, 1992). The case of Rome clearly shows as the new extended grid of leisure/shopping centralities significantly (adaptively) change spatial behavior and daily practices, in new relations between housing (more and more abstracted from its territory) and leisure, in an extremely transcalar form. Path–space dependence, in this case, shows a dynamic of de-territorialization and re-territorialization, overcoming the traditional link between home and other places. The traditional space dependence of family/work/leisure is a path interrupted, the daily life is deployed in many places at the same time, perhaps producing new "worldlifes" and spatiality, in fact one of the many forms of the regionalization of the space.

In the regional portraits, path dependence (alongside space dependence) is well depicted, both in the negative and positive consequences of the lock-in. Path and space dependences are processes which imply reproduction and conservation (positive or negative lock-in, lock-in as a trap or as opportunity), or vice versa creation of new trajectories and a break with history. The case of Milan's urban region may be read, at least in the age of globalization and post-Fordism, as a case of positive lock-in, which reinforces itself through economies of agglomeration (network of learning), linkage and inter-dependencies at many scales, specific institutions. Over time, Milan (and in part Turin) experienced a dramatic break in the path (from Fordist industries to advanced producer services and creative industries) and the creation of a new path, perhaps thanks to the so-called Jacobsian externalities, a heterogeneity and diversity of local industries and organizations in dense urban agglomerations that facilitates innovation and economic reconfiguration – "avoiding complete adaptation and lock-in to a fixed structure" (Molina-Morales & Expósito-Langa, 2013, p. 744) – policy/technology/ideas transfer through external linkages, and so on (on Jacobsian externalities see, among others, Jacobs, 1961; Lucas, 1988; Glaeser, 2012). Such processes have profoundly changed the social, economic and physical character of the Milan region, its position in the international urban networks, and the spatial organization of the urban region, with a transition from a monocentric structure toward a complex grid of highly provisioned centralities. In comparing the transformations of Milan, Rome and Turin, one will find quite different models of urban regionalization, in which similar (general) trends produce quite different spatializations.

The game of creative/destructive/conservative time-spatial lock-in is quite apparent in the Third Italy. The cases of Tuscany and the Veneto show a profound crisis and restructuring of the Marshallian industrial districts, and the emergence of a plurality of socio-economic trajectories which contribute to the diversification of the regional economies. The quite introverted Marshallian district has broken beyond its boundaries, and in some cases disappeared; firms and clusters of firms locate themselves differently in the global value chain and the necessary (Marshallian) link with the territory has become significantly weakened. A cognitive proximity has partially replaced the geographic one. In Tuscany, a regionalization of the economic structure seems to emerge from the crisis of districts. The Veneto appears more and more a patchwork of different path–space-dependence situations, as the effects of globalization and economic crises are felt, where very old ways of production/reproduction/consumption co-exist with the hypermodernity of the locally global networks and lifestyles, producing a vast variety at every scale. Marshallian and Jacobsian agglomeration economies seem no longer to present opposing alternatives but rather co-exist (even in terms of spatial policy: see Frenken & Boschma, 2007). In Italian hypermodernity, specialization (not so much in the form of Marshallian districts but rather of more-or-less related functional clusters connected to the global value chain) and variety co-exist, influencing each other. Redundancy, slack and sometimes weak ties (in comparison with the strong Marshallian ties) seem to be facilitating innovations.

Such a situation produces profound differences in the configurations of Italian urban regions (in part global urban regions) particularly in comparison with non-European situations. This calls for a more profound analysis of the link between the micro and the macro. In fact, the Italian regions are a sort of blending between a historical (physical) legacy and their reproduction as relational entities in which different arenas, social and economic practices, and institutional arrangements co-evolve.

Fourth remark: the ambiguity of development and the role of the territory

The issue of path dependence, and the dependence on the historical development of the settlement, must then be framed in an Italian context. The weight these have in Italy is particularly significant, because it not only structures the forms of settlement, but strengthens cultures, economies and social systems. It is often in deep-rooted cultures with strong identities, real, alleged or claimed, that we find the traces of a long-term path dependence in Italy. This often results in negative components of a localist type, which can also take on an exclusive and exclusionary character, based on presumptions of (strategically re-invented) identity.

Beyond these general considerations, we see on the contrary, even in Italy (and in Italy this is a particularly significant factor), a breakdown of the historical pattern of settlement, a process that actually has been under way for a long time. And the most significant factor of this breakdown is not so much the emergence of new centers or new polarities, which is albeit as important a dynamic as settlement processes historically unknown in Italy (traditionally considered a land of minor centers, the renowned "hundred cities" of the *Bel Paese*, and so on). These processes include urban sprawl (in the north-east, and so on), the development of settlements in agricultural areas, urban fragmentation, and so on. In south-central Italy this type of settlement development has been characterized and supported by illegal settlements that have upset entire areas of the national territory, from rural Nocera and Sarno near Naples to the Roman countryside.

This dynamic interacts to produce profound changes in urban culture, in the form of lifestyles and ways of conceiving of urban life. This transformation has already had a deep effect on the reality of Italian cities.

What is important to note, as a significant factor that emerges from the Italian context, is rather the deep conflict, perceived and implemented, between human settlement, on the one hand, overwhelmed with the economies and cultures that accompany it, and the system of values, on the other hand. Whether real or imagined, these values are connected to a certain path dependence that also plays out in terms of a wide demand for new patterns of living and sociability. This conflict is therefore at the same time an ambiguity, one which seems suddenly to strongly characterize the current neo-liberally oriented territorial development.

The improvement policies of the major Italian historic cities (but also of minor centers and rural areas), and their related economies, provide a powerful example. Impacted by varying forms of tourism and by huge financial flows, included in international circuits and in globalized economies that uproot meaning and values, these local realities are often turned into "city-museums" or "postcard-territories" (Soja's simulacra). The emptying of significance of these places and these territories often turns them into simulacri of worlds that are then sold and marketed, offering experiences based on impressions and feelings. In some cases this path dependence can transform them into a massive theme park. Even if the physical structures are maintained or even improved, their internal contents are emptied or transformed, creating ambiguous and contradictory situations. As mentioned above, therefore, it is important to clarify what we mean as a path dependence and what it entails.

On the other hand, we are witnessing continuous processes of re-rooting, even within those areas of urban sprawl or squatter settlements, or within the new urban realities being formed, even if they lack the favorable characteristics for the construction of urban fabric conducive to social development of forms of appropriation and re-signification of places. Yet such re-rooting is constantly sought and expressed as a socially and widely felt need. Again it creates an ambiguous and contradictory dynamic; the results and meanings are yet to be understood or interpreted.

Against this background, the national research on the Italian context has detected a centrality of the territory, whose weight and texture is not so much (and not solely) based on path dependence. Almost in contradiction with the process of dematerialization, or with an idea of the development of post-metropolis indifferent to place, it exhibits how the characteristics and materials of historical stratification of territories (in terms of the environment and landscape, but also in terms, for example, of stratification of the historic centers, consolidated axes, and so on) also clearly influence the regionalization of the urban, its development and its structure. This is well illustrated in the regional portrait of Tuscany, but also in others. The territory has a consistency, its structure and therefore its autonomy. It causes a friction in the mediation between global processes and local settlements and social organization. In this sense, it is not just "determined," but it is "decisive."

The elements of the local "milieu," tied to history, to local relationships and identity (including the "negative" or "conservative" connotation these occasionally take on) and other immaterial dimensions, analogously influence the development and shape of urban form (Dematteis, 2008).

Fifth remark: Resilience

Resilience, as path dependence, is not a property of a system, but rather a dynamic process (Boschma, 2014; Dawley et al., 2010). Resilience and path–space dependence are closely interwoven, particularly through the degree of connectedness of a system (Simmie & Martin, 2010, p. 33). High resilience and low connectedness produce a phase of re-organization, innovation and economic restructuring (through the virtues of the weak ties) that can evolve toward a phase of exploitation (growth and capacity to seize opportunities). Vice versa, low resilience and high connectedness (as in the case of negative lock-in) may more or less quickly generate decline and destruction. Italian urban regions, as they are depicted in the regional portraits, appear fairly resilient. Such resilience is not apparent only in the economic domain of the more industrialized northern regions (where the strong ties peculiar to the Marshallian district have been broken, creating in part new paths, or in the Turin and Milan urban regions in their different path to post-Fordist arrangements), but also in the socio-economic practices of daily life.

Naples is a case in point: in a situation of significant social heterogeneity, with substantial degrees of poverty, informality, illegality and deregulation, the city appears very resilient. In a sort of bricolage between old and new, some inhabitants use tactics and strategies in an interesting mix of pre-modernity, modernity and hypermodernity. Naples may be considered as a special case of deployment of Jacobsian externalities, where path and space dependence are not distinguishable and are co-produced in co-evolutionary processes.

In the Italian context, resilience appears to be closely connected to a social type of resilience, that is, to an adaptive capacity on the part of different social bodies, capable of more or less rapidly absorbing or responding to situations of stress, of change, of crisis, but also of dealing with the difficulty, if not the shortcomings, of public authorities to respond adequately and effectively to emerging problems and their functions. In Italy this has, in some ways, anticipated the effects of the global abolition of the welfare state, so much so that some European states are observing carefully this type of process that in Italy has mobilized social energies and forms of adaptation. It is not unexpected that resilience appears to grow in the face of a major degree of "deregulation" or forms of behavior considered illegal, or even the presence of forms of cooperation between secondary subjects of the territorial government. Vice versa, it appears more problematic where strong players persist and attempts are made to coordinate policy among relevant bodies of the territorial government. This situation provides a possible explanation of the rigid/elastic relationship of the social bodies and the institutions.

The effect of this trend on the territories leads one, however, to question the generally positive value of resilience, especially in terms of a weakening of social protection, but also the waning of solidarity (in favor of a progressive individualism), as well as a negative environmental impact, in terms of the unregulated consumption of resources (with negative, often nearly irrevocable effects of the long term). Think of the problems of urban sprawl. This line of reasoning should not so much call for a return to greater rigidity or greater top–down control, as it should promote a move toward greater complexity in territorial government, where the capacity for social adaptation should be measured and coordinated with a more organic and collectively shared vision.

Sixth remark: regions between normative and interpretative perspectives, and some tentative conclusions

The case studies clearly show a variety of regions and processes of regionalization. The social and economic landscape appears as a multidimensional palimpsest. The many layers refer to co-existence of the past (which influences the dynamic in many ways, particularly important being the inertia of the physical structures) and new elements. Such a palimpsest combines differences linked to historical events (with different social and economic timing that overlap each other), but it also refers to the overlapping of a large variety of models and trajectories, whose evolution depends on the capacity to exploit or escape the lock-in opportunities or traps.

For Soja, the post-metropolis represents a historical phase, still in progress, the transition from the modern (in particular, industrial and Fordist) metropolis to a radically different configuration (see, among others, Soja, 1999, 2005, 2011). The metropolis explodes, it extends at a global scale; the hinterland is no longer defined in terms of proximity and, therefore, neither in traditional terms of transportation relationships between center and suburbs. A new metropolis form emerges, one that radicalizes the characters of the modern city, reaching unusual levels of heterogeneity and diversity (social, economic, cultural, life forms), in a radically different context from a spatial point of view. Soja puts particular emphasis on overcoming the drastic dualism between city and suburbs (suburbs now being affected by an unprecedented process of spatial, economic and social transformations, from edge cities to technoburbs, in a direction of propagation of various types of centers and the construction of new spheres of life (from gated communities to large business parks or theme parks), which together reshape our social geography in a new way.

Everything appears everywhere as new form-metropolis, and locations can contain everything, offering a seemingly contradictory mix of variables of de-industrialization and re-industrialization, centralization and decentralization, combinations and hybrids, producing, from the traditional monocentric form to regional, polycentric systems (another distinction that is dissolving, according to Soja, is that between city and region). For Soja, this not only leads to forms of regionalization of the urban, but the region seems to take on a character which is not only interpretive but also administrative, as the context in which to treat or revise, in a unified manner, several important differences. These include the difference between traditional and innovative forms of production of goods and services, between populations, between competitiveness and solidarity, and so on. On these points seem to converge the positions of Sassen (as well as other important authors that, for brevity, we do not name), in which the regional dimension (with some of its characteristic features, such as the sense of belonging) seems almost in opposition to the dark side of the post-global city (Sassen, 2001). The region appears to be the place where forms of territorial solidarity could be exercised with respect to the intra-urban inequalities which seem to some extent inevitable in the dynamics of globalization.

In the American case, the exercise of solidarity also seems somewhat problematic, partly because of the constitutive fragmentation of city administrations, the effects of legal mechanisms of incorporation, and the intentional constitution of incorporated towns (often suburbs, which acquire the legal status of municipalities) in the processes of exclusion of "undesirable" social segments (see, for example, as a historical reconstruction, Teaford, 1975) and attraction of desired populations and activities. The case of Europe, however, leaves significant room for regional action (albeit with many and sometimes contradictory facets, from the European Union to the national states and regions).

The preceding paragraphs have shown how (and why) the notion of post-metropolis should be used with caution in the case of Italy. Without doubt, globalization has acted with force on the territories (which often posed resistance and creative interpretation), but the spatial results are quite different from those reported in the literature on the American city. There is evidence of similarities, but the processes of formation of new spaces appear quite singular, as in the transition to a polycentric system (but historically almost all urban realities in Italy are polycentric) or the increase of density of in-between spaces forming in the intercity connective tissues (already densely anthropic and punctuated by dense settlement pattern consisting of a variety of social and economic landscapes, radically different from the former suburbs) that are forming complex corridors. The social outcomes, by contrast, see a dramatic growth in inequality, in which Milan emerges as by far the most unequal city in Italy, while other urban situations appear much less unequal.

Economic restructuring has therefore impacted the city in a variety of ways, producing very different structures. The inequalities instead to a very limited degree regard the in-between space now under development, despite the significant presence of immigrants. In these areas there is actually a post-metropolitan, and even post-urban, stratification of practices, from reverse commuting, to post-rural economic practices (niche agriculture, with high added value and new business operators), to re-signification of places in a bricolage of pre-modern and hyper-modern (see the case of Sardinia), to environmental conflicts that bring into play the plausibility of different models of development, to new forms of living in relation to work (and to changes in the labor markets, now much more flexible than before, and families, increasingly multi/single-person, and so on) to changing types of consumption. All these are aspects of a post-metropolitan and, simultaneously, a post-rural landscape. All this tends to "regionalize" (at various scales) ways of life and economic and social practices and, from the point of view of governance, the region appears, in Italy as in other contexts, as the designated place to exercise solidarity and forms of social and spatial justice.

References

Boschma, R. (2014). *Towards an evolutionary perspective on regional resilience* (Papers in Evolutionary Economic Geography (PEEG), No. 1409). Utrecht University, Section of Economic Geography.

Braudel, F. (1992). *Civilization & capitalism, 15th–18th century* (Vol. 3). Oakland: University of California Press.

Brenner, N. (Ed.) (2014). *Implosions/explosions: towards a study of planetary urbanization.* Berlin: Jovis Verlag GmbH.

Brenner, N., and Katsikis, N. (2014). Is the Mediterranean urban? In Brenner N. (Ed.), *Implosions/explosions: towards a study of planetary urbanization* (pp. 428–459). Berlin: Jovis Verlag GmbH.

Cacciari, M. (2008). Nomades en prison. Réflexions sur la post-métropole. In P. Simay and S. Fuzessery (Eds.), *Le choc des metropoles. Simmel, Kracauer, Benjamin* (pp. 243–252). Paris: Editions de l'Eclat.

Dawley, S., Pike, A., and Tomaney, J. (2010). *Towards the resilient region? Policy activism and peripheral region development* (Serc Discussion Paper No. 53). University of Newcastle.

Dematteis, G. (Ed). (2008). *L'Italia delle città. Tra malessere e trasfigurazione.* Roma: Società Geografica Italiana.

Diener, R., Herzog J., Meili M., de Meuron P., Schmid C., and ETH Studio Basel, Contemporary City Institute (2006). *Switzerland: an urban portrait.* Basel-Boston-Berlin: Birkhäuser.

Florida, R., Gulden, T., and Mellander, C. (2008). The rise of megaregions. *Cambridge Journal of Regions, Economy and Society,* 1(3), 459–476.

Frenken, K., and Boschma, R. (2007). A theoretical framework for economic geography: industrial dynamic and urban growth as a branching process. *Journal of Economic Geography,* 7(5), 635–649.

Friedman, T. (2005). *The world is flat: a brief history of the twenty-first century.* New York: Farrar, Straus, and Giroux.

Glaeser, E. (2012). *Triumph of the city.* London: Pan Books.

Goonewardena, K., Kipfer, R., Milgrom, R., and Schmid, C. (Eds). (2008). *Space, difference, everyday life: reading Henri Lefebvre.* New York: Routledge.

Harrison, P. (2007). The space between us: opening remarks on the concept of dwelling. *Environment and Planning D: Society and Space*, 25, 625–647.

Harvey, D. (2006). *Spaces of global capitalism: towards a theory of uneven geographical development*. London-New York: Verso.

Jacobs, J. (1961). *The death and life of great American cities*. New York: Random House.

Jacobs, J. (1969). *The economy of cities*. New York: Random House.

Jessop, B., Brenner, N., and Jones, M. (2008). Theorizing sociospatial relations. *Environment and Planning D: Society and Space*, 26, 389–401.

Lefebvre, H. (1970). *La révolution urbaine*. Paris: Gallimard.

Lefebvre, H. (1974). *La production de l'espace*. Paris: Éditions Anthropos.

Lucas, R.E. (1988). On the mechanics of economic development. *Journal of Monetary Economics*, 22(1), 3–42.

Madden, D.J. (2012). City becoming world: Nancy, Lefebvre, and the global-urban imagination. *Environment and Planning D: Society and Space*, 30(5), 772–787.

Marshall, A. (1890). *Principles of economics*. London: MacMillan.

Martin, R. (2010). Roepke Lecture in Economic Geography: Rethinking path dependence: beyond lock-in to evolution. *Economic Geography*, 86(1), 1–27.

Martin, R., and Simmie, J. (2010). The economic resilience of regions: toward an evolutionary approach. *Cambridge Journal of Regions, Economy and Society*, 3(1), 27–43.

Martin, R., and Sunley, P. (2006). Path dependence and regional economic evolution. *Journal of Economic Geography*, 6(4), 395–437.

Massey, D. (1992). Politics and space/time. *New Left Review*, 196, 65–84

Molina-Morales, F.X., and Expósito-Langa, M. (2013). Overcoming undesirable knowledge redundancy in territorial clusters. *Industry and Innovation*, 20(8), 739–758.

Reps, J.W. (1965). *The making of urban America*. Princeton: Princeton University Press.

Rodriguez-Posé, A., and Crescenzi, R. (2008). Mountains in a flat world: why proximity still matters for the location of economic activity. *Cambridge Journal of Regions, Economy and Society*, 1(3), 371–388.

Sassen, S. (2001). Global cities and global city-regions: a comparison. In A.J. Scott (Ed.), *Global city-regions* (pp. 78–95). Oxford: Oxford University Press.

Schmid, C. (2012). Henri Lefebvre, the right to the city, and the new metropolitan mainstream. In N. Brenner, P. Marcuse, and M. Mayer (Eds.), *Cities for people, not for profit: critical urban theory and the right to the city* (pp. 42–62). New York: Routledge.

Simmie, J., and Martin, R. (2010). The economic resilience of regions: toward an evolutionary approach. *Cambridge Journal of Regions, Economy and Society*, 3(1): 27–43.

Soja, E.W. (1999). *Postmetropolis: critical studies of cities and regions*. Oxford: Blackwell.

Soja, E.W. (2005). On the concept of global city region. *Artefact*, 4, 1–10. Retrieved from artefact.mi2.hr/_a04/lang_en/theory_soja_en.htm.

Soja, E.W. (2011). Regional urbanization and the end of the metropolis era. In G. Bridge and S. Watson (Eds.), *New companion to the city* (pp. 679–689). Chichester: Wiley-Blackwell.

Soja, E., and Kanai, M. (2007). The urbanization of the world. In R. Burdett and D. Sudjic (Eds.), *The endless city: the urban age project by the London School of Economics and Deutsche Bank's Alfred Herrhausen Society* (pp. 54–69). New York: Phaidon.

Teaford, J.C. (1975). *The municipal revolution in America: origins of modern urban government, 1650–1825*. Chicago and London: University of Chicago Press.

18 Conclusions

Alessandro Balducci, Valeria Fedeli and Francesco Curci[1]

John Friedmann, introducing his book *The Prospects of Cities* in 2002, wrote: "The city is dead. It vanished sometime during the 20th century" (2002, p. XI), and proposed to define the emerging forms of the human habitat simply as "the urban." In the last 30 years, there has been a relentless search for new words capable of expressing what has been happening to cities: the endless city, "la città diffusa," disurbia, outer city, rurban, dispersed urbanization, urban region, regional urbanization, mega-city-region, and so on. What is clear is that the conceptual terms "city" and "metropolis," with their hierarchical and dichotomous implications, are no longer useful for understanding what is happening to the spatial organization of society.

The group of researchers that has coordinated the project we are presenting in this book at Politecnico di Milano already had this fact clear in 2004, when they decided to title the departmental research conference "Milano dopo la Metropoli" (tr. *Milan after the Metropolis*, 2004). Holding that Milan could no longer be described as a city based upon its historical radiocentric spatial structure, nor as a metropolis, the term used to designate the relationship between the central city and the cluster of cities depending upon it. In that conference we underlined the vanishing of the traditional center–periphery patterns, the emergence of a new form of urbanization based upon conurbations and discontinuities – a phenomenon that could be grasped only by an aerial view, because of its scale and dimension.

We observed that the spatial complexity and discontinuity was accompanied by discontinuity in time: the pace of change in the last 30 years has been steady and at the same time difficult to be recorded in a traditional way. In fact, it is possible to perceive the changes taking place in the former countryside and in the periphery of small- and medium-sized centers only by looking at aggregate data or using geographic information systems. Although the population of cities was stable or decreasing, and although one could not notice the great changes taking place at ground level (which were so fragmented and scattered that they appeared almost imperceptible), there had been an incredible acceleration in construction activity and related land consumption.

This book is the result of a large research effort produced by a network of scholars in different Italian universities interested in delivering a significant output for both the scientific and policy communities about new ways to describe this discontinuity in time and space in significant urban areas across Italy. Trying to interpret at its best the rationale of the projects funded by the Italian Ministry for Education, Universities and Research, in the national project "Progetti di ricerca di interesse nazionale" (tr. *Research projects of national interest*), the network really wanted to produce an output of national interest working in the first place on the production of an atlas of urban change in Italy and on this basis constructing new representations and new descriptions of the Italian socio-spatial structure.

In our perspective, this collection of chapters has provided at least three relevant research results: (1) presenting the Italian case in the international debate about contemporary urban change; (2) offering a series of in-depth regional portraits that could construct an image of the urban Italy; and (3) contributing to the definition of a new agenda for contemporary urban space.

Contributing to the international debate about the contemporary "urban"

The post-metropolis perspective introduced by Edward Soja (2011) has been a functional and strategic way to enter in the international academic debate and to organize a dialogue with a number of other conceptualizations confirming or opposing Soja's perspectives, emerging along the journey. The idea of suburbanization formulated by Keil (2011), but in particular the more recent thesis of a planetary urbanization formulated by Brenner (2014), in fact, hybridized consistently our original approach, as this book shows.

In this respect, first of all, the *regional portrait* chapters together with the transversal chapters provide arguments concerning the need to reframe the ideas of the city accumulated over the last century, trying to acknowledge *new/old urban forms and forms of urbanity taking place*. The *urbanoid galaxy* discussed in Chapter 16 by Fregolent and Vettoretto (with Bottaro and Curci) opens the way for interpreting forms/processes with a dynamic nature that do not correspond linearly to different levels of cityness. In fact, there is no hierarchical or evolutionary ideal-type dimension in this conceptualization. The *urbanoid galaxy* is neither a form of city-to-be nor a not-yet-city (Bonomi, 2013); it is rather a new form of the urban that deserves analysis and research, but also policies and governance of its own. Its conceptualization must be read in connection with the role and in relation with the other forms of the urban accumulated during the centuries, especially in Italy, and that are experiencing significant changes. On the one hand, the more traditional cities, which seem to have, not only in Italy, a new recentralizing role, probably linked to the effects of the crisis, have produced a new urban concentration of resources together with the difficulties of decentralized organization of functions, jobs and families. On the other hand, the more traditional metropolitan dynamics/patterns are still playing a central role, through concentrated and concentrating urbanization, producing metropolitan nodes and corridors.

In this perspective, the research shows the importance of exploring ways for coexistence and interplay between different historical forms/processes of cityness, between path(space) dependence and innovation. As shown by the contributions of both Cellamare and Vettoretto (Chapter 17) and Paba and Perrone (Chapter 13), space still matters. In a world that is becoming more and more urban, in which we have largely exceeded the potentialities of urbanization provided by territories and have invented new forms of immaterial proximities, space – and cities – still matter. If, in fact, there is an ongoing production of urbanity in fairly non-traditional urban places – the Alps as well as the Mediterranean islands – nevertheless space remains a relevant variable in the production of the urban. Mobility practices in this respect show the crucial dilemmas of a post-metropolitan world, where being mobile offers the opportunity to live a (multiple, satisfying, challenging) urban experience, whereas being non-mobile is synonymous with voluntary or forced segregation more than in the past (Urry, 2007).

In all cases, a challenging character of the post-metropolitan seems to be its *pace of change*. In a post-metropolitan world, change seems to occur in a quick and intense way. As a result, social practices suddenly and unexpectedly can design new geographies, evident in particular for mobility spaces. These new geographies quickly deposit on the territory elements of un-bundling and re-bundling (Keil et al., 2012) that are capable of producing disruptive changes in a few years, consistently subversive of traditional orders.

A second and related interesting aspect on this point is the fact that the urbanity produced by these processes is fragmented and distributed, following, much more than demographic and building density, steep profiles from the center to the outskirts. As highlighted by the Milan regional portrait, one of the few real metropolitan cases in Italy, we record fairly gentle curbs, enabling the possibility to find diffuse answers to the demand of urbanity in large urban regions. In a post-metropolitan perspective, peripheries cannot be found in the usual places; at the same time, distance still matters, but not so consistently as in the past. Urbanity can be found in very different places. What is evident, though, is that this diffusion does not reduce conflicts and imbalances. If, on the one hand, indicators, like the Gini Index, seem to talk about less sharp cleavages between the center and the peripheries, new centers and peripheries are emerging, together with new forms and ideas of urbanity and cityness that deserve respect and attention (Rosanvallon, 2013). If distance and differences still matter, boundaries are changing and mobile. The boundary between urban and non-urban fades, in some cases completely, while in others it changes forms, location and meaning: a new set of boundaries emerge, between dynamic and non-dynamic places, between attractive and non-attractive ones, between highly homogeneous and highly differentiated societies. These new geographies are more and more mobile and transcalar. Distance between the center and the periphery can no longer be used to explain social differentiation or to impute social differentiations to the regional dimension. Nevertheless, the regional dimension seems to be the new necessary perspective for understanding processes and dealing with the urban question. It seems to play an interesting role in reshaping the urban question: when, in fact, the regional dimension is not taken into consideration, problems, conflicts and processes cannot be recognized as they should be to understand and include them in a new public agenda. In this perspective, as argued by Fedeli in this book (Chapter 14), it is not possible to conclude that the regional dimension per se generates new spatial injustices of its own. At the same time, lacking conceptualization and acknowledgment, new spatial injustice and a new urban question could be generated.

A national-regional portrait

A second general result of this project is the production of a national-local inter-pretation of several relevant urban processes occurring in the Italian context. In fact, the general chapters, interacting with the regional portraits, build a mul-tiscale portrait of urban regionalization processes in Italy, where a complex interplay between path dependence and change is not only conceptualized, but also exhibited in detail.

In this respect, a valuable aspect of this contribution is, from our perspective, the fact of being based not only on theory, but also on a wide and in-depth quanti-tative and qualitative research campaign, producing a large set of information only partially and fragmentally available until today and ready to provide materials for in-depth interpretations. The operationalization of theoretical concepts has been a challenging test-field, generating a set of hypotheses not to be taken for granted on how the contemporary urban should be investigated. The research and the book offer an interesting methodological perspective suggesting how to try to deal with traditional data (census) and non-traditional ones in order to explore phenom-ena that largely exceed the administrative boundaries and propose the regional as the necessary scale of observation of urban processes. At the same time, the research tries to demonstrate the need to move a step forward in how the urban is studied: a number of factors that have been studied separately – increase in mobil-ity, decentralization of residential and commercial functions, explosion of digital communication, fragmentation of families and firms – are now displaying their combined effects and producing a profound reconfiguration of "the urban" and its structure. Not many years ago, Manuel Castells, in his seminal work *The Rise of the Network Society* (Castells, 1996), said, ironically, that there were probably more scholars researching telework than there were actual teleworkers. However, now we cannot deny that the new spatial configuration is composed of an unedited combination of distance and face-to-face communication in the labor market that is evident in the changing patterns of mobility.

As a result, the national-regional portrait collected in this book enables the measurement of the peculiarities of the Italian case toward the planetary dimen-sion of urban change. We succeeded in producing a portrait of Italy critically respectful of both traditional imaginaries on "the country of the one hundred cities" and recent scholarly interpretations concerning the emergence of mega-city-regions (Hall & Pain, 2006; Martinotti, 1999; Florida, 2008). In Italy regional urbanization processes are taking place in a specific tension between local and non-local, which is reshaping the traditional urban structure, and between urban and non-urban, which has never been simple to conceptualize in an ordinary and linear way. Beyond any extreme position affirming or denying an epochal trans-formation of cities, the new configuration of urban spaces results in a co-existence rather than in a substitution or opposition. Despite the extraordinary explosion of social networks and Internet communities at the global level, a great number of exchanges are locally based. A new combination of material and immaterial relationships are greatly impacting the use of space. Spatial and physical relationships have not disappeared, but distance relationships are creating new types of "communities" and networks. The dynamism of former peripheral areas has often been interpreted as an alternative and a threat to the role of central cities. However, it is now evident that this is not true: it is not a development against the wealth of central cities, rather it is part of the same new form of urban development. Peripheral centers are growing because of their internal vitality and attractiveness and the delocalization of activities from the central cities, thus creating a new spatial pattern. Cities of different sizes in emerging urban regions are not losing their role as urban communities where residents are also local workers; but they even belong to a space of flows at regional and global scales.

At the end of the day, the national picture that can result from the combination of the regional portraits in this book talks about difference: differentiated dynamics of post-metropolization that do not correspond to a unique post-metropolitan form of the urban.

Dynamic phenomena, produced by incomplete, overlapping and highly interconnected processes of transcalar nature, are producing forms of polynuclear urbanization, such as in the Veneto and Tuscany cases. This expresses a path dependence on historical patterns and more recent socio-economic models, proposing a form of diffuse and archipelago urbanization, which presents hardly any real trace of metropolitan nature. Therefore it cannot be considered simply post-metropolitan in a chronological perspective. However, it is somehow post-metropolitan because of the way regional urbanization is taking place, producing a highly interconnected polynuclear urban formation. Post-metropolitan appears also in cases such as eastern Sicily and north Sardinia, contexts that have never been metropolitan in any sense, but where peaks of urbanity, rather than simple urbanization, are completely redefining the organization of space: flows of people, connectivity and accessibility, social and demographic dynamism; heterogeneity of people and functions.

The squares of Turin and Rome seem to represent more traditional processes of transition from a monocentric to a polynuclear urban structure. Although keeping a metropolitan spatial structure, as well as often social and actor-related, with a strong role of the central cities in structuring the interplay between centralization and decentralization, they locally present interesting forms of a post-metropolitan nature: awkward local conflicts, new political–social alliances, unexpected sociospatial assemblages are evidence of post-metropolitan nature.

The square of the Milan urban region appears easier to be conceptualized and observed, because of the historic interplay between polycentrism and metropolization that has shaped the regional space in the last century. It is an apparent urban *continuum*, where new discontinuities emerge exceeding all traditional urban and metropolitan kinds of boundaries, imaginary and shapes. Similar dynamics can be observed in the square of Naples, as the outcome of a clash between the historical monocentrism of the regional chief lieu and the polycentrism of internal areas, toward the formation of an urban continuum constrained only by the complex geo-morphology of the area.

Finally, what is more, and argued by the perspective of corridors proposed by Perulli and others (Chapter 12), but also by Vettoretto and colleagues (Chapter 16), these phenomena are part of a complex process of regional urbanization that must be read at a national scale, producing large urban regions.

A regional imaginary for a new urban agenda

The third result – in the making and still the most open – is related to the restructuring of the urban agenda, which could derive from this updated national/regional portrait. The conclusion of this research project coincided with a peculiar moment for Italy. In fact, the Pact of Amsterdam concerning an EU urban agenda was just signed (EU, 2016), while the new EU programming cycle had already introduced a specific focus on cities in the national operational programs. Italy took its first steps in this direction, with the publication of an official document for the implementation in Italy of the Cohesion Policy (CIPU, 2013) indicating Mezzogiorno (tr. southern regions), metropolitan areas and internal areas as the three strategic priorities for cohesion policy. At the same time, in 2015, the first steps for implementing a national reform introducing metropolitan governments were made.

The results of this research project interact with the Italian approach to an urban focus of cohesion policies and the Italian way to address the governance dimension raised by the new law.

As regards the first direction, the national government document suggested, first of all, to address the citizenship deficit and private entrepreneurship in southern Italian regions, where the logic of place-based and territorial approach are strongly supported. Second, it proposed supporting cities against social imbalances and toward development and competitiveness, especially in global sectors, supporting the supply of services for citizens. It also introduced the need to look at functional cities, rather than administrative units, distinguishing between different urban forms (great cities/metropolitan areas, medium-sized cities, and systems of small towns) and investing in the network of large metropolitan cities in order to reinforce competitiveness in Europe. Finally, it made reference to internal areas, 60 percent of the Italian territory, where 25 percent of the population is concentrated, far from large agglomerations and characterized by instable development trajectories, highly polycentric and with high potentialities of attractiveness for a number of resources available different from the central areas (Ministro per la Coesione Territoriale, 2012). This threefold interpretation of the Italian territorial cohesion strategic options introduced a new focus on metropolitan cities, on the basis of which Italy structured its National Operative Program (PON Metro, 2014) document, assuming metropolitan cities as the main focus for cohesion policy. Actually, notwithstanding the establishment in the last four years of a committee destined to elaborate a urban agenda, Italy is still lacking from this viewpoint, producing scattered and fragmented urban policies (Urban@it, 2016; in particular Pasqui et al., 2016; see also Dematteis in CSS, 2011, for the foundation of this debate).

This new focus on the metropolitan dimension is confirmed by the approval of law 56/2014, which has finally paved the way for the implementation of metropolitan cities, constitutionally founded since 2001 but never implemented. The original rationale of the law is far from proposing what Calafati defined as a missing "pensiero metropolitano" (Calafati, 2014). Originally adopted in 2012 during the most recent economic and political crisis in Italy and suffering from a delay in implementation because of a non-constitutionality judgment in relation to the parallel cancellation of provinces, the law was tightly bounded with the need to reduce public expenditures, rather than to promote a new urban imaginary. In this perspective, it simply introduced new "metropolitan cities" within the boundaries of an old provincial government in most large urban areas.

Within this complex framework, the research project contributes to highlight the need of a new regional-transcalar urban governance and the shortcomings of a phase in which a traditional metropolitan-urban imaginary still seems at play. In this respect the project dialogues with the new debate concerning the redefinition of the regional geography, present in Italy since the 1990s (Brosio et al., 1994) and relaunched by the European Union's indications based on the concept of macroregions and functional regions (Richardson, 1971). The proposal by Società Geografica Italiana of 36 new regions, based on the identification of urban systems and trying to address both the reconfiguration of regions and provinces (SGI, 2014; Bruzzo, 2016; Ferri, 2016), actually seems far from being able to grasp the consequences of the regionalization of the urban observed by this project, in line with the limited result of the government commission in charge of it.

As a second challenging conclusion, the research highlights the need to redefine the urban agenda in Italy, in particular introducing a new transcalar and regional focus, capable of intercepting and studying dynamics and processes at the right scale. This means the need in the first place to go beyond, both in terms of problem-setting and problem-solving, center–periphery, urban–non-urban, concentration–decentralization policy models. Second, there is the need to adopt a regional perspective, not just as an enlargement of the scale, but as a challenging mind capable of reading and dealing with the transcalar nature of the urban. In other words, the main input for urban policies concerns the nature of their main object: the urban, in its different forms. This means of course reducing the distance among territories, practices, problems and institutions, introducing innovative forms of governance capable of building the territory of policies as the outcome of local and interscalar processes, producing new social, economic and political efficacy and legitimacy.

Finally, there are also implications of our research activity for spatial planning, which is a central concern of many research units in our network. Planning has always been based on a homogeneous and linear relationship between territory and authority, while according to our descriptions of the Italian urban space it is now being called to work across territories, without any stable reference to defined authorities and boundaries. It is called to work upon difference and not homogeneity. In the metropolitan phase, planning was mainly concerned with growth at the edge and new developments in uninhabited territories. Whereas in the post-metropolitan phase, planning has to involve the in-between spaces and the reuse and recycling of sites that have traditionally been inhabited by populations, residents or users.

Assuming the new perspective, we are suggesting that planning should commit itself to giving shape to this fragmented and discontinuous space by:

—   strengthening the multi-centric nature of urban regions;
—   encouraging the recognition of significant intermediate aggregations of former territorial authorities capable of organizing themselves into meaningful urban areas where complementarities and the integration of service systems can be sought;
—   limiting the consumption of land and working for territorial sustainability;
—   enhancing agricultural, green and natural areas as constitutive urban functions;
—   encouraging the construction of coalitions around important territorial projects;
—   creating new conditions of habitability for resident or temporary populations across the urban space;
—   producing new public spaces at the regional scale, a new "urbanity" based upon economic and social complexity;
—   producing new systems of centrality capable of enhancing the old framework of existing centers as a means for giving structure to the emerging urban settlements.

The debate on the negative or positive nature of urban transformation is progressively losing its meaning. We have tried to show what the contemporary urban space is in Italy. It is not the deterioration of the modern city or metropolis; it is something else. Images are persistent, and if we continue to name this new socio-spatial phenomenon a city or a metropolis, we may unconsciously incur a number of implicit consequences. If we continue to look for the reconstruction of an order that has been lost forever, we will miss the opportunity to explore the potential and appropriateness of the post-metropolitan space in dealing with emerging societal challenges.

Note

1   Although this chapter should be considered a result of the common work and reflection of the three authors, A. Balducci took primary responsibility for the introduction, V. Fedeli took primary responsibility for the section "Contributing to the international debate about the contemporary 'urban'", and F. Curci took primary responsibility for the section "A national-regional portrait". They co-authored the section "A regional imaginary for a new urban agenda".

References

Balducci, A. (2004). Milano dopo la metropoli. Ipotesi per la costruzione di un'agenda pubblica. *Territorio*, 29–30, 9–17.

Bonomi, A. (2013). *Il capitalismo in-finito: Indagine sui territori della crisi*. Torino: Einaudi.

Brenner, N. (Ed.). (2014). *Implosions/Explosions: Towards a Study of Planetary Urbanization*. Berlin: Jovis Verlag GmbH.

Brosio, G., Pola, G., and Bondonio, D. (Eds.). (1994). *Una Proposta Di Federalismo Fiscale*. Torino: Edizioni della Fondazione Giovanni Agnelli.

Bruzzo, A. (2016). Riferimenti teorici per la delimitazione territoriale delle Regioni. *Argomenti. Rivista di economia, cultura e ricerca sociale*, 3, 31–56.

Calafati, A. (2014). *Città e aree metropolitane in Italia* (GSSI Urban Studies Working Paper No. 1). L'Aquila: Gran Sasso Science Institute. Retrieved from http://ssrn.com/abstract=2369323

Castells, M. (1996). *The Rise of the Network Society*. Malden, MA: Blackwell.

CIPU, Comitato interministeriale per le politiche urbane. (2013). *Metodi e contenuti sulle priorità in tema di agenda urbana*. Retrieved from http://recs.it/it/news-detail/metodicontenutiintemadiagendaurbana.

CSS, Consiglio italiano per le Scienze Sociali. (2011). *Società e territori da ricomporre. Libro bianco sul governo delle città italiane*. Roma.

EU. (2016). *Establishing the Urban Agenda for the EU 'Pact of Amsterdam'. Agreed at the Informal Meeting of EU Ministers Responsible for Urban Matters on 30 May 2016 in Amsterdam, The Netherlands*. Retrieved from http://ec.europa.eu/regional_policy/sources/policy/themes/urban-development/agenda/pact-of-amsterdam.pdf.

Ferri, V. (2016). La delimitazione territoriale dei governi sub-centrali: un'analisi comparata a livello europeo con particolare riferimento a Francia e Italia. *Argomenti. Rivista di economia, cultura e ricerca sociale*, 3, 57–92.

Florida, R. (2008). The Rise of the Mega-region. *Cambridge Journal of Regions, Economy and Society*, 1(3), 459–476.

Fondazione Agnelli. (1996). *Un federalismo dei valori Percorso e conclusioni di un programma della Fondazione Giovanni Agnelli (1992–1996)*. Torino: Edizioni della Fondazione Giovanni Agnelli.

Friedmann, J. (2002). *The Prospect of Cities*. Minneapolis: University of Minnesota Press.

Hall, P., and Pain, K. (2006). *The Polycentric Metropolis: Learning from Mega-City Regions in Europe*. London: Earthscan.

Keil, R. (2011). Global Suburbanization: The Challenge of Researching Cities in the 21st Century. *Public*, 43, 54–61.

Keil, R., Olds, K., and Addie, J-P. (2012, May 15). *Mobilizing New Urban Structures to Increase the Performance and Effect of R&D in Universities and Beyond*. SSHRC Knowledge Synthesis Grant Leveraging Public Investments in HERD. Retrieved from: http://discovery.ucl.ac.uk/1425766/1/Addie_KeilOldsAddieFinalMay15%20copy.pdf.

Martinotti, G. (Ed.). (1999). *La dimensione metropolitana*. Bologna: il Mulino.

Ministro per la Coesione Territoriale. (2012). *Metodi e obiettivi per un uso efficace dei fondi comunitari 2014–2020*. Rome. Retrieved from: http://www.dps.tesoro.it/documentazione/comunicati/2012/Doc%2014–20%20Master_27%20dic%202012.pdf.

Pasqui, G., Briata, P., and Laino, G. (2016). Risorse. Fondi comunitari per le città metropolitane. In Urban@it, Centro nazionale di studi per le politiche urbane. (Ed.), *Rapporto sulle città, Metropoli attraverso la crisi*. Bologna: il Mulino.

PON Metro, Programma Operativo Nazionale Città Metropolitane 2014–2020 (2014, July 22). *Documento di programma*. Dipartimento per lo Sviluppo e la Coesione Economica.

Richardson, H.W. (1971). *Economia regionale*. Bologna: il Mulino.

Rosanvallon, P. (2013). *Le parlament des invisibles. Raconteur la vie*. Paris: Seuil.

Sassen, S. (2006). *Territory, Authority, Rights: From Medieval to Global Assemblages*. Princeton, NJ: Princeton University Press.

SGI, Società Geografica Italiana (2014). *Per un riordino territoriale dell'Italia*. Roma.

Soja, E.W. (2011). Regional Urbanization and the End of the Metropolis Era. In G. Bridge and S. Watson (Eds.), *New Companion to the City* (pp. 679–689). Chichester: Wiley-Blackwell.

Urban@it, Centro nazionale di studi per le politiche urbane. (Eds.). (2016). *Rapporto sulle città. Metropoli attraverso la crisi*. Bologna: il Mulino.

Urry, J. (2007). *Mobilities*. Cambridge: Polity.

Index